Gender Studies

Gender Studies

New Directions in Feminist Criticism

Judith Spector, Editor

Bowling Green State University Popular Press
Bowling Green, Ohio 43403

Acknowledgment is made to the following journals for permission to reprint articles and portions of articles in this collection:

College English, for "Gender Studies: New Directions for Feminist Criticism" (by Judith Spector).

Critical Inquiry, Univ. of Chicago Press, for " 'The Blank Page' and the Issues of Female Creativity" (by Susan Gubar) and "Costumes of the Mind: Transvestism as Metaphor in Modern Literature" (by Sandra M. Gilbert).

The Centennial Review, for "Heroes, Earth Mothers, and Muses: Gender Identity in Barth's Fiction" (by Cynthia Davis).

Pacific Coast Philology, for "Through Greene-Land in Drag; Joan Didion's *Book of Common Prayer*" (by Patricia Merivale).

Literature and Psychology, for "Science Fiction and the Sex War: A Womb of One's Own" (by Judith Spector).

The Midwest Quarterly, for "Civilization as Emasculation: The Threatening Role of Women in the Frontier Fiction of Harold Bell Wright and Zane Grey" (by Fritz H. Oehlschlaeger).

Science Fiction Studies, for *"Amor Vincit Foeminam:* The Battle of the Sexes in Science Fiction" (by Joanna Russ).

*This book is for Hutch and Sam,
and for all of my good friends
who realize that to transcend gender is
not an easy proposition.*

Contents

GENDER AND GENRE

Preface

THIS COLLECTION OF GENDER STUDIES came about as the result of a suggestion by Donald Gray that I develop my article for *College English* ("Gender Studies: New Directions for Feminist Criticism") into a tangible demonstration of gender studies in the form of an anthology. Donald Gray often has terrific ideas, and I thank him for this one; he is a continuing source of encouragement and inspiration to all of us in the profession.

The contributors to the collection have been no less inspiring. Some of them perfected their essays during hectic semesters, in the middle of very heavy teaching loads, without grants or release time. They have demonstrated their commitment to the concept of gender studies and to the difficult task of working on the anthology. I thank them for their patience, perseverance, and help.

I have been fortunate to have additional help and advice from my colleagues and friends. I am grateful to Marilyn Breiter for her suggestions on the prospectus for the book, and on the technicalities of the publication process. Marilyn Tanger, Sharon Dean, Ray Keller, and Margaret Myers helped with "readings" of the introduction and with other advice, and colleagues at IUPUI Columbus were positive and helpful. I thank Paul Bippen, Director at IUPUI, for his support and enthusiasm for the project. I must also thank my secretaries Dee Herrmann and Judy Stohler, and Mitzi Graham, our word processor operator, for the production of the manuscript on a machine which we not-so-affectionately refer to as "the dinosaur."

Every author with an essay in the collection generously offered to waive permission fees for essays which had been published previously. The President's Council on the Humanities at Indiana University has awarded a publication subsidy to the collection to cover a portion of the fees requested by some of the journals, and I thank the Council for its assistance.

The collection would not have been possible at all without the support of Pat Browne and all of the people at The Popular Press; their enthusiasm for ideas makes me feel the way I feel about my work when I'm happiest about it, when I know I'd never want to do anything else.

Introduction

AFTER THE POPULARITY in the sixties and early seventies of Kate Millett's *Sexual Politics*, Mary Ellmann's *Thinking About Women*, and Katharine Rogers' *The Troublesome Helpmate*, there seemed to be a clear feminist directive to avoid the study of male authors and their psychology. There is some evidence that this trend in feminist criticism is beginning to change. Recently, feminist criticism has not only permitted but graciously accepted Nina Auerbach's *Communities of Women: An Idea in Fiction* (Cambridge, Mass.: Harvard Univ. Press, 1978) and Judith Fetterley's *The Resisting Reader: A Feminist Approach to American Fiction* (Bloomington: Indiana Univ. Press, 1978). These books are not feminist studies of male authors per se; however, they are inclusive of literature written by men. Auerbach examines the notion of communities of women within the work of Henry James and others, while Fetterley comes very close to a study of sexual politics in the works of Henry James, Hemingway, Hawthorne, Fitzgerald, Mailer and others.

Sandra Gilbert's article, "Life Studies, or, Speech After Long Silence: Feminist Critics Today" (*College English*, 40, April 1979, 849-863) closes with an exhortation to "speak to our male counterparts, even to our antagonists" now that women have spoken to women. That sentiment seems to be a healthy one, if feminist criticism is to survive to be other than self-limiting. Ultimately, feminist criticism must adapt to changing times, changing sexual politics, and the changing academic community, or risk increasing specialization in a world of increasing generalism.

To understand adequately possible future trends and the necessity for change in the eighties, one must first understand the ways in which feminist criticism has evolved and defined itself. In the first place, feminist criticism of the sixties and early seventies started with *Sexual Politics* as a critique of mainstream criticism, of the prevailing attitudes toward literature written by men. In that sense, feminist criticism defined itself initially as intellectual antagonist to the male establishment. Feminist critics stated that style and content were separate issues, that beautifully written fiction, regardless of the power of the prose, was less than satisfactory aesthetically if the content of the prose were sexist. The fear and/or hatred of women inherent in the works of major twentieth century American writers such as Faulkner and Hemingway, and major British writers such as Lawrence and Joyce was a phenomenon which had to be noted. But there were problems with this stance so far as the future development of feminist criticism was concerned.

2

The biggest problem seemed to be that feminist criticism couldn't develop or advance unless it had a subject matter of its own. One could stand slightly to the side forever, haranguing about the injustice of sexual attitudes in mainstream modern authors. The authors couldn't change their attitudes, since they were dead, presumably, and feminist criticism couldn't change the fact that mainstream literature was well-written, even if, in some respects, hateful. The literature would still be included in English department curricula because even its detractors recognized it as the basis of the mainstream literary tradition. Regardless of the number of women authors one attempted to add to that tradition and to recognize as part of it, the tradition itself remained a male-dominated historical fact.

At that point, separatism or specialization in the study of women authors seemed the only option. It was a way out of the dilemma, but it was also a way out of the mainstream tradition. Studies of women writers proliferated in an attempt to establish a literature which belonged exclusively to women and to counter the male-dominated tradition which failed to take adequate notice of women writers. Studies like Elaine Showalter's *A Literature of Their Own* (Princeton: Princeton Univ. Press, 1977), Patricia Meyer Spacks' *The Female Imagination* (New York: Knopf, 1975) and Ellen Moers' *Literary Women* (New York: Doubleday, 1976) became the focus of women's studies in literature. Why read beautifully crafted insults written by men, when there was a wealth of literature written by women? Studies of major women authors, the Brontes in *The Madwoman in the Attic* (Sandra M. Gilbert and Susan Gubar, New Haven: Yale Univ. Press, 1979) and Virginia Woolf in *Woman of Letters* (Phyllis Rose, New York: Oxford Univ. Press, 1978) constitute the most recent and appropriate form of specialization in an area previously not recognized wholeheartedly by the male-dominated establishment.

In addition to the critical focus on building a revised tradition, contemporary fiction writers have provided a new politically conscious women's literature for feminist critics to read and to teach. Doris Lessing, Margaret Atwood, Marge Piercy, Gail Godwin, Toni Morrison, Marilyn French and many other writers responded to the chance to discuss issues that related exclusively to women, with the result that it will be impossible for any literary scholar to talk about the literature of the sixties and seventies without recognizing as mainstream literature the "women's" literature written during this time.

The problem, and one reason for this collection, is that we have been talking about history instead of facing the eighties and the changes which this decade may bring to contemporary fiction, to feminist criticism, to women's studies and to academe. Feminist critics must and will continue to supplement tradition with revised perspectives of previously little known or inadequately studied women authors. As critics, they must also continue to select for study those women writers who deal with issues which are particularly relevant to women. But to continue these endeavors exclusively now seems to be an impossibility, for several reasons.

One such reason is that the decline in student enrollment is creating a movement away from specialized programs such as women's studies. We all are sorry to see that happen, but we must make the commitment to seek ways in which to preserve and communicate the message of women's studies, even without funding of special programs. One of the most effective means of fostering the feminist critical approach is to include works by women writers within traditional curricula, where that is possible, certainly, but also to point out attitudes toward gender within traditional works of literature. That tactic brings us back to the original dialogue with the male-dominated tradition. This time around, though, the feminist critic can, in addition to critiquing an obviously masculine sexist perspective, also teach literature by women writers in a positive manner. We are not back where we started as mere detractors on the sidelines; we are in danger of remaining on the sidelines only if we insist on teaching and studying literature only by women.

A recently published feminist critic who supports this point of view is Minda Rae Amiran who writes rather indignantly that she finds

the present interest in 'women's literature' degrading, and the teaching of women's literature in English departments a subversion of women's liberation. The whole point of leaving the doll's house, I would have thought, was to become a person among people, to be what one wanted to be. If one chose to be an English teacher, it was because one had an interest in literature; one didn't have to astonish the professors, or to decorate a campus, or to confine oneself to books on childbirth. (*College English*, 39, February 1978, 653-461)

Minda Rae Amiran has no quarrel with those who wish to pursue the study of women authors, but rather with male-dominated departments which perceive that keeping women professionals occupied with "women's literature" is one way of keeping them out of the establishment. It may also be a way of eliminating women whenever women's studies programs are seen as too expensive or as "extra" features added to basic programs.

So far as literature by women is concerned, there is no guarantee that such literature will continue to be separatist, either. Feminist critics who have taken a separatist stance and who have specialized in the study of, say, Margaret Atwood, may be left behind when Atwood ceases to undermine her male characters by depicting them as solely childish, pathetic, foolish, inept, or even predatory. It was easy, when fiction by women was concerned with getting as far away from men as emotionally possible, to get away from dialogue with men. There is a world of difference, however, between Atwood's *Lady Oracle* and *Life Before Man* in Atwood's characterization of men. The contemporary feminist critic must deal with the changes. Men are an issue which has always been a part of some women's concerns. As such, the study of men is a perfectly legitimate focus for feminist criticism.

Just as Marge Piercy, in *Vida* (New York: Summit, 1979), has Vida describe her husband in a restaurant, "He was being his old dominating self, his manner before feminists had filed down his edges, when he would never hesitate to order for anybody" (p. 24), so feminist critics must begin to interact with all of literature in order to "file down" the rough edges. The essence of this interaction must be dialectical. We need to focus on and to discuss differences far more than we need to dwell on similarities. At one point in the recent past before feminist criticism shifted its predominant focus to literature by and about women, there was frequent talk about androgyny. We owe a great deal to Carolyn Heilbrun (*Toward a Recognition of Androgyny*, New York: Knopf, 1973) for the development of the concept as part of literary critical theory. Many other feminist critics, however, found the notion too difficult to work with. As one critic states of androgyny,

> As an ideal image of liberation from traditonal sex-role stereotypes, it is false. We cannot discuss the myth, in psychological terms, without resorting to sexist polarizations for the definition of identity ("My intellect is my masculine self; my intuition, my feminine self"); simply from a linguistic point of view, the myth is self-defeating.
>
> (Daniel A. Harris, *Women's Studies*, 2, 1974, 171)

The sentiment at the core of the work on androgyny was a good one—one which was inclusive of the study of both genders and which recognized a fact which used to be at the core of feminist study—women and men are equally human, equally entitled to full privileges within the human race, literature and academe. However, and this is the second fact that made androgyny an unsuitable focus for feminist critics, men and women are equally influenced by differences in perspective which result from gender-related differences in culture. That makes men and women "equally different," and it's only a short step from there to separatism.

The exclusivity of women's studies is profoundly separatist and, in a sense, that elitism is a glorious thing after so many years of oppression and neglect dumped upon issues in literature which are gender-related to women in particular. Yet there are forces at work, now more than in the recent past, which are taking away from academe some of the elitist tendencies which were previously possible; these forces militate against separatism and the survival of women's studies and all other forms of elitism. The movement back to "basics" is a movement away from specialization.

Feminist scholars at small or poorly funded institutions have always operated within non-separatist systems, either because enrollments were not large enough to create women's studies programs, or because funding simply wasn't available. Funding and enrollments may become increasing problems for all institutions. But the point is that it is possible to live with these conditions and simultaneously to enrich and develop the study of gender—including feminist study. Feminist scholars with an interest in opposite gender foci, and those simply with an interest in infiltrating traditional curricula as completely as possible should consider that while some continue the fight to establish funding and priority for the study of women authors and issues which relate particularly to women, the following rather obvious alternatives are also possible:

1. The study of male authors is wholly legitimate for the feminist scholar. It is crucial to engage in dialogue with authors, critics (and students) of the opposite sex. That exploration of differences is at the center of gender study and at the center of criticism itself. We also have the right to be different in perspective from those of the same as well as of the opposite gender.
2. In the area of teaching, we should be working to insure that students never again complete a program of literary study without an awareness of works by both women and men, and without an awareness of the differences in sexual perspective in those works. Sexism as literary content should always be explained.
3. Instructors must feel free to modify traditional courses by teaching them from a feminist critical perspective and by including works which are well-suited for gender study. In a recent science fiction course, for example, I used works by Arthur Clarke and Kurt Vonnegut, Jr., but also included Mary Shelley's *Frankenstein*, Marge Piercy's *Woman on the Edge of Time*, Joanna Russ' *The Female Man* and Doris Lessing's *The Memoirs of a Survivor*. If one takes the attitude that there's no such thing as a separate women's science fiction, then science fiction by women is simply legitimate science fiction. A course which explores sexual attitudes in science fiction is that much richer than one which overlooks a feature which has always been prominent in the genre.

There is a great difference between sexual and sexist study, and the acute scholar, critic and teacher must be prepared to see that women's studies is a vital part, but only a part, of gender studies. By the same token, the study of gender within literature is of general importance to everyone.

*   *   *

Since the preceding position statement appeared in longer form in *College English* in 1981, "everyone" has, in fact, moved toward an acceptance of gender studies. That they have done so is an indication, in part, of the extent to which the concept of such studies is critically useful. We do not live in worlds of our own, safely segregated by gender or by gender preference, although we sometimes feel as if we do or wish that we did. We live in a world in which our only hope of escaping the fact of sexism is in recognizing it, studying it, sharing our findings with one another, and engaging in dialogue, even if that involves confrontation. It is appropriate for women to study—and to critique—gender-related aspects of the works of male authors (as the essays by Doan and Hodges, Myers, Gilbert, Davis, Spector and Russ so clearly demonstrate). Critical dialogue between genders has a potential for humor, for involvement, and for a kind of gender-related pride in one's own insights. It is clear that such dialogue is a psychological exercise, as one gender-based mind, aware of its bias, tries simultaneously to "read" an opposite-gender mentality and to express—or to overcome—its own gender bias.

Similarly, the study of gender-related aspects of literature by critics who are of the author's same gender can—although it needn't—involve an exhilarating feeling of empathy with the text and an eagerness to explain one's insights to others and "opposites." In this collection, Gubar's essay on female creativity and Voss' work on female autobiography exemplify the best clarificatory function of gender studies. We also see this clarification in Oehlschlaeger's study of women as a threat to the men in frontier fiction, in Bodmer's essay on identity and the masculine tradition in some contemporary fiction, and in Boone's work on the male quest. These three essays, which are really pioneer attempts at "men's studies," share very comfortably in the critical concept of gender study, and that concept is a valid description of the sort of criticism in which all of the essayists are engaged. Furthermore, there needn't be either a special gender-related empathy or a gender-related antipathy between authors and critics in gender studies; that is a subjective matter of reading for the critic to determine personally. The only "rule" which comes into play is that the critic must recognize and consider all gender-related factors which have a bearing on his/her study. Anything less is deceptive, or less than "objective" in this arena which is so often perceived and experienced as "subjective."

An awareness of these "subjective" elements often manifests itself in critical perspectives and techniques which seem to be explicitly or implicitly psychoanalytic, in these essays. Judith Fetterley's study of Cather's *My Antonia*, for example, is also a study of the way in which the psychology of sexual preference is reflected in the text; Ann Parson's work on "The Self-Inventing Self" is an analysis of the psychology of the sexually oppressed victim struggling to be creator and artist. Most of the essays, some of them mentioned previously in other contexts, participate in this psychoanalytic and social milieu.

Gender study addresses psychological issues—the relationships between gender and creativity, gender and identity, and gender and genre. I have chosen these areas as "categories" for the arrangement of this collection, although they are clearly arbitrary; most of these essays address at least two of these three issues to a greater or lesser extent. Merivale's essay on Didion, like Archer's study of Woolf's *Jacob's Room*, concerns the issue of gender and the creative bias of the authors under consideration, the question of identity of the characters, and the definition of genre. That these issues do not remain distinct is another indication of the comprehensive nature of gender studies. Two issues which gender studies also typically address, but which I have not included in the collection, are relationships between gender and reading, and gender conflicts. So much is currently being done on gender and reading that, apart from my discussion of this issue in the introduction, I felt it was best to leave this area to be a primary concern of other collections which are to appear soon, and of Judith Fetterley's *The Resisting Reader*. The question of conflict between the genders in literature is one which, for the moment, has become the focus of my own ongoing study.

It will be interesting to see what new insights and critical perspectives develop as the awareness of gender becomes increasingly a part of the way in which we study literature. The essays in this collection demonstrate that the influence of gender on literature is a fundamental and complex interaction which no intelligent critic can afford to overlook, and one which represents a comprehensive "new direction" for feminist criticism in years to come.

Judith Spector

Indiana University, 1986

Gender And Creativity

Susan Gubar

"The Blank Page" and the Issues of Female Creativity

When the "Mona Lisa" was stolen from the Louvre in Paris in 1911 and was missing for two years, more people went to stare at the blank space than had gone to look at the masterpiece in the 12 previous years.

Barbara Cartland, *Book of Useless Information*

"The female genital, like the blank page anticipating the poem, is an absence, a not me, which I occupy."

Sandra McPherson, "Sentience," *The Year of Our Birth*

CONSIDER FOR A MOMENT Ovid's story of Pygmalion: a king, shocked at the vices of the female disposition, creates a beautiful statue, significantly an ivory statue white as snow, with which he falls in love. Pygmalion brings his lovely statue presents, dresses it, bedecks it with jewels, fondles its curves, takes it to bed, and prays to Venus that his wife be (or be like) his "ivory girl." When he feels the ivory under his fingers soften, "as wax grows soft in sunshine, made pliable by handling," Pygmalion is astonished with joy: "It is a body!"[1] Not only has he created life, he has created female life as he would like it to be—pliable, responsive, purely physical. Most important, he has evaded the humiliation, shared by many men, of acknowledging that it is *he* who is really created out of and from the *female* body.

Our culture is steeped in such myths of male primacy in theological, artistic and scientific creativity. Christianity, as feminist theologians have shown us, is based on the power of God the Father, who creates the natural world of generation out of nothing.[2] Literary men like Coleridge, Shelley, Keats and Ruskin describe the author as priest, prophet, warrior, legislator, or emperor, reinforcing the idea most lucidly articulated by Gerard Manley Hopkins that "the male quality is the creative gift."[3] The example of scientific overreachers from the Faust of Marlowe and Goethe and Mann to the most recent DNA biologists implies that scientific ingenuity also seems to usurp the generative powers of the womb, even as it tries to re-create the female in the male's image. But if the creator is a man, the creation itself is the female, who, like Pygmalion's ivory girl, has no

10

name or identity or voice of her own. Margaret Atwood's prose poem about two boys who construct a woman out of mud ("She began at the neck and ended at the knees and elbows: they stuck to essentials") seems far removed from Ovid's ivory girl. Yet the boys continually "repair her, making her hips more spacious, enlarging her breasts with their stone nipples," as they make use of "her brown wormy flesh" ("They would take turns, they were not jealous, she preferred them both")[4]: both the ivory girl and the mud woman are products of the male imagination, objects created for the use of men. As Simone de Beauvoir has demonstrated in *The Second Sex*, the phallus as the transcendent incarnate turns woman's self into an object, an other.[5]

Woman is not simply an object, however. If we think in terms of the production of culture, she is an art object: she is the ivory carving or mud replica, an icon or doll, but she is not the sculptor. Lest this seem fanciful, we should remember that until very recently women have been barred from art schools as students yet have always been acceptable as models. Both Laura and Beatrice were turned into characters by the poems they inspired. A poet as sensitive as Chaucer to this reification of the female allowed Criseyde to recognize and lament her own dilemma: "Allas, of me, unto the worldes ende, / Shall neyther ben., ywriten nor ysonge / No good word; for these bokes wol me shende" (bk. 5, st. 152). Like the words written about her, she fears she will be "rolled on many a tongue."[6] Shakespeare also studied this entrapment of the woman: looking at Desdemona, whom he imagines dishonest, Othello asks, "Was this fair paper, this most goodly book, / Made to write 'whore' upon?" (4. 2. 71-72).[7] The appropriation of the female "read" or "written" into textuality makes one wonder about many another heroine's fate. On more than one occasion, Dorothea Brooke in *Middlemarch* bemoans her inability to become a poet; how much of a comfort is Will Ladislaw's assurance to her that "You *are* a poem"?[8] Ezra Pound quotes a similar line to the poet H.D.: "You are a poem, though your poem's naught."[9] When the metaphors of literary creativity are filtered through a sexual lens, female sexuality is often identified with textuality.

We can see this clearly in Henry James' *Portrait of a Lady*, where the ideal *jeune fille* is described as "a sheet of blank paper." So "fair and smooth a page would be covered with an edifying text," we are told, whereas the experienced woman who is "written over in a variety of hands" has a "number of unmistakable blots" upon her surface.[10] In *To the Lighthouse*, egotistical Mr. Ramsay sees his wife in a window "as an illustration, a confirmation of something on the printed page to which one returns, fortified and satisfied."[11] In Conrad's *Victory*, Axel Heyst saves a girl called Lena (after the seductress Magdalena) from "murdering silence" in an all-female orchestra by renaming her Alma (soul). Converted from artist to accompanist to accomplice, she seems "like a script in an unknown language" or "like any writing to an illiterate." Looking at her Heyst feels like a "man looking this way and that on a piece of writing which he was unable to decipher, but which may be big with some revelation."[12] From *The Waste Land*, in which a woman's hair "glow[s] into words," to *The Great Gatsby*, in which the "black rivulets" of mascara on a weeping woman lead to the "humorous suggestion ... that she sing the notes on her face," the female body has been feared for its power to articulate itself.[13] More recently, Ishmael Reed describes sex in this way: "He got good into her Book tongued her every passage thumbing her leaf and rubbing his hands all over her binding."[14] And John Berryman sums up the implications of this metaphor when he concludes a sequence of sonnets written to his mistress with the emphatic admission, "You are the text."[15]

In fact contemporary critics not infrequently write about the act of reading in sexual terms. A "passage" of a text is a way of knowing a "corpus" or "body" of material that should lead us on, tease us—but not too obviously. "Knowing" a book is not unlike sexual knowing, as Roland Barthes has demonstrated in *The Pleasure of the Text*, his erotics of reading.[16] Not only do we experience gratification orally as we "devour" books voraciously, but we also respond subliminally to the "rhythms" of the plot, looking forward to a "climax." Furthermore, Claude Levi-Strauss implies that the female must be identified with language used by men in the perpetuation of culture when he explains in *Structural Anthropology* that women are "*circulated* between clans, lineages, or families, in place of *the words of the group*, which are *circulated* between individuals."[17] Similarly, William Gass argues that "ordinary language ought to be like the gray inaudible wife who services the great man: an ideal engine, utterly self-effacing, devoted without remainder to its task; but when language is used as an art it is no longer used merely to communicate. It demands to be treated as a thing, inert and voiceless."[18] The connection between women and words is less explicit but just as significant in David Lodge's *Language of Fiction*. Lodge asserts that the medium of fiction "is never virgin: words come to the writer already violated by other men...."[19] This corrupt lexicon presumably can be redeemed by the semantics of the text, for its seminal meaning is almost always closely associated with the seed or semen of the author's mind brooding on the repository of the page that bodies this meaning forth: Pound, for example, describes ideal creativity as a result of "the balance of the ejector [male] and retentive media [female]."[20] And in an effort to criticize what he calls phallocentrism, Jacques Derrida describes the literary process in terms of identification of the pen with the penis, the hymen with the page. As Gayatri Spivak explains in her introducion to *Of Grammatology*, "The hymen is always folded ... space in which the pen writes its dissemination."[21]

This model of the pen-penis writing on the virgin page participates in a long tradition identifying the author as a male who is primary and the female as his passive creation—a secondary object lacking autonomy, endowed with often contradictory meaning but denied intentionality. Clearly this tradition excludes women from the creation of culture, even as it reifies her as an artifact within culture. It is therefore particularly problematic for those women who want to appropriate the pen by becoming writers. Especially in the nineteenth-century, women writers, who feared their attempts at the pen were presumptuous, castrating, or even monstrous, engaged in a variety of strategies to deal with their anxiety about authorship. Sandra M. Gilbert and I discuss some of these strategies in *The Madwoman in the Attic*. But just as important as the anxiety the male pen produces in the would-be woman writer is the horror she experiences at having been defined as his creation. Indeed, this problem seems to explain the coherence of nineteenth- and twentieth-century writing by women. Isak Dinesen's short story "The Blank Page" addresses this question with brilliant clarity.[22] This story can be used to illustrate how woman's image of herself as text and artifact has affected her attitudes toward her physicality and how these attitudes in turn shape the metaphors through which she imagines her creativity.

Briefly, the story of "The Blank Page" centers on the sisters of a Carmelite order of nuns who grow flax to manufacture the most exquisite linen in Portugal. This linen is so fine that it is used for the bridal sheets of all the neighboring royal houses. After the wedding night, it is solemnly and publicly displayed to attest to the virginity of the princess and is then reclaimed by the convent where the central piece of the stained sheet "which bore witness to the honor of a royal bride" is mounted, framed, and hung in a long gallery with a plate identifying the name of the princess. These "faded markings" on the sheets are of special interest to female pilgrims who journey to the remote country convent, for "each separate canvas with its coroneted name-plate has a story to tell, and each has been set up in loyalty to the story." But pilgrims and sisters alike are especially fascinated by the framed canvas over the one nameless plate which displays the blank, snow-white sheet that gives the story its title.

Before approaching the mysterious promise of the blank page, let us consider the framed, bloodied sheets in the convent gallery, which is both a museum of women's paintings (each sheet displays a unique, abstract design and is mounted in a heavy frame) and a library of women's literary works (the bloodstains are the ink on these woven sheets of paper). Collected and cherished by a female community that has seen better days, a kind of paradigmatic women's studies department, these bloodstained marks illustrate at least two points about female anatomy and creativity: first, many women experience their own bodies as the only available medium for their art, with the result that the distance between the woman artist and her art is often radically diminished; second, one of the primary and most resonant metaphors provided by the female body is blood, and cultural forms of creativity are often experienced as a painful wounding. Although I will deal with each point separately, they are clearly related, for the woman artist who experiences herself as killed into art may also experience herself as bleeding into print.

As to my first point, the objects of art in "The Blank Page" are quite literally made out of the bodies of the royal princesses whose internal fluids are the print and the paint. Not only are artist and art object physically linked but also the canvases in the nuns' gallery are a direct response to the princesses' private lives. Royal ladies and highborn spinsters would proceed "on a pilgrimage which was by nature both sacred and secretly gay" to read the canvas bearing the name of a princess they had once served and to review the bride's life as a wife and mother. The stained pages are therefore biographical remnants of otherwise mute existences, a result of and response to life rather than an effort at producing an independent aesthetic object. Indeed, were the female community less sensitive to the significance of these signs, such stained sheets would hardly be considered art at all. Dinesen implies that woman's use of her own body in the creation of art results in forms of expression devalued or totally invisible to eyes trained by traditional aesthetic standards. She also seems to imply that, within the life of domesticity assigned the royal princess from birth, the body is the only accessible medium for self-expression.

Certainly women's limited options—expressed in the parable by the fact that all royal (privileged) women marry while all single women are nuns—have shaped the art they create. Unable to train themselves as painters, unable to obtain the space or income to become sculptors, gifted women in these areas have had to work in private, using the only materials at hand—their bodies, their selves. If, as Dinesen implies, female creativity has had to express itself within the confines of domesticity (in part because of the emphasis on the personal in female socialization), women could at the least paint their own faces, shape their own bodies, and modulate their own vocal tones to become the glass of fashion and the mold of form. To make up, for such women, means not only making up stories but making up faces. In terms of the Pygmalion myth with which I began, the woman who cannot become an artist can nevertheless turn herself into an artistic object.

Nowhere is this better illustrated than in the novels of George Eliot, in which many female characters squander their creativity on efforts to reconstruct their own images. From Hetty Sorrell in *Adam Bede* (1859), who peers at her earrings and ribbons in a blotched mirror as she sits at a dressing table where the brass handles hurt her knees, to Gwendolen Harleth in *Daniel Deronda* (1876), who poses as Saint Cecilia in a glass exquisitely framed in black and gold, Eliot analyzes the ways in which women's creativity has been deformed by being channeled into self-destructive narcissism. Eliot criticizes the idea that beauty is an index of moral integrity by demonstrating how narcissism infantilizes the female, turning her from an autonomous person into a character in search of an author (or a page in search of a pen, to keep up the metaphor with which I began). Such a woman is always and only "becoming"—that is, she is beautiful but she is always imagining some future identity that she is unable to realize by herself.

Hetty, for example, is like a hopeful child waiting to be adopted and adapted by Arthur Donnithorne. Gwendolen's case is even clearer. After arranging at a party a series of *tableaux vivants* to gain the admiration of prospective suitors, she chooses to represent herself imitating a character who looks like a statue. Instead of turning back to life on cue, Gwendolen is terrified by a picture of a dead face that unexpectedly springs out of a movable panel before her eyes; when she returns to herself, she looks "like a statue into which a soul of Fear had entered: her pallid lips were parted; her eyes, usually narrowed under their long lashes, were dilated and fixed."[23] The dead face, Eliot implies, is Gwendolen's own. For in the process of turning herself into an artistic object, she makes herself autistic. Increasingly enmeshed in dreadful hallucinatory visions of her own distress, Gwendolen eventually is impelled to desire the death of her husband and her own death. Eliot's conviction that female creativity has been perverted (here as female narcissism and elsewhere in Eliot's fiction as enthrallment to male authority) helps us understand why she never wrote a *Kunstlerroman*.

Many female modernists have studied the deflection of female creativity from the production of art to the re-creation of the body,[24] but Edith Wharton, especially in *The House of Mirth* (1905), was most clearly influenced by Eliot. Cynthia Griffin Wolff has already brilliantly shown how Wharton's first title, "A Moment's Ornament," captures "the decorative imperative of that aspect of femininity that Lily embodies and the ultimate fragility of a self that has grown out of that imperative."[25] Lily Bart's gracefulness, her stylish clothing, her belief in the power of her own beauty to do good, her use of furniture and nature as backdrop scenery, even the lines on her face she traces with dismay in the mirror justify Diana Trilling's view that "Lily herself possesses the quality of a fine work of art."[26] Because financially she cannot afford to maintain herself as a work of art without the money of a man, Lily's artful presentation resembles Gwendolen's; she too must attract a husband. Furthermore, the only man in the novel who could possibly save her from becoming a commodity on the marriage market is himself incapable of viewing her as anything but a collectable in the aesthetic market: "As a spectator, Lawrence Selden had always enjoyed Lily Bart," making "use of the 'argument from design'," for he knows that "she must have cost a great deal to make" (p. 3). In fact, he believes that "even her weeping was an art"

(p. 69). While he is correct that her self-presentation empties her of spontaneity and makes her relationships duplicitous, Selden only further imprisons her in this ornamental behavior by characterizing it as so uniquely her own.

Although Lily's art does not procure her security in the form of a husband, and although she is quite destitute on her deathbed at thirty years of age, Lily seems to triumph at the end of *The House of Mirth*, for her death is the logical extension of her life. Having turned herself into an artistic object, she now literally kills herself into art. Significantly, before taking the overdose that lulls her to sleep and death, Lily goes through her wardrobe of dresses which "still kept the long unerring lines, the sweep and amplitude of the great artist's stroke, and as she spread them out on the bed the scenes in which they had been worn rose vividly before her" (p. 211). She remembers specifically the party at which she, like Gwendolen, participated in *tableaux vivants*; when Lily turned herself into Reynolds' portrait of "Mrs. Lloyd," she looked "as though she had stepped, not out of, but into, Reynolds' canvas" (p. 131), thereby demonstrating to Selden and the other onlookers "the touch of poetry in her beauty" (p. 131).

While Lily waits in bed for the drug to bring oblivion, she thinks that there is "some word she had found" to tell Selden that would make everything well (p. 317). On entering her room, Selden sees "a narrow bed along the wall, and on the bed, with motionless hands and calm, unrecognizing face, the semblance of Lily Bart." He kneels by this semblance for a final moment, "drain[ing] their last moment to the lees; and in the silence there passed between them the word which made all clear" (p. 323). This word is Lily's dead body; for she is now converted completely into a script for his edification, a text not unlike the letters and checks she has left behind to vindicate her life. She submits to being thus defined, although she liberates her lover from such a degradation by destroying his letters. Lily's history, then, illustrates the terrors not of the word made flesh but of the flesh made word. In this respect, she illuminates the problems Wharton must have faced in her own efforts to create rather than be created—efforts not always successful, if we can trust the reported comments of as important a contemporary critic as Percy Lubbock who, in comparing her to Henry James, quipped: "She was herself a novel of his, no doubt in his earliest manner."[27]

Like Kafka's victim in "The Penal Colony," women have had to experience cultural scripts in their lives by suffering them in their bodies. This is why Maxine Hong Kingston writes so movingly about her resemblance to the mythic woman warrior who went into battle scarred by the thin blades which her parents literally used to write fine lines of script on her body.[28] For the artist, this sense that she is herself the text means that there is little distance between her life and her art. The attraction of women writers to personal forms of expression like letters, autobiographies, confessional poetry, diaries and journals points up the effect of a life experienced as an art or an art experienced as a kind of life, as does women's traditional interest in cosmetics, fashion and interior decorating. Many books by women writers (like Dorothy Richardson's *Pilgrimage* and Olive Schreiner's *From Man to Man*) cannot be finished because they are as ongoing and open-ended as the lives of their authors. The mythic lives of women artists from Emily Dickinson (who played out the Gothic fiction of the white-dressed maiden imprisoned in daddy's house) to Isadora Duncan (whose costumes and affairs and death express her creed as well as her autobiography does) also reveal the close identification experienced between the female artist and her art. Duncan's medium, dance, has always been acceptable for women, I suspect, because the body of the dancer becomes an instrument or icon on stage.

Not a few of the most exciting experiments of women artists, moreover, grow out of a self-conscious attempt to obliterate aesthetic distance. The insistence that the domestic is artistic is illustrated, for example, by Katherine Mansfield, who writes lovingly about the ways in which a kitchen is decorated with utensils and food.[29] It finds a kind of culmination in the performative art of Mierle Laderman Ukeles, whose "Maintenance Art Activity" consists in washing museum floors with a damp mop, over and over again, and even more to the purpose here, Carolee Schneemann, who reads from a long scroll she removes from her vagina in her performance of *Up To and Including Her Limits* (1975).[30] Writing about Eleanor Antin's videotape in which she applies makeup to the "canvas" of her face and her photo sequence in which she documents "carving" ten pounds off her body, Arlene Raven and Deborah Marrow explain that "Antin's work is of the verb rather than the object" in its effort to illuminate how "in this culture women themselves are the art product."[31] Judy Chicago's *The Dinner Party* celebrates creative women who, refusing conventional definitions of the female, are in a privileged position to question the definitions of art that our culture accepts.[32] But *The Dinner Party* plates also imply that women, who have served, have been served up and consumed. They therefore remind us of the sacrificial nature of the body "dressed" as art. Indeed, in *The House of Mirth* the fashion plate often lifts a face "like an empty plate held up to be filled" (p. 45); Lily's beauty is described as a "glaze," (pp. 3, 51), reminding us of the fragility and vulnerability of Chicago's "service."

The stain that darkens the reputation of a girl like Lily and the stains of vaginal imagery at the center of the porcelain plates turn us to my second point, the centrality of blood as a symbol furnished by the female body. Luce Irigaray has argued recently that women are made vulnerable by their inability to express their delirium: "Women do not manage to articulate their madness: they suffer it directly in their body."[33] In "The Blank Page," the sacrificial suffering of the inarticulate female body is revealed in the bloody ink print, which is the result of the hymen's penetration and which is so valued by the community; the high steward to the royal house proclaims, *"Virginem eam tenemus*—'we declare her to have been a virgin'." While bloodstains can be a certification of freedom from pregnancy or the mark of entrance into puberty, in the Dinesen story they call to mind the more tragic associations of blood for women, especially for women writers. Unlike the blood of menstruation which presumably defiles like a curse or the blood of childbirth which is also taboo, the blood on the royal sheets is holy, for it certifies purity. By making the sheets into objects as sacred as altar cloths, the nuns sanctify the sacrifice of the virgin, and by reading the stains as if they were hieroglyphs, they imply that we must come to terms with the fact of blood before we can understand the nature of female art.

Lest this seem too gothic a pronouncement, let me point to as pious and proper a poet as Christina Rossetti, for this Victorian conspicuously offers her song as a virginal blood sacrifice.[34] At least part of Rossetti's plan came from her sense that she was the model not the painter, the character not the author. She has been represented, moreover, "Not as she is, but as she fills his dream" ("In an Artist's Study"). Rossetti therefore experiences herself as "Dead before Death," to quote the title of a characteristic poem. In "From the Antique" she is explicit about her life's being "Doubly blank in a woman's lot." As in Dinesen's tale of the convent, Rossetti's speaker on the doorstep of "The Convent Threshold" feels caught between sexuality and chastity. Choosing to become a nun because there is mysterious "blood" between her lover and herself, she looks down to see her lily feet "soiled with mud, / With *scarlet* mud *which tells a tale*" [my italics]. The same identification of bleeding with telling or singing appears in the vision of the suffering poet in "From House to Home." Beginning with a sense of sinfulness, of being stained, Rossetti transforms herself in a number of religious poems into the bride of Christ and into a female Christ (she had modelled for a painting of the Virgin Mary). Imitating his blood sacrifice, she testifies repeatedly to the "mark of blood" that distinguishes her door ("Despised and Rejected"). But this sign also recalls the tokens of virginity on the cloth brought before the elders of the city to redeem the honor of a slandered bride, as described and prescribed in Deuteronomy.[35]

The blood sacrifice of the royal princesses in Dinesen's story represents the sacrifice of virginity not through martydom but through marriage, although the stained sheets also seem to imply that marriage may be a martyrdom. The blood on the royal sheets is considered holy because it proves that the bride is a valuable property, given by father to husband for the production of sons. In other words, before the sheet is collected by the convent sisters and assumes the status of art, the bloodstains are a testimony to the woman's function as a silent token of exchange. But this blood wedding transforms the marriage bed into a kind of coffin in which the virgin is sacrificed. Dinesen may have considered her own marriage deathly because she believed her many illnesses in later life were related to the syphillis she unwittingly contracted from her husband, but she implies that many women in a patriarchy experience a dread of heterosexuality. The storyteller of "The Blank Page," who has told "one more than a thousand" tales, is thereby associated with Scheherazade, who told stories in the night to circumvent the death awaiting her after sexual initiation in the bridal chamber.[36] Not only a surrogate for her own body, her stories save the daughters of the land who have been threatened with penetration and execution by the misogynist king who is enraged by the infidelity of women.

The framed stained sheets imply, then, that all the royal princesses have been "framed" into telling the same story, namely, the story of their acquiescence as objects of exchange. The American poet H.D. treats this confinement as a primary plot (conspiracy) against women and an effective plot (burial mound) for women.[37] She has therefore dedicated her late poems to excavating the female by creating alternative scripts, as she explains in *Trilogy* (1944-46), where her muse carries "the blank pages / of the unwritten volume of the new."[38] In *Helen in Egypt* (1961), H.D. begins with a character who is a phantom because she has barely survived being turned into a heroine. Basing her epic on a seventh-century palinode by Stesichorus that claims Helen never got any further than Egypt—it was merely an image of Helen that accompanied Paris to Troy to give the pretext for war—H.D. shows us a Helen haunted by stories told about the war, specifically, the blame heaped on her for presumably causing it and the role allotted to her as an object of exchange; war booty, gift, ransom.[39] Helen realizes at the beginning of H.D.'s revisionary epic that her own imagined role in the war was a sacrifice inflicted on her, that "the script was a snare" (p. 220). But it is terribly difficult for her to evade the snare or escape it, because, like Eliot's and Wharton's heroines and Dinesen's royal princesses, she feels that "*She herself is the writing*" (p. 91). She tries to rescue herself by considering other stories of growing up female, but these turn out to be the same story of the blood sacrifice of daughters and virgins: Iphigenia, Polyxena, Chryseis, Cassandra and Persephone.

"Helen returns constantly to this theme of sacrifice" (p. 84) because the daughters "were all sacrificed in one way or another" (p. 173). Inside this blood factory, she mourns the "bridal pledge at the altar" as a "pledge to Death" (p. 73). Her blood consciousness harkens back to the mythic female artist, Philomela: raped by Tereus who cut out her tongue, Philomela took her revenge by weaving her story for all to see with "purple / On a white background."[40] In addition, Helen's blood consciousness also reaches forward to contemporary poems (by writers like May Swensen and Marge Piercy) in which the phallus is a weapon. The desecrated female body that feels like the self of the poet bleeds into print.[41] Anne Sexton

therefore associates her female anatomy with the absence of control: in her
female revision of *The Waste Land*, "Hurry Up Please It's Time," she
identifies herself with Eliot's wasted, working-class women, for she knows
"I have ink but no pen." As a result, Sexton feels that her poems "leak"
from her "like a miscarriage."[42] Likewise, Frida Kahlo, who presents
herself as bound by red cords that are not only her veins and her roots but
also her paint, is a painter whose tragic physical problems contributed to
her feeling wounded, pierced and bleeding.[43]

Mired in stories of our own destruction, stories which we confuse with
ourselves, how can women experience creativity? In Dinesen's story, the
creation of female art feels like the destruction of the female body. Because
of the forms of self-expression available to women, artistic creation often
feels like a violation, a belated reaction to male penetration rather than a
possessing and controlling. Not an ejaculation of pleasure but a reaction to
rending, the blood on the royal marriage sheets seems to imply that
women's paint and ink are produced through a painful wounding, a literal
influence of male authority. If artistic creativity is likened to biological
creativity, the terror of inspiration for women is experienced quite literally
as the terror of being entered, deflowered, possessed, taken, had, broken,
ravished—all words which illustrate the pain of the passive self whose
boundaries are being violated. In fact, like their nineteenth-century
foremothers, twentieth-century women often describe the emergence of
their talent as an infusion from a male master rather than inspiration from
or sexual commerce with a female muse. This phallic master causes the
woman writer to feel her words are being expressed for her rather than by
her. Like Mary Elizabeth Coleridge who sees her lips as a silent wound, or
Charlotte Bronte who suffers from a "secret, inward wound" at the
moment she feels the "pulse of Ambition," or Emily Dickinson who is
bandaged as the empress of Calvary in some poems and as the wounded
deer in others, women writers often dread the emergence of their own
talents.[44]

If writing feels as if "the ink was pouring on to the sheets like blood,"
as it does for the heroine of Margaret Drabble's *The Waterfall*, then the
poet can easily become frightened by her sense of victimization: "I was
unnaturally aware of my own helpless subjugation to my gifts, my total
inability to make a poem at will." Drabble's poet explains. "I resented
this helplessness as I resented a woman's helplessness with a man."[45]

The twentieth-century prototype of this anxious sense that poetry
comes from being possessed and wounded is, of course, Sylvia Plath. Like
Drabble's heroine, whose creativity is released by giving birth to a second
child, Plath begins *Ariel* with a relatively cheerful poem about childbirth
that seems to promise a more positive way of imagining creativity for
women. But even here in "Morning Song," the new birth of morning
seems converted into grief and mourning, for the child is a "New statue"

and the parents "stand round blankly as walls." This statue, confined by blank walls, is transformed into the far more terrible wife of "The Applicant": "Naked as paper to start," she is "A living doll." Like Pygmalion's ivory girl, Atwood's mud woman, Eliot's living statues, Lily Bart who really is a living doll, or Sexton who is her own dead doll, Plath's wife is a kind of automaton in the clutches of someone else's will. Plath herself is not infrequently filled with a "thin / Papery feeling" which helps explain the thousands of paper dolls she played with as a child, and her poems lend sinister insight into Mansfield's perception that "Female dolls in their nakedness are the most female things on earth."[46] From Maggie Tulliver, who tortures her doll in the attic in *The Mill on the Floss*, to Pecola Breedlove in Toni Morrison's *The Bluest Eye*, who tortures herself because she cannot look after her doll, the heroines of women's fiction have played with dolls to define themselves.

Plath can only escape the dread that she has been created as an object (as she says in "Lady Lazarus," "I am your opus") by self-inflicted violence, by watching the bloodstain darkening the bandages, proving she is alive. A sense of helplessness seems inextricably related to the emergence of her voice: "By the roots of my hair some god got hold of me," Plath exclaims in "The Hanging Man"; "I sizzled in his blue volts like a desert prophet." As terrible as her muse is, however, her pain at his violation also proves she is alive. But the jolting words snapped out by these electric charges mean that the poetry Plath creates will kill her: "The blood jet is poetry, / There is no stopping it" ("Kindness"). She has had the blood sucked out of her by "Daddy," who "Bit [her] pretty red heart in two." While she has killed "The vampire who said he was you / And drank my blood for a year," she is still haunted by the black bat airs, and having been bitten, she has herself become a bloodsucker, for "The blood flood is the flood of love" ("The Munich Mannequins"). The redness of the "Tulips" in her hospital bed therefore "talks to [her] wound, it corresponds." If she sees herself as "flat, ridiculous, a cut-paper shadow / Between the eye of the sun and the eyes of the tulips," she knows she will eventually fly into these eyes which are, of course, "the red / Eye, the cauldron of morning" ("Ariel"). The only way to escape papery perfection in "Stings" is to become the "red / Scar in the sky." At the end of *Ariel*, she is finally perfected into a statue: "The illusion of a Greek necessity / Flows in the scrolls of her toga" as she accepts her role as heroine in the tragedy that is not only her art but her life ("Edge"). The dialectic between perfection and blood destruction means finally that Plath's "Words" are "Axes" from whose rhythmic strokes she will never recover.[47]

Adrienne Rich also identifies blood with the female body: "Sometimes every / aperture of my body / leaks blood. I don't know whether / to pretend that this is natural." In other words, Rich is aware that even her most intimate attitudes toward her own blood have been defined by male voices:

> You worship the blood
> you call it hysterical bleeding
> you want to drink it like milk
> you dip your fingers into it and write
> you faint at the smell of it
> you dream of dumping me into the sea.[48]

Rich seeks a way of experiencing the blood through her own sensibilities. In "Women," she sees three Fates who seem to represent her sense of women's progress in history: the first sister is sewing a costume for her role as Transparent Lady when "all her nerves will be visible"; the second is sewing "at the seam over her heart which has never healed entirely"; and the third is gazing "at the dark-red crust spreading westward far out on the sea."[49] Her beauty and her vision promise a time when women can automatically deny that our "wounds come from the same source as [our] power."[50] Refusing a poetry that implies performance, competition, or virtuosity, Rich strives in her most recent volume for "the musings of a mind / one with her body," within

> . . . the many-lived, unending
> forms in which she finds herself,
> becoming now the sherd of broken glass
> slicing light in a corner, dangerous
> to flesh, now the plentiful, soft leaf
> that wrapped round the throbbing finger, soothes the wound.[51]

Rich's promise returns us to Dinesen's poetry, for the snow-white sheet of the nameless princess also seems to promise a breakthrough into new beginnings for new stories that can soothe the wound. The singular blank sheet that so fascinates pilgrims and nuns alike in the convent library-museum seems an alternative to the bloody sheets that surround it. Thus, in terms of the patriarchal identification of women with blankness and passivity with which we began, Dinesen's blank page becomes radically subversive, the result of one woman's defiance which must have cost either her life or her honor. Not a sign of innocence or purity or passivity, this blank page is a mysterious but potent act of resistance. The showing of the sheet, moreover, proves that the anonymous princess has forced some sort of acknowledgment or accommodation in the public realm. On a literal level, the blank sheet may mean any number of alternative scripts for women: Was this anonymous royal princess not a virgin on her wedding night? Did she, perhaps, run away from the marriage bed and thereby retain her virginity intact? Did she, like Scheherazade, spend her time in bed telling stories so as to escape the fate of her predecessors? Or again, maybe the snow-white sheet above the nameless plate tells the story of a young woman who met up with an impotent husband, or of a woman who learned other erotic arts, or of a woman who consecrated herself to the nun's vow of chastity but within marriage. Indeed, the interpretation of this sheet seems as impenetrable as the anonymous princess herself. Yet Dinesen's old storyteller, who learned her art from her grandmother such as her grandmother learned it from her own mother's mother, advises her audience to "look at this page, and recognize the wisdom of my grandmother and of all storytelling women!"

The storyteller says this, I think, first of all because the blank page contains all stories in no story, just as silence contains all potential sound and white contains all color. Tillie Olsen's *Silences* and Rich's *On Lies, Secrets, and Silences* teach us about the centrality of silence in women's culture, specifically the ways in which women's voices have gone unheard. While male writers like Mallarme and Melville also explored their creative dilemmas through the trope of the blank page, female authors exploit it to expose how woman has been defined symbolically in the patriarchy as a tabula rasa, a lack, a negation, an absence. But blankness here is an act of defiance, a dangerous and risky refusal to certify purity. The resistance of the princess allows for self-expression, for she makes her statement by not writing what she is expected to write. Not to be written on is, in other words, the condition of new sorts of writing for women. The nuns and the storyteller recognize wisdom in the place where the uninitiated see nothing, in part by removing their attention from the traditional foreground to what is usually relegated to background, much as we might radically revise our understanding of the 1,001 blank days during which Scheherazade silently bore the king three sons whose surprise appearance at the end of the 1,001 nights wins her a reprieve from the death sentence. But the old crone also praises the blank sheets because it is the "material" out of which "art" is produced. Women's creativity, in other words, is prior to literacy: the sisterhood produces the blank sheets needed to accomplish writing.

Olive Schreiner, the great feminist theorist, explains what this implies about English culture when one of her heroines holds up a book and theorizes about literary history:

When I hold these paper leaves between my fingers, far off across the countless ages I hear the sound of women beating out the fibres of hemp and flax to shape the first garment, and, above the roar of the wheels and spinnies in the factory, I hear the whirr of the world's first spinning wheel and the voice of the woman singing to herself as she sits beside it, and know that without the labor of those first women kneeling over the fibres and beating them swiftly out, and without the hum of those early spinning wheels, neither factory nor paper pulp would ever have come into existence .... little book!—it has got its roots down, down, deep into the life of man on earth; it grows from there.[52]

If we take Schreiner's claim seriously, then, as Sandra Gilbert has argued in a slightly different context, no woman is a blank page: every woman is author of the page and author of the page's author.[53] The art of producing essentials—children, food, cloth—is woman's ultimate creativity. If it is taken as absence in the context of patriarchal culture, it is celebrated within the female community by the matrilineal traditions of oral storytelling. The veiled, brown, illiterate old woman who sits outside the city gates in Dinesen's tale therefore represents her grandmother and her grandmother's grandmother: "they and I have become one." Existing before man-made books, their stories let us "hear the voice of silence."

The blank page is created in Dinesen's story through the silent act of "sowing" the flax seed and "sewing" the linen, acts traditionally performed by the female community. This is the subversive voice of silence, and we can associate it with the silent sound of Philomela's shuttle. The process whereby "the seed is skillfully sown out by labor-hardened virginal hands" and the "delicate thread is spun, and the linen woven" is the secret of Dinesen's society of convent spin-sters. For the nuns who have raised the production of flax into art, then, the blank page is a tribute to what has been devalued as mere craft or service. The nuns refuse to relegate the domestic or the decorative to a category outside the realm of true creativity. At the same time, moreover, they sanctify their own creative efforts; for the germ of the story, the first seed of the flax, comes from the holy land of the daughter Achsah who sought and received a blessing—specifically, the blessing of springs of water. When the flax blooms, we are told, the valley becomes "the very color of the apron which the blessed virgin put on to go out and collect eggs within St. Anne's poultry yard, the moment before the Archangel Gabriel in mighty wing-strokes lowered himself onto the threshold of the house, and while high, high up a dove, neck-feathers raised and wings vibrating, stood like a small clear silver star in the sky."

Members of this "blithe sisterhood" thus preserve the history of lesser lives in the blood markings and glorify the blank page as a sacred space consecrated to female creativity, thereby pulling heaven down to earth. While the bloodstained sheets resemble the true icon of suffering divinity as seen on Veronica's veil, the virgin-blue flax blossoms remind us of Mary at the time before the Annunciation—Mary waiting, about to become pregnant with divinity.[54] In her readiness for rapture, she represents the female community, and its blank page is therefore hers. The convent in Dinesen's story is a Carmelite order, the order which propagates a special devotion to our Lady; indeed, in the Middle Ages, Carmelite theologians were among the earliest defenders of the Immaculate Conception, the doctrine that Mary was conceived without original sin. But the Carmelites have also produced the greatest Christian mystics, most importantly Saint Theresa, who inspired Dorothea Brooke's, and George Eliot's, quest for a life of significant action. Like Mary, whose sanctity is hidden in the ordinary, Theresa's mysticism was grounded in the everyday. The vows of poverty, chastity and obedience taken by the Carmelite nuns are strenuous attempts to aid contemplation, to achieve Theresa's ordinary mysticism. Not martyrs who suffer death but prophets who suffer inspiration, the convent virgins spend much time in silence, seeking to duplicate Mary's receptivity to bearing and giving birth to the Incarnate Word.[55] Thus, the blank place, a female inner space, represents readiness for inspiration and creation, the self conceived and dedicated to its own potential divinity.

Many of the late-Victorian and twentieth-century women writers whom I have mentioned were involved in the creation of a revisionary theology that allowed them to reappropriate and valorize metaphors of uniquely female creativity and primacy. I have space here only for a few examples. Florence Nightingale in *Cassandra* (1852), pronounced her audacious belief that "the next Christ will perhaps be a female Christ."[56] Schreiner claimed by extension that God is female when she argued that "the desire to incarnate" in the true artist "is almost like the necessity of a woman to give birth to her child."[57] From the blessed Lady who carries the new Bible of blank pages in H.D.'s *Trilogy* to Gertrude Stein's liturgical drama in praise of *The Mother of Us All*, modernist texts by women appear to corroborate the contemporary French feminist Helene Cixous' sentiment that the woman writer sanctifies herself when she gives birth to "an amniotic flow of words that reiterates the contractual rhythms of labor."[58] Margaret Anderson and Jane Heap's desire for a radically new kind of art is brilliantly illustrated by the *Little Review* volume that consisted of sixty-four blank pages.[59] The substitution of the female divinity for the male god, the womb for the penis, as the model of creativity was so pronounced by the turn of the century that it posed a real problem for such male modernists as T.S. Eliot, Lawrence, and Joyce. But of course, many women writers remained sensitive to the fact that such a mother-goddess myth was compensatory and that—unless freed from any biological imperative—it could entrap women in destructive stereotypes. To celebrate uniquely female powers of creativity without perpetuating destructive feminine socialization is the task confronted by writers as dissimilar as George Eliot, Rossetti, Schreiner, Wharton, H.D., and Mansfield, all of whom are involved in efforts to sanctify the female through symbols of female divinity, myths of female origin, metaphors of female creativity, and rituals of female power. "The Blank Page" is only one of many parables in an ongoing revisionary female theology.[60]

Since I have here persistently and perhaps perversely ignored history, I feel it is only fair to conclude by acknowledging that certain historical factors helped make this modulation in valuation possible. The shift in metaphors from the primacy of the pen to the primacy of the page is a late nineteenth-century phenomenon. The Romantic movement in poetry, the suffrage movement in politics, the rise of anthropology with its interest in fertility gods and goddesses, the myth of Mother Right coming at a time when the infant mortality rate was significantly lowered and birth control became more widely available, and finally World War I—all of these need to be studied, for we are only just beginning to read the patterns and trace the figures in what all too recently has been viewed as nothing but the blank pages of women's cultural and literary history.

Denise Levertov expresses my own sense of excitement at engaging in such a task, even as she reminds us how attentive and patient we must be before the blank page to perceive genuinely new and sustaining scripts. Like Dinesen, moreover, Levertov seeks to consecrate her own repeated efforts to contribute to the blank pages of our future history. Recognizing the strenuous and risky readiness at the moment before conception is itself an art, a kind of balancing act. Levertov praises the discipline that allows the poet to stand firm on "one leg that aches" while upholding "the round table" of the "blank page." Such diligence receives its just reward when the round table of the blank page is transformed into living wood that sighs and sings like a tree in the wind. This attitude toward creativity substitutes for the artistic object an act or process. Furthermore, just as sexuality was previously identified with textuality, the text itself now becomes infused with potent sexual energy, or so Levertov claims in what we can now recognize as a decidedly female vision:

> One at a time
> books, when their hour is come
> step out of the shelves.
> Heavily step (once more, dusty, fingermarked,
>   but pristine!)
> to give birth:
>
> each poem's passion
> ends in an Easter,
> a new life.
>   The books of the dead
> shake their leaves,
> word-seeds fly and
> lodge in the black earth.[61]

Notes

I am indebted to Sandra M. Gilbert for her insights and encouragement on this paper.
[1]Ovid, *Metamorphoses*, trans. Rolfe Humphries (Bloomington, Ind., 1955), pp. 241-43.
[2]See Mary Daly, *Beyond God the Father* (Boston, 1973), and *Womanspirit Rising: A Feminist Reader in Religion*, ed. Carol P. Christ and Judith Plaskow (San Francisco, 1979).
[3]Hopkins, letter to Richard Watson Dixon, 30 June 1896, *The Correspondence of Gerard Manley Hopkins and Richard Watson Dixon*, ed. C.C. Abbott (London, 1935), p. 133. For a fuller discussion of the identification of paternity and creativity, see Sandra M. Gilbert and Gubar, *The Madwoman in the Attic: The Woman Writer and the Nineteenth-Century*

Literary Imagination (New Haven, 1979), pp. 3-44.

[4]Margaret Atwood, untitled poem in the Circle / Mud sequence, *You Are Happy* (New York, 1974), p. 61.

[5]See Simone de Beauvoir, *The Second Sex*, trans. H.M. Parshley (New York, 1970).

[6]I am indebted for this view of Criseyde to Marcelle Thiebaux's "Foucault's Fantasia for Feminists: The Woman Reading" (Paper delivered at the MMLA Convention, Indianapolis, 8 Nov. 1979).

[7]The symbolic value of the "handkerchief / Spotted with strawberries" (3.3.434-45) is closely identified with Othello's fear that his "lust-stained" bedsheets must "with lust's blood be spotted." For a brilliant discussion of male sexual anxiety in *Othello* see Stephen J. Greenblatt, "Improvisation and Power," in *Literature and Society: Selected Papers from the English Institute*, ed. Edward W. Said (Baltimore, 1980), pp. 57-99.

[8]George Eliot, *Middlemarch* (Boston, 1968), pp. 57-99.

[9]Pound, quoted by H.D., *End to Torment* (New York, 1979), p. 12.

[10]Henry James, *The Portrait of a Lady* (New York, 1978), pp. 238, 268. It is interesting to compare this view of the blank female text with the horror Margaret Laurence's heroine, Morag, feels at the dying, fat and servile stepmother whose "face is as blank as a sheet of white paper upon which nothing will ever now be written" (*The Diviners [Toronto, 1978], p. 250*).

[11]Virginia Woolf, *To the Lighthouse* (New York, 1955), p. 53.

[12]Joseph Conrad, *Victory* (Garden City, 1957), p. 183.

[13]T.S. Eliot, *The Waste Land and Other Poems* (New York, 1962), sec. 2, l. 110; see also sec. 5, ll. 378-90: "A woman drew her long black hair out tight / And fiddled whispered music on those strings." F. Scott Fitzgerald, *The Great Gatsby* (New York, 1953), p. 34; see also p. 119 where Jordan Baker is described as "a good illustration."

[14]Ishmael Reed, *Mumbo Jumbo* (New York, 1978), pp. 208-9.

[15]John Berryman, *Berryman's Sonnets* (New York, 1967), p. 114. Russell Baker recently compared women to books, bemoaning the fact that "it is common nowadays to find yourself confronting a woman no thicker than a slim volume of poetry while buying a book wider than a piano" ("Sunday Observer," *New York Times Magazine*, 2 December 1979. p. 28).

[16]See Roland Barthes, *The Pleasures of the Text*, trans. Richard Miller (New York, 1975), p. 32: "There are those who want a text (an art, a painting) without a shadow, without the 'dominant ideology'; but this is to want a text without fecundity, without productivity, a sterile text (see the myth of the Woman without a Shadow)." Barthes' next book, *A Lover's Discourse*, makes the connection explicit by moving directly from the eroticism of texts to the eroticism of bodies.

[17]Claude Levi-Strauss, *Structural Anthropology* (trans. Claire Jacobson and Brooke Grundfest Schoepf (New York, 1963), p. 61.

[18]William H. Gass, *Fiction and the Figures of Life* (New York, 1971), p. 93.

[19]David Lodge, *Language of Fiction* (New York, 1966), p. 47.

[20]Pound's postscript to his translation of Remy de Gourmout's *Natural Philosophy of Love* is discussed and quoted by Lawrence S. Dembo in *Conceptions of Reality in Modern American Poetry* (Berkeley, 1966), p. 158.

[21]Gayatri Chakravorty Spivak, introduction to Derrida, *Of Grammatology* (Baltimore, 1976), pp. lxv-lxvi. See also Derrida's discussion of how "woman is (her own) writing" in *Spurs: Nietzsche's Style / Eperons: Les Styles de Nietzsche* (Chicago, 1979), p. 57.

[22]Isak Dinesen, "The Blank Page," *Last Tales* (New York, 1957), pp. 99-105. Because of the frequent quotations and the brevity of the fable, I have omitted page numbers entirely. For useful criticism of this story, see Thomas R. Whissen, *Isak Dinesen's Art: The Gayety of Vision* (Chicago, 1975), p. 219; and Florence C. Lewis, "Isak Dinesen and Feminist Criticism," *The North American Review* 264 (Spring 1979), 62-72.

[23]Eliot, *Daniel Deronda* (Baltimore, 1967), p. 91.

[24]Elinor Wylie (herself a beautiful woman) wrote a series of poems and novels about the "firing" of girls into porcelain artifacts. For a fuller discussion of Wylie's attraction to formal perfection, see Celeste Turner Wright, "Elinor Wylie: The Glass Chimaera and the Minotaur," *Women's Studies*, 7, nos. 1 and 2 (1980): 159-70 (special issue on women poets, ed. Gilbert and Gubar).

[25]Cynthia Griffin Wolff, *A Feast of Words: The Triumph of Edith Wharton* (New York and Oxford, 1977), p. 109; all further references to Wharton's *The House of Mirth*, ed. R.W.B. Lewis (New York, 1977), will be included in the text. Wharton's second provisional title, "The Year of the Rose," points up the ways in which the Jew Rosedale is a double for Lily, in part because his Semitism allows him to glimpse the sordid economic realities behind the veneer of culture, much as Wharton's feminism did for her. For a useful consideration of Wharton's debt to Eliot, see Constance Rooke, "Beauty in Distress: *Daniel Deronda* and *The House of Mirth, Women and Literature*, 4, no. 2 (Fall 1976): 28-39.

[26]Diana Trilling, "*The House of Mirth* Revisited," in *Edith Wharton*, ed. Irving Howe (Englewood Cliffs, N.J., 1962), p. 109.

[27]Lubbock, quoted in Millicent Bell, *Edith Wharton and Henry James: The Story of Their Friendship* (New York, 1965), p. 21.

[28]See Maxine Hong Kingston, *The Woman Warrior: Memoirs of a Girlhood among Ghosts* (New York, 1977), pp. 41-42 and 62-63.

[29]Domestic artistry is repeatedly celebrated in Mansfield's stories, most especially in the figure of Mrs. Fairfield in "Prelude" (*The Short Stories of Katherine Mansfield*, ed. John Middleton Murry [New York, 1976]), but also throughout the letters in which Mansfield writes about the culinary skills of a maid or the interior decorating she herself performs on a hotel room.

[30]For a photograph of Mierle Laderman Ukeles performing her *Washing, Tracks, Maintenance: Maintenance Art Activity III* (22 July 1973), see Lucy R. Lippard, *From the Center: Feminist Essays on Women's Art* (New York, 1976), p. 60; for her discussion of Carolee Schneemann, see p. 126.

[31]Arlene Raven and Deborah Marrow, "Eleanor Antin: What's Your Story?" *Chrysalis* 8 (Summer 1979): 43-51.

[32]See Judy Chicago, *Through the Flower: My Struggle as a Woman Artist* (New York, 1975) and her book on the work, *The Dinner Party* (Garden City, 1979).

[33]Irigaray, quoted by Diana Adlam and Couze Venn in "Women's Exile: Interview with Luce Irigaray," *Ideology and Consciousness* (Summer 1978): 74.

[34]See *The Complete Poems of Christina Rossetti*, ed. R.W. Crump (Baton Rouge, La., 1979).

[35]See Deut. 22:13-24. I am indebted to Stephen Booth for pointing out the relevance of this biblical passage. The issue of blood and sacrifice is a complicated one in the Catholic tradition, as this quotation from Charles Williams illustrates: "There is also, of course, that other great natural bloodshed common to half the human race—menstruation. That was unclean. But it is not impossible that that is an image, naturally, of the great bloodshed on Calvary, and perhaps, supernaturally, in relation to it. Women share the victimization of the blood; it is why, being the sacrifices, they cannot be the priests. They are mothers, and, in that special sense, victims; witnesses, in the body, to the suffering of the body, and the method of Redemption" (*The Forgiveness of Sins* [London, 1950], p. 138).

[36]Scheherazade is an important model of the female storyteller for Dinesen. See the conclusion of "The Deluge at Dorderney," *Seven Gothic Tales* (New York, 1972), p.79, and Hannah Arendt's foreword, "Isak Dinesen, 1885-1962," to Dinesen's *Daguerreotypes* (Chicago, 1979), p. xiv. See also Gilbert's poem "Scheherazade," *Poetry Northwest* 19, no. 2 (Summer 1978): 43.

[37]On women's entrapment in erotic plots, see Elizabeth Hardwick, *Seduction and Betrayal: Women and Literature* (New York, 1974), pp. 175-208, and Joanna Russ, "What Can a Heroine Do; or, Why Women Can't Write," in *Images of Women in Fiction: Feminist Perspectives*, ed. Susan Koppelman Cornillon (Bowling Green, Ohio, 1972), pp. 3-20.

[38]H.D., *Trilogy* (New York, 1973), p. 103.

[39]H.D., *Helen in Egypt* (New York, 1961); all further references to this poem will be included in the text.

[40]Ovid, *Metamorphoses*, trans. Humphries, pp. 148-51. Significantly, once Procne reads Philomela's story, she kills her own son and cooks him up for Tereus who is made to eat him. The sisters are transformed into birds, "And even so the red marks of the murder / Stayed on their breasts; the feathers were blood-colored."

[41]See May Swenson, "Cut," *Iconographs* (New York, 1970), p. 13, and Marge Piercy, "I Still Feel You," in *Psyche: The Feminine Poetic Consciousness*, ed. Barbara Segnitz and Carol Rainey (New York, 1973), pp. 187-88.

[42]Anne Sexton, "Hurry Up Please It's Time," *The Death Notebooks* (Boston, 1974), p. 62; "The Silence," *Book of Folly* (Boston, 1972), p. 32.

[43]See Joyce Kozloff, "Frida Kahlo," *Women's Studies* 7 (1978), 43-58.

[44]See Mary Elizabeth Coleridge, "The Other Side of a Mirror," *The World Split Open: Four Centuries of Women Poets in England and America, 1552-1950*, ed. Louise Bernikow (New York, 1974), p. 137; Charlotte Bronte, *The Professor* (New York, 1964), p. 195; and the Discussion of Emily Bronte in Gilbert and Gubar, *The Madwoman in the Attic*, pp. 581-650.

[45]Margaret Drabble, *The Waterfall* (New York, 1977), pp. 114-15.

[46]Katherine Mansfield to Violet Schiff, October 1921, *Letters*, ed. Murry (New York, 1932), pp. 405-6. It is significant in this regard that both Mansfield and H.D. can only imagine the reeducation and redemption of boys in terms of their learning to play with dolls.

[47]See Sylvia Plath, *Ariel* (New York, 1965). Plath's paper doll collection can be seen in the Lilly Library at Indiana University.

[48]Adrienne Rich, "Waking in the Dark," *Adrienne Rich's Poetry*, ed. Barbara Charlesworth Gelpi and Alpert Gelpi (New York, 1975), p. 61.

[49]Rich, "Women," in *Psyche*, ed. Segnitz and Rainey, p. 152.

[50]Rich, "Power," *The Dream of a Common Language* (New York, 1978), p. 3.

[51]Rich, "Transcendental Etude," ibid., p. 77.

[52]Olive Schreiner, *From Man to Man* (Chicago, 1977), p. 409.

[53]Sandra Gilbert's forthcoming paper "Potent Griselda: D.H. Lawrence's *Ladybird* and Literary Maternity."

[54]I am indebted to Mary Jo Weaver for informing me that the image on Veronica's headcloth has been associated by the gnostics with the woman cursed by blood in Matt. 9:20-22.

[55]See Thomas Merton, *Disputed Questions* (New York, 1960), pp. 222x and 227. For a feminist discussion of the usefulness of the figure of the Virgin Mary to Catholic women, see Elisabeth Schussler Fiorenza, "Feminist Spirituality, Christian Identity, and Catholic Vision," in *Womanspirit Rising*, ed., Christ and Plaskow, pp. 138-39, and Drid Williams, "The Brides of Christ," in *Perceiving Women*, ed. Shirley Ardener (London, 1975), pp. 105-26. The most important feminist analysis of how the Virgin Mary is exalted for virtues men would like women to exhibit is Marina Warner, *Alone of All Her Sex: The Myth of the Virgin Mary* (New York, 1976). While I agree that Mary has been used against women who cannot be virgin and mother, I am arguing here that women have reclaimed her image in positive ways.

[56]Florence Nightingale, *Cassandra* (Old Westbury, 1979), p. 53.

[57]Schreiner, *From Man to Man*, p. 453.

[58]Helene Cixous, quoted by Verene Andermatt, "Helene Cixous and the Uncovery of a Feminine Language," *Women and Literature* 7 (Winter 1979): 42.

[59]See Margaret Anderson, *The Unknowable Gurdjieff* (London, 1962), p. 75.

[60]Gilbert's two brilliant papers, "Potent Griselda: D.H. Lawrence's *Ladybird* and Literary Maternity" and "Soldier's Heart: Literary Men, Literary Women, and the Great War" (both unpublished), document the importance to women of rising anthropological theories of mother right and the significance of World War I to women writers.

[61]Denise Levertov, "Growth of a Poet," *The Freezing of the Dust* (New York, 1975), pp. 83, 78-79. See also Susan Fromberg Schaeffer, "The Nature of Genres," *Granite Lady* (New York, 1974), p. 136.

Jane Archer

The Characterization of Gender-Malaise:
Gazing up at the Windows of *Jacob's Room*

But there were many more influences than anger tugging at her imagination and deflecting it from its path. Ignorance for instance. The portrait of Rochester is drawn in the dark. We feel the influence of fear in it; just as we constantly feel an acidity which is the result of oppression, a buried suffering smoldering beneath her passion, a rancour which contracts those books, splendid as they are, with a spasm of pain.

Virginia Woolf, A Room of One's Own[1]

A young man has nothing to fear. On the contrary, though he may not have said anything brilliant, he feels pretty confident he can hold his own.

Virginia Woolf, Jacob's Room[2]

THE IGNORANCE, FEAR, BURIED SUFFERING and rancour which Woolf read in the "blighted" works of Charlotte Bronte sends its spasm through her works as well. Her third novel, *Jacob's Room*, is informed by a consciousness of ignorance and limitation. Jacob's room, the narrator finds, cannot be her room, and Jacob, as a male, is too privileged to be accessible to her understanding. She attempts to make him visible by surrounding him with images, impressions and opinions, but he remains invisible. Jacob and his gender are the irritants which the narrator, oyster-like, surrounds with conjecture.

Like Woolf's older brother Thoby, Jacob escapes into a life of privilege, knowledge and intellectual communion at Cambridge and the world beyond. Woolf felt her exclusion from that society as a severe limitation in her work as a novelist. Her first-hand knowledge of experience in the world was necessarily fettered by the rigid upbringing and casual education afforded women in the late Victorian era. In *A Room of One's Own*, Woolf addresses this issue in her comparison of George Eliot (shut off from the world because of her socially unacceptable relationship with a married man) to Tolstoi:

At the same time, on the other side of Europe, there was a young man living freely with this gypsy or that great lady; going to wars; picking up unhindered and uncensored all that varied experience of human life which served so splendidly later when he came to write his books. Had Tolstoi lived at the Priory in seclusion with a married lady "cut off from what is called the world" however edifying a moral lesson, he could scarcely, I thought, have written *War and Peace* (p. 74).

For a young man of Woolf's class, the beginning of experience in the world was school, and the flowering of intellectual life took place at Cambridge or Oxford. For Woolf, however, Cambridge represented exclusion, and a Cambridge education pointed up her own sense of intellectual inadequacy. She came by her vision of Cambridge through Thoby, who was sent there as a matter of course. She coveted the freedom available to him as a male, and admired what she thought was his resulting superior intelligence. In a letter to Thoby at college, she discusses her reading and her sense of inadequacy: "I shall want a lecture when I see you; to clear up some points about the plays. I mean about the characters. Why aren't they more human? . . . I find them beyond me.—Is this my feminine weakness in the upper region? But really they might have been cut out with a pair of scissors."[3] Already, as a girl, Woolf experiences literary characters as cut-outs, an image to which she returned in her short stories. In "The Lady in the Looking-Glass," as we have seen, the character is mercilessly shorn of embellishment by scissors, and cut off by the rim of a mirror, the emblem of traditional characterization in the story. As a young girl writing to Thoby, however, Woolf assumes that her perception is flawed, and a sign only of her ignorance.

Thoby was the distant and admired older brother leading a life of mystery and excitement at Cambridge. He had about him "a look of one equipped, unperturbed, knowing his place, relishing his inheritance and his part in life, aware of his competence, scenting the battle; already, in anticipation, a law maker; proud of being and playing his part among Shakespeare's men."[4] As she wrote "A Sketch of the Past," late in life, Thoby had become for Woolf a literary character, literally "among Shakespeare's men." During her youth, Woolf saw Thoby as a characterizer. His visits home were filled with stories of the characters and exploits of his friends, as vivid to his sister as characters in Shakespeare. She made up her own stories about them in Thoby's absence. These romanticized friendships reappear in *Jacob's Room*. As Jacob and his friend Timmy Durrant walk the London streets, "They were boastful, triumphant; it seemed as if they had read every book in the world; known every sin, passion, and joy. Civilizations stood round them like flowers for the picking. Ages lapped at their feet like waves fit for sailing" (p. 76).

After Leslie Stephen's death, when the younger Stephens set up house together in Bloomsbury, Woolf had a chance to enter this romanticized world of intellectual communion. She frequently found it uninspiring—often amusingly so. But, at least as frequently, as her letters, diaries and essays indicate, she felt her own lack of education. She, after all, had not sat in smoke-filled rooms at Cambridge, but had made her isolated way through the Victorian library of her father.

In that they are both about Woolf's sense of exclusion and limitation, *Jacob's Room* and *A Room of One's Own* are companion pieces. In each book, the narrator wanders the paths of Cambridge, ghostlike, unseen and unwanted by the masculine academic community. And in each book, her sense of exclusion results in a meditation on gender and its effect on writers, writing and, most specifically in *Jacob's Room*, the process of characterization. The two works are widely enough separated in time that their parallels at first seem surprising. *Jacob's Room*, published in 1922, is followed by *Mrs. Dalloway*, *To the Lighthouse* and *Orlando*. *A Room of One's Own* does not appear until 1929. Its concerns echo those of *Jacob's Room*, however, more strikingly than those of the intervening novels.

Woolf's diary indicates a common origin for both books. The seeds for *A Room of One's Own* were planted in 1920 while she struggled with *Jacob's Room*. On September 20, 1920, she reports a conversation she and Leonard had with T.S. Eliot: "Now in all this L[eonard] showed up much better than I did," she writes, "but I didn't much mind." Her next diary entry, however, dated September 26, reads: "But I think I minded more than I let on; for somehow Jacob has come to a stop .... I reflected how what I'm doing is probably being better done by Mr. Joyce."[5] Clearly, Woolf's sense of intellectual inadequacy was a life-long torment. More directly, her informal woman's education was a disadvantage when she attempted to characterize Jacob Flanders who, like Thoby, was an inheritor of the culture which excluded her or, at best, rendered her marginal. In any case, late in September 1920, she found her progress on *Jacob's Room* blocked. At about that time, Arnold Bennett published a book called *Our Women*.[6] He claimed to be a feminist, and his book claimed sympathy with women. But he concluded, in 264 pages of sanguine misogyny, that women are physically, intellectually and morally inferior to men. Woolf's diary entry for September 26 continues: "I now find myself making up a paper upon Women, as a counterblast to Mr. Bennett's adverse views reported in the papers. Two weeks ago I made up Jacob incessantly on my walks. An odd thing, the human mind! So capricious, faithless, infinitely shying at shadows. Perhaps at the bottom of my mind, I feel I'm distanced by L[eonard] in every respect."

This, then, was the climate of her mind as she struggled with *Jacob's Room*. Mr. Bennett's views, it seems, have been internalized; she finds herself inadequate when she compares herself to Leonard. The counterblast to Mr. Bennett does get written, however, in the form of two letters to the editor of the *New Statesman*. The letters were a running debate with Desmond MacCarthy, who had favorably reviewed Bennett's book under his pen name, Affable Hawk. He agreed with Bennett that " 'no amount of education and liberty of action will sensibly alter' the fact that women are inferior to men in intellectual power, and that women's indisputable 'desire to be dominated is ... a proof of intellectual inferiority'." In her letters, Woolf points out that the number of remarkable women is increasing century by century. Thus, she argues, education does make a difference. She suggests several reasons why women don't write. Women who want to excel are confronted with the opposition of their fathers. No young man, she asserts, would ever be confronted with such "tortures at home." Citing other oppressed groups, she says that it is difficult to create in a hostile culture. In addition, she points out: "The fact, as I think we shall agree, is that women from the earliest times to the present day have brought forth the entire population of the universe. This occupation has taken much time and strength." Women simply need education, she concludes, and the freedom to differ from men without their differences being considered faults. And they need to be free from assertions of their inferiority. Such productions as Bennett's, she says, hinder women as much as anything.[7] The two letters thus read like early studies for *A Room of One's Own.* She touches briefly on the range of issues she was to develop in the book—the unwritten history of women, their poverty, their oppression on all levels of society, from the family to the university to the streets of London. And Arnold Bennett's book, the catalyst for these meditations on the condition of women, is the original for *The Mental, Moral, and Physical Inferiority of the Female Sex,* that book which so infuriates the speaker of *A Room* as she researches the status of women in the British Museum. The one fact that the speaker retrieves from her research is the fact of anger—her own, and that of Arnold Bennett's fictional representative.

This anger speaks throughout *Jacob's Room.* Most pervasive and least obvious is the voice of the narrator, but other voices contribute their notes of rage and frustration as well. After Woolf resumes her work on the novel, Jacob finds himself in the British Museum. One of his neighbors is "Miss Julia Hedge, the feminist" (p. 106). She sits, waiting for her books, reading the names of the great which surround the dome: " 'Oh damn,' said Julia Hedge, 'why didn't they leave room for an Eliot or a Bronte?' "

Julia Hedge's research is the same as the research conducted by the speaker in *A Room of One's Own,* and she pursues it with the same frustration and sense of inadequacy: "Unfortunate Julia! wetting her pen in bitterness and leaving her shoe laces untied. When her books came she applied herself to her gigantic labours, but perceived how composedly, unconcernedly, and with every consideration the male readers applied themselves to theirs. That young man for example" (p. 106). The narrator of *A Room* directly links this feeling of inadequacy to a lack of education:

Now the trouble began. The student who has been trained in research at Oxbridge has no doubt some method of shepherding his question past all distractions till it runs into its answer as a sheep runs into a pen. The student by my side, for instance, who was copying assiduously from a scientific manual was, I felt sure, extracting pure nuggets of the essential ore every ten minutes or so. His little grunts of satisfaction indicated so much. But if, unfortunately, one has had no training in a university, the question far from being shepherded to its pen flies like a frightened flock hither and thither, helter skelter, pursued by a whole pack of hounds.

(*A Room*, p. 28)

So hounded, Julia Hedge works, with "death and gall and bitter dust ... on her pen-tip" (*Jacob*, p. 106). Jacob, however, is smug in his confidence that he is an inheritor. Julia Hedge dislikes him, and so, it seems, does the narrator. When she posits thoughts for Jacob, they are the thoughts of one who would read and agree with *The Mental, Moral, and Physical Inferiority of the Female Sex*. Jacob, sitting in the King's College Chapel, wonders why women are allowed in church: "No one would think of bringing a dog into church. For though a dog is all very well on a gravel path ... a dog destroys the service completely. So do these women" (p. 33). The speaker of *A Room of One's Own* is banished from the libraries and chapels of Oxbridge and allowed to set foot only on the gravel paths. Jacob, the inheritor of the libraries and the chapels, upholds this judgement with a confidence that the narrator describes with mingled admiration and anger. Jacob infuriates her as he infuriates Julia Hedge, yet she has chosen him as the magnet of her attention.

Why? Her narrator's admitted ambivalence about Jacob certainly has a profound effect on the process of characterization, yet Woolf's critics fail to address the issue. Rather than study this ambivalence as a technique of the narration or even as a major theme of the novel, the majority of the critics who study *Jacob's Room* treat it as an annoyance. The book is a failure, many decide, because Jacob is vague, incomprehensible, ghost-like. Jacob's invisibility is at the center of a confusion in the critical commentary of the novel. What is its subject? What is its intent? What, finally, is it about? Plot summaries of *Jacob's Room* refer to Jacob's sea-shore childhood, his boyhood insect collections, the quickening of his awareness in the fertile intellectual atmosphere of Cambridge, his love affairs, his travels, and his death in the first World War. But these brief sketches which are part of most readings of *Jacob's Room*, though ostensibly accurate, are strangely unsatisfactory. The events listed may be "what happens," but they are not what the book is "about." Critics frequently express frustration with Woolf's technique, calling it "nebulous"[8] and "incoherent."[9] Yet in *Jacob's Room* technique and subject are melded so that the "confusion" of Woolf's style becomes the subject of the novel rather than obscuring it, and the frustration of the reader parallels the frustration of the narrator in her own efforts to discover her plot and its character.

The role of the narrator may be the most misunderstood part of this novel which has confused Woolf's critics more than any of her other books. Despite repeated direct commentary by the narrator of the novel, Joan Bennett insists that in *Jacob's Room* Woolf "makes her first attempt to remove the narrator from the scene, so that the reader may seem to see the subject solely through the eyes of the people in the book. But elimination is not yet completely effected. There are passages of description, events are recorded, comments are made not by the characters themselves, but by their author."[10] The narrator confuses Jean Guiget as well. He expresses a strange enthusiasm for her "omniscience," despite her repeated assertions that Jacob remains a mystery because she is excluded from his world. Undeterred by the narrator's declarations of frustration and ignorance, Guiget writes:

The focus of observation is everywhere and yet nowhere; it is at the disposal of the novelist, taking up her stand here or there, for a second or an hour, according to whether a single word or gesture is needed or a whole scene. No obstacle impedes the author's godlike mobility, her changing moods; she stands beside her characters, listening to them, watching them; she is inside them, following their words and thoughts simultaneously.[11]

In fact, several serious obstacles impede the author's mobility. For one thing, the walls of Jacob's room are not transparent, and just as the narrator of *A Room* was not allowed on the grass or in the libraries of Oxbridge, this narrator is denied access to the rooms of young male students. Here is a sample of her omniscience: "The young men were now back in their rooms. Heaven knows what they were doing" (p. 42). As a matter of fact, whenever the narrator attempts to describe Jacob's activities at Cambridge, she resorts to the language of uncertainty:

The laughter died in the air. The sound of it could scarcely have reached any one standing by the Chapel, which stretched along the opposite side of the court. The laughter died out, and only gestures of arms, movements of bodies, could be seen shaping something in the room. Was it an argument? A bet on the boat races? Was it nothing of the sort? What was shaped by the arms and bodies moving in the twilight room? (p. 44)

The grey walls are formidable obstacles to the narrator stationed outside the Chapel, gazing at Jacob's windows on the opposite side of the court, reading shadows and gestures, catching fragments of speech. In short, she is guessing.

Although her project confuses many critics, Woolf herself is unusually forthright about her intentions in her diary. She explains her project as she embarks on it, and she predicts the misreadings of the critics:

Suppose one thing should open out of another—as in An Unwritten Novel—only
not for 10 pages but for 200 or so—doesn't that get closer & yet keep form & speed &
enclose everything, everything? My doubt is how far it will [include] enclose the
human heart—Am I sufficiently mistress of my dialogue to net it there? For I figure
that the approach will be entirely different this time: no scaffolding; scarcely a brick
to be seen; all crepuscular, but the heart, the passion, humour, everything bright as
fire in the mist. Then I'll find room for so much—a gaiety—an inconsequence—a
light spirited stepping at my sweet will. Whether I'm sufficiently mistress of
things—that's the doubt; but conceive mark on the wall, K[ew]. G[ardens]. &
unwritten novel taking hands & dancing to unity (AWD, p. 22).

Woolf's description of her new form is reminiscent of the world
outside the looking-glass in "The Lady in the Looking-Glass." There is
"no scaffolding; scarcely a brick to be seen." The new form represents the
less focused, more complex truths rather than the "brick wall." Like
Isabella Tyson's room this form is a twilight world, "in which lights
advanced and retreated, came pirouetting and stepping delicately."[12]
Commentators on *Jacob's Room* frequently quote this passage,
particularly the description of the new novel as the unified dance of the
three short stories. The wealth of information about the narrative
perspective in *Jacob's Room* which this comment implies, however, is
overlooked. The narrators in these stories are neither absent nor
omniscient. They are actively creative intelligences confronted by an
unknowable world, it itself potentially meaningless and "bare as bone."[13]
In their efforts to posit meaning for the subjects of their stories—an
unknown woman opposite on the train, a mysterious mark on the wall—
they describe and exuberantly display their own creative processes. Woolf's
diary entry indicates that, far from trying to eliminate the narrator from
Jacob's Room, the narrator is as important a focus of attention as Jacob
himself.[14] Yet this narrator is precisely not omniscient. *Jacob's Room*, after
all, is not truly about Jacob; rather, it is about the impossibility of
characterizing Jacob.

The narrator of *Jacob's Room* explores many obstacles to the process
of characterization. Besides the obvious existential isolation of the
individual, there are the blinders of age, class and temperament. Most
baffling to the narrator, however, is the difference of gender: "Then
consider the effect of sex—how between man and woman it hangs wavy,
tremulous, so that here is a valley, there is a peak, when in truth, perhaps,
all's as flat as my hand" (*Jacob*, p. 73).

Significantly, despite its ostensible subject, *Jacob's Room* opens with
the wavy, tremulous perspective of a woman writing: "Slowly welling
from the point of her gold nib, pale blue ink dissolved the full stop; for
there her pen stuck; her eyes fixed, and tears slowly filled them. The entire
bay quivered; the lighthouse wobbled; and she had the illusion that the
mast of Mr. Conner's little yacht was bending like a wax candle in the sun"

(p. 7). Thus, in the opening scene of the book, it is made clear that vision is distorted and distorting. What is presented is not some absolute outside world, but a world of subjective relativity, where the mast of a yacht is bent by the tears of a woman writing.

In fact, in *Jacob's Room* we never escape the perspective of the woman watching and writing. The entire first chapter of the book deals primarily with women's concerns. Betty Flanders worries in her letter about where to store the perambulator, the difficulty of keeping three young children in lodgings, and the meat for dinner. Mrs. Flanders and Rebecca are "conspirators plotting the conspiracy of hush and clean bottles" (p. 13). Mrs. Jarvis looks at Mrs. Flanders in church and thinks "marriage is a fortress and widows stray solitary in the open fields, picking up stones, gleaning a few golden straws, lonely, unprotected, poor creatures" (p. 8). And the narrator steps in with a lyrical paean to women: " ... who shall deny that this blankness of mind, when combined with profusion, mother wit, old wives' tales, haphazard ways, moments of astonishing daring, humour, and sentimentality—who shall deny that in those respects every woman is nicer than any man?" (p. 11).

An obsession with gender thus lurks close beneath the surface of *Jacob's Room*, even in those sections which ostensibly deal with Jacob as a very small boy. Gender-based power structures and gender-inspired hostilities appear on nearly every page. Betty Flanders looks at the red cat, Topaz, a gift from Mr. Floyd, the red haired man who once proposed to her: " ... she smiled, thinking how she had had him gelded, and how she did not like red hair in men" (pp. 22-23). Mr. Dickens, the attendant of "civilization's prisoner," the invalid Ellen Barfoot, relishes his bit of power over the old woman as proof of his own tenuous sense of superiority: "He, a man, was in charge of Mrs. Barfoot, a woman" (p. 26).

This gender-malaise is present in all attempts to represent Jacob. The first time he is actually described, he is seen through the eyes of an elderly lady. Like Mrs. Brown in Woolf's essay on characterization or Minnie Marsh in the short story "An Unwritten Novel," Mrs. Norman is riding a train, observing her fellow passenger. But Mrs. Norman, like Mrs. Brown, is not free to enjoy her voyage and her observations. Both of these travelers are shut up in the railway carriage with a threatening man. In "Mr. Bennett and Mrs. Brown" this bullying figure is closely identified with Bennett, Galsworthy and Wells—Woolf's straw men in her protest against what she called the "materialist" approach to characterization. For Mrs. Norman, Jacob, the inheritor, is the threatening male presence. She is nervous and feeble; Jacob is powerfully built and energetic. He is, on first impression, a threat: "The train did not stop before it reached Cambridge, and here she was shut up alone, in a railway carriage with a young man" (p. 30). Before she can stop to consider Jacob's possible character, Mrs. Norman must see to her physical defense. She can throw a book and pull the alarm cord, she decides. With this in mind, she can relent a bit and see Jacob with a little more familiarity, a little less fear: "She was fifty years of age, and had a son at college. Nevertheless, it is a fact that men are dangerous" (p. 30). By thinking of her own son and musing about Jacob's appearance, Mrs. Norman is able to lay her fear to rest; she cannot, however, transcend some basic ignorance about Jacob. Her perception is poisoned by fear. The narrator explains: "Nobody sees any one as he is, let alone an elderly lady sitting opposite a strange young man in a railway carriage. They see a whole—they see all sorts of things—they see themselves...." (pp. 30-31). Mrs. Norman's attention is necessarily riveted on Jacob because of her initial fear. He is an imposing young man; she is an insignificant old woman. She cannot ignore him; he, on the other hand, "seemed absolutely indifferent to her presence ... she did not wish to interrupt" (p. 31).

The effect of fear is not limited to feeble old women, however; the narrator falls prey to it as well. After Jacob has been jilted by Florinda, the narrator despairs of being able to comprehend his response: "Whether we know what was in his mind is another question. Granted ten years seniority and a difference of sex, fear of him comes first; this is swallowed up by a desire to help" (pp. 94-95). Thus, we learn that the narrator is approximately thirty-five years old—but her seniority means nothing in terms of the balance of power in any interaction with Jacob, since she is also a woman. Like Mrs. Norman, the narrator initially responds with fear. Her next response is maternal—"a desire to help"—just as Mrs. Norman is reminded of "her own boy." Which is the more distorting perspective— defensively fearful recoil, or maternal concern? In any case, the narrator is unable to imagine what is going on in Jacob's mind.

If fear and maternal concern are distorting responses to a male character, the narrator's physical desire further complicates her project. Sex, she finds, is unavoidable.

Not a square in the snow or fog lacked its amorous couple. All plays turned on the same subject. Bullets went through heads in hotel bedrooms almost nightly on that account. When the body escaped mutilation, seldom did the heart go to the grave unscarred. Little else is talked of in theatres and popular novels. Yet we say it is a matter of no importance at all. (p. 79)

As Jacob engages in sexual experimentation, the narrator notes the signs of conflict and unrest around him. A couple in a restaurant fight, the streets are filled with prostitutes, the alleys seethe with an undercurrent of violence: "The voices, angry, lustful, despairing, passionate, were scarcely more than the voices of caged beasts at night. Only they are not caged, nor beasts" (p. 81). Jacob's response to the contradictions and frustrations of heterosexual relations is "a violent reversion towards male society, cloistered rooms, and the works of the classics ..." (p. 82). But, the narrator decides, "The problem is insoluble. The body is harnessed to a brain."

And in any case, the cloistered rooms and the classics are not available to the narrator. Her brain—the life of her mind—is more severely limited because it is harnessed to the body of a woman. Hence, the way she sees young men is not the way that the laws of fiction decree that they should be seen. She begins to describe Timmy Durrant in her way, but stops: " ... the sight of him sitting there, with his hand on the tiller, rosy gilled, with a sprout of beard, looking sternly at the stars, then at a compass, spelling out quite correctly his page of the eternal lesson book, would have moved a woman. Jacob, of course, was not a woman" (p. 47).

If the subject of *Jacob's Room* is in part the narrator's attempt at characterization and her sense of inadequacy in the face of her task, a conflict arises. In *A Room of One's Own*, Woolf emphasizes the necessity of avoiding gender grievances in writing:

... it is fatal for anyone who writes to think of their sex. It is fatal to be a man or a woman pure and simple; one must be womanly-manly or manly-womanly. It is fatal for a woman to lay the least stress on any grievance; to plead even with justices any cause; in any way to speak consciously as a woman. And fatal is no figure of speech; for anything written with that conscious bias is doomed to death (p. 108).

Jacob's Room is certainly a book narrated with a grievance. The woman who enviously stalks Jacob through his privileged life is thwarted by fear and ignorance. The novel itself, however, is not fatally blighted precisely because the condition of limitation is exploited. The bias becomes a self-conscious narrative stance, and the subject of the narration is literally doomed to death. The free-ranging novels of men, according to Woolf, fail in their attempts at characterization as well. In *A Room*, the narrator picks up a novel written by a man: "One had a sense of physical well-being in the presence of this well-nourished, well-educated free mind which had full liberty from birth to stretch itself in whatever way it liked" (p. 103). Even this privileged narrative voice, however, is unable to transcend the limitations of gender in characterization: "the worst of it is that in the shadow of the letter 'I' all is shapeless as mist. Is that a tree? No, it is a woman. But ... she has not a bone in her body, I thought, watching Phoebe, for that was her name, coming across the beach. Then Alan got up and the shadow of Alan at once obliterated Phoebe. For Alan had views and Phoebe was quenched in the flood of his views" (p. 104).

Does Woolf demonstrate this gender-malaise or fall prey to it in *Jacob's Room*? The above passage seems to describe what happens in *Jacob's Room* with a great deal of accuracy. Jacob, critics frequently complain, is "shapeless as mist." The shadow of the narrator and her views obliterates a clear sense of him. *Jacob's Room*, according to a great deal of its critical commentary, is as "arid" in its characterization as the novels written by men which leave the narrator of *A Room* so dissatisfied. The difference, however, is the degree of self-consciousness in the narration. The fictional male novelist in *A Room* believes that he is characterizing Phoebe. This "well-nourished, well-educated, free mind which had never been thwarted" doesn't notice that Phoebe doesn't have a bone in her body. In his confidence, he fails to realize that Alan's views obliterate her. The failure to characterize is not a self-conscious narrative stance in this case.

It is precisely its apparent lack of confidence which makes Woolf's narration a success. The voice in *Jacob's Room* is a character Woolf developed to work out in fiction the points about gender and writing which she later made polemically in *A Room of One's Own*. She deliberately exposes the foibles and limitations of *Jacob's* narrator because, as she writes later in *A Room*, " ... when a subject is highly controversial—and any question of sex is that—one cannot hope to tell the truth. One can only show how one came to hold whatever opinion one does hold. One can only give one's audience the chance of drawing their own conclusions as they observe the limitations, the prejudices, and the idiosyncracies of the speaker" (p. 4).

In Woolf's progress as a novelist, *Jacob's Room*, with its treatment of the issues of gender and characterization, is a turning point. Writing in her diary, two years almost to the day after her "counterblast" to Arnold Bennett appeared in the *New Statesmen*, Woolf writes: "I think Jacob was a necessary step for me, in working free" (AWD, p. 51). The freedom to which Woolf refers is not simply a freedom of style. As Phyllis Rose points out, the form of the novel was a sexual issue for Woolf. Her essays on form and technique in fiction written between 1919 and 1924 prefigure her feminist tracts of 1929 and 1938.[15] The young girl who wrote to Thoby in 1901 saw the limitation of literary forms, but she could only interpret her perceptions as evidence of her own inadequacy. She was apologetically exploring traditional literature—Thoby's domain: Jacob's room. In writing *Jacob's Room*, she confronted her feelings of exclusion and inadequacy, spurred on by Arnold Bennett and "Affable Hawk." By 1924, when she wrote "Mr. Bennett and Mrs. Brown," Woolf, far from asking for a lecture on literature from a masculine inheritor like Thoby, lectures her readers to obey their own instincts, despite the tyranny of the literary tradition:

Nevertheless, you allow the writers to palm off upon you a version of all this, an image of Mrs. Brown, which has no likeness to that surprising apparition whatsoever. In your modesty, you seem to consider that writers are of different blood and bone from yourselves; that they know more of Mrs. Brown than you do. Never was there a more fatal mistake. It is this division between reader and writer, this humility on your part, these professional airs and graces on ours, that corrupt and emasculate the books which should be the healthy offspring of a close and equal alliance between us.[16]

In *Jacob's Room*, Woolf works free of her own humility, and in moving beyond her sense of inadequacy, she also works free of the rigidly limiting effect of gender in her writing. Yet despite her frequent and often defensive claims that "it is fatal for anyone who writes to think consciously of their sex," and fatal for women "in any way to speak consciously of their sex," Woolf never actually purged all indications of gender from her writing.

When Woolf's speaker in *A Room* reaches the shelves which hold contemporary literature, she picks up a novel written by a Mary Carmichael. The failings of this hypothetical novelist are the limitations many critics find in Woolf's books: "Mary Carmichael will still be encumbered with that self-consciousness in the presence of sin which is the legacy of our sexual barbarity. She will still wear the shoddy fetters of class on her feet" (p. 92). But Mary Carmichael has made some progress in surmounting the obstacle which gender presented to the narrator of *Jacob's Room*: "Men were no longer 'the opposing faction': she need not waste her time railing against them .... Fear and hatred were almost gone ... she wrote as a woman, but as a woman who has forgotten that she is a woman, so that her pages were full of the curious sexual quality that comes only when sex is unconscious of itself" (p. 96). If insistence upon one's gender leads to sterility and death in literature, the refusal of sexuality in writing has the same effect. Woolf uses the metaphor of intercourse between man and woman to express not only the relationship between writer and reader, but also to describe the process which takes place in the mind of the writer: " ... a woman must have intercourse with the man in her .... It is when this fusion takes place that the mind is fully fertilized and uses all its faculties" (p. 102).

In *Jacob's Room*, Woolf's narrator is shut off from the male portion of her mind. In subsequent novels, however, her increased receptivity to "the man in her" serves as a catalyst. Clarissa Dalloway has her epiphany because of some affinity with Septimus Warren Smith, who was driven insane because he lost contact with the woman in himself. Lily Briscoe has her vision after she has discovered her own satisfactory mode of interaction with Mr. Ramsay. Woolf wrote from the perspective of a woman with a grievance in *Jacob's Room*. Like the male novelists whose depictions of women are "too simple" according to the speaker of *A Room*, she "observes through the black or rosy spectacles which sex puts upon [her] nose" (p. 86). As a result, "So much has been left out, unattempted." But Woolf's narrator is explicitly self-conscious about these limitations and omissions. *Jacob's Room*, read in this way, is not simply a failed experiment. It is only by consciously experiencing her exclusion from Jacob's room that Woolf can demonstrate the necessity of a style, tradition and room of her own.

Notes

[1] Virginia Woolf, *A Room of One's Own* (New York: Harcourt, Brace and World, 1929), p. 76. All subsequent references appear in the text.

[2] Woolf, *Jacob's Room* (New York: Harcourt, Brace and World, 1923), p. 112. All subsequent page references appear in the text.

[3] Woolf, *The Flight of the Mind: The Letters of Virginia Woolf,* ed. Nigel Nicholson (London: Hogarth Press, 1975), I, 45.

[4] Woolf, "A Sketch of the Past," in *Moments of Being* (New York: Harcourt Brace Jovanovich, 1976), p. 119.

[5] Woolf, *The Diary,* ed. Anne Olivier Bell (New York: Harcourt Brace Jovanovich, 1978), II, 68-69.

[6] Arnold Bennett, *Our Women* (New York: George H. Doran, 1920).

[7] Woolf, *The Diary,* II, 339-42.

[8] Joan Bennett, *Virginia Woolf: Her Art as a Novelist* (Cambridge: Cambridge University Press, 1964), p. 96.

[9] James Hafley, *The Glass Roof: Virginia Woolf as Novelist* (New York: Russell and Russell, 1963), p. 58. See also J.K. Johnstone, *The Bloomsbury Group* (London: Seck and Warburg, 1954), p. 336.

[10] Joan Bennett, p. 91.

[11] Jean Guiget, *Virginia Woolf and Her Works,* trans. Jean Stewart (New York: Harcourt, Brace and World, 1965), p. 222.

[12] Woolf, "The Lady in the Looking-Glass," in *A Haunted House and Other Stories* (New York: Harcourt, Brace and World, 1949), p. 92.

[13] Woolf, "An Unwritten Novel," in *A Haunted House,* p. 21.

[14] See Barry Morgenstern's article, "The Self-Conscious Narrator in *Jacob's Room,*" in *Modern Fiction Studies,* 18, No. 3 (Autumn 1972), 351-61. His is one of the only studies to analyze the narration which most critics reject as unsatisfactory: "*Jacob's Room* is a book about a twenty-five year old man—Jacob—and a thirty-five year old woman—the narrator" (p. 352).

[15] Phyllis Rose, *Woman of Letters: A Life of Virginia Woolf* (New York: Oxford, 1978), pp. 94, 100-01.

[16] Woolf, "Mr. Bennett and Mrs. Brown," in *The Captain's Deathbed and Other Essays* (New York: Harcourt Brace Jovanovich, 1950), p. 114.

Judith Fetterley
My Antonia,
Jim Burden and the Dilemma of the Lesbian Writer

I

IN "TO WRITE 'LIKE A WOMAN': Transformations of Identity in Willa Cather" (forthcoming in *Journal of Homosexuality*), Joanna Russ claims Cather as a lesbian writer and essays to understand the central situation in many of her novels and stories as an indirect expression of a lesbian sensibility. Not unlike most readers of Cather, I have long thought *My Antonia* both a remarkably powerful and a remarkably contradictory text and have long suspected that its power was connected with its contradictions.[1] Russ' thesis, while controversial,[2] is hardly startling once stated; and it provides an admirable framework within which to understand this connection and thus the meaning of Cather's text. As Deborah Lambert has demonstrated, *My Antonia* is a watershed book for Cather, marking the transition between her ability to write as a woman about women and her decision to write as a man about men.[3] In *My Antonia*, the transition and transformation are still in process and the process is incomplete. What marks *My Antonia*, then, as a central, if not the central Cather text, is not so much the evidence it contains of Cather's capitulation to convention, but rather the evidence it contains of her deep-seated resistance to such capitulation. It is, if you will, the force-fed loaf but partially chewed. As such, it defines the nature of Cather's situation as an American writer who is a lesbian writer. And in defining so sharply that situation, *My Antonia* enables us to grasp the essence of Cather's art and of her achievement.

II

In Book IV, the Widow Steavens informs Jim of the fate of their Antonia: "My Antonia, that had so much good in her, had come home disgraced. And that Lena Lingard, that was always a bad one, say what you will, had turned out so well, and was coming home every summer in her silks and her satins, and doing so much for her mother. I give credit where credit is due, but you know well enough, Jim Burden, that there is a great difference in the principles of those two girls. And here it was the good one that had come to grief!"[4] One might well ask where the Widow's certainties are coming from, what principles are determining the comfortable clarity of her moral universe. How is it that she can so easily distinguish the good woman from the bad one? Surely, Antonia's goodness comes straight from her conventionality; she is all that one could ask for in the way of traditional womanhood. She is smart as a whip, but will never attend school; eager and quick to learn the language of her new country, she will always speak broken English with an accent which marks her as foreign; eventually she will speak no English at all; nurturant in the extreme, she saves even the insects, making a nest in her hair for the protection of the sole surviving cricket. Above all, she identifies with men and against women. She is passionately devoted to her father whom she ennobles, in a moment of extraordinary disclosure, for having married her mother when he could have bought her off. Since Antonia herself will recapitulate her mother's experience, her idealization of her father and denigration of her mother is as painful as it is predictable. She pads about after Charley Harling, "fairly panting with eagerness to please him" (p. 155); and she equally "pants" after Jim and his approval, hoping that "maybe I be the kind of girl you like better, now I come to town" (p. 154). With Lena she is cold and distant because Lena "was kind of talked about, out there" (p. 164); Tony is not one to give a sister the same uncritical support she gives men.

In Book II, we learn that Tony is all heart: "everything she said seemed to come right out of her heart," and this is the source of her power (p. 176). In Book IV, we learn the limitations of the power of "heart." "The trouble with me was," she later explains to Jim, "I never could believe harm of anybody I loved," thus indicating how radical is her severance of head from heart (p. 344). Tony's "all heart, no head" approach to life leads her directly into the arms of Larry Donovan, for whom she performs the conventional female function of becoming the mirror in which one is seen as large ("His unappreciated worth was the tender secret Larry shared with his sweethearts," p. 305); against her better judgment, she participates in the mythology of the transforming power of women's love: "I thought if he saw how well I could do for him, he'd want to stay with me" (p. 313). The arms of Larry Donovan open directly onto the realm of the seduced and abandoned and "my" Antonia is "poor" Antonia now. Though Jim professes anger at this convention, there is a direct connection between the qualities he values in Antonia and her abandoned state, between being "good" and being "poor." At the end of Book I, Jim murmurs, "why aren't you always nice like this, Tony?" (p. 140). Previously, she has not been so nice: "Antonia ate so noisily now, like a man" (p. 125), and "like a man" she works, competing daily with Ambrosch and boasting of her strength. From the "fate" of acting like a man and losing "all her nice ways" (p. 125), **Grandmother** Burden "saves" her, getting Antonia a job in town serving the Harlings. Tony's salvatory tenure at the Harlings is abruptly terminated, however, by another incursion of not-niceness. Forced to choose between working for the Harlings and going dancing, Tony "set[s] her jaw" and leaves: "A girl like me has got to take her good times when she can. Maybe there won't be any tent next year. I guess I want to have my fling, like the other girls" (p. 208). To which Jim responds, "Tony, what has come over you?" Tony is unrecognizable when not "nice," that is, when she uses her head to have some fun and puts herself, her desires and her needs before the approval and service of others.

But, of course, Tony's "badness" is only a temporary deviation from her trajectory towards apotheosis as earth mother, in which image she is fully delivered up in Book V, fittingly titled "Cuzak's Boys." Defined not only as the mother of sons but as the mother of the sons of her husband, so completely does "niceness" require the elimination of self, Antonia admits, in an aside reminiscent of Aunt Polly, "That Leo; he's the worst of all .... And I love him the best" (p. 335). Obviously, in boys badness is goodness. Though "a rich mine of life" to others, Antonia is herself somewhat depleted. She is a battered woman, whose grizzled hair, flat chest and few remaining teeth reflect the toll exacted of one who plays the role of earth mother.

This is a role which Lena, "coming home here every summer in her silks and satins, and doing so much for her mother," has firmly refused, eliciting thereby the Widow's fiery denunciation of her as "bad." From the moment she first appears at the Harlings' back door, Lena presents a marked contrast to Antonia. While Tony pants after approval in broken English, Lena moves through the world with "perfect composure" and perfect English (p. 160). Unlike Tony, Lena is "crazy about town" (p. 164) because she sees it as the way up and out, and up and out Lena intends to get. "Through with the farm" and through with family life and resolutely anti-marriage, Lena is determined to be economically and personally independent; she has come to town to learn a profession. Lena's clear head is clearly harnessed to her vision of her own self interest and, while she "gave her heart away when she felt like it,... she kept her head for her business and had got on in the world" (p. 298). Though Lena's success is in itself sufficient to draw the Widow's ire, her definition of "good" requiring an element of failure in which head is submerged in heart and self is deferred to other, the personal focus of the success is equally enraging. It's bad enough that Lena wants to take care of herself; worse yet is her desire to take care of her mother. To Antonia's male-identification and glowing commitment to father-right and brother-right, Lena opposes the image of a woman-identified-woman whose hidden agenda is rescuing her mother. Lena's resistance to marriage derives from her perception of it as bad for women—too much work, too many children, too little help: "she remembered home as a place where there were always too many children, a cross man and work piling up around a sick woman" (p. 291). Further, "it's all being under somebody's thumb" (p. 292), and when that somebody is cross or sullen, "he'll take it out on her," wives serving for men, as Lena knows, as live-in-victims (p. 162). On the same occasion in which Tony builds a shrine to her father for actually having married a girl he seduced, Lena reveals the heart of her hidden agenda: "I'm going to get my mother out of that old sod house where she's lived so many years. The men will never do it" (p. 241). Not only does Lena identify with her mother; she sees her mother identifying with her: "She'd get away from the farm, too, if she could. She was willing for me to come" (p. 161). The handkerchiefs Lena would buy for her mother carry the letter "B" for Berthe, not "M" for mother.

III

Though the moral universe of the Widow Steavens is simple, that of the text of *My Antonia* is not. At several points and in several ways, *My Antonia* fails to confirm or ratify the Widow's easy differentiation. Indeed, to read *My Antonia* is to be visibly confronted with a series of contradictions, to be forced to raise a series of questions, and to be required to realize that these contradictions and questions, as they are central to the act of reading the text, are central to the text's meaning. One such question emerges from Jim's final apotheistic tribute to Antonia: "It was no wonder that her sons stood tall and straight. She was a rich mine of life, like the founders of early races" (p. 353). But where are these sons? Even a cursory examination of *My Antonia* reveals nothing to support the validity of Jim's assertion; on the contrary, it reveals much that subverts it. If one examines the various men who appear in *My Antonia*, the cumulative picture is one of weakness, insubstantiality, and self-destruction. Sons in *My Antonia* are neither tall nor straight nor well-fed. Either they are being starved to death or they are constitutionally incapable of assimilating offered nourishment or both or more. Emblematic is the nameless tramp whose story Tony recounts in Book II. Arriving out of nowhere, he offers to run the threshing machine and minutes later jumps into it head first. Tony's response emphasizes the peculiar maleness of this behavior: "What would anybody want to kill themselves in summer for? In threshing time, too! It's nice everywhere then." And besides, she adds, "the machine ain't never worked right since" (pp. 179, 178). Bewildered Tony may well be as to the cause of this behavior but hardly as to its existence; her own father, in an act which anticipates the demise of Wick Cutter, has blown his head off because life is simply too much for him. He becomes daily less substantial until there remains only enough energy to mark the fact of his existence by the violence of its termination. Consumptive rather than consuming describes the men in this text, as witness the example of Gaston Cleric. Are we then to assume that Antonia herself comprises an entire category, no other earth mother existing, all these men being the sons of women who are something other than earth mothers? Yet whom has Antonia nourished?

Not her father certainly. Cuzak?—"a crumpled little man" who lifts "one shoulder higher than the other ... under the burdens of life" and looks "at people sidewise, as a work-horse does at its yokemate" (pp. 356, 358). Jim, who seems to have no life at all? Where are Antonia's tall, straight sons?

If there are no well-fed sons, no end products to validate Jim's assertion of nourishment, there is evidence to suggest that when women feed men they poison them. Female nourishment is linked to death. Wick Cutter's viciousness, which culminates in his wife's murder and his own suicide, runs on the energy generated by Mrs. Cutter's outrage: "he depended upon the excitement he could arouse in her hysterical nature" (p. 253). Mrs. Harling feeds Mr. Harling: "Before he went to bed she always got him a lunch of smoked salmon or anchovies and beer. He kept an alcohol lamp in his room, and a French coffee pot, and his wife made coffee for him at any hour of the night he happened to want it" (p. 157). She feeds him ego food too: "Mr. Harling not only demanded a quiet house, he demanded all his wife's attention.... Mrs. Harling paid no heed to anyone else if he was there" (pp. 156-7). The result of this feast is an arrogant imperialism which stops life: "We had jolly evenings at the Harlings' when the father was away" (p. 156). And what are the consequences of Antonia's whipping up cakes for "Charley"? Charley/Larry doesn't seem to have benefitted much from her hot lunches. He is last seen disappearing toward Mexico where he may get rich, "collecting half-fares off the natives and robbing the company," and where he may just as easily get killed (pp. 312-313). And Charley/Jim? The most elaborate exposure of the dangers of female nourishment occurs in a scene which involves Jim, the architect of the earth mother image. In Book I, Jim kills a snake and Antonia is unrelenting in her praise of his courage; singlehandedly she creates monster and hero, dragon and George, feeding Jim's ego until "I began to think that I had longed for this opportunity, and had hailed it with joy.... Her exultation was contagious. The great land had never looked to me so big and free. If the red grass were full of rattlers, I was equal to them all" (pp. 47-48). Back at the ranch, Otto, the cowboy, succinctly punctures Antonia's windy distortion: "Got him in the head first crack, didn't you? That was just as well" (p. 49). Later Jim learns how lucky he really was: "A snake of his size, in fighting trim, would be more than any boy could handle. So in reality it was a mock adventure; the game was fixed for me by chance, as it probably was for many a dragon-slayer. I had been adequately armed by Russian Peter; the snake was old and lazy; and I had Antonia beside me, to appreciate and admire" (pp. 49-50). But what if there were no Otto? What if Antonia's was the only voice Jim ever heard? Might he not, thus stuffed with heroic imagery, set off on other adventures where, not so lucky, he would return on his shield rather than with it?

The point here is not to suggest that Cather is writing an anti-feminist text which demonstrates how bad women are for men, a position implicit if not explicit in Blanche Gelfant's truly provocative and insightful essay[5] and one which finally reinforces the apotheosis of the earth mother. Rather it is to suggest that the text of *My Antonia* radically undercuts the premises of the image which occupies its center, thus calling into question the value of the very conventions it asserts. Women are not under attack here for failing to be earth mothers. Nor are earth mothers under attack for failing to fulfill their promises or, more insidiously, for masquerading as nourishers while enacting emasculation. Rather under attack is the apotheosis of the earth mother image. The pressure the text resists is the pressure embodied in the voice of the Widow Steavens with her easy assurance of good and bad and it resists this pressure by undermining the bases of the earth mother image. Like a system responding to the implantation of a foreign body, *My Antonia* surrounds Antonia with anti-stories.

One such features as heroes Russian Peter and Pavel who, for daring to act out a powerful though non-conventional truth, have suffered banishment and stigmatization. Can the apotheosis of the earth mother work without a positive attitude toward heterosexual marriage? For the Widow Steavens, Lena's badness is directly connected to her resistance to marriage; yet much of the text of *My Antonia* supports Lena's badness, not Tony's goodness. The significance of the Russians' story may be taken, as Gelfant suggests, from its mode of presentation.[6] Like any highly explosive material it is carefully contained. Dying, Pavel tells his story to Mr. Shimerda; Antonia overhears it and, translating first from Russian to Bohemian and then from Bohemian to English, she repeats it to Jim who tells it to us. And what is the content of this highly explosive tale? A hatred of marriage as pure as the snow onto which the bride and bridgroom are thrown and as intense as the hunger of the wolves who consume them. Pavel and Peter's priorities are ratifed by a text whose hostility to marriage would be hard to exceed. Examples of destructive marriages abound: Cutters, Shimerdas, Harlings, Crazy Mary and just as crazy Ole, Jim and the woman who "for some reason" wishes to remain Mrs. Burden. Good marriages exist only when essential to maintaining the surface tone of the text, as is the case with Jim's family. Note, however, that Jim's parents are conveniently dead; his family is his *grand*parents, safely distanced by a generation from his generation. Further, we see very little of the actual texture of this relationship. That necessarily good relationship whose texture we do partially witness in fact confirms, though more moderately, the vision of marriage as a structure of mutually conflicting interests: "It did rather seem to me that Cuzak had been made the instrument of Antonia's special mission. This was a fine life, certainly, but it wasn't the kind of life he had wanted to live. I wondered whether the life that was right for one was ever right for two!" (p. 345).

Attitudes toward sexuality obviously inform the attitude toward marriage. While more complex, they are equally hostile. Antonia's extraordinary fecundity finds neither resonance nor reinforcement in a text whose sexual emblems are Crazy Mary, Wick Cutter and Lena with the reaping hook. The act required for the "rich mine of life" motif is fraught with danger and repugnance. Mr. Shimerda's dalliance with the servant girl who comes to work for his mother terminates in the gruesome scene in a Nebraska barn, a frozen corpse on the floor and "bunches of hair and stuff" stuck to the roof (p. 98). Like father, so daughter, whose brief moment of eroticism, those nightly trips to the dancing tent, finds an equally painful conclusion in the house attached to the barn. Haunting the landscape of sexual passion is the figure of Crazy Mary, whose jealousy of Lena reduces her to a caricature with a corn knife in danger of being re-committed. The pathetic object of her passions is no more fortunate in his relation to sexual longing; having married his Mary to keep him steady, he finds the remedy insufficient and himself wandering the prairies looking for Lena.

Though the sexual impulse in *My Antonia* dooms men as well as women, a loathing of male, not female, sexuality informs the negative context. Emblematic here is Wick Cutter, whose name reveals at once his phallic identity and the narrative attitude toward it. In Wick male sexuality emerges as unrestrained, unrestrainable and rapacious, preying on those women who must serve him to survive. Through him is articulated the hidden, and shameful, sexual history of Black Hawk, a history of exploitation and abuse which spawns an endless series of pregnant "Marys," some of whom return to town after being "forced to retire from the world for a short time" and some of whom do not return but move on to Omaha and Denver where they are "established in the business" for which they have been "fitted" (pp. 203, 210). Though less obvious than the abuse of the hired girls, the anemia, paralysis and unlived lives of the "white," middle-class town girls must also be laid in part at the door of a sexuality which requires "purity" in wives and mothers and vents its lust on the bodies of servants. Yet there is in *My Antonia* a loathing of male sexuality that transcends the presumably political. The disgust which Wick Cutter's flesh elicits, "his pink, bald head, and his yellow whiskers, always soft and glistening" (p. 210), is adumbrated in the nausea elicited by the extraordinarily phallic snake of Book I: "His abominable masculinity, his loathsome, fluid motion, somehow made me sick. He was as thick as my leg, and looked as if millstones couldn't crush the disgusting vitality out of him . . . . He seemed like the ancient, eldest Evil" (pp. 45-47).

Up to this point in the analysis, we have a paradigm which, while somewhat complicated, is nevertheless easy to grasp: the conventional enshrinement of the conventional image of the earth mother undermined by a critique of the premises upon which the convention is based; or, if you will, a patriarchal story co-existing with a feminist story. We must now move to a level of analysis which is more complex, one which engages the contradictions within the two stories as well as those between them and one which understands the two stories not simply as co-existing but as coinciding, both inevitably present because dynamically related. For surely neither sexual politics nor phallic loathing, though richly informative of the attitude toward marriage, is adequate to explain the aura of fear which encircles sexual experience in *My Antonia* and creates a radical contradiction within the conventional story between the romanticization of earth mother fecundity and the attribution of "goodness" to her stance of asexuality. The key rests with the figure of Lena Lingard, whose "badness" is related to her sexuality and whose sexuality reveals the erotic asymmetry at the heart of the novel. If Wick Cutter's flesh elicits loathing and disgust, Lena's elicits desire—in crazy Ole; in the Polish musician who lives across the hall; in old Colonel Raleigh, her landlord; in Jim himself; and in the narrative voice which describes her. The fear Lena arouses can only be understood as a response to the desire she has first aroused. And most certainly she arouses fear. The landscape of Antonia's "rich mine of life," the fruit cave whose veritable "explosion of life" dizzies Jim temporarily, finds no complement in the erotic landscape of Jim's dream life. Rather this landscape is bare, cut and full of shocks. In the dream Jim dreams "a great many times," Lena appears to him as the grim reaper, armed with the hook which he, at least, never forgets. Though Jim says he wished he could have this "flattering" dream about Antonia, it is obvious that his ability to idealize her, like the Widow's ability to define her as "good," is directly connected to her refusal to appear to him in the imagery of sexual desire. Moreover, it is connected to the fact that she serves him as the agent of sexual repression and prohibition, reinforcing that part of him which needs to set the erotic in the landscape of dream and surround it by an aura of fear. Shortly before Jim tells us about his dream, he records an equally significant exchange between himself and Antonia. Attempting to kiss Tony as "Lena Lingard lets me kiss her," Jim experiences a sharp rebuff (p. 224). Tony gasps with indignation and snarls protectively, "If she's up to any of her nonsense with you, I'll scratch her eyes out" (p. 224). To which Jim responds with an outburst of pride and the avowal that now he knows "where the real women were, though I was only a boy; and I would not be afraid of them, either!" (p. 225).

It would be a thankless, if not hopeless, task to attempt to unravel the contradictions and confusions of this particular bit of textual sequence. But it would be irresponsible to fail to note their existence or to fail to observe that this abundance of confusion coincides precisely with the most overtly sexual moment in the text. Surely, if not answers, questions are being forced upon us. Why is Jim's pride in Antonia tied to her protecting him from Lena? How can an earth mother be idealized both for her fecundity and for her asexuality? And behind these, and the welter of similar questions, is the overriding issue of the source of the imperative against responding to female sexuality. Women's resistance to male sexuality is adequately explained by sexual politics and phallic loathing. But why can't Jim have erotic dreams about Tony or see Lena without her reaping hook?

In Book III, Jim, accompanied by Lena, attends the theatre and on one particular afternoon encounters for the first time the transcendant power of art. The initiating play is *Camille* whose theme, significantly enough, is renunciation. Why, we may well ask, is Jim so transfixed by the dream of renunciation and why does this drama enable him to grasp the meaning and function of art? What, we might equally well ask, is being renounced here and who is doing the renouncing?

IV

Jim Burden has presented a problem to many readers of *My Antonia*.[7] Indeed, Cather's own uneasiness on the subject of her point of view is apparent, not simply in her various explanations/rationalizations of her narrative choice but also within the text itself.[8] How else can one understand the "Introduction" save as an effort to substantiate Jim Burden, explain his relation to story and character, and make him credible as a narrator? "Unlike the rest of the book," Brown tells us, Cather found the introduction "a labor to write."[9] Her difficulty may well suggest something false in the nature of the task, an inability to say what needs to be said, an unwillingness to explain where explanation is essential. Her discomfort was such that for the 1926 reissue of *My Antonia* she revised the introduction, improving the effect, according to Brown, and most particularly by removing from "the reader's mind a question that could do the book no good—whether in fact it would not have been better told by another woman, the query Miss Jewett had raised about 'On the Gull's Road'."[10] Cather's revisions may indeed have improved the "Introduction," but not because they solved its problems. Rather her revisions re-focus the questions which the "Introduction" will inevitably raise so as to more accurately reflect and engage these problems. The ultimate effect of the revised "Introduction" is to focus the reader's attention on the problematic nature of the narrative voice in the text, for instead of explaining Jim Burden the "Introduction" leaves us wondering who has made the attempt. The "I" who introduces our "eye" is not now Willa Cather who, as a "little girl" had watched Antonia "come and go" and who has made a feeble attempt to write Antonia's story herself, but is rather a nameless, faceless, sexless voice. Three pages into the story and we itch for definition, crave knowledge of who is speaking to us. Neither itch nor craving is satisfied here or later and this, I would propose, is precisely the point of Cather's excisions and final "solution." While putatively existing to solve a problem, the "Introduction" in fact serves to identify a problem and to indicate that the problem is the point. Indirect in its strategy, the "Introduction" further reveals that the inability to speak directly is the heart of the problem which is the point.

In revising the "Introduction" Cather removed all references to herself. Dramatized in the act of revision and embedded thus in the revision itself, palimpset sub-text informing the super-imposed surface text, is the renunciation of Cather's own point of view and of the story that could be told from that point of view. To return to the motif of *Camille*, I would suggest that the renunciation at issue is Cather's own. In *My Antonia* Cather renounces the possibility of writing directly in her own voice, telling her own story, and imagining herself in the pages of her text. Obviously autobiographical, the obvious narrator for *My Antonia* would be Cather herself. Yet for Cather to write in a female voice about Antonia as an object of intense and powerful feelings would require that she acknowledge a lesbian sensibility and feel comfortable with such a self-presentation—a task only slightly easier to do now than then.[11] Indeed, in the context of early 20th century self-consciousness of sexual "deviance" and thus of the potentially sexual content of "female friendships,"[12] Jewett's directive to Cather to avoid the "masquerade" of masculine impersonation and write openly in her own voice of women's love for women—("a woman could love her in that same protecting way—a woman could even care enough to wish to take her away from such a life, by some means or other"[13])—seems faintly specious. In fact, it was not "safer" for Cather to write "about him as you did about the others, and not try to be he!"[14] Her "safety" lay precisely in her masquerade.

Yet *My Antonia* is not simply "safe." Choosing to transpose her own experience into a masculine key, Cather nonetheless confronts us with a transposition which is radically incomplete. At the end of Book IV, Jim confesses to Antonia, "I'd have liked to have you for a sweetheart, or a wife, or my mother or my sister—anything that a woman can be to a man" (p. 321). Why, then, does he not so have her? No reader of *My Antonia* can avoid asking this question because Cather makes no attempt to answer it and thus prevent us. For the contradiction between speech and act cracks open the text and reveals the story within the story, the story which can't be told directly, the essence of whose meaning is the fact that it can't be told.

Though nominally male, Jim behaves in ways that mark him as female. From the start he is anomalous. On the farm, he rarely leaves the kitchen; he inhabits women's space: "When grandmother and I went into the Shimerdas' house, we found the women-folk alone . . . . The cold drove the women into the cave-house, and it was soon crowded" (pp. 114, 115). Yet Cather can't have him doing women's work; thus Jim does virtually nothing, a fact which at once contributes to his insubstantiality and provides a context for understanding its source. Jim's most active moment comes, not surprisingly, when he is left alone. With no one to observe him and with responsibility for all tasks of both sexes, he throws himself into housework and barn work with equal vigor. There is a moment in Book II which similarly defines his ambiguity. Realizing that he is about to leave Black Hawk, Jim delivers a reminiscent tribute to his life as a Black Hawk boy: "For the first time it occurred to me that I should be homesick for that river after I left it. The sandbars, with their clean white beaches and their little groves of willows and cottonwood seedlings, were a sort of No Man's Land, little newly created worlds that belonged to the Black Hawk boys. Charley Harling and I had hunted through these woods, fished from the fallen logs, until I knew every inch of the river shores and had a friendly feeling for every bar and shallow" (p. 233). To which peroration we can only murmur, "really?" For we have seen no part of this boys' world. Instead, we have seen Jim hanging out at the Harlings, participating in female-centered family life; Jim playing with the hired girls and getting a reputation for being "sly" and "queer" (p. 216); Jim studying his books at home alone; Jim walking the streets at night and sneering at the cowardice and hypocrisy of these very Black Hawk boys who are supposedly his fishing and hunting buddies. Nor does Jim identify with Black Hawk men. Toward an obvious role model, he manifests the most intense dislike. How are we to explain Jim's hatred of Mr. Harling, a figure who represents his own possibilities for future power, dominance, self-assertion and self-gratification? It is particularly significant that Jim's hostility focuses precisely on those aspects of Mr. Harling which are most patriarchal—the subservience of his wife and children, their absolute catering to his every whim, his ownership of time and space; in short, his "autocratic" and "imperial" ways, the ways of a man "who felt that he had power" (p. 157). Jim's hostility, reminiscent of his earlier contempt for the arbitrary predominance accorded Ambrosch, though unintelligible in a male, is thoroughly intelligible in a female who understands patriarchal privilege as tyranny.

Equally revealing of gender ambiguity is Jim's sexual self-presentation. With Harry Paine, the town boy who loses Tony her job by forcing her to kiss him on the Harlings' back porch, as the "norm" for adolescent male sexuality, Jim's behavior stands out as "queer" indeed. Attempting to kiss Tony himself and meeting with a similar rebuff, he responds not with force but with petulance and then support. "Lena Lingard lets me kiss her," he weakly asserts, disclosing thus his essential sexual passivity and foreshadowing the postures of his erotic dream. After listening to Tony's lecture on the dangers of playing with Lena, Jim capitulates completely, submerging his dissent in a rush of pride at the "true heart" of his Antonia. The conflict produced by the oppositional nature of male and female sexual interests collapses at this point; it cannot survive the stronger pull of Jim's implicit sympathy for and identification with Tony's position. As Antonia knows, sexuality can be dangerous for women. It is she who has paid the price of Harry Paine's desire and it is she who will be left with child and without money at the end of her affair with Larry Donovan. Jim's pride in Antonia's warning is worthy of a mother or a sister or a friend, but not of a suitor whose interest lies in undermining her perceptions and making her ashamed of her resistance.

There are two scenes in *My Antonia*, both explicitly about sex and gender, which define unmistakably the essential femaleness of Jim Burden. In Book I Jim tells us of an incident which made a change in his relationship with Antonia, a change which he claims to have welcomed and relished. Through this event Antonia presumably learns that gender means more than age; thus taught, she abandons her tone of superiority and assumes her appropriately subservient place: "Much as I liked Antonia, I hated a superior tone that she sometimes took with me. She was four years older than I, to be sure, and had seen more of the world; but I was a boy and she was a girl, and I resented her protecting manner. Before the autumn was over, she began to treat me more like an equal and to defer to me in other things than reading lessons. This change came about from an adventure we had together" (p. 43). Jim's sexism here is so unlike anything we know of him before or after that, for this reason alone, the snake episode would invite our closer scrutiny. Yet even a cursory glance reveals an agenda very different from the one Jim asserts. Not masculine superiority and the validity of masculine privilege but the fraudulence of male heroics and hence of the feminine worship that accompanies and inspires it are the subjects of this episode. Jim responds to the sudden appearance of the snake with sheer terror and he kills it by sheer luck. From his experience he learns that a stacked deck makes heroes and a chorus of female praise obscures the sleight of hand. The aura of the impostor colors the scene and explains the absence of any sequel to it. Once again, the disjunction between speech and act points us in the direction of gender ambiguity. Jim's experience is far more intelligible as that of a girl, who, while temporarily acting a boy's part, discovers the fraudulence of the premises on which the system of sexism is based and thus comes to see all men as imposters; but who nevertheless recognizes that, though she may play male roles and sign herself William Cather, her signature is a masquerade and her identity a fake.

The second scene occurs in Book II when Tony, made nervous by the more than usually bizarre behavior of her employer, Wick Cutter, asks Jim to take her place. And take her place is precisely what Jim does. In theory, Antonia's request ought to provide Jim with a golden opportunity, a chance to demonstrate that masculine superiority which is the putative lesson of the earlier scene by protecting the woman whom he continually tells us he loves. Further, since Cutter's intention is rape and since the whole town loathes the man, the situation carries with it the additional possibility of becoming a local hero. Knight in shining armor, defender of fair womanhood, Black Hawk avenger—Tom Sawyer would jump at it. Jim Burden turns and runs, straight home to grandmother where he puts his face to the wall and begs, "as I had never begged for anything before," that she allow no one else to see him, not even the doctor (p. 249). To her reiterated note of thankfulness "that I had been there instead of Antonia," Jim responds with pure hatred: "I felt that I never wanted to see her again. I hated her almost as much as I hated Cutter. She had let me in for all this disgustingness" (p. 250). Surely Jim has literally taken Antonia's place and experienced the rape intended for her. The physical repulsion, awareness of sexual vulnerability, sense of shame so profound as to demand total isolation—all are intelligible as the responses of a woman to an attempted rape. Jim's identification with Antonia structures the scene, undermining his pretense to masculinity and maleness. Is it not obvious why Jim can't marry Antonia?

At the end of his story, Jim returns to the landscape of his youth. Setting out, north of town, into "pastures where the land was so rough that it had never been ploughed up," Jim has "the good luck to stumble upon a bit of the first road that went from Black Hawk out to the north country; to my grandfather's farm, then on the Shimerdas' and to the Norwegian settlement. Everywhere else it had been ploughed under when the highways were surveyed; this half-mile or so within the pasture fence was all that was left of that old road which used to run like a child across the open prairie, clinging to the high places and circling and doubling like a rabbit before the hounds" (pp. 369, 370-371). Formless, unploughed and unsurveyed, with possibilities for wildness, this landscape, so steeped in nostalgia, reflects a longing for a time before definition, before roads have been marked and set and territories rigidly identified. Not surprisingly, at the end of the book Jim has returned to a psychological state parallel to that of his beloved landscape. Reunited at last to Antonia, he is also reunited with a past before the domination of sexual definition where one might be a tomboy and love one's Antonia to one's heart's content. The attendant spirit on the longing for gender ambiguity is a profound uneasiness in the face of actual manifestations of this desire. Like a threatened animal tracked to its lair, the text exudes the stench of trauma at those moments when gender crossing actually occurs—for example, when Antonia begins to dress and act like a man and grandmother Burden determines to "save" her. This tension between impulse and repression, desire and renunciation determines the various trajectories described by the text of *My Antonia*. "The Pioneer Mother's Story" is not the only tale this text is telling. Though *My Antonia* may have at its center a massively romanticized earth mother, the surrounding context denies both condition and consequence of that role. Profoundly non-heterosexual in its view of men, male sexuality and marriage, the text embodies the feeding not of sons but daughters. In *My Antonia* daughters, not sons, stand tall and straight for they alone have access to the shelves of jars, the barrels of food, stored in the fruit cave of the womb, the rich mine of life.

The text as a whole recapitulates the burden of narrative choice—a forced feeding only partially swallowed; a transposition only partially completed; a story, a sensibility, an eroticism only partially renounced. Emblematic of the unrenounced is the character of Lena Lingard. If the idealization of Antonia in "the pioneer woman's story" requires the steady denial of her sexuality,[15] Lena remains convincingly sexual to the end. More significantly, her sexuality is neither conventionally female nor conventionally male but rather some erotic potential only possible outside the heterosexual territory of rigid definitions and polar oppositions. Characterized by a diffused sensuality rooted in a sense of self and neither particularly aggressive nor particularly passive, Lena represents a model of lesbian sexuality. Her presence in the text as a symbol of desire, felt as desireable and allowed to be desired, "flushed like the dawn with a kind of luminous rosiness all about her" (p. 226), provides occasional moments of pure sensual pleasure and indicates the strength of Cather's resistance to renouncing her lesbian sensibility.

V

In the foreword to his biography of Willa Cather, James Woodress writes: "Although Willa Cather wrote an old friend in 1945 that she never had any ambitions, the truth was just the opposite. Her entire career down to the publication of *O Pioneers!*, her first important book, shows a very ambitious young woman from the provinces, determined to make good."[16] Certainly that "determination" to "make good" must have played a large role in Cather's decision to renounce her own point of view, masquerade as a male, and tell a story which is not her own. As critics from Leslie Fiedler to Carolyn Heilbrun and, most recently, Nina Baym[17] have demonstrated, American literature is a male preserve; the woman who would make her mark in that territory must perforce write like a man. The pressure which converted Willa Cather into Jim Burden was not simply homophobic; equally powerful was the pressure exerted by the definition of the American "I" as male and the paradigm of American experience as masculine. Yet perhaps the ultimate irony of Cather's career lies in the fact that she is best remembered, not for her impersonations of male experience, her masculine masquerades, but rather for the strategies she evolved to maintain her own point of view and tell her own story within the masquerade. In a word, she is less remembered for the consequences of her renunciation than she is for the results of her resistance.

In *My Antonia*, Cather reveals the face of that ambition which she later declared the book to have satisfied: "The best thing I've done is *My Antonia*. I feel I've made a contribution to American letters with that book."[18] It is not surprising that the book in which Cather reveals her artistic ambitions should be her most powerful work. Nor is it surprising that this book is marked by the theme of renunciation and defined by the tension between the pressure to renounce and the equally imperative need to resist this pressure. Nor finally is it surprising that it is here, in this text, that Cather works out the terms of her compromise with her context—the context of an ambitious American writer who is also female and lesbian.

At the opening of Book III, Jim sits musing on the lines from Virgil's *Georgics*: " 'Primus ego in patriam mecum ___ deducam Musas'; 'for I shall be the first, if I live, to bring the Muse into my country' " (p. 264). He remembers that his teacher, Gaston Cleric, had explained "that 'patria' here meant, not a nation or even a province, but the little rural neighborhood on the Mincio where the poet was born"; and he wonders if "that particular rocky strip of New England coast about which he had so often told me was Cleric's *patria*" (pp. 264, 265). Surely Jim's musings illustrate Cather's ambition—to be, like Virgil, the first to bring the muse into her own country. But if Virgil's country is a *patria*, Cather's Nebraska is ardently female, envisioned and embodied in a lavishly feminine imagery, metaphor, and analogy, which culminates in the identification of the Bohemian girl with the American land.

Equally female is Cather's muse. Jim's musing on poets and poetry is interrupted by a knock at the door and the entrance of Lena Lingard. After she leaves, "it came to me, as it had never done before, the relation between girls like those and the poetry of Virgil. If there were no girls like them in the world, there would be no poetry" (p. 270). It would be hard to overestimate the significance of this moment for the career of Willa Cather or for the history of the woman artist in America. Locating the source of poetic inspiration in the figure of Lena Lingard—the unconventional, the erotic, the lesbian self retained against all odds—instead of in the figure of Antonia—the conventional, the desexed, the self distanced and defined as Other (for Antonia, unlike Lena, could never have written *My Antonia*), the location one would expect if one read the entire text as "The Pioneer Woman's Story," Cather reverses the transposition which produced Jim Burden, drops her masquerade, and defines a woman's love for women as the governing impulse of her art. Lesbian eroticism is at the heart of her concept of artistic creation. Moreover, if muse and country are both female, and if the function of the writer is to bring muse and country together, then the textual act itself is in this formulation equally lesbian. Yet, in what sense does *My Antonia* validate Cather's aesthetic theory? In what sense, beyond anything yet observed, is *My Antonia* an expression of lesbian eroticism, a story of women's love for women—in other words, a lesbian book?

In the "Introduction" to *My Antonia*, we hear a voice that is marked as neither male nor female. This voice recurs throughout the text. Often we forget that we are listening to Jim Burden—his masculinity, as suggested above, has been made easy to forget—and we assume instead that we are hearing the voice of Willa Cather. This slippage occurs most frequently and most easily when the subject of contemplation is the landscape. A woman's voice making love to a feminine landscape—here, I would suggest, is the key to Cather's genius and achievement. Unable to write directly of her own experience and to tell her own story in her own voice, and thus baffled and inhibited in the development of character and plot, Cather turned her attention elsewhere, bringing the force of her talent to bear on the creation of the land, her country, her *matria*. In the land, Cather created a female figure of heroic proportions, proportions adequate to both her lived experience as a woman and to her imaginative reach as a woman writer. In the land, Cather successfully imagined herself; in the land, she imagined a woman who could be safely eroticized and safely loved. Thus the story she could not tell in terms of character and character is told in terms of narrator and country, and the flattening and foreshortening of personality which is the consequence of her renunciation of her own voice has as its corollary a complementary lengthening and enriching of landscape. Cather made her mark in the territory of American literature with her landscape; we remember her *matria* long after we have forgotten her masquerade. Though she may have sold her birthright, the price she got for it was gold.

Notes

[1]See, for example, E.K. Brown and Leon Edel, *Willa Cather: A Critical Biography* (New York: Knopf, 1953; pb. rpt. New York: Avon, 1980), pp. 152-159; Blanche Gelfant, "The Forgotten Reaping Hook: Sex in *My Antonia*," *American Literature*, 43 (1971), 60-82; William J. Stuckey, "*My Antonia*: A rose for Miss Cather," *Studies in the Novel*, 4 (1972), 473-483.

[2]In *Lesbian Images* (Garden City: Doubleday, 1975), Jane Rule explicitly denounces a lesbian approach to Cather's work, suggesting that it violates Cather's sense of herself as an artist and a person and fulfills her worst fears of the critical act as merely an effort to "reduce great artists to psychological cripples, explaining away their gifts and visions in neuroses and childhood traumas" (p. 74). Rule shares Cather's fears about the motives of critics; she presents a series of "readings" which she labels "grossly inaccurate" and which she claims "can only be explained by a desire of each of these men to imply that Willa Cather's 'basic psychology,' 'personal failure,' or 'temperament' negatively influenced her vision" (pp. 75, 76). Obviously Rule has reason to assume that masculinist critics will seek to find in Cather's lesbianism the "flaw" which explains what's "wrong" with her work. Rule's solution to this situation, however, is absurd. Reciting the biographical evidence for viewing Cather as a lesbian, she nevertheless severs the life from the work, refusing to imagine the possibility that Cather's lesbianism might have influenced her art and resolving the paradox she has thus created by resorting to a mystical mumbo-jumbo, as in the following statement, which means as far as I can tell, absolutely nothing: "What actually characterizes Willa Cather's mind is not a masculine sensibility at all but a capacity to transcend the conventions of what is masculine

and what is feminine to see the more complex humanity of her characters" (p. 80). Rule's anxiety to protect Cather against the masculinist misreadings which result from patriarchal homophobia lead her, unfortunatley if predictably, to commit similar atrocities, as when she calls *My Antonia* Cather's "most serene and loving book," proving thereby that, though Cather was emotionally devastated by Isabelle McClung's marriage to Jan Hambourg, her personal torment as a lesbian in no way interfered with her ability to write a classic of heterosexual love. Homophobia can go no further. It is not surprising that David Stouck in his review essay, "Women Writers in the Mainstream," *Texas Studies in Literature and Language*, 20 (1978), 660-670, gleefully seizes on Rule's analysis as proof of the limits of feminist criticism for illuminating the work of Willa Cather.

[3]"The Defeat of A Hero: Autonomy and Sexuality in *My Antonia*, *American Literature*, 53 (1982), 676-690.

[4]Willa Cather, *My Antonia* (Boston: Houghton Mifflin, 1918; rev. 1926; pb. rpt. 1980), p. 313. All subsequent references are to this edition and will be included parenthetically in the text.

[5]See, for example, pp. 70, 74.

[6]See Gelfant, p. 74. Gelfant must be credited with first according this scene the attention it deserves. It is, however, interesting that in her interpretation of it as a "grisly acting out of male aversion" to women, she overlooks the fact that the groom as well as the bride gets eaten.

[7]See, for example, E.K. Brown and Leon Edel, pp. 153-154.

[8]See James Woodress, *Willa Cather: Her Life and Art* (Lincoln: University of Nebraska Press, 1970), p. 176: "She felt obliged to defend her use of a male point of view, however, when she wrote her old friend and editor Will Jones. Because her knowledge of Annie came mostly from men, she explained, she had to use the male narrator, and then she rationalized that she felt competent to do this because of her experience in writing McClure's autobiography." Or Mildred Bennett, *The World of Willa Cather* (Lincoln: University of Nebraska Press, 1961), pp. 46-47: "One of the people who interested me most as a child was the Bohemian hired girl of one of our neighbors, who was so good to me. She was one of the truest artists I ever knew in the keenness and sensitiveness of her enjoyment, in her love of people and in her willingness to take pains. I did not realize all this as a child, but Annie fascinated me and I always had it in mind to write a story about her. But from what point of view should I write it up? I might give her a lover and write from his standpoint. However, I thought my Antonia deserved something better than the Saturday Evening Post sort of stuff in her book. Finally, I concluded that I would write from the point of a detached observer, because that was what I had always been. Then I noticed that much of what I knew about Annie came from the talks I had with young men. She had a fascination for them, and they used to be with her whenever they could. They had to manage it on the sly, because she was only a hired girl. But they respected and admired her, and she meant a good deal to some of them. So I decided to make my observer a young man."

[9]Brown and Edel, p. 153.

[10]Brown and Edel, p. 153.

[11]For a fuller exploration and discussion of the issues involved in such a decision, see the first several pages of Deborah Lambert's essay.

[12]For a discussion of the emergence of this self-consciousness and of the loss of "innocence" attendant on it, see Lillian Faderman, *Surpassing The Love of Men: Romantic Friendship and Love Between Women from the Renaissance to the Present* (New York: William Morrow, 1981), pp. 297-331.

[13]*The Letters of Sarah Orne Jewett*, ed. Annie Fields (Boston: Houghton Mifflin, 1911), p. 247.

[14]*Jewett*, p. 246.

[15]See Deborah Lambert's essay for a detailed analysis of the stages by which Antonia is "reduced to an utterly conventional and asexual character."

[16]Woodress, p. 13.

[17]"Melodramas of Beset Manhood: How Theories of American Fiction Exclude Women Authors," *American Literature*, 33 (1981), pp. 123-139.

[18]Bennett, p. 203.

Janice Doane
Devon Hodges

Women and the Word According to *Garp*

UNTIL RECENTLY, many feminist critics have defined the feminist novel on the basis of theme and character. One such critic, for example, writes that a novel "can serve the cause of liberation" and "earn feminist approval" if it performs "one or more of the following functions: 1) serves as a forum for women, 2) helps achieve cultural androgyny, 3) provides role models, 4) promotes sisterhood, 5) augments consciousness raising."[1] The importance of focusing on the relation between gender and narrative structure, rather than on character, can be shown through an examination of a novel that seems to make feminism a central concern, John Irving's *The World According to Garp*.

The hero of that novel receives this rave review for one of his books: "The women's movement has at last exhibited a significant influence on a significant male writer."[2] Irving's *Garp* begs for a similar review. It sympathetically discusses feminist issues such as rape, single motherhood, the aspirations of women for political power, domestic role reversal. In a gesture toward androgyny, it provides characters who prove the viability of transsexuality. Its major women characters are strong and capable. One of them, Garp's mother Jenny Fields, is a champion of feminists, who authors her life and insists upon directing her own destiny. The other, Garp's wife Helen, is an exemplar of intelligence and cool professionalism. She supports the family while Garp minds the children, cooks and cleans—an arrangement that satisfies them both.

Yet surely even a cursory feminist analysis of this novel would reveal a strong ambivalence about feminism. All of the strong female characters are uncomfortable with the label "feminist," although, in their words, they are "not antifeminist!" (p. 552). The narrator tells the reader that Jenny "felt discomfort at the word *feminist*. She was not sure what it meant but the *word* reminded her of feminine hygiene and the Valentine treatment" (p. 185) (the torturous treatment for syphilis in males). In the text, *feminism* always designates a simplistic ideology and those who embrace the term are extremists. But the deeper evidence of ambivalence about feminism is built, as we shall show, into the novel's form. Despite *Garp's* thematic performance of feminist criteria, the book ignores the fact that feminists formulate such criteria to challenge the male hegemony over

writing and to end the silence of women. But though American feminists
know that the male control of writing must be challenged, they rarely
explicitly consider what *The World According to Garp* so self-consciously
plays upon: the conventions of narrative and writing. We propose to open
a feminist discussion of male control over writing by revealing how *Garp*
protects narrative conventions and with them reinforces patriarchal
power.

At first it seems that *The World According to Garp* defends women's
right to claim traditionally male prerogatives. The book begins with a
description of Garp's mother, Jenny. Jenny competently defends herself
against "male lust" and staunchly commits herself to single motherhood,
thus undercutting the male's traditional rights over her body and his place
as head of the family. She is neither a dutiful daughter nor anyone's wife
and we are encouraged to admire her because of this. Furthermore, she
recounts her rebellion against traditional sex roles in an autobiography
that "bridges the usual gap between literary merit and popularity" (p. 13).
The book, entitled *A Sexual Suspect*, is popular because it speaks for a
multitude of women who soon become Jenny's followers. All this seems to
suggest that women can have control over themselves and writing—but
what is the status of Jenny's writing?

Although she is an influential writer, Jenny's book is "no literary
jewel" (p. 168). Garp puts it more bluntly when he says that the book has
"the literary merit of the *Sears Roebuck* catalog" (p. 13). His metaphor
points out what he considers to be the book's main flaws: a mundane prose
style and simple-minded organizational scheme. The only way that Jenny
can bind her story together ("the way fog shrouds an uneven landscape,"
the narrator tells us [p. 157]) is with this opening sentence: "In this dirty-
minded world, you are either somebody's wife or somebody's whore, or fast
on the way of becoming one or the other" (p. 157). This sentence provides
the book with a unity of tone—strident assertiveness—presumably
appropriate to her thesis: the right of individual women to refuse their two
traditional options. Garp's literary assessment of Jenny's style thus
becomes an unspoken commentary on her thesis. We are led to believe that
Jenny's literary prose style is evidence of a dogmatic and somewhat simple-
minded view of the world. "Disharmonious," "rambling," "messy,"
Jenny's book is a testament to her failure to produce a truly coherent work
that could capture the "complexity" of "human behavior." Unlike "art,"
A Sexual Suspect can only catalogue experience—it is "about me"—and
render it in a literal-minded way.

Jenny is the central woman character in the novel, and *A Sexual
Suspect* is the most powerful instance of women's writing. In order to limit
the authority of this writing, the novel retains, in order to denounce, the
idea of "literal writing." The notion that literal writing even exists rests
upon the assumption that language is transparent so that words are able to

represent accurately their referents—the world or the self. This assumption informs much literary criticism, including feminist literary criticism which valorizes women's writing that is somehow particularly close to life. Elizabeth Janeway, for example, writes in the *Harvard Guide to Contemporary American Writing* that "If there is a woman's literature, it will derive from an area of experience, worthy of exploration which is known pretty exclusively to women and largely overlooked by men."[3] She goes on to say that "authentic literature reflects actual life."[4] Her second statement, less cautious than her first, binds her to a view of literature that Irving easily denounces in the name of "art," although, as we will show, his "art" also claims to represent the world. But it is in his interest to set up this false opposition to give his own writing a special value. Literature based solely on experience is proved to be shapeless and timebound through Jenny's book. Her messy story is timely but ephemeral: after Jenny's death, *The Sexual Suspect* is never printed again. Irving further critiques "literature that reflects actual life" by suggesting that the writer devoted to actual life cannot sustain the act of writing: having captured and depleted her subject matter—"me"—Jenny has no more to write.

In *The World According to Garp*, autobiographical writing is called the "worst" kind of writing (p. 225). With this judgment, the most powerful form of women's writing in the novel is discredited. But to be fair, *Garp* does provide alternative forms of writing by "better" women writers, though these alternatives are withdrawn as soon as they are offered. One character, Alice, writes beautifully. She cares about language as a thing in itself, rather than as a mere tool for reflecting life, but she is unable to finish a single novel. Another, Ellen James, is a good poet. But her collection of poems, *Speeches Delivered to Animals and Flowers*, and her genre, the lyric poem, are made to seem peripheral in a novel whose very subject matter privileges the narrative rendering of complex human behavior.

The writing of the major male character, Garp, is set in opposition to the writing of all these women. It is imaginative rather than literal, beautifully written, complete and complex—in short, it makes Garp into what the narrator calls a "real writer" (p. 223). The opposition between male and female writing is set in sharpest relief at the beginning of the novel through the contrast of Jenny's writing with Garp's. Irving juxtaposes the ease with which Jenny steadily produces her 1,158 page life story with the difficulty with which T.S. Garp writes a short story that has very little to do with his own experience. While Jenny's story comes from memory, Garp's story, "The Pension Grillparzer," is drawn from an interior source that is privileged in the novel—imagination. "Imagination, Garp realized, came harder than memory" (p. 124).

Though serious reviewers "chide" Jenny for "her actual writing," her book becomes a "household product." Garp's story, on the other hand, "would first appear in a serious journal where nobody would read it" (p.

156). But even though he initially lacks an audience, Garp's is the more fecund mode of writing. "The Pension Grillparzer" is the first of several "serious stories" published in "a serious way" that culminate in a book, *The World According to Bensenhaver*, which wins him everything: it is both serious and popular. Still (because it is so "imaginative"), "The Pension Grillparzer" is considered his best work by everyone in the novel whose judgment seriously counts. This high evaluation of Garp's work, placed next to derogatory remarks about Jenny's book, is Irving's way of teaching us the importance of "imagination" in writing. And this lesson is repeated over and over in the novel.

All that is said about imaginative fiction in Garp invites the reader to admire rather than understand it. As in literal writing, language is transparent in the fictional world but its referent is different: literal writing reveals the "real world" whereas good fiction reveals "imagination." Claiming that a work that is "imaginative" is an important maneuver because distancing writing from the world elevates its status. The "imaginative" work is freed from the exigencies of history and thus enters the realm of eternal objects. Furthermore, the apparent autonomy of the imaginative work insures its "wholeness"—imaginative work is true to itself. This "inner truth" must be worshipped rather than articulated. Reviewers who use redemptive strategies of interpretation are the objects of Garp's scorn: he mutters about "The destruction of art by sociology and psychoanalysis" (p. 525). Immutable, whole, true, the work of art is "better" than the known and knowable world.

Yet for all of Garp's insistence on the separateness of the imaginative work, he also claims that it is "better" than literal-minded fiction because it is closer to the world. A leap of faith is required if we are to accept this paradox. Apparently the creation of an autonomous work requires such mastery and artistry that the work is assured of being mysteriously complex. And since life itself is mysterious and complex, the work is true to life. This logic bestows a god-like power on the author and helps us accept the *thesis* that art is a sacred ideal. For all his efforts to differentiate fictional and literal writing, the two forms converge: Garp insistently promotes a theory of writing that depends on his notion of "reality"—his writing, so we are encouraged to believe, is the "real" thing.

What is women's relationship to this valorized realm of writing? In the novel, women are destined to consume rather than produce "art." Garp, the incarnation of the active male imagination, is a "natural storyteller" (p. 155), while his audience consists of women, who like his wife Helen seem to be "natural" spectators for this writing. Jenny, a prolific "bad" writer, is simply awed by "real writing." Upon reading her son's first story, "Jenny marvelled at her son's imagination" (p. 170). She is not only awed, but silenced: she reads many boosk, but "she had nothing to say about them" (p. 36). Helen, too, is a voracious reader, but acknowledges she cannot write. Nevertheless, her fine critical intelligence allows her to appreciate fully works of imagination. In fact, all of the women readers—including Alice, the babysitter Cindy, and Mrs. Ralph—are cast into the role of born consumers and spectators, awed and seduced by the display of male authority.

Men, on the other hand, are active, productive readers and writers. Garp reads only to produce fiction and writes fiction to seduce women. When Garp's writing does not seduce women—be it Helen, Alice or Cindy—it still functions in a procreative way to increase his family. At the end of the novel, he attracts Ellen James by *The World According to Bensenhaver* and eventually adopts her. *The World According to Garp* clearly advocates, then, a familiar dichotomy between an active male principle and a passive female principle. This familiar sexual dichotomy, assumed by the novel to be a fact of nature, determines who will write and who will read. "Real" writing, in this novel, is intimately connected with the "active" male and his sexuality.

It is not only this particular novel, of course, that makes the claim that only men can produce "art." Men have long appropriated the power of writing by maintaining as natural and inevitable the metaphorical link between pen and penis, author and patriarch.[5] In *Garp*, the thematic opposition between male and female writers serves this end. But finally it is the very structure of the novel itself, its narrative conventions, that most strongly defends the equation of author and patriarch. Several modern theorists have pointed out the ways in which the conventions of narrative, and particularly of the novel, give expression to and serve the interests of patriarchy. "The purpose of narrative," writes Dianne Sadoff, "including the narrative about purpose or vocation, is to seek the figure of the father, to write the paternal metaphor and to acquire paternal authority."[6] This paternal authority is inscribed in narrative form through the structuring of a significant sequence of events that moves toward a conclusion which bestows both finality and integrity on the text. The conventions of the novel—sequence, finality, integrity—are therefore not neutral. "The novel," as Edward Said points out, "most explicitly realizes these conventions, gives them coherence and imaginative life by grounding them in a text whose beginning premise is paternal."[7]

The story of Oedipus, which has become the patriarchal myth par excellence, is the paradigm for narrative structure. Without Oedipus, Roland Barthes tells us, story-telling is impossible:

The death of the Father would deprive literature of many of its pleasures. If there is no longer a Father, why tell stories? Doesn't every narrative lead back to Oedipus? Isn't storytelling always a way of searching for one's origins, speaking one's conflicts with the Law, entering into the dialectic of tenderness and hatred? .... As fiction, Oedipus was at least good for something: to make good novels, to tell good stories.[8]

The passage from ignorance to knowledge, the familiar trajectory of the realistic novel, re-enacts the Oedipal drama. But this passage of discovery, it is important to note, is specifically dependent upon the discovery of sexual difference. In the Oedipal drama, the son moves from the naive assumption that everyone has a penis to the discovery of women's lack. This discovery of castration and the anxiety it provokes propel him towards reconciliation with the Law of the Father, the Symbolic Order.

The plot of *The World According to Garp* perfectly re-enacts the classical trajectory of the traditional novel. It is the story of the life and development of a male writer, who, by learning his craft, which entails writing stories that become more and more obviously the Oedipal story (*My Father's Illusions* is his last novel), finally acquires patriarchal authority. But Garp also literally represents what the structure of this dream depends upon: the fear of castration and the corresponding insistence upon sexual differences defined by "castration" (or lack). This fear is represented when Helen bites off Michael Milton's penis; but more threatening to Garp is the graphic equation of castration and silence in the figures of the Ellen Jamesians—women who cut off their own tongues. Here women seem to choose what the Oedipal drama makes necessary: women are defined by silence and by a lack that is perceived as mutilation. The familiar trajectory of the novel, then, depends as much upon the drama of silencing and castrating (mutilating) the female as it does upon reconciling the son to the father. It is the demands of the novelistic structure itself which inscribe, not only male authority and female silence, but the violence done to women as well.

Irving not only relies on this structure but defends it in a way that Roland Barthes does not. Roland Barthes poses his questions about the death of the father and its consequences for narrative as part of a meditation on modern writing that both performs and subverts the conventions of traditional narrative. In some sense, *The World According to Garp* is also a meditation on the death of the father and its consequences for narrative and the male writer. Certainly because it is about the development of a writer, the book has occasion to perform and comment upon the conventions of narrative writing. *Garp* opens with the death of the father (Garp's), like nineteenth-century novels which often begin by presenting the reader with fatherless orphans. But unlike the nineteenth-century novel, *Garp* connects the death of the father to the rise of woman, particularly the rise of the mother to power. In response to his shift of power, Garp, the hero-writer, becomes more and more adamant about protecting patriarchy, not only, as we have seen, by equating "real writing" with male writing, but also by protecting traditional narrative conventions.

One of Garp's early experiences demonstrates Irving's defensive response to challenges to traditional conventions. When the young Garp submits his first story for publication, it is rejected by one journal because the story "does nothing new with language or with form" (p. 181). Puzzled, Garp consults his teacher, Mr. Tinch, who taught him how to write by teaching him respect for "good old-fashioned grammar." But Mr. Tinch, who reeks of death and decay, is simply as puzzled as Garp. The rotting Mr. Tinch seems to embody Irving's awareness of the decay of "old-fashioned" standards and conventions; nonetheless, Irving valorizes Garp's adherence to them. When Garp's writing becomes more "successful," i.e., popular, the same journal requests one of his stories. Garp triumphantly shoots back a nasty rejection on the rejection slip he had received so many years ago: "I am still doing nothing new with language or with form. Thanks for asking me though" (p. 182). Success has vindicated Garp's inflexibility with form. Experimenting with narrative convention, we are meant to understand, is simply a fad. What really counts—to everybody—is success, which becomes a validation for the truth of traditional narrative form.

By adhering to conventions which meet expectations and insure our pleasure, a writer is likely to be successful. Unconventional writing sacrifices the pleasure of structuring meaning in familiar ways and by doing so, challenges the status of any particular meaning as absolute. Irving cannot acknowledge that conventions of writing create the impression of truth because that acknowledgement would threaten his belief in his truthfulness and his seriousness. For Irving, narrative structure is a natural way to achieve and reflect the truth. But narrative is not natural; Irving simply naturalizes an important narrative convention—the convention of narrative sequence, of the significant accumulation of events toward an inevitable "truth." Thus Irving's conventionalism, which parallels Garp's, becomes a way of defending his own seriousness and a success that accompanies his adherence to the familiar.

Garp achieves his success with a book entitled *The World According to Bensenhaver*. Both the book's title and its major concerns, of course, are meant to parallel *The World According to Garp*. The sequence of events in both books is generated by sexual violence: both depend upon erotic polarization and the violence that ensues from it to make things happen. In the beginning of *The World According to Bensenhaver* Hope Standish is raped. *The World According to Garp* is powered by a first sentence that sets men and women in opposition: "Garp's mother, Jenny Fields, was arrested in Boston in 1942, for wounding a man in a movie theatre." A simple plot summary demonstrates that the rest of the novel continues to rely on the war between the sexes: Jenny does not want to have anything to do with men. She writes a book in defense of this position. Her book attracts a group of feminist extremists, the Ellen Jamesians, to Jenny and Garp. These women have banded together to make the raped and mutilated eleven-year-old Ellen James a political cause, and in the end kill Garp. The battle of the sexes is reproduced within Garp's family where sexual tensions between Garp and Helen lead to a catastrophe in which Helen sexually mutilates a man and Garp kills one of his own children. In sum, sexual violence is what happens in the novel.

In each book, the sequence of events seems contrived to fulfill the popular demand for violence, but Irving works to extol the "seriousness" of his violent narrative by defending the seriousness of Garp's novel. Jillsey Sloper, in her defense of *The World According to Bensenhaver*, acts as Irving's mouthpiece. Jillsey Sloper is a reader who has an intuitive access to what makes a work popular as well as a feeling for the deeper truths of literature. She finds "sick" (i.e., violent) books compelling: "This book is so *sick*. You *know* somethin's gonna happen, but you can't imagine *what*" (p. 452). But she dignifies this perversity by saying that "it feels so true" (p. 453)—the narrator comments later that Jillsey uses "true" in the "good way," not as in "real life" (p. 457). Here we have it again: Garp's writing is not like life and yet it is a perfect representation of it; as Jillsey explains, with "true" books one can say, "Yeah! That's just how damned people *behave* all the time!" (p. 453).

There are several "truths" being defended here. One is that Garp is a serious writer, who can capture the "truth" of human behavior. Another is that narrative sequence, what happens, is natural—there is a compelling human "instinct" to want to know what happens—and this narrative sequence is fully adequate to expressing human behavior.[9] Finally, male power is necessary and inevitable, so sexual violence is as well. For their "truth," Irving and Garp depend upon the "naturalness" of an active male principle and a passive female principle, a polarization that is erotic, violent, hierarchical, and gives rise to women's victimization. Irving's narrator is clearly unhappy about this victimization and insists on decrying male violence in the form of rape. But it doesn't matter. Irving's explanation for rape, finally, is male lust, an extreme form of the active male principle. Rape, then, is another consequence of the facts of nature. And in the figure of the Ellen Jamesians, who cut off their own tongues in sympathy with Ellen James, Irving entertains the notion that the extreme of female "nature"—masochism—is also a cause of the victimization of women. This victimization in turn generates a "natural" sequence of events—a true narrative. Narrative is naturalized, is itself the truth.

Because in classical narrative it is so important to know "what happens," and to know the meaning of what happens, the conclusion is always privileged. "Truth, these (traditional) narratives tell us, is *at the end* of expectation."[10] This truth is conventionally embodied in the hero's death—the moment when meaning is conferred upon his entire life, giving the narrative—normally the story of his life—coherence as well. "A novelist is a doctor who sees only terminal cases" (p. 570) is the way Garp chooses to formulate this convention. Having naturalized narrative sequence by naturalizing violence between the sexes, Irving makes seemingly inevitable the novel's conventional momentum toward death. Our hero, Garp, must die as a result of sexual violence, and his death confers meaning upon the novel.

If we were to pay attention only to the subject matter, it would seem as though Irving were proposing something like the following: feminism is exacerbating the battle between the sexes, and bringing more violence into society. The best-intentioned men are becoming weaker, are less emotionally capable of dealing with this violence. They are mutilated or killed—they cannot endure. The best of women are stronger. They deal with violence wisely and they will survive, just as Helen and Hope do. But when we see the importance of the form of narrative, that death is what confers meaning on the whole of the narrative, we can see how, in fact, Irving is saying that the survival of women is insignificant since men will endure in more important ways. Garp's death serves only to make his life more important. In death, Garp becomes the all-powerful father that he could never quite be in life.

The last chapter, "Life After Garp," tells how the surviving characters of the novel devote the rest of their lives to making Garp's life more important and meaningful by remembering it. Helen, Roberta, Duncan, Jenny, various biographers and critics, all join in a chorus dedicated to singing Garp's praises. Having apparently conceded the loss of the father in the beginning of his novel, Irving reminds us here that the father, in his death, simply becomes more important.

An analysis of traditional narrative conventions teaches us how the death of the father can make him larger than life. Paradoxically, patriarchy can be served by assaults on it, and this means that feminism can be made the obstacle of its own ends. In *Garp*, not only does the death of the father at the hands of a feminist extremist dignify the hero at the expense of feminist ideology, but Irving can also use the feminist issue of rape to entrench patriarchal power by making sexual violence seem "natural" and by using it to generate and naturalize narrative sequence. Irving easily writes a book that meets thematic criteria for the "feminist" novel—he includes strong female characters who are attractive survivors—without ever jeopardizing the patriarchal power inscribed in traditional narrative conventions. So rather than concentrating on whether or not a work of fiction truthfully represents women—a critical focus which assumes that a transparent writing is possible—feminist critics should examine how writing creates the illusion of truth. In the novel, and in *The World According to Garp*, truth is structured in such a way as to guarantee paternal authority and to silence women no matter how much they seem to speak.

Notes

[1]Cheri Register, "American Feminist Literary Criticism: A Bibliographical Introduction," *Feminist Literary Criticism*, ed. Josephine Donovan (Lexington: University

Press of Kentucky, 1975), p. 13.

[2]John Irving, *The World According to Garp* (New York: Pocket Books & Simon Schuster, 1979), p. 476.

[3]"Woman's Literature," *Harvard Guide to Contemporary American Writing*, ed. Daniel Hoffman (Cambridge: Belknap Press, 1979), p. 342.

[4]*Ibid.*, p. 346.

[5]Sandra Gilbert and Susan Gubar discuss this at length in *The Madwoman in the Attic* (New Haven: Yale University Press, 1979), particularly pp. 3-16.

[6]"Storytelling and the Figure of the Father in Little Dorrit," *PMLA*, 95, No. 2 (1980), 235.

[7]Edward Said, *Beginnings: Intention and Method* (New York: Basic Books, Inc., 1975), p. 163.

[8]Roland Barthes, *The Pleasure of the Text*, trans. Richard Miller (New York: Hill and Wang, 1975), p. 47.

[9]Elsewhere, Garp wonders: "What is the instinct in people that makes them expect something to *happen*?" p. 265.

[10]Roland Barthes, *S/Z*, trans. Richard Miller (New York: Hill and Wang, 1974), p. 76.

Sandra M. Gilbert

Costumes of the Mind:
Transvestism as Metaphor in Modern Literature

What is the current that makes machinery, that makes it crackle, what is the current that presents a long line and a necessary waist. What is this current.

What is the wind what is it.

Where is the serene length, it is there and a dark place is not a dark place, only a white and red are black, only a yellow and green are blue, a pink is scarlet, a bow is every color. A line distinguishes it. A line just distinguishes it.

Gertrude Stein, "A Long Dress"[1]

"THERE IS MUCH TO SUPPORT the view that it is clothes that wear us and not we them," declared Virginia Woolf in *Orlando* (1928), adding that "we may make them take the mould of arm or breast, but [clothes] mould our hearts, our brains, our tongues to their liking."[2] In the same year, however, W.B. Yeats published a collection of poems that included a very different, and far more famous, statement about costumes: "An aged man is but a paltry thing, / A tattered coat upon a stick, unless / Soul clap its hands and sing, and louder sing, / For every tatter in its mortal dress." Where Woolf's view of clothing implied that costume is inseparable from identity—indeed, that costume creates identity—Yeats' metaphor, repeated throughout his career, posits a heart's truth which stands apart from false costumes. For Woolf, we are what we wear, but for Yeats, we may, like Lear, have to undo the last button of what we wear in order to dis-cover and more truly re-cover what we are.

It is not surprising that literary men and women like Yeats and Woolf should have speculated on the significance of costume, for both were living in an era when the Industrial Revolution had produced a corresponding revolution in what we have come to call "fashion." Though there has always been a tradition of theatricality associated with the expensive clothing of aristocrats and wealthy merchants as well as a long literary tradition exploring the implications of transvestism, until the middle or late nineteenth century most people wore what were essentially uniforms: garments denoting the one form or single shape to which each invididual's life was confined by birth, by circumstance, by custom, by decree. Thus the widow's weeds, the peasant's Sunday embroidery, the governess' sombre gown, the servant's apron, and the child's smock were signs of class, age and occupation as fated and inescapable as the judge's robes, the sergeant's stripes, and the nun's habit.[3]

With the advent of the spinning jenny and the sewing machine, common men and women, along with uncommon individuals from Byron to Baudelaire, began to experience a new vision of the kinds of costumes available to them and, as a corollary to that vision, a heightened awareness of the theatrical nature of clothing itself.[4] By 1833 Thomas Carlyle was writing obsessively about the mystical significance of tailoring, and by the 1890s *fin de siècle* literary circles were dominated by poets who defined themselves at least in part as dandies, poets whose art increasingly concerned itself with style in every sense of the word. In our own century that literary concern with costume has, of course, continued, accompanying and in a sense commenting on the rise and fall of hemlines and governments, houses of fashions and fashions of thought.

There is a striking difference, however, between the ways female and male modernists define and describe literal or figurative costumes. Balancing self against mask, true garment against false costume, Yeats articulates a perception of himself and his place in society that most other male modernists share, even those who experiment more radically with costume as metaphor. But female modernists like Woolf, together with their post-modernist heirs, imagine costumes of the mind with much greater irony and ambiguity, in part because women's clothing is more closely connected with the pressures and oppressions of gender and in part because women have far more to gain from the identification of costume with self or gender. Because clothing powerfully defines sex roles, both overt and covert fantasies of transvestism are often associated with the intensified clothes consciousness expressed by these writers. But although such imagery is crucially important in works by Joyce, Lawrence and Eliot on the one hand, and in works by Barnes, Woolf and H.D. on the other, it functions very differently for male modernists from the way it operates for feminist modernists.

Literary men, working variations upon the traditional dichotomy of appearance and reality, often oppose false costumes to true clothing. Sometimes they oppose costume (seen as false or artificial) to nakedness (which is true, "natural," and the equivalent of a suitable garment or guise). Frequently, moreover, they see false costumes as unsexed or wrongly sexed, transvestite travesties, while true costumes are properly sexed. In defining such polarities, all are elaborating a deeply conservative vision of society both as it is and as it should be, working, that is, on the assumption that the sociopolitical world should be hierarchical, orderly, stylized. Often, indeed, in their anxiety about the vertiginous freedom offered by an age of changing clothes, these men seem nostalgic for the old days of uniforms, and so they use costumes in poems and novels in part to abuse them. Even more important, their obsessive use of sex-connected costumes suggests that for most male modernists the hierarchical order of society is and should be a pattern based upon gender distinctions, since the ultimate reality is in their view the truth of gender, a truth embodied or clothed in cultural paradigms which all these writers see as both absolute and Platonically ideal and which the most prominent among them— Joyce, Lawrence, Yeats, Eliot—continually seek to revive.

The feminist counterparts of these men, however, not only regard clothing as costume, they also define all costume as false. Yet they don't oppose false costume to "true" nakedness, for to most of these writers that fundamental sexual self for which, say, Yeats uses nakedness as a metaphor is itself merely another costume. Thus where even the most theatrical male modernists differentiate between masks and selves, false costumes and true garments, most female modernists and their successors do not. On the contrary, many literary women from Woolf to Plath see what literary men call "selves" as costumes and costumes as "selves," in a witty revision of male costume metaphors that can be traced back to such nineteenth-century foremothers as Charlotte Brontë and Emily Dickinson. Moreover, just as male modernist costume imagery is profoundly conservative, feminist modernist costume imagery is radically revisionary in a political as well as literary sense, for it implies that no one, male or female, can or should be confined to uni-form, a single form or self. On the contrary; where so many twentieth-century men have sought to outline the enduring, gender-connected myths behind history, many twentieth-century women have struggled—sometimes exuberantly, sometimes anxiously—to define a gender-free reality behind or beneath myth, an ontological essence so pure, so free that "it" can "inhabit" any self, any costume. For the male modernist, in other words, gender is most often an ultimate reality, while for the female modernist an ultimate reality exists only if one journeys beyond gender.

I want to illustrate these points by considering both well-known male modernist transvestite fantasies and famous feminist fantasies which employ similar themes and plot devices but toward very different ends. One of the most dramatic transvestite episodes in modern literature, for example, appears in the Nighttown episode at the heart of Joyce's *Ulysses*. Here Leopold Bloom encounters a Circe named Bella Cohen, the whorehouse madam, who turns herself into a male named Bello and transforms Bloom first into a female, then into a pig, and finally into an elaborately costumed "charming soubrette." Significantly, it is the last of these transformations, the one depending upon costume, which is the seal of Bloom's humiliation, just as Bello's dreadful ascendancy is indicated by her/his clothing. "With bobbed hair, ... fat moustache rings, ... alpine hat ... and breeches," Bello becomes a grotesque parody of masculinized female mastery, what she/he calls "petticoat government," hunting and beating the tremblingly masochistic Bloom.[5] Even more ludicrous clothing defines Bloom's disgrace. Pointing to the whores, Bello growls that "as they are now, so will you be, wigged, singed, perfumesprayed, ricepowdered, with smoothshaven armpits. Tape measurements will be taken next your skin. You will be laced with cruel force into vicelike corsets ... to the diamond trimmed pelvis ... while your figure, plumper than when at large, will be restrained in nettight frocks, pretty two ounce petticoats, and fringes..." (p. 523).

These sadomachistic passages are important for several reasons. Besides parodying fashion magazine descriptions of clothing and reminding us thereby that for the modernist both literary style *and* costume are often tools of ironic impersonation, Joyce is here specifically parodying Leopold von Sacher-Masoch's famous *Venus in Furs*; but in doing so, he is also parodying a distinctively nineteenth-century pornographic genre:

Closely allied to [erotic histories of] spanking and whipping, were the underground Victorian epics about bondage that usually recount how recalcitrant and unmanageable boys were put into tight corsets and educated to be docile and feminine and lived more or less happily as women. Two such works are *Miss High Heels* and *Gynocracy* ..... In the first, Dennis Evelyn Beryl is transformed under the supervision of his stepsister Helen into a properly trained young woman. As part of his corset discipline, he [is] sent to a girls' school, where he [is] punished with canes, riding whips, birch rods, and ever more restrictive corsets .... In the second novel, Julian Robinson, Viscount Ladywood ... had showed too much energy as a boy, and so his parents shipped him to a [similar] school. The novel concluded: "The petticoat...I consider extremely beneficial.... There is a wonderful luxuriousness and sensuality in being made to bow down before a woman.... My lady's stockings and drawers upon me give me...an electrifying thrill.... This world is woman's earth, and it is petticoated all over. Theirs is the dominion, turn and twist the matter as you will!"[6]

In the dialogue between Bloom and Bella/Bello, Joyce almost literally echoes some of this language. ("Married, I see," says Bella to Bloom. "And the Missus is Master. Petticoat government"; "That is so," Bloom replies, adding encomia to Bella as "Powerful being" and "Exuberant female" [pp. 515-16].)

Does Joyce's parody suggest a serious if covert acceptance of the original pornography, a reinterpretation of the work in a spirit in which it was not intended? Might we decide, for instance, as several recent critics have suggested, that the grotesque androgyny Joyce imagines for Bloom in Nighttown and elsewhere in *Ulysses* hints through veils of parody at the possibility of a nobler and more vital androgyny?[7] I would like to agree with such an optimistic, and implicitly feminist, interpretation of the Nighttown episode, but it strikes me as largely mistaken.

For one thing, Bloom's female costume is a sign that he has *wrongly* succumbed to "petticoat government" and thus that he has become weak and womanish himself; his clothing tells us, accordingly, not of his large androgynous soul but of his complete degradation. For Joyce's parodic narrative implies that to become a female or femalelike is not only figuratively but literally to be de-graded, to lose one's place in the preordained hierarchy that patriarchal culture associates with gender. If this is so, however, Joyce is also hinting that to *be* a woman is inevitably to be degraded, to be "a thing under the yoke." And certainly the language of the Nighttown episode supports this depressing notion, for as Joyce (and all his readers) knew perfectly well, it was not just Bella/Bello's whores who were "wigged, singed, perfumesprayed, ricepowdered," shaven, corseted, and "restrained in nettight frocks"; this degrading reality of female costume is in fact the reality at the heart of the pornography Joyce is parodying in *Ulysses*. (The sadism associated with the male/female role reversal in transvestite Victorian pornography suggests, moreover, that the pornography itself is perversely reversing, exaggerating, and thereby parodying the male dominance/female submission that the authors of these works believe to be quite properly associated with male/female relationships.)

In other words, just as Kate Millett extrapolated a true societal evaluation of femaleness from the parodic posturings of Jean Genet's male homosexual transvestites,[8] we can extrapolate Joyce's vision of society's vision of femaleness from Bloom's degraded androgyny. It is significant therefore, that after this episode the traveling salesman returns home and, instead of increasing his commitment to nurturing wholeness, femaleness, and androgyny, the figuratively, if only temporarily, expels the suitors, gives the "viscous cream" ordinarily reserved for "his wife Marion's breakfast" to his mysteriously mystical son Stephen, and asserts his proper male mastery by ordering Molly to bring him eggs for his own breakfast the next morning. Casting off his false female costume, he has begun to dis-cover and re-cover his true male potency, his masterful male self. "From infancy to maturity he had resembled his maternal procreatrix," but from now on he will "increasingly resemble his paternal creator" for he has at last taken his place in a patrilineal order of success and succession (p. 692).

Bloom's dramatic recovering of power is, however, curiously associated not only with his repudiation of the female and the female costume but also with his wearing of that costume. But this is not because his new power is in any way androgynous. On the contrary, Bloom's regained authority seems to have been energized by the sort of ritual sexual inversion that, as Natalie Davis notes, traditionally accompanied festive misrule. In sixteenth-century France, Davis tells us, the ceremonial functions of such sexual inversion were mostly performed by males disguised as grotesque cavorting females, and the primary purpose of their masquerades was usually to reinforce the sexual/social hierarchy.[9] Through enacting gender disorder, men and women learned the necessity for male dominant/female submissive sexual order. At the same time, through a paradoxical yielding to sexual disorder, the male, in particular, was thought to gain the sexual energy (that is, the potency) he needed for domination. For since women were traditionally defined as "the lustier sex"—the sex made for sex—it was only natural, if paradoxical, that a man could achieve sexual strength by temporarily impersonating a woman. Through grotesque submission, he would learn dominance; through misrule, he might learn rule; through a brief ironic concession to "petticoat government," he would learn not androgynous wholeness but male mastery.

Moreover, Bloom's revitalized male mastery might not derive just from the essentially conservative psychodramas of misrule that Davis describes but also from a transvestite enigma recently analyzed by the psychoanalyst Robert Stoller. Discussing the phenomenon of "the phallic woman," Stoller argues that the male transvestite uses the degrading apparatus of female costume to convert "humiliation" to "mastery" by showing himself (and the world) that he is a woman with a penis. Unlike the transsexual, Stoller notes, the transvestite is constantly and excitedly "aware of the penis under his women's clothes and, when it is not dangerous to do so, gets great pleasure in revealing that he is a male-woman and [proving as it were] that there is such a thing as a woman with a penis. He therefore can tell himself that he is, or with practice will become, a better woman than a biological female if he chooses to do so."[10] Such a "phallic woman" does not merely, as Davis suggested, gain female sexual power by impersonating femaleness, he assimilates femaleness into his maleness—not his androgyny—so that he mysteriously owns the power of both sexes in a covertly but thrillingly male body.

In an analysis of transvestite masochism which is also obviously important for understanding Leopold-von-Sacher-Masoch-Bloom's behavior, Stoller reviews the pornography "that repeatedly shows cruelly beautiful [women] ... bullying the poor, pretty, defenseless transvestite." This image is associated, he notes, with the terrifying ascendancy of women (usually mothers or older sisters) in the lives of transvestites, Gea Tellus-women—like Molly Bloom—who have made their man-children impotent as little girls: "they hang those bosom-bombs heavily over his head," says Stoller; "they are cruel and haughty; they are sure of themselves; their gigantically voluptuous bodies are strong, hard, slim, long, and smooth, i.e., phallic .... [And] it takes little imagination," he remarks, "to recognize in the transvestite man's erotic daydream the little boy's impression of the woman or older girl, who, in her greater power, so damaged his masculinity." Yet, he adds, "by a remarkable tour de force [the transvestite] takes the original humiliation and converts it into an active process of sexual mastery and pleasure .... [For while the archetypal pornographic] illustration makes him appear like a poor cowering wretch, the fact is that the [transvestite] man who is excitedly masturbating while looking at such a picture is ... filled with a sense of triumph as he is successful in producing an erection, excitement, and orgasm."[11]

The transvestism in Joyce's Nighttown, like much of the costume play imagined by Victorian pornographers, almost exactly recapitulates the spirit of such sexually compensatory transvestism even while it depends upon the energy of the traditional ritual transvestism Davis analyses. Because this transvestism is the parodic product of an age of costumes rather than an era of uniforms, both its private/neurotic and its public/ritual functions are of course disguised, ironic and oblique compared to those impicit in Stoller's case histories and Davis' social histories. Nevertheless, Leopold Bloom's imaginary escapade in the Dublin whorehouse is a kind of parodic Feast of Misrule from which this exiled husband regains the strength for true rule. Recovering himself in his proper male costume, he finds a spiritual son (Stephen), remembers a lost real son (Rudy), and returns from his wanderings to a moderately welcoming Penelope. Just as the ritual magic plant *Moly* saved Homer's Ulysses from the degradation threatened by Circe, Joyce's Bloom saves himself from the depravations of Bella/Bello Cohen by not only having but ironically pretending to *be* his own *Molly*, a covertly but triumphantly phallic version of the recumbent *Ewig-Weibliche*, a "new womanly man" (p. 483) whose secret manliness must ultimately co-opt *and* conquer all insubordinate "new women."[12]

*   *   *

D.H. Lawrence's "The Fox," another transvestite work, tells the tale of Banford and March, two "new women" from the city who try to run a farm together but who fail when a literal fox attacks their chickens and a figurative fox, in the form of a young soldier, attacks them, first by making love to March and thus disrupting the women's relationship, and later by accidentally-on-purpose felling a tree in such a way that it kills Banford. Thus the foxy soldier, Henry, and his two vulnerable female opponents, Banford and March, form a love/hate triangle whose tension is resolved only when Henry manages to divest the transvestite March of her male clothing, her female companion, and her autonomous power.

In the beginning of the story, Lawrence tells us, March is dressed in "putties and breeches ... belted coat and ... loose cap," a costume in which "she looked almost like some graceful, loose-balanced young man." But he adds that "her face was not a man's face, ever," and it is not surprising that shrewd, foxily masculine Henry soon decides that he should marry her and take over the farm. "What if she was older than he? It didn't matter. When he thought of her dark, startled, vulnerable eyes, he smiled subtly to himself. He was older than she, really. He was master of her."[13]

March's change of dress is the most dramatic sign that Henry's appraisal of her is correct. Coming in to tea one day, he finds her "in a dress of dull, green, silk crepe," and as if to emphasize the sexual revelation this costume change represents, Lawrence comments that "if she had suddenly grown a moustache he could not have been more surprised" (p. 156). Despite the surprise, however, March's dress confirms Henry's mastery and definitively transforms the two of them into the true male and true female each had been all along.

Seeing her always in the hard-cloth breeches ... strong as armours ... it had never occurred to [Henry] that she had a woman's legs and feet. Now it came upon him. She had a woman's soft, skirted legs, and she was accessible.... He felt a man, quiet, with a little of the heaviness of male destiny upon him. (p. 157).

But if March's dress emphasizes her true womanliness, it also reveals, by comparison, the unwomanliness of Banford, who, with her little "iron breasts" and her chiffon costumes, is a sort of grotesque female impersonator of a male impersonating a female (p. 155). Thus Henry's murder of Banford is his most powerful assertion of his "destiny" as well as the final sign that he has achieved the virility he needs in order to dominate March. Seeming "to flash up enormously tall and fearful" (p. 173), he fells Banford by felling "a weak, leaning tree" which had appeared, in its attempt at upright assertiveness, to impersonate the phallic strength that must by rights belong to him. Once again, though rather more painfully than in *Ulysses*, a male modernist has shown the way to rule by elaborating a costume drama of misrule. And once again, the hierarchial principle of an order based upon male dominance/female submission has been recovered from transvestite disorder.

   That order undergoes a similar process of testing and regeneration in *The Waste Land*, a poem that is obviously about sexuality but not quite so clearly about the horrors of transexuality. It is certain, of course, that, as Carolyn Heilbrun notes, Tiresias' androgyny "made him of special interest to Eliot."[14] But this is not necessarily because the author of *The Waste Land* wanted to elide traditional gender definitions. On the contrary, it seems likely that Eliot was using sexual costumes to promote a vision of rule and misrule comparable to the visions that underlie "The Fox" and *Ulysses*. For though androgyny—or, more accurately, hermaphroditism—of the sort Tiresias possesses is not quite the same as transvestism, metaphorically speaking the two are close indeed. Certainly when Tiresias describes himself as an "Old man with wrinkled female breasts," he is defining his sexuality in much the same way that Joyce defines Bloom's in Nighttown. But if, as Eliot himself noted, "what Tiresias *sees*, in fact, is the substance of the poem," we must assume that the vision offered by *The Waste Land* is in some sense a comment on the consciousness through which it is filtered. Just as a dream of Tiersias' would speak to us primarily of Tiresias, so "what Tiresias *sees*" must reveal more about Tiresias than about anyone else.

What Tiresias sees, however, is a Dantesque Inferno of sexual misrule, an unreal (and unroyal) City enthralled by the false prophetess Madame Sosostris and laid waste both by its emasculated king's infertility and by the disorderly ascendancy of Belladonna, the Lady of Situations (whose name, whether intentionally or not, echoes Bella Cohen's). Moreover, just as the perverse ceremonies of Joyce's female-dominated Nighttown inevitably organized themselves into a Black Mass in celebration of the unholy "Dooooog!" who is God spelled backward, Eliot's infertile London is haunted by a sinister Dog, who threatens to dig up corpses. For like Nighttown, this unreal City is a topsy-turvy kingdom where towers that should be upright hang "upside down in air" and baby-faced bats crawl "head downward down a blackened wall." And like Nighttown, it is ruled (and may indeed have been magically created) by a magical woman, a kind of sorceress, who draws "her long black hair out tight" and fiddles terrifyingly sacrilegious "whisper music on those strings."[15] Even the central scheme Tiresias "sees" in the upside-down world he describes—the seduction of the typist by the young man carbuncular—is merely a grotesquely disorderly parody of the male dominance/female submission that should be associated with fertility and order, for the young man is "One of the *low* on whom assurance sits / As a silk hat on a Bradford millionaire," and the typist is not really submissive but simply indifferent. Both, therefore, represent a society where everything and everyone are out of place, not just women on top but shopclerks unruly and carbuncular young men strutting in the false costume of the nouveau riche.

Some of the passages Pound and Eliot excised from the original manuscript of *The Waste Land* make it, finally, quite clear that both Tiresias' terrible vision and Eliot's vision of Tiresias' anomalous sexuality arise from sexual anxiety and specifically from anxiety about a blurring of those gender distinctions in which human beings ought properly to be clothed. The first draft of "The Burial of the Dead," for instance, begins with a description of a visit to a whorehouse called "Myrtle's Place," a house not unlike Bella Cohen's establishment—for Madame Myrtle proves frighteningly independent, even masterful. Announcing that "I'm not in business here for guys like you," she explains, as if anticipating Banford and March, that she's going to "retire and live on a farm."[16] And though she is ultimately kinder than Bella—refusing to give the speaker a woman, she does give him "a bed, and a bath, and ham and eggs"—her kindness is disturbingly matriarchal. "Now you go get a shave," she tells her would-be customer as she turns him out into the barren nighttime streets of the wasteland. Her emasculating sexual autonomy foreshadows the frightening sexual dominance of sibylline Madame Sosostris, of enthroned Belladonna—that chess queen who moves in all directions, unlike her paralyzed king—and of the freewheeling, unladylike ladies in the pub. It also adumbrates the obscenely perverse power of another character who was summarily cut from the final draft: "white-armed Fresca."

Appearing voluptuously "between the sheets," like insubordinate Molly Bloom, Fresca "dreams of love and pleasant rapes" in a series of antiheroic "heroic couplets" that parody Pope's often equally disturbing eighteenth-century parodies of the lives and aspirations of "Blue Stockings." Fresca's perverse dreams comment interestingly on those literal and figurative rapes (of Philomel, the Thames daughters, and the typist) which actually occur in Eliot's Waste Land. When she enters her "steaming bath," moreover, she does not strip or purify herself; rather costuming herself in deceptive "odours, confected by the artful French," she wilfully disguises what Eliot describes as her "good old hearty female stench."

Worse still, although Eliot/Tiresias tells us that "in other time or other place" Fresca would have been her proper self, a creature devised by male poets, "A meek and lowly weeping Magdalene; / More sinned against than sinning, bruised and marred, / The lazy laughing Jenny of the bard" (and at the same time "a doorstep dunged by every dog in town"), in the upside-down realm Fresca now rules she is, of all improper things, a woman poet, the inevitable product of an unnatural age of transvestite costumes, masks, disguises:

> Fresca was baptized in a soapy sea
> Of Symonds—Walter Pater—Vernon Lee ....
> From such chaotic misch-masch potpourri
> What are we to expect but poetry?
> When restless nights distract her brain from sleep
> She may as well write poetry, as count sheep. (p. 27)

Thus, "by fate misbred, by flattering friends beguiled, / Fresca's arrived (the Muses Nine declare) / To be a sort of can-can salonnière," and, significantly, the immediate consequence of her literary triumph for the speaker is that "at my back from time to time I hear / The rattle of the bones, and chuckle spread from ear to ear." For as this speaker—Tiresias, Eliot, the lost disinherited son of the Fisher King—had earlier reminded us, "Women grown intellectual grow dull, / And lose the mother wit of natural trull." Losing nurturing *mother* wit, however, and artificially separating themselves from the natural trull in themselves, such women separate their men from the fertile and properly mythologized order of nature, precipitating everyone, instead, into a chaotic No Man's Land of unnatural, transvestite women.

It is no coincidence, then, that the third in the series of nineteenth-century aesthetes who "baptized" Fresca into her unholy religion of art was, in an important sense, a female transvestite: Vernon Lee was the male pseudonym under which a woman named Violet Paget achieved considerable literary success in the late nineteenth and early twentieth centuries. Her fleeting appearance here is yet one more detail which suggests that, rather than implying an optimistic vision of androgyny, *The Waste Land* is precisely the *Walpurgisnacht* of misplaced sexuality that a conservative male modernist like Eliot would define as the fever dream of the hermaphrodite, the nightmare of gender disorder. Ultimately, after all, Eliot yearns with Joyce and Lawrence for "the violet hour, the evening hour that strives homeward," to bring a thoroughly male Ulysses home from the sea to his soft-skirted, definitively female Penelope. Because both time and Tiresias are out of joint, such a consummation does not happen in *The Waste Land*. But it is devoutly wished, and thus it represents a patriarchal sexual rule which is as implicit in the sorrowful misrule that haunts Eliot's poem as it is in the Jovian voice of thunder that virtually concludes the work and in the triumphantly orderly endings of *Ulysses* and "The Fox."

*   *   *

Virginia Woolf knew, of course, these three works—*Ulysses*, "The Fox" and *The Waste Land*—and it is to her use of metaphorical transvestism that I will now turn, for her radical revisions of male costume dramas provide an extraordinarily useful paradigm of the gleeful skepticism with which feminist modernists questioned, subverted and even repudiated the conservative, hierarchical views of their male counterparts.

When "Great Tom" Eliot came to Hogarth House and "sang" and "chanted" and "rhythmed" *The Waste Land*, Woolf was so impressed by its "great beauty" that Hogarth Press published the poem in book form the following year.[17] When Eliot defended *Ulysses* to her, however, her feelings about Joyce's novel were considerably less charitable. Though Eliot was eventually to praise not only Joyce's literary abilities but also his "ethical orthodoxy,"[18] Woolf insisted in her diary that *Ulysses* was "brackish" and "underbred," adding that "one hopes he'll grow out of it; but as Joyce is 40 this scarcely seems likely."[19] But she herself was forty when she made this remark, and, for herself, she considered the age advantageous: "At forty I am beginning to learn the mechanism of my own brain" (*WD*, p. 46). Clearly, then, Joyce's "orthodox" but "underbred" novel inspired her with sufficient irritation to cause her thinking to become uncharacteristically inconsistent. Could the sexual psychodrama embedded in *Ulysses* and manifested in its transvestite fantasies have anything to do with these feelings? Considering both Woolf's feminism and her developing "Sapphism" such a possibility seems reasonable. Certainly within a few weeks of her assertion that *Ulysses* was "underbred," she noted in her diary that when "Tom said '[Joyce] is a purely literary writer'," she had scornfully responded that he was "virile—a he-goat . . . (*WD*, p. 49). Five years later, when Woolf herself wrote a transvestite novel—*Orlando*— she seems to have deliberately set out to shatter the "he-goat" vision of male mastery upon which Joyce based *Ulysses*.

Orlando, a work that is nominally about a transsexual, depicts transsexualism through sardonic costume changes rather than through actual physical transformations. In fact, as if to emphasize that costume, not anatomy, is destiny, Woolf comically eschews specific descriptions of the bodily changes that mark Orlando's gender metamorphosis. As "man become woman" Orlando stands naked before a mirror, but Woolf merely remarks that he/she looks "ravishing," then brings on three parodic "virtues" personified as ladies—Chastity, Purity and Modesty—who throw a towel at the unclothed being.[20] That the towel bearers are *ladies* suggests at once the connection between self-definition, sexual definition and costume, a connection that Woolf makes more clearly as her narrative unfolds. Her transsexual, she agrees, is no more than a transvestite, for though Orlando has outwardly become a woman, "in every respect [she] remains precisely as he had been" (p. 138), and this not because sexually defining costumes are false and selves are true but because costumes *are* selves and thus easily, fluidly, interchangeable.

Unlike Leopold Bloom's humiliation, then, or the "corset discipline" imposed upon Dennis Evelyn Beryl and Viscount Ladywood, Orlando's metamorphosis is not a fall; it is simply a shift in fashion (so that Woolf associates it with shifts in literary style, shifts in historical styles, changing modalities of all kinds which remind us that, like Orlando, all is in flux, all is appearance, no fixed hierarchy endures or should endure). As a shift that is not a fall, moreover, Orlando's metamorphosis, and indeed the whole of her history, seems to comment on Bella/Bello Cohen's threat to Bloom that "As they are now, so shall you be"—wigged, powdered, corseted, de-graded. Although Orlando's female costume discomfits her at times, it never degrades her, for, declares Woolf, "it was a change in Orlando herself that dictated her choice of a woman's dress and of a woman's sex [because] different though the sexes are, they intermix" (p. 188). Orlando, in other words, really is androgynous (as Tiresias, for instance, is not) in the sense that she has available to her a sort of wardrobe of male and female selves, "far more," says Woolf, "than we have been able to account for . . . since a person may well have [thousands]" (p. 309). Making herself up daily out of such costumes, Orlando rejoices in the flux and freedom of a society where there need be no uni-forms, for indeed (as if confusing nakedness and costume) Woolf remarks that Orlando's own "form combined in one the strength of a man and a woman's grace" (p. 138).

Thus, unlike Tiresias, upon whom the worst of both sexes has been inflicted as if to suggest that any departure from the fixity of gender implies disorder and disease, Orlando has the best of both sexes in a happy multiform which she herself has chosen. And in accordance with this visionary multiplicity, she inhabits a world where almost anyone can change his or her sexual habits at any time. Yet this is not, like Tiresias' Waste Land, a kingdom of gender disorder but a realm of insouciant shiftings. After Orlando has become a woman, for instance, the Archduchess Harriet becomes Archduke Harry; he/she and Orlando act "the parts of man and woman for ten minutes with great vigour, and then [fall] into natural discourse" (p. 179). Similarly, marriage for Orlando need not be the affair of pure masterful maleness embracing pure submissive femaleness that it was for Lawrence's foxy Henry. Wed to the magical sea captain Marmaduke Bonthrop Shelmerdine, Orlando comically accuses her simpatico husband of being a woman, and he happily accuses her of being a man, "for ... it was to each ... a revelation that a woman could be as tolerant and free-spoken as a man, and a man as strange and subtle as a woman" (p. 258). Thus a question with which Bella Cohen's Fan surrealistically initiated the phantasmagoria of sick horror that overtook Bloom in Nighttown aptly summarizes not the disease but the delight of *Orlando*: "Is me her was you dreamed before? Was then she him you us since knew? Am all them and the same now we?" (*Ulysses*, p. 516).

Orlando is, of course, in one sense a utopia, a revisionary biography of society not as Woolf thinks it is but as she believes it ought to be; and in another sense *Orlando* is a kind of merry fairy tale, its protagonist an eternally living doll whose wardrobe of costume selves enables her to transcend the constraints of flesh and history. But though Woolf defined the book as a happy escapade, satiric and wild, *Orlando*'s carefully plotted transvestism contrasts so strikingly with the transvestism we have seen in major works by male modernists that I believe we must consider this futuristic historical romance more than merely a lightheartd *jeu*. How, in fact, can we account for the extraordinary divergence between the transvestism depicted in *Ulysses*, "The Fox" and *The Waste Land*, on the one hand, and in *Orlando* on the other?

There is a major sense, of course, in which *Orlando* is first and foremost a costume drama of wish fulfillment, a literary pageant (comparable to the one in *Between the Acts*) designed to prove to Everywoman that she can be exactly who or what she wants to be, including Everyman. In this regard, it is significant that the tale forced its way out like a mirage of health just when Woolf was preparing to defend Radclyffe Hall's *The Well of Loneliness* and settling down to confront the painful problems of female subordination in the treatise on *Women and Fiction* that was to become *A Room of One's Own*. "How extraordinarily unwilled by me but potent in its own right...*Orlando* was!" she exclaimed in her diary. "As if it shoved everything aside to come into existence" (*WD*, p. 118). Yet if *Orlando* is primarily a fantasy of wish fulfillment which can be explained as a feminist pipe dream, a self-deceptive response to the anxieties instilled in women by a society structured around male dominance/female submission, what *male* anxieties energize the nightmare fantasies of *Ulysses*, "The Fox" and *The Waste Land*? And what engendered such anxieties in artists like Joyce, Lawrence, and Eliot, all of whom lived in a world that was still, as Woolf knew to her sorrow, comfortably patriarchal?

Obviously this last question is not one that can be answered hastily. Unique biographical irritants contributed, for instance, to the sexual worries of each of these men: Lawrence's mother-dominated childhood, and perhaps ambiguous sexuality, and maybe even his large, strong-willed motherly wife; Joyce's ambivalent relationship to his mother, his church and his old gummy granny of a country; Eliot's clouded and cloudy first marriage, perhaps his somewhat beclouded relationship to the Frenchman Jean Verdenal, and maybe even his poet mother, who so strongly disapproved of the vers libre her son had been writing.[21] History, too, must have intensified these male anxieties, history which—as Eliot wrote in "Gerontion"—"gives with such supple confusions / That the giving famishes the craving." Certainly the nineteenth century's incessant contrivance of costumes may have bewildered these writers, along with what must often have seemed the threatening effeminacy of the decadent *fin de siècle* and the threatening rise of serious feminism in England and America. Yet another important irritant may have been the hidden but powerful attraction that the modernists' ancestors, the Romantic poets, felt for matriarchal modes and images.[22] In addition, many men of letters were obviously disturbed by the fact that "scribbling women" on both sides of the Atlantic had begun to appropriate the literary marketplace.[23] These speculations are necessarily vague, however, and in place of further generalities I would like briefly to consider one significant event which is in any case always associated with the characteristics displayed by modernism: World War I.

Surely that Great War which so haunts modern memory has something to do with the different costume metaphors I have been reviewing here and with their very different implications: male gloom and female glee; male sexual anxiety and female sexual exuberance; male yearnings to get *back* to myth and female desires to get *beyond* myth. For World War I, after all, is a classic case of dissonance between official, male-centered history and unofficial female history.[24] Not only did the apocalyptic events of the war have very different meanings for men and women, such events *were* in fact very different for men and women.

As Paul Fussell has shown, World War I fostered characteristically "modernist" irony in young men by revealing to them exactly how spurious were their visions of heroism and, by extension, history's images of heroism.[25] For these doomed young soldiers, history's "cunning passages" (Freudianly female!) had deceived "with whispering ambitions" (like Belladonna's hair) and had guided "by vanities." But of course young women had never had such illusions, either about themselves or about history. Whether or not they consciously articulated the point, almost all had always shared the belief of Jane Austen's Catherine Morland that "history, real solemn history...tells me nothing that does not either vex or weary me. The quarrels of popes and kings, with wars or pestilences, in every page; the men all so good for nothing, and hardly any women at all— it is very tiresome."[26] With nothing to lose, therefore, women in the terrible war years of 1914 and 1918 had everything to gain. And indeed when their menfolk went off to the trenches to be literally and figuratively shattered, the women on the home front literally and figuratively rose to the occasion and replaced them in farms and factories. While their brothers groped through the rubble of *No Man's Land* for fragments to shore against the ruins of a dying culture, moreover, these women *manned* the machines of state, urging more men to go off to battle. At times, in fact, these vigorous, able-bodied young women, who had so often been judged wanting by even the weakest of young men, became frighteningly censorious judges of their male contemporaries. Speaking with some bewilderment and disgust of "the gratification that war gives to the instinct of pugnacity and admiration of courage that are so strong in women," Bernard Shaw complained that "civilized young women rush about handing white feathers to all young men who are not in uniform."[27] But though such behavior may have offended Shaw's (or anyone's) pacifism, it is easy to understand once we recognize the different meanings World War I had for men and women. Every feather given to a young man, after all, might mean another job, another *position*, for a young woman.

This is hyperbolic, of course, but it is worth considering that even the most conventionally angelic woman's ministrations—jobs like rolling bandages, nursing the wounded, and entertaining the troops—must have reminded both sexes that while men were now wounded, partial, invalid, maybe even in-valid, women were triumphant survivors, gold star mothers who might inherit the very state which had for so long disinherited them. Consciously or not, then, even the "best" of women must have seen themselves as living out a tradition first imagined in Victorian fiction by the male novelist Charles Dickens who was obsessed, as Alexander Welsh has argued, by female angels of death, and by the female novelist George Eliot who was obsessed, as several critics have demonstrated, by female angels of destruction.[28] Indeed, in a triumph of ambiguity, Eliot declared that the happiest hour of her life was the hour she spent at her father's deathbed—and such a statement might well have been made by even the most devoted of World War I sisters. For to many of these women the war was, yes, a horror and a nightmare, but it was also, alas, a nightmare from which they might awake (as Florence Nightingale did from the Crimean War) to find themselves on the sofa, permanently invalid and in-valid. Thus, like Edith Wharton (whom Henry James actually did shiveringly describe as an "Angel of Desolation"),[29] the noblest of women rushed about in the service of the Red Cross, tending the wounded with the sinister tenderness displayed by Isolde of the White Hands in *Tristan and Isolde*—a work with which writers like T.S. Eliot and D.H. Lawrence were obsessed.

In this connection it is surely significant that the women's movement in England recognized quite early a connection—though, as Emily Dickinson would say, a "slant" one—between feminist goals and the effects of the war. In 1915, *The Suffragette*, the newspaper of the Women's Social and Political Union, was renamed *Britannia*, with a new dedication: "For King, For Country, For Freedom." At last, it must have seemed, women could begin to see themselves as coextensive with the state, and with a female state at that, a Britannia not a Union Jack. And, as we know, the female intuition expressed in that renaming was quite accurate: in 1918, when World War I was over, there were 8.5 million European men dead, and there had been 37.5 million male casualties, including killed, wounded and missing, while all the women in England over the age of thirty were finally, after a sixty-two year struggle, given the vote. For four years, moreover, a sizable percentage of the young men in England had been imprisoned in trenches and uniforms, while the young women of England had been at liberty in farm and factory, changing their clothes.

In an analysis of Austen's novels, Susan Gubar and I have used Rudyard Kipling's "The Janeites" to show that Austen's heroines inhabit "a tight place" not unlike the constricted trenches of World War I.[30] But of course the converse of the proposition is also true. If eighteenth- and nineteenth-century women occupied a place as narrow as a trench, the soldiers of World War I kept house in trenches as constricting as what had heretofore been woman's place.[31] Paradoxically, then, the war to which so many men had gone in the hope of becoming heroes ended up emasculating them, depriving them of autonomy, confining them as closely as any of Austen's heroines, or any Victorian women, had been confined. It is not surprising, therefore, that the heart of darkness Yeats confronts in "Nineteen Hundred and Nineteen" is the nightmare of the return of Herodias' castrating daughters together with the horror of the ascendance of that fiend Robert Artisson, a low and no doubt carbuncular creature "To whom the love-lorn Lady Kyteler brought / Bronzed peacock feathers, red combs of her cocks." For while the Jake Barneses of the early twentieth century were locked up like Victorian girls in the trenches of No Man's Land, their female counterparts were coming out of the closet as flappers like Lady Brett, barelegged, short-haired, corsetless, in simple shifts, knickers and slacks.[32] For many, indeed, "wearing the pants" in the family or even stepping into "his" shoes had finally become a real possibility.

It is no wonder, then, that Lawrence's Henry, like Homer's Ulysses (if not Joyce's), is a soldier from the wars returning—and returning specifically to a home and farm that have been taken over by undutiful Penelopes. It is no wonder, too, that Joyce's Stephen feels himself haunted by the powerfully reproachful ghost of a mother who refuses to lie down in the grave where she belongs and no wonder that in one version of *The Waste Land* Eliot wrote that he had "spelt" these fragments from his ruin, as one would painfully spell truths out of the sibyl's leaves.[33] Finally, it is no wonder that toward the end of the last draft of *The Waste Land* a wounded voice babbles that "London Bridge is falling down falling down falling down," hinting at and simultaneously repressing the next line of the nursery rhyme: "Take a key and lock *her* up, My Fair *Lady*" (my italics). Coerced by women, at the mercy of women, bedded *down* in the terrible house of women, all these male modernists must have felt they had painfully to extract the truth of their gender's ancient dominance from an overwhelming chaos of female leaves and lives and leavings. For the feminist redefinitions fostered by World War I had reminded them that even the brothel, ostensibly an institution designed to serve men, had served—as it does in *Ulysses*—both to test men and to reinforce female power, autonomy, sisterliness.[34] Finally, therefore, it is no wonder that when Woolf came to write those twin meditations on gender, *Orlando* and *A Room of One's Own*, she had to set herself against what Rebecca West astutely called "an invisible" but unfriendly "literary wind." Woolf's argument, wrote West in an early review of *A Room*, "is all the more courageous because anti-feminism is so strikingly the correct fashion of the day among the intellectuals." And West's explanation accurately summarizes what has been my speculation here: "Before the war conditions were different. The man in the street was anti-feminist but the writers of quality were pro-suffrage. Now the case is reversed. The man in the street accepts the emancipation of women.... But a very large numer of the younger male writers adopt a [misogynistic] attitude."[35]

In fact, the misogyny (or, more accurately, the sexual anxiety) of these young male writers led them in the postwar years to just the obsession with false and true costumes, deceptive history and true myth, and transvestism and true "vestism" that we have observed in *Ulysses, The Waste Land* and "The Fox." For inevitably, in the aftermath of the emasculating terrors of the war, the male modernist insists that the ultimate reality underlying history—the myth or ontology or, as Robert Scholes would put it, "cybernetic" pattern—is and must be the Truth of Gender.[36] In Joyce's system, Bloom and Molly can and must be boiled down, as it were, to Ulysses and Penelope, the "childman weary" and the "unfulfilled, recumbent" woman, Sinbad the Sailor and Gea Tellus (*Ulysses*, pp. 720,

721). For Lawrence, all men, together with (or, more accurately, over against) all women, can and should be reduced to the paradigmatic polarities of "man-life and woman-life, man-knowledge and woman-knowledge, man-being and woman-being."[37] And Eliot, seeking beneath the sexual chaos of the Waste Land the ultimate beginning which is his true end, quite logically yearns toward the "significant soil" of gender, imagining that on a summer midnight he can hear the Ur-music "of the weak pipe and the little drum / And see them dancing around the bonfire / The association of man and woman / In daunsinge, signifying matrimonie— / A dignified and commodious sacrament."

Eliot's "East Coker," from which these last lines were drawn, is one of the major works to which Woolf was responding in *Between the Acts*. But this novel's Miss La Trobe, an ironic version of the lost Shakespearean sister Woolf imagined in *A Room*, holds many mirrors up to the nature of Western culture in order to show that all our roles, even those which appear most fated, are merely costumes. Indeed, rather than shoring fragments of history against her ruin, Miss La Trobe, like the revisionary feminist Shakespeare, seems to want to fragment history in order to ruin it. Together, she and her author imply that to find real truth one must "tunnel" back, back to the night of the dinosaurs and the mud, the "night before roads were made,"[38] the night before costumes and gender, the sacred shamanistic night of what Djuna Barnes' Dr. O'Connor calls "the third sex."[39] Woolf insisted that her own novelistic art was based upon a "tunneling" process (*WD*, p. 60), but such tunneling has long been a technique common to female writers, many of whom wish either to identify "selves" with costumes or to strip away all costumes (and selves) and to reveal the pure, sexless (or third-sexed) being behind gender and myth.

As early as 1847, for instance, Charlotte Brontë's Rochester dresses himself as a female gypsy not to degrade himself but to try to "get at" the truth about Jane; in *Villette*, moreover, Brontë's Lucy Snowe discovers ultimate truths about herself, first, when she impersonates a man for the school play and, later, when she perceives that the nun who has haunted her is really no more than a costume worn by a transvestite male. Just as Rochester is trying to communicate with the "savage free thing" trapped in Jane, Lucy is trying to uncover that purely powerful element in herself and her life. Similarly, throughout the middle years of the century, Emily Dickinson defines herself variously as Emily, Emilie, Uncle Emily, Brother Emily and Dickinson,[40] as if attempting to name not what is fixed but what is fluid in herself; in the same years Florence Nightingale continually calls herself a "man of action" or a "man of business."[41] Like latter-day gnostics, moreover, many of these women see the transformation or annihilation of gender as theologically necessary. "The next Christ will perhaps be a female Christ," writes Nightingale in *Cassandra* in 1852, and in 1917 the feminist theorist Olive Schreiner fantasizes a mystical encounter with "a lonely figure" standing "on a solitary peak," about whom she notes that "whether it were man or woman I could not tell; for partly it seemed the figure of a woman but its limbs were the mighty limbs of a man. I asked God whether it was man or woman. God said, 'In the least Heaven sex reigns supreme, in the higher it is not noticed; but in the highest it does not exist."[42]

More recent writers have elaborated the transvestite metaphors Brontë, Dickinson, Nightingale and Schreiner only provisionally imagined. For example, Barnes' *Nightwood* (1937) hurls us back through tunnels of history and literature to the third-sexed figures of Robin Vote and Dr. O'Connor. Both star in a novel that was, ironically, introduced by Eliot himself, but despite the Jacobean eloquence that must have appealed to the admirer of Webster and Beaumont and Fletcher, Dr. O'Connor is an anti-Eliotian witch doctor or medicine man, half Circe-half Ulysses, who wears women's skirts and wigs. Robin Vote, moreover, is described as "outside the 'human type'—a wild thing caught in a woman's skin" (p. 146), whose first name connects her with nature and whose last name associates her with the triumphs of the women's movement and the voting powers of the sacred. She is "my heart," says Robin's lesbian lover Nora Flood, implying that Robin represents the wild reality beyond gender, the pure potency to be found in what Yeats, less optimistically, called "the rag and bone shop of the heart." "I, who want power," says Nora, "chose a girl who resembles a boy," and Dr. O'Connor glosses this line as follows: "The last doll, given to age, is the girl who should have been a boy, and the boy who should have been a girl! The love of that last doll was foreshadowed in that love of the first. The doll and the immature have something *right* about them, the doll because it resembles but does not contain life, and, the *third sex* because it contains life but resembles the doll" (p. 148). If we read *Nightwood* in the aftermath of this speech—the way it seems we must—as a revisionary response to male modernist touchstones like Nighttown and *The Waste Land*, it is not surprising that by the end of the novel Robin actually does become a kind of sacred Dog, a reversed God (or Goddess) of the third sex, parodically barking before a conventional statuette of the Madonna.

Even more recently, H.D.'s *Helen in Egypt* (1961) suggests that Helen and Achilles, the archetypal seductive female and the paradigmatic warrior male, must be redeemed as "New Mortals," a phrase that seems to be a revision of the earlier "New Woman." Their salvation begins in the sacred precincts of the Amen Temple and ends with a rediscovery of the lost androgyny they had as children.[43] Helen, for instance, recalls that as Helen of Sparta she spoke in a "heroic voice," praising war, while the narrator reminds us that Achilles' mother—the sea nympth Thetis—dressed her heroic boy as a girl to hide him from the men who would make him into a warrior, and she argues that such transvestism, far from being degrading, was appropriate and necessary. Indeed, at the end of this enigmatic epic, H.D. suggests that the vulnerable New Mortal Achilles, freed from the iron ring of his Myrmidons through his mother's lucky failure to dip his heel into the river Styx, will be reborn in Helen's arms as the potentially transvestite or third-sexed boy he once was, "the child in Chiron's cave" who cherished a wooden doll carved in his mother's image, a "Thetis-eidolon" (p. 284).

When we consider this last, fetishistic doll in the context of the dolls, witch doctors, and magical third-sexed beings of *Nightwood* as well as in connection with the visionary multiplicity of the costumes depicted in *Orlando* and *Between the Acts*, it becomes quite clear that many feminist/modernists are concerned not only with "savage free things" or "wild things caught in women's skins" or "third sexes" but obsessed with a kind of utopian ceremonial androgyny whose purpose is very different from the ritual transvestism more "ethically orthodox" artists like Joyce, Eliot and Lawrence have used to maintain or reassert a fixed social order. For in the view of such women as Woolf and Barnes, that social order is itself fallen or at least misguided. Thus the only redemption that they can imagine from the dis-order and dis-ease of gender is in the symbolic chaos of transvestism, a symbolic chaos that is related not to the narrow power of male mastery but, as in Miss La Trobe's play, to the androgynous wholeness and holines of prehistory. For, as Mircea Eliade has noted, the ceremonial transvestism practiced in many non-Western societies is "a coming out of one's self, a transcending of one's own historically controlled situation...in order to restore, if only for a brief moment, the initial completeness, the intact source of holiness and power...the undifferentiated unity that preceded the Creation."[44]

Although Woolf would not have had access to most of the anthropological materials with which Eliade worked, she would have been introduced to such ideas by at least one contemporary thinker—and a thinker who links her not only with Schreiner but also with, of all unlikely peers, Lawrence. I am referring, of course, to Edward Carpenter, the well-known Fabian writer who was also in his own time a famous Whitmanite and a major homosexual theorist of gender. The friend of Havelock Ellis, Bernard Shaw, Lowes Dickinson and E.M. Forster as well as of Schreiner, Carpenter wrote two widely read books on the so-called third-sexed beings he called "Uranians" or "Urnings," meaning "children of heaven": *The Intermediate Sex: A Study of Some Transitional Types of Men and Women* (1908) and *Intermediate Types Among Primitive Folk* (1914). In both works, but especially in the latter, he postulated a connection between the third sex and what Eliade calls the ahistorical "Great Time" of the sacred, a link between the bisexual or "homosexual temperament and divinatory or unusual psychic powers."[45] Carpenter's notions of the "man-womanliness" of such artists as Shelley, Shakespeare and Michelangelo clearly influenced Woolf (probably through Forster but perhaps more directly), for they are exactly analogous to the ideas she defines in *A Room of One's Own*.[46] Even more to the point here, the ameliorative and mystical vision of sacred transvestism that he offers in *Intermediate Types* seems closely connected to the magical transvestism depicted in *Orlando* and, by implication, in *Between the Acts*.

As Emile Delavenay has pointed out, Lawrence was also deeply influenced by Carpenter's sermons on sexuality, even by the Victorian theorist's beliefs in the undifferentiated sexual energy that manifests itself as "femaleness" in males and "maleness" in females.[47] At the same time, however, Delavenay suggests, Lawrence withdrew as anxiously as Eliot or Joyce did from a final commitment to Carpenter's "intermediate sex"— leaving the concept free and powerful for Carpenter's feminist disciples like Woolf.[48] For Lawrence, as for Eliot and Joyce, the "cybernetic" patterns of dominance/submission associated with paradigms of gender were not only inevitable but necessary, not just irrefutable but consoling.

That a male modernist should have wanted the consolation of orthodoxy is not surprising, for it is, after all, only those who are oppressed or repressed by history and society who want to shatter the established paradigms of dominance and submission associated with the hierarchies of gender and restore the primordial chaos of tranvestism or genderlessness. Such political devotees of "the third sex" wish to say "I am not that fixed self you have restrained in those nettight garments; I am all selves—and no selves." Given even a modicum of power, as they were, for example, by the Great War, these women—for of course I am talking mainly about women—will enact their ceremonies of ritual tranvestism with what we might call "a vengeance." Those to whom the social order has traditionally given power, however, will inevitably use ceremonies of transvestite misrule to recapture rule; they seek not a third sex but a way of subordinating the second sex, and in their anxiety they play with costumes to show that costumes are merely plays, seeking reassurance in what they hope is the reality behind appearances.

Though I do not have space here to bring this argumentative history up to the present, I want in conclusion to suggest that even for post-modernist women both the identification of self with costume and the search for an ontological "savage free thing," a third sex beyond gender, may be healthy rituals, enabling the sex that is still subordinated to stand ironically outside subordination, like customers in a dress shop refusing to buy uncomfortable clothes. In her marvelously witty *The Left Hand of Darkness*, Ursula K. Le Guin has created a ceremonial and gender-free planet whose inhabitants may be alternately described with the English pronouns "he" and "she"—as their author actually has described them in different versions of the same romance.[49] And although Sylvia Plath in one of the *Ariel* poems sees her world as a series of civilized suitcases "Out of which the same self unfolds like a suit / Bald and shiny, with pockets of wishes,"[50] in another poem this paradigmatic post-modernist transcends the pain of her own life by imagining her "selves dissolving [like] old whore petticoats"—the old whore petticoats, for instance, of the "tuppenny uprights" whose degradation Barnes describes with such nightmarish precision in *Nightwood.*[51] And in the fierce monologue of reborn "Lady Lazarus," Plath boasts that she is a "big striptease," a savagely naked shamanistic spirit who "eats men like air."

In the end, Plath may have been killed by the fixity of her situation, her imprisonment in an identity the world refused to see as a costume. But she fought by trying to throw away costumes, trying to redefine herself as a "savage free thing," sexless and "pure as a baby," rather than as "a thing under the yoke" like the masochistic female Bloom had impersonated (*Ulysses*, p. 523). In *The Bell Jar*, for instance, Plath has Esther Greenwood enact a Woolfian utopian fantasy on the roof of the Amazon Hotel in New York City. Biblically queenly in her first name, green with the untried chaotic power of forests and wishes in her last, this cynical but feminist heroine renounces both true and false costumes as casually as Orlando adopts them. "Piece by piece, I fed my wardrobe to the night wind, and flutteringly, like a loved one's ashes, the gray scraps were ferried off . . . ."[52] To Bella Cohen's "As they are so shall you be," she replies, like Orlando, *no I shall not.*

Notes

[1]"A Long Dress," *Tender Buttons: Selected Writings of Gertrude Stein* (New York, 1972), p. 467.

[2]Virginia Woolf, *Orlando* (New York, 1928), p. 188.

[3]Lawrence Langner, in *The Importance of Wearing Clothes* (New York, 1959), notes that in ancient Greece "women were not permitted . . . to wear more than three garments at a time. In Rome . . . the law restricted peasants to one color, officers to two, commanders to three . . . . In the reign of Charles IX of France, the ornamentation of clothing was regulated according to the rank of the wearer, and most of these laws remained in force until the French Revolution. In England Henry VIII insisted that a countess must wear a train both before and behind, while those below her in rank might not have this distinction" (p. 179).

[4]The first of Yeats' visionary "Fragments," though probably intended as a comment on the Industrial Revolution, mythologizes the transformative power of the spinning jenny: "Locke sank into a swoon; / The Garden died; / God took the spinning-jenny / Out of his side" (*The Collected Works of W.B. Yeats* [New York, 1955], p. 211).

[5]James Joyce, *Ulysses* (New York, 1934); all further citations to this work will be included in the text.

[6]Vern Bullough, *Sexual Variance in Society and History* (New York, 1976), pp. 554-55.

[7]See, e.g., Carolyn G. Heilbrun, *Toward a Recognition of Androgyny* (New York, 1974), p. 95, and Suzette Henke, *Joyce's Moraculous Sindbook: A Study of Ulysses* (Columbus, Ohio, 1978), pp. 7, 93, 194-97.

[8]See Kate Millett, *Sexual Politics* (New York, 1970), pp. 336-61. Discussing Genet, Millett suggests that "as she minces along a street in the Village, the storm of outrage an insouciant queen in drag may call down is due to the fact that she is both masculine and feminine at once—or male, but feminine. [And thus] she has . . . challenged more than the taboo on homosexuality, she has uncovered what the source of this contempt implies—the fact that her sex role is sex rank" (p. 343). See also Maria Ramas, "Freud's Dora, Dora's Hysteria: The Negation of a Woman's Rebellion," *Feminist Studies* (forthcoming), for a useful analysis of

the connections between sex role, sex rank and sadomasochistic fantasies. "Ultimately," Ramas suggests, "heterosexual desire cannot be separated from what psychoanalysis terms 'primal scene' fantasies [which] are sado-masochistic in content and have rigidly defined masculine and feminine positions. They are cultural and are perhaps the most profound ideology, precisely because they are erotised."

⁹Natalie Davis, "Women on Top," *Society and Culture in Early Modern France* (Stanford, Calif., 1975), p. 129.

¹⁰Robert Stoller, *Sex and Gender* 2 Vols. (New York, 1975), 1:177. Significantly (in view of the connections I have been examining between sex roles, sex rank and transvestism), Stoller asserts that "fetishistic cross-dressing is almost non-existent in women" (1:143).

¹¹Because it is so important to an understanding of the phenomenon Joyce describes in Nighttown, here is Stoller's key passage on transvestism in toto:

The transvestite, his sense of wholeness and worth in himself damaged, often *before* the Oedipal phase, by the powerful feminizing effect of the woman who dressed him or who otherwise scorned his maleness, has a disturbance in his sense of identity, in his taken-for-granted feeling of wholeness as a male. Because of this, he senses that the prime *insignia* of maleness, his penis, is in danger. Then, knowing of the biological and social "inferiority" of women, and also knowing that within himself there is a propensity toward being reduced to this "inferior" state, he denies that such creatures exist and invents the "phallic" woman. In a way, he does not have to invent such a person, for the living prototype actually has existed in his life—that is, the fiercely dangerous and powerful woman who already so humiliated him as a child. But he will have his triumph over her and all women, in the process of which he will reestablish his masculinity, the scar of the perversion remaining as a permanent sign of the original traumatic relationship. While it seems paradoxical, this triumph comes when he dresses up as a woman, for then, appearing like a woman, he can nonetheless say that he is a whole person, since he is the living proof that there is such a thing as a woman who has a penis (p. 215).

For a slightly different but related analysis of compensatory transvestism, see Freud's analysis of Senatsprasident Schreber, who believed that he had been magically transformed into a semidivine woman and even after his "cure" continued at times to cross-dress ("Psycho-analytic Notes on an Autobiographical Account of a Case of Paranoia," *The Standard Edition of the Complete Psychological Works of Sigmund Freud*, ed. James Strachey, 24 vols. (London, 1958), 12:3-82.

¹²It is quite clear that Joyce is referring consciously and sardonically to the turn-of-the-century idea of the "new woman." He even introduces a bit of comic dialogue for "a feminist" who comments on Bloom's fantasied achievements as a political leader (p. 472):

A Millionairess: (*Richly.*) Isn't he simply wonderful?
A Noblewoman: (*Nobly.*) All that man has seen!
A Feminist: (*Masculinely.*) And done!

¹³D.H. Lawrence, "The Fox," *Four Short Novels* (1923; New York, 1965), p. 130; all further citations to this work will be included in the text. "Tickets, Please," which Lawrence wrote during World War I, is an interesting mirror image of "The Fox." In this tale, a group of uniformed young women tram conductors attack an inspector who is given the significant Lawrentian name of "John Thomas"; like vengeful Bacchae, they strip him of the official tunic that is a sign of his power over them, and the mock rape-murder they enact suggests, as dramatically as the scene in Bella Cohen's whorehouse, the horror and disorder associated with female ascendancy (see *The Complete Short Stories of D.H. Lawrence*, 3 vol. [New York], 2:334-46).

¹⁴Heilbrun, *Toward a Recognition of Androgyny*, p. 11.

¹⁵It is interesting to speculate that some of the imagery of *The Waste Land* unconsciously (or consciously?) echoes the mythic imagery of Rider Haggard's extraordinarily influential *She* (1887; New York, 1976), the best-selling tale of a sinister, "upsidedown" African matriarchy ruled by a semiimortal, raven-haired *femme fatale* known as "She-who-must-be-obeyed." In addition, it is also interesting to consider the connection between Bram Stoker's

Dracula and the upside-down bats described in "What the Thunder Said." In early drafts of
The Waste Land these were "a man/form" which "crawled head downward down a
blackened wall," and Valerie Eliot has noted the link between this figure and the scene in
Dracula where the count crawls in a similar way (see Leonard Wolf, *The Annotated Dracula*
[New York, 1975], p. 37, n. 29). Count Dracula is, of course, a dead man who must depend for
sustenance on the blood of living women; after he has converted his female victims to
vampires, moreover, they prey on infants, unnaturally reversing woman's maternal role.
Finally, *The Waste Land*'s "voices singing out of empty cisterns and exhausted wells" are
reminiscent of the voice of John the Baptist, who was the victim of yet another "woman-on-
top"—Herodias' unruly daughter Salome.

[16]Eliot, *The Waste Land: A Facsimile and Transcript of the Original Drafts Including
the Annotations of Ezra Pound*, ed. Valerie Eliot (New York, 1971), p. 5; all further citations to
this work will be included in the text. The Augustine allusions in "The Fire Sermon"—"To
Carthage then I came" and "Burning burning"—also of course recall "unholy loves" in a sort
of ancient Nighttown.

[17]See Quentin Bell, *Virginia Woolf: A Biography*, 2 vols. (New York, 1972), 2:86.

[18]T.S. Eliot, *After Strange Gods* (London, 1934), p. 38.

[19]Virginia Woolf, *A Writer's Diary*, ed. Leonard Woolf (New York, 1954), p. 48; all
further references to this text, abbreviated as *WD* will be included in the text.

[20]*Orlando*, p. 138; all further citations to this work will be included in the text.

[21]For a discussion of Eliot's relationship with Jean Verdenal, see James E. Miller, Jr.,
T.S. Eliot's Personal Waste Land (University Park, Pa., 1977).

[22]See Leslie A. Fiedler, "The Politics of Realism: A Mythological Approach,"
Salmagundi 42 (Summer/Fall 1978): 31-43,and Northrop Frye, "The Revelation to Eve," in
Paradise Lost: A Tercentenary Tribute, ed. Balachandra Rajan (Toronto, 1969), pp. 18-47.
There is, of course, a significant nineteenth-century tradition of writing about androgyny,
hermaphroditism, transvestism, and even transsexualism, with some key texts being
Swinburne's lyric poem "Hermaphroditus" (1863) and Balzac's two short novels *Sarrasine*
(1831) and *Seraphita* (1835). (For a brilliant, though in some respects evasive, reading of
Sarrasine, see Roland Barthes, *S/Z*, trans. Richard Miller [New York, 1975].) In addition,
Theodore Roszak has noted the powerful but neglected impact of nineteenth-century
feminism in his "The Hard and the Soft: The Force of Feminism in Modern Times," in
Masculine/Feminine: Readings in Sexual Mythology and the Liberation of Women, ed. Betty
Roszak and Theodore Roszak (New York, 1969), pp. 87-104. An important twentieth-century
transvestite fantasist who seems to have actually enacted many of Balzac's (and Joyce's)
fictions was Marcel Duchamp. Photographed by Man Ray as Rose Sselavy, his female alter
ego, Duchamp asked essential gender questions for many contemporary dadaists and
surrealists (see Calvin Tompkins, *The World of Marcel Duchamp* [New York, 1966]).

[23]For a discussion of Hawthorne's "scribbling women" and their appropriation of the
literary marketplace in America, see Nina Baym, *Woman's Fiction: A Guide to Novels by and
About Women In America, 1820-1870* (Ithaca, N.Y., 1978), esp. chaps. 1 and 2.

[24]For a useful discussion of such "dissonance," see Joan Kelly-Gadol, "Did Women Have
a Renaissance?" in *Becoming Visible: Women in European History*, ed. Renate Bridenthal
and Claudia Koonz (Boston, 1977), pp. 137-64.

[25]See Paul Fussell, *The Great War and Modern Memory* (New York, 1975), esp. chap. 1.
For equally telling analyses of the war, see also Eric J. Leed, *No Man's Land: Combat and
Identity in World War I* (Cambridge, 1979).

[26]Jane Austen, *Northanger Abbey* (New York, 1965), chap. 14.

[27]Shaw, quoted by Virginia Woolf in *Three Guineas* (New York, 1938), p. 182.

[28]See Alexander Welsh, *The City of Dickens* (London, 1971), pp. 182-90 passim. For a
discussion of Eliot's stance as an "angel of destruction," see Carol Christ, "Aggression and
Providential Death in George Eliot's Fiction," *Novel* (Winter 1976): 130-40, and Gilbert and
Susan Gubar, "George Eliot as an Angel of Destruction," *The Madwoman in the Attic: The
Woman Writer and the Nineteenth-Century Literary Imagination* (New Haven, 1979), pp.
478-535.

[29]See Cynthia Griffin Wolff, *A Feast of Words: The Triumph of Edith Wharton* (New
York, 1977), pp. 144-45. Henry James' epithets for Wharton included "The Princess

94   Gender Studies

Lointaine, the whirling princess, the great and glorious pendulum, the gyrator, the devil-dancer, the golden eagle, the Fire Bird, the Shining One, the angel of desolation and of devastation, the historic ravager."

[30]See *The Madwoman in the Attic*, pp. 110-12.

[31]For a brilliant analysis of spatial symbolism in World War I, see Leed, *No Man's Land*, pp. 17-24. It is, of course, true that feminists like Woolf and Crystal Eastman were also passionate pacifists whose anger at patriarchal culture was often specifically channeled into contempt for masculine war-making, while such other literary women as Katherine Mansfield and H.D. hated the Great War because they had suffered severe personal losses. Nevertheless, the paradox of the war's asymmetrical effect on men and women must have unconsciously (if not consciously) struck all these women. To many of them, moreover, the devastation wrought by war may have seemed a punishment (for men) exactly fitted not only to the crime of (masculine) war-making but to other (masculine) crimes. In a draft of *Three Guineas* that is now part of the New York Public Library's Berg Collection, Woolf wrote: "you [men] must help us. because that is the only way we can help you. if you allow us to earn enough to live on to be indepednent you have a great instrument to prevent w. [war?] *We should say let there be war. We should go on earning our libings. We should say it is a ridiculous and barbarous but perhaps nec aary little popgun.* The atwould be a help. Then we should live ourselves the sight of happiness is very make you envious" (my italics; Woolf's spelling and punctuation).

[32]In the unpublished essay "Original Sin in 'The Last Good Country'; or, the Return of Catherine Barkley," Mark Spilka speculates, however, that Hemingway saw "Lady Brett's defiance" as an "implicit tribute to male superiority: the girls were more like men, they were copying male styles," and he adds that "androgyny . . . was for Hemingway a reassurance of manly superiority which allowed him to be womanly" (p. 25).

[33]See *The Waste Land: A Facsimile*, p. 81.

[34]For a discussion of the covertly feminist function of late nineteenth-century brothels, see Ruth Rosen, *The Lost Sisterhood: Prostitution in the American Past* (Ph.D. diss., Univ. of Calif., Berkeley, 1976).

[35]Rebecca West, "Autumn and Virginia Woolf," *Ending in Earnest: A Literary Log* (New York, 1971), pp. 212-13.

[36]Robert Scholes, *Structuralsm In Literature: An Introduction* (New Haven, 1974), pp. 180-90.

[37]Lawrence, *The Letters of D.H. Lawrence*, ed. Harry Moore, 2 vols. (New York, 1962), 1:280.

[38]Woolf, *Between the Acts* (New York, 1941), p.219.

[39]Djuna Barnes, *Nightwood* (1937; New York, 1961), p. 146; all further citations to this work will be included in the text.

[40]See Dickinson, *The Letters of Emily Dickinson*, ed. Thomas Johnson, 3 Vols. (Cambridge, Mass, 1965). In a few poems, Dickinson speaks of an "it" with which she seems to identify her ontological being, as if to emphasize a secret belief that ultimately her true self is gender-free. See, for instance, "Why make it doubt—it hurts it so—" and "I want—it pleaded—All its life—."

[41]See Myra Stark's introduction to Florence Nightingale's *Cassandra* (Old Westbury, N.Y., 1979), p. 17.

[42]Nightingale, *Cassandra*, p. 53; Olive Schreiner, *Stories Dreams, and Allegories* (London, 1924), pp. 156-59. For further discussion of Schreiner's work, see Joyce Berkman, "The Nurturant Fantasies of Olive Schreiner," *Frontiers: A Journal of Women's Studies* 3, no. 3 (Fall 1977): 8-17.

[43]H.D., *Helen in Egypt* (New York, 1961).

[44]Mircea Eliade, *Mephistopheles and the Androgyne* (New York, 1965), p. 113.

[45]See Edward Carpenter, *Intermediate Types among Primitive Folk: A Study in Social Evolution* (New York, 1914), p. 48.

[46]See Carpenter, *The Intermediate Sex* (London, 1908), pp. 170-71.

[47]Emile Delavenay, *D.H. Lawrence and Edward Carpenter* (New York, 1971), pp. 190-235.

[48]Ibid., pp. 243-44.

[49]See Ursula K. Le Guin, *The Left Hand of Darkness* (New York, 1969), esp. p. 17: "For it was impossible to think of him [Estraven] as a woman . . . and yet whenever I thought of him as a man I felt a sense of falseness . . . ." For a revision of an early story about Winter, in which Le Guin uses "she" instead of "he" to describe her androgynes, see her "Winter's King," *The Wind's Twelve Quarters* (New York, 1976), pp. 85-108. See also Dorothy Gilbert, "Interview with Ursula Le Guin," *California Quarterly*, 13/14: 48-51.

[50]Sylvia Plath, "Totem," *Ariel* (New York, 1963), p. 76.

[51]Plath, "Fever 103," *Ariel* p. 55; Barnes, *Nightwood*, pp. 130-31.

[52]Plath, *The Bell Jar* (New York, 1972), p. 91. From *Jane Eyre* and *The Mill on the Floss* to Kate Chopin's *The Awakening* and Margaret Atwood's *Surfacing*, ruining, tearing, or throwing away clothes is of course a general female metaphor for defiance of sex roles, but Plath, especially in her poems, presses it farther than most of her precursors and contemporaries.

Gender and Identity

Ann Parsons

The Self-Inventing Self:
Women Who Lie and Pose in the Fiction of
Margaret Atwood

ONE OF MARGARET ATWOOD'S poems tells a story about two boys who make a woman out of mud. "She began at the neck and ended at the knees and elbows: they stuck to the essentials."[1] Every day that the sun shines and warms her, they make love to her, repairing her afterwards and making her breasts and hips ever more spacious for their use. At the end of the poem the speaker asks, "Is this what you would like me to be, this mud woman? Is this what I would like to be?" These two questions, and the sardonic comment—"they stuck to the essentials"—invest this wry version of the creation myth with a concern central to much of Atwood's work. She investigates how the two questions interact to affect the lives of women, how male notions of essential femininity enter into women's thinking about themselves, how the expectations of some *other*—culture, a man, a parent—interfere with the processes of self-naming and autonomy in women. If choice about identity is constantly subject to other-defined expectations, then internal self-image and external self-presentation will be affected in complex ways.

In two of her novels, *The Edible Woman* and *Lady Oracle*, Atwood focuses in particular on a kind of behavior for which women are often condemned. She explores the truism, more ancient than Eve, that women are by nature devious, deceitful, conniving and sly. The central characters put on masks, create fictions of themselves, and perpetrate so ingenious an array of frauds upon themselves and others as to seem to support this stereotype. Marian MacAlpin, in *The Edible Woman*, is a consummately sensible young woman who prides herself on functioning at all times with a coolly dexterous responsiveness to what situations and people seem to expect of her; her friend, Ainslie, a college graduate who masquerades as a dewy-eyed innocent in order to seduce a man who prefers seventeen-year-olds, is a caricature of Marian's subtler methods. Joan Foster, in *Lady Oracle*, fabricates so intricate a series of false selves that the only way out of the troubles they cause is to simulate her own death. Both Marian and Joan view themselves and their predicaments humorously, and as narrators invest the novels with a comic tone which is often playful and sometimes seems like mockery of female antics.

But more deeply than mockery of a stereotype, the comedy serves as in itself a layer of subterfuge which both women use to ease fear and insecurity. To see the world and the self as funny, to refuse to take things seriously, is a means of protection against that which threatens and terrifies. Marian frequently comments flippantly on what she fears: her fiance's clothes closet, for example, amuses her because it reveals how image-conscious Peter is; but resentment, and something "more like fear" color the amusement at clothes "smugly asserting so much invisible silent authority."[2] The comic tone, and the stereotypical images of deceiving women, work not to corroborate but to question and explore the stereotype.

The two novels join much serious modern fiction by women, in asking whether women are coerced or conditioned into deceitful behavior, and if so, by what forces. The heroine of Lois Gould's *Final Analysis*, who is trying to stop using cosmetics, remarks: "Make up. Meaning invent. Make up something more acceptable, because that face you have on right there will not do, I'm afraid."[3] Her comment typifies what much recent literature has targeted as a leading source of oppression in the lives of women, and a major handicap in any effort toward female growth and self-definition: cultural pressures to make oneself over, body and soul, in the prevalent cultural image of acceptable femininity. From ex-prom-queen and termite queen, from heroines who are housewives and career women and English professors, from voices ranging through insouciance, wry humor, defiance, hurt, madness to the bitter rage, for instance of Marge Piercy's "The Friend":

> he said, cut off your hands
> they are always poking at things
> they might touch me.
> I said yes.[4]

we hear how insecure women become, how afraid of their own colors, shapes, smells, talents and temperaments, and how addicted to pretense and masquerade.

Margaret Atwood's novels dramatize the forces that stunt growth to produce the lying and cheating behavior which the culture then righteously deplores as an innate female characteristic. In both the novels under discussion, she also explores how women may indirectly benefit from and therefore connive at their own oppression; and further, how they may, if only gradually and painfully, begin to realize their own complicity in victimization, and stop playing the game by others' rules. In her second novel, *Surfacing*, Atwood depicts two separate women: one who remains "closed in the gold compact,"[5] the cosmetic agent of the demand that she reject her natural self, and who is stuck in the image of "a seamed and folded imitation of a magazine picture that is itself an imitation of a woman who is also an imitation, the original nowhere . . . captive princess in someone's head";[6] and another, who is able after much suffering to rediscover her original self, and understand: "This above all, to refuse to be a victim. Unless I can do that I can do nothing . . . . The word games, the winning and losing games are finished; at the moment there are no others but they will have to be invented, withdrawing is no longer possible and the alternative is death."[7] *The Edible Woman* and *Lady Oracle* each explores more fully how one central character moves through all the stages from unconscious captivity to self-awareness and hope of self-determination.

In *The Edible Woman* a slightly crazed male graduate student offers a commentary on *Alice in Wonderland*:

'Of course everybody knows *Alice* is a sexual identity-crisis book. . . . What we have here, if you only look at it closely, this is the little girl descending the very suggestive rabbit-burrow, becoming as it were prenatal, trying to find her role,' he licked his lips, 'her role as a Woman. Yes, well that's clear enough. These patterns emerge. Patterns emerge. One sexual role after another is presented to her but she seems unable to accept any of them, I mean she's really blocked . . . . So anyway she makes a lot of attempts but she refuses to commit herself, you can't say that by the end of the book she has reached anything that can be definitely called maturity.' (199)

This is enjoyably wicked mockery of a certain style of literary criticism; but it also takes its place in the novel in an array of disquisitions and comments by men upon the essential nature, role and problems of Woman. Joe, the gentle harassed husband who fears maternity destroys a woman's "core . . . the centre of her personality, the thing she's built up" (242); Len, the seducer of young girls who sees all women as pure until he has corrupted them; Duncan, the intellectual lost soul who assumes all women want to mother him and make him whole; Peter, the image-conscious young-man-on-the-move who generalizes freely about "most women"—the comments of all these men create an environment in which options for women are clearly demarcated by men. Their prescriptions are reinforced throughout the novel by the presence of minor women characters who seem helplessly encased in stereotyped images: three office virgins, a rigidly corseted woman boss, a bemusedly fecund young mother, a faceless cluster of "successful and glittering" wives of soap-men (240), a professedly emancipated young woman who decides she wants a baby without the bother of a husband but panics when voices of authority proclaim that babies need a father-figure.

Among these limiting choices, Marian seems at first to pick her way with all the independence, poise, confidence and sturdy common sense of an Alice or an Elizabeth Darcy. She seems to have freely chosen to be the sensible one, observing the vagaries of others with amused and sympathetic detachment, and always calmly in charge of her own affairs. But gradually we see how important it is to her to be normal in every way, and how rigorously she tries to guard herself against any sign to the contrary. The novel's central subject is the way in which her decision to get married, itself arrived at with uncharacteristic haphazardness, undermines her faith first in the self-command which protects her normality and second in the value of such rigid self-control. Early in the novel, even before the decision to marry, we begin to see that Marian's sedateness is a careful construct, a pose so habitual as to seem natural but nevertheless one which is carefully maintained as a defense, and one which she herself eventually finds repressive of important aspects of her full self. "It had snowed earlier, fine powdery snow, and the park was a white blank space, untracked. Suddenly she wanted to go down and run and jump in it, making footmarks and mazes and irregular paths. But she knew that in a minute she would be walking sedately as ever across it toward the station" (208). We see that the composed face she turns to the world is at least partly a mask, worn as a defense against social pressures which she fears as traps. Fearing pressure to conform with unattractive role expectations, she traps herself in an identity which allows little freedom to be spontaneous and impulsive. The novel explores how she comes to realize, if imperfectly, that the effort to evade uncongenial roles has led only to a different and constricting role-playing.

"Ainslie says I choose clothes as though they're a camouflage or a protective colouration" (12). It is clear that Marian has chosen a self for camouflage, too, in her often expressed fear of losing control over her own future. Forced to join her company's pension plan, she reacts very strongly:

It was a kind of superstitious panic about the fact that I had actually signed my name, had put my name to a magic document which seemed to bind me to a future so far ahead I couldn't think about it. Somewhere in front of me a self was waiting, preformed, a self who had worked during innumerable years for Seymour Surveys and was now receiving her reward . . . . I told myself not to be silly, I reminded myself I could walk out of there the next day and get a different job if I wanted to, but that didn't help. I thought of my signature going into a file and the file going into a cabinet and the cabinet being shut away in a vault somewhere and locked. (20)

Marian tells herself not to be silly quite frequently, and has to discover that not being silly is a frail bulwark against her fears.

She has two central fears. One is the loss of freedom to choose her own identity and life-style. Marriage, like the pension plan, will make her fit into a preformed role. At the end of Part One of the novel, she tries to begin to fit by listing all the things she should do to tidy up her affairs in preparation for marriage. "I must get organized. I have a lot to do" (106). She must be efficient: "I can't let my whole afternoon dribble away, relaxing though it is to sit in this quiet room gazing up at the empty ceiling with my back against the cool wall, dangling my feet over the edge of the bed" (106). The tone here suggests how aversive the proper action is to her; in fact, in Part Two, she manages to perform almost none of it. Her other fear is of total loss of identity. The competent facade is her protection against dreams and hallucinations that she is "dissolving, coming apart layer by layer like a piece of cardboard in a gutter puddle" (224). "She was afraid of losing her shape, spreading out, not being able to contain herself any longer" (225). At an office party, surrounded by women co-workers, "She felt them, their identities, almost their substance, pass over her head like a wave. At some time she would be—or no, already she was like that too; she was one of them, her body the same, identical, merged with that other flesh that choked the air in the flowered room with its sweet organic scent; she felt suffocated by this thick sargasso-sea of femininity. She drew a deep breath, clenching her body and her mind back into herself" (172). Against this fear, the idea of marriage seems at times a safeguard: "She slid her engagement ring back onto her finger, seeing the hard circle for a moment as a protective talisman that would help keep her together" (224-5). But the complexity of her dilemma lies in the fact that the hard circle also closes her into one of the preformed identities she dreads.

The Edible Woman explores the predicament, then, of a woman who presents a deceptive face to the world, who creates a fiction of self in an attempt to control her own reality, and who then has to deal with the ways in which her own fiction controls her. Atwood sets her exploration of this psychological dilemma, however, in an environment whose social victimization of women is made very clear. The dominant image of the novel, appearing repeatedly in event, motif and metaphor, is an image of consumption, of woman as chief commodity in a world where everything is commodity. Everything and everybody is packaged for consumption, and Marian comes to see the main purpose of the packaging as a disguise for various forms of more or less ugly and violent exploitation. For a while, she maintains a whimsical detachment from all the manifestations of ersatz, packaged identity which surround her: from her own market research job, which manipulates words to sell products; from Ainslie's expert and predatory "latest version of herself" (69), designed to trap Len; from Peter's meticulously detailed self-presentation in his desired image; and from her own skillful maintenance of an "aura of independence and common sense" (62) to please Peter, who believes, " 'Most women are pretty scatterbrained, but you're such a sensible girl. You may not have known this but I've always thought that's the first thing to look for when it comes to choosing a wife' " (91). But the detachment begins to break down when, drinking with friends and listening to Peter talk about hunting—" 'You know how to gut them, you just slit her down the belly and give her a good hard shake and all the guts'll fall out' " (70)—she has a sudden vision of Peter as blood-splashed predator and herself as prey. "Something inside me started to dash about in dithering mazes of panic, as though I had swallowed a tadpole" (71). First weeping unexpectedly, and then running away from the group, she regains control of her behavior by regarding it as a momentary, inexplicable aberration, not to be repeated.

But this glimpse of herself as quarry, as consumer item, though firmly repressed, is the beginning of change in Marian. Later, at dinner with Peter, she suddenly sees herself, too, as predator:

She looked down at her own half-eaten steak, and suddenly saw it as a hunk of muscle. Blood red. Part of a real cow that once moved and ate and was killed, knocked on the head as it stood in a queue like someone waiting for a streetcar. Of course everyone knew that. But most of the time you never thought about it. In the supermarket they had it all pre-packaged in cellophane, with name-labels and price-labels stuck on it, and it was just like buying a jar of peanut butter or a can of beans, and even when you went into a butcher shop they wrapped it up so efficiently and quickly that it was made clean, official. But now it was suddenly there in front of her with no intervening paper, it was flesh and blood, rare, and she had been devouring it. Gorging herself on it. (155)

This vision is a turning point in Marian's experience. She becomes progressively unable to eat more and more foods, and finally connects this neurotic awareness of even carrots as suffering victims with her own situation. She is an edible woman, an object of consumption. After a party from which she has again fled in panic, she confronts Peter with a cake she has shaped and frosted in the image of a woman, and says, " 'You've been trying to destroy me, haven't you . . . . You've been trying to assimilate me. But I've made you a substitute, something you'll like much better. This is what you really wanted all along, isn't it?' " (279).

What Marian herself has really wanted all along becomes clear to her only very gradually. She has persuaded herself to want marriage, and evades as long as possible the meaning of all the clues, the fearful images of victimization and entrapment, that prompt her erratic behavior. The sensible, calm self, so carefully constructed to keep her safe, has almost betrayed her into the paralyzed, stereotyped identity she most fears. Although she notices how frequently other people exist in narrow fabrications of self—Ainslie, for instance, who "had constructed her image and now she had to maintain it" (122), and Peter, "having exchanged the free-bachelor image for the mature-fiance one and adjusted his responses and acquaintances accordingly" (123)—she is slow to recognize her collusion in her own identity-freeze. She persuades herself that the "nicely packaged" (150) Peter is what she ought to want, that marriage can be as

practical and well organized as she believes her own personality is—"Peter
and I should be able to set up a very reasonable arrangement" (104)—and
she represses all the signs that the truth of her personality is being very ill-
served by all this common sense, that in fact the common sense has itself
become a constricting camouflage.

When Peter begins to take pictures at his party, she is terrified. She
equates the camera with a lethal weapon, herself in her red dress "a perfect
target" (251). Evading several of his efforts to photograph her, she runs
away: "She could not let him catch her this time. Once he pulled the trigger
she would be stopped, fixed indissolubly in that gesture, that single stance,
unable to move or change" (252). This party, Peter's conventional gesture
of farewell to bachelorhood, precipitates, finally, the full realization that
she cannot let herself be "stopped" in this way in her life, and that she is
herself partly responsible for her danger. She has passively allowed herself
to be corseted, coiffed, dressed, hung with ornaments, made up and made
over to please Peter, who is among several people at the party to tell her she
looks absolutely marvelous. But she is aware of discomfort with this
invented image:

Now she wondered whether or not she did look absolutely marvelous.... The
difficulty was that she couldn't grasp the total effect: her attention caught on the
various details, the things she wasn't used to—the fingernails, the heavy ear-rings,
the hair, the various parts of her face that Ainslie had added or altered .... What
was it that lay beneath the surface these pieces were floating on, holding them all
together? She held both of her naked arms out toward the mirror. They were the
only portion of her flesh without a cloth or nylon or leather or varnish covering,
but in the glass even they looked fake, like soft pinkish-white rubber or plastic,
boneless, flexible (235).

She is dressing and acting as she is supposed to, she is being "smiling and
efficient" (240) as a good hostess, and she is briefly amazed and pleased that
she is performing her role so well. But finally she has to ask, "Who was that
tiny two-dimensional small figure in a red dress, posed like a paper woman
in a mail-order catalogue, turning and smiling, fluttering in the white
empty space .... This couldn't be it; there had to be something more"
(250). She completes her escape and regains her equilibrium by making an
image of her fake party-pretty self in sponge cake ("She decided on sponge.
It was more fitting" [275]) and offering it to both the men she has been
involved with. When Ainslie sees the cake as a symbolic rejection of her
femininity, she says, delightfully, " 'Nonsense .... It's only a cake' " (280).

For its brief last section, *The Edible Woman* returns to the first-person
narrative of Part One. Part Two, the long central section of the novel,
suggests alienation from self in its use of third-person narrative: at the end,
Marian congratulates herself happily on her return to thinking of herself

in the first person singular again. The switch, obviously, reinforces a sense of self regained. Duncan, Marian's eccentric student friend, remarks, " 'You're back to so-called reality. You're a consumer' " (287), and we are reminded—perhaps: it is never safe to take Duncan too seriously—that in the novel's consumer society, Marian has successfully avoided being swallowed into the nonentity or the stereotyping of identity she has dreaded. The victory may be precarious, but it is real: an edible woman, she has not been eaten. A series of fears, motivating her role-playing, has been faced, explored and surmounted in the novel: a lack of confidence which is masked by the will to be cool under all conditions, a fear of disintegration, a need for security and stability, and a fear of losing freedom to define oneself both psychologically and as a social being.

Lady Oracle, Margaret Atwood's third novel, pays similarly subtle attention to the difficulties of female self-definition, and to the interplay of social pressures and expectations with private, inner emotional and psychological needs. *Lady Oracle* goes further than *The Edible Woman*, in exploring the causes and consequences in a woman's life of habitual posing, lying and dissimulation about herself. *Lady Oracle* also suggests the possibility that behavior with defensive, negative sources may become an agent of positive growth toward self-fulfillment.

We first meet Joan Foster when, in despair at the tangled web of studied deceptions she has been practising, unable to maintain all her identities separately, and totally panicked at the idea of letting the truth be known, she has just fled to Europe, having left behind her, most intricately contrived, her own dead self. The novel's plot alternates between Joan's continuing intricate, desperate and comic efforts to maintain this fiction of her death, and a more or less chronological account of the series of events and role playings which have culminated in this rather final metamorphosis.

By the age of seven, fat little red-headed Joan knows that her mother has "decided that I would not do."[8] She defies her mother and grows fatter, but discovers inevitably that this response makes her just as fully the puppet of her mother's expectations as any other. After this one act of overt defiance, she spends the next twenty years or so inventing selves that will "do." Dancing school tells her that she should be better than other people, Brownies that she should be just like other people. Unable to believe she can successfully follow either prescription, uncertain about what her "real" self is, certain only that if the real Joan Foster stood up she would be ridiculed and unloved—these are the conditions of her maturation. "In my experience, honesty and expressing your feelings could lead to only one thing. Disaster" (37). She becomes adept at creating and enacting new selves, usually with detailed fictitious autobiographies, in response to each new situation and each new man she meets. Almost always, she creates her roles at the dictation of external circumstances: what kind of mistress would a Polish emigre count want? What is an appropriate wife for a serious radical intellectual? What is appropriate background, appearance, behavior and even name, for a writer of costume Gothic romances? and so on. "Make up something more acceptable, because that face you have on right there will not do, I'm afraid."

Lady Oracle is an extraordinary biography of a chameleon self. The novel documents in great detail how strong the need to evade self by inventing selves can be. As Joan endlessly, sometimes in the panic of emergency, sometimes with lovingly thorough care, spins and inhabits new selves, we come to understand her behavior as a survival mechanism, a response to heavy inner and outer pressures. But we also come to understand that there are motives at work here that go beyond fear and self-doubt and anxiety. The novel opens up further dimensions of this deceitful behavior, and explores them richly and complexly. The self-creating Joan becomes not only the self-defeating neurotic, the hermit crab wasting all its energy in hunting up protective shells; the self-creating activity becomes also an energetically productive, positive creative act. We come to see that in Joan, woman as con artist and woman as artist grow from the same psychological sources.

Joan has two literary *personae* as well as her sequence—sometimes simultaneous sets—of actual-life selves. She is a successful writer of costume Gothic romances, and an equally successful *avant-garde* poetess; she is Louisa K. Delacourt and "Lady Oracle," as well as Joan Foster. There are many parallels among the stories of these three. Joan herself comments that the book of poems, except for the diction, "seemed a lot like one of my standard costume Gothics, but a Gothic gone wrong. It was upside-down somehow. There were the sufferings, the hero in the mask of a villain, the villain in the mask of a hero, the flights, the looming death, the sense of being imprisoned, but there was no happy ending, no true love" (259). She does not recognize, but we do, the half-likeness of all this to her own life: the masks; the flights into fantasy and deception; the love-affair with the fantastically self-creating Royal Porcupine, a self-styled "con-create artist" (293) who seems a Byronic hero to waltz and wear black net stockings with, but turns disappointingly into a villain when he grows "gray and multi-dimensional and complicated like everyone else. Was every Healthcliff a Linton in disguise?" (300); the imprisonment in insecurity; the looming death. The important point about this triple identity and its paralleled experiences is that Joan's writing is created out of the same feelings and experiences that also produce her fantasies and subterfuge.

The making up, inventing impulse is strong in Joan. If its origin is neurotic, at least some of its productions are healthy. A life-enhancing, positive, even joyful spirit sometimes pervades even the escapes from self. The act of making up new selves can be an exuberant experience for Joan.

She deceives out of mistrust of herself and others, to win love, to escape, to avoid pain, to get power, to hide unpleasant truths. But amongst all the hiding from reality there is also the impulse to seek a richer reality, and to express the potential of self more fully than reality seems to allow. At nineteen, for instance, Joan has dieted away her "magic cloak of blubber," and chooses to create a new identity and past—"a more agreeable one" in a new place, not only because she wants to discard her old self, but also because "I wanted to have more than one life" (157). Later, on the brink of a love affair with the Royal Porcupine, she feels both afraid of danger and exhilarated at the prospect of adventure and new experience: "That was the beginning of my double life. But hadn't my life always been double? ... It was never-never land she wanted, that reckless twin. But not twin even, for I was more than double, I was triple, multiple, and now I could see that there was more than one life to come, there were many. The Royal Porcupine had opened a time-space door to the fifth dimension ... and one of my selves plunged recklessly through" (274). Although she qualifies at once, "Not the others, though," she asserts here a healthy expansion into the experiencing of multiplicity; not a frightened turning away from deficiency, but a reaching for more."

This "reckless twin" is a very important part of Joan, born from the same origin as the timid, self-defensive, compulsive liar and cheat. Her career as a poet begins in a gesture and mood very similarly blended. Stalled in a Gothic chapter she is writing, in which a helpless captive heroine is being hypnotized by candle-flames in a mirror, Joan decides to act out the scene. She sets up candle and mirror in a dark room, and experiences a kind of trance, during which, "in a scrawly handwriting that was certainly not my own" (246) she writes a word. Thoroughly shaken, she nevertheless repeats the experiment: "I wanted to go down that dark, shining corridor again, I wanted to see what was at the other end ..." (246). The reckless twin takes her to the poems at the other end, to the creating of Lady Oracle.

Sometimes, even when Joan is fabricating new selves neurotically, she notices how much she enjoys it. Camouflaging her past for the serious intellectual boyfriend Arthur, she performs what has become her usual stunt to hide her insecurity; but she also comments, "What lies I told him, and it wasn't just in self-defense: already I'd devised an entire spurious past" (98). Her pleasure in her own inventive skill rings true, even though she also admits, "I suppose I couldn't trust him" (99). Told at her wedding that "you should love each other for what you are and forgive each other for what you are not" (227), Joan can never quite bring herself to trust herself or others enough to tell the truth. But although she despises herself as a "sorry assemblage of lies and alibis" (236) she often savors her inventive capacities in both life and art. When, for instance, she is burying the evidence of her fake death, she imagines: "Perhaps, hundreds of years from now, someone would dig up my jeans and T-shirt and deduct a forgotten rite, a child murder or a protective burial. The idea pleased me" (18). The play of imagination pleases her: she goes on to drink a toast of Cinzano "To life," and comments, "I could start being another person entirely." That this anticipatory attitude is undercut immediately by fear that people will think she is a secret drinker does not destroy its zestful self-approval.

Nothing in *Lady Oracle* reveals this simultaneous presence of health and neurosis better than some of Joan's fantasies. Her fantasizing is itself a hiding-place from reality. But sometimes the source of growth and confidence flourishes in the fantasy. As a fat adolescent in high school, for instance, she fantasizes a Fat Lady who will triumph in all her fatness:

... I was sitting in a circus tent. It was dark, something was about to happen, the audience was tense with expectation. I was eating popcorn. Suddenly a spotlight cut through the blackness and focused on a tiny platform at the top of the tent. Upon it stood the Fat Lady from the freak show at the Canadian National Exhibition. She was even fatter than I had imagined her, fatter than the crude picture of her painted on the hoarding, much fatter than me. She was wearing pink tights with spangles, a short fluffy pink skirt, satin ballet slippers and, on her head, a sparkling tiara. She carried a diminutive pink umbrella; this was a substitute for the wings which I longed to pin on her. Even in my fantasies I remained faithful to a few ground rules of reality.

The crowd burst out laughing. They howled, pointed and jeered; they chanted insulting songs. But the Fat Lady, oblivious, began to walk carefully out onto the high wire, while the band played a slow, stately melody. At this the crowd stilled, and a murmur of dismay arose. It was obvious this was a dangerous thing for her to be doing, she was so enormously fat, how could she keep her balance, she would topple and fall. "She'll be killed," they whispered, for there was no safety net.

Gradually, inch by inch, the Fat Lady proceeded along the wires, pausing to make sure of her balance, her pink umbrella raised defiantly above her head. Step by step I took her across, past the lumbering enterprises of the West Coast, over the wheatlands of the prairies, walking high above the mines and smoke stacks of Ontario, appearing in the clouds like a pink vision to the poor farmers of the St. Lawrence Valley and the mackeral fishermen of the Maritimes. "Good Christ, what is it?" they muttered, pausing in the endless hauling-in of their nets. Several times she faltered and the crowd drew in its breath; the wire oscillated, she concentrated all her forces on this perilous crossing, for a fall meant death. Then, just before the bell went and the period was over—this was the trick—she would step into safety on the other side and the people would rise to their feet, the roar of their voices her tribute. A large crane would appear and lower her to the ground. (111-112)

The fantasy is a lovely assertion of an impulse toward open, unashamed delight in self-acceptance.

Lady Oracle is about Joan Foster's search to accept and enjoy and use herself. It explores Joan's compulsively habitual role-playing not only as the struggles of an insecure woman playing hide and seek with her own psychological health, but also as the processes of a creative imagination discovering its strength. Joan is presented as a victim of sexist social pressures; but the novel richly extends this theme in its probing of how Joan as a writer can draw an exuberant creative energy from the same sources as those which prompt the devious, deceitful, frightened-chameleon behavior. As a teen-ager, when her contemporaries are idolizing male pop singers, Joan feels an "idealized lust" (104) for the figure of Mercury on the Toronto telephone book; very appropriately, Mercury is both the god of thieves and trickery, and of speed, quicksilver, inventiveness, "making up."

The novel is an exploration of Joan's difficult growth. The five-year-old who was not allowed to be a butterfly at dancing school, because she was too fat, seeks a way to earn wings, in her own right. At the end of the novel, "From now on, I thought, I would dance for no one but myself" (368). This resolution is immediately sabotaged—she dances, and cuts her feet, and asks "How could I escape now, on my cut feet?" (369). But her "escape" this time, is her readiness to face exposure of the truth about herself, both to husband Arthur and to the public. She is no longer planning a "story" that will account creditably for her behavior. She is still planning a new self, but drawing on the positive rather than the negative aspects of her talent for fakery. Willing to "feel like an idiot with all the publicity," she turns her attention, not to camouflage for idiocy, but to plans about her writing. "I won't write any more Costume Gothics, though; I think they were bad for me. But maybe I'll try some science fiction. The future doesn't appeal to me as much as the past, but I'm sure it's better for you" (379). Finally, too, she is feeling comfortable, rather than, as in the past, uncomfortable to the point of panic and subterfuge, with a man who really knows something about her. Perhaps all the making up and inventing are beginning to achieve more creative than cosmetic results.

One of Margaret Atwood's poems begins:

> I'm telling the wrong lies,
> they are not even useful.
>
> The right lies would at least
> be keys, they would open the door.[9]

Essentially, telling lies about the self becomes a means of growth for both Marian and Joan. Through painful experience, they discover what the wrong lies cost in terms of stunted identity and surrendered autonomy. They learn to distinguish between lies which entrap and lies which empower: a difference which is at least partly a matter of the crucial difference between lying to oneself and to the world. With a clearer understanding of the pressures from the world which have made posing and pretending habitual both as defense and as counterattack, the two women begin to open the doors on their prisons, and take truer control of their images of self and their future directions.

Notes

[1] Margaret Atwood, *Selected Poems* (New York: Simon and Schuster, 1976), p. 214.

[2] Margaret Atwood, *The Edible Woman* (New York: Popular Library, 1969), p. 236. Page references in parentheses after subsequent quotations from this novel are to this edition.

[3] Lois Gould, *Final Analysis* (New York: Avon, 1975), p. 77.

[4] Marge Piercy, "The Friend," in *No More Masks*, ed. Florence Howe (New York: Anchor, 1973), p. 244.

[5] Margaret Atwood, *Surfacing* (Ontario: Paperbacks, 1972), p. 175.

[6] Atwood, *Surfacing*, p. 165.

[7] Atwood, *Surfacing*, p. 191.

[8] Margaret Atwood, *Lady Oracle* (New York: Avon, 1976). All page references in parentheses after quotations from this novel are to this edition.

[9] Atwood, *Selected Poems*, p. 168.

Cynthia Davis

Heroes, Earth Mothers and Muses: Gender Identity in Barth's Fiction

I

JOHN BARTH'S FICTIONS have always used male-female relationships to explore questions of identity. Barth's characterizations have escaped criticism, however, because his fictions have gradually abandoned the pretense of realism, in favor of parodic and self-conscious techniques. The "self-reflexive" approach allows Barth to explore the deeply traditional structures—the myths—that he finds at the heart of fiction, of experience, and of perception. This pursuit of fundamental form has led him to a mythic definition of male and female identities, one that underlies all the work but becomes most explicit in *Chimera*. The notions of gender identity revealed in Barth's work are important first because they *are* traditional; they reflect the assumptions inherent in a male-centered mythology. But Barth extends the myth, employing it as metaphor for the condition of the artist/perceiver. That "new" myth contains more than the dangers of the old male-female dichotomy; it is a fascinating example of the ways that contemporary subjective relativism can support a myth even more deadening to women. Thus Barth's ideas of gender identity are important not only in illuminating his own fictional views, but also in tracing the emergence of old sex roles in new disguises.

The most common Barthian situation is the romantic triangle. The first two novels offer the simplest versions: Todd Andrews' long affair with Jane Mack in *The Floating Opera* has the active collaboration of her husband Harrison; Jake Horner's "seduction" of Rennie Morgan in *The End of the Road* provokes the crisis in the Morgan marriage. In later novels, the triangle, though complicated by parallel characters, is still central: in *The Sot-Weed Factor*, Ebenezer Cooke competes with his tutor Henry Burlingame for Eb's sister Anna (and with others for prostitute Joan Toast); and in *Giles Goat-Boy*, Giles' love for Anastasia involves rivalry with first her husband, then her other lovers, and finally the "false prophet" Bray. *Chimera* reverses the triangle to show a male with two women: the first triangle, including Dunyazade, Scheherazade, and Shah, is complicated by the intervention of the Genie and then made a quadrangle by the sisters' double marriage, but the book's other two novellas give clearer versions of the situation. Because of *Chimera*'s special situations and because it raises the question of heterosexual love most

110

directly, it must be considered as an extension of ideas and patterns first
broached in the earlier work. Before *Chimera*, certain obvious similarities
link the fictions and offer a key to later problems.[1]

First, in all the earlier novels, the competition between male
characters for possession of the woman is clearly representative of a basic
conflict in attitude. The woman is desired less for herself than as a means of
self-assertion and triumph over the rival. She becomes a potential proving-
ground for the man, and any opinions she may express echo those of the
dominant male. The basic conflict of which she is symbol and prize also
has a clear pattern; the protagonists of the novels—Todd, Jake, Giles, and
Eb—are (at first) all detached from life and from personal involvement,
unable or unwilling to commit themselves, whereas their rivals take hold
of life by defining and controlling the woman. So the struggle over her is
symptomatic of a struggle between two very different approaches to life.

The protagonists' detachment has several causes. One is that they are
generally too concerned with defining their own identities to give much
thought to anyone else's. All the early "heroes" have projects or problems
so all-consuming that the woman is at best a shadowy figure to be
assimilated into their perspective, not an individual. Todd is writing his
Inquiry, Jake following his program of therapy, Giles struggling to
become a Grand Tutor and Eb to become a poet. In all these cases, the
woman's dependence on them for opinions and identity makes her little
more than a reflection of their own lack of definition. The hero's problem,
in addition, takes a form that makes personal commitment nearly
impossible; he tends to suffer from what Jake calls "cosmopsis"—a sense of
possibility so overwhelming that he is unable to choose at all for fear of
eliminating alternative choices (ER 74). Jake and Eb are paralyzed by
cosmopsis, Todd almost led to suicide by it. Even Giles, the most directed,
wants everything: choice and destiny, mundane life and mythic meaning,
personality and fulfilled prophecy. No single choice seems necessary or
desirable, for all these heroes have discovered, like Todd, that "Nothing
has intrinsic value" (FO 232), and they have no standard for selection.
Their life-products are atttempts to surmount that problem, but by self-
definitions uncontrolled by the outside world. The hero's attitude toward
women, then, is his attitude toward everything, the result of a free-floating
self-concept logically unconnected to anything external. (The more
recently published "first" version of *The Floating Opera* stresses this lack
of connection even more.) Without necessary values, all choices hopelessly
arbitrary and subjective, the protagonist is trapped in a mirror maze; just as
all experiences are equally valuable, so all other persons are equal objects
of indifference. So it is with women, anyway; parts of the world to which
the hero refuses to attach value, they remain tools for his experiments with
point of view. Eb demonstrates the interchangeability of women in this
world when he changes Joan's name in his poem to the all-purpose

"*Heart*" (SWF 67). And the same is true of minor female characters: Peggy Rankin in *The End of the Road* and Dorothy Miner in *The Floating Opera*, for example, provide opportunities for Jake and Todd to try out attitudes and make points against their rivals, and so are mini-models of the major females' functions. But other men, like the hero, are seers rather than seen; challenging his view, they cannot become merely objects in it. Instead of the Other, the not-self equated with external reality, they become alternative selves. They force the hero out of paralysis by embodying a choice, undermining his inclusive view; then they challenge his chosen identity by representing its alternative. So they must be either defeated or imitated for the hero to define himself. Bray's usurpation of Giles' prophet-role is an extreme version, but Harrison and Todd, Joe and Jake, and Burlingame and Eb all act out the patterns of rivalry as sexual contest, philosophical argument, and creative struggle.

Because the woman is symbol of the reality over which the men struggle, her primary qualities are passivity and emptiness. The typical situation is described in Herbert P. Smith's discussion of *The End of the Road* as a "logical paradigm," with Jake and Joe as representatives of conflicting ethical positions and Rennie as an "ethical vacuum," waiting to be filled by the winner. Her purely symbolic quality is shown by the fact that "Once the adultery has been consummated, Rennie is no longer the central concern" of the men.[2] Once possessed, the female is of little interest, since the struggle itself was of prime importance. Her "emptiness" invited choice and action, but the act of choosing really matters. Repeatedly Barth's fictions depict the hero being forced out of cosmopsis by the male challenge and the female shapelessness. The woman's lack of positive qualities makes an implicit demand on the hero, and her passivity provokes both fascination and irritation. At first, it seems a wonderful mystery, promising new discovery and possibility, but finally it becomes annoying: Todd surrenders Jane with relief, Giles grows away from Anastasia, even the deaths of Rennie and Joan, though unwanted, release Jake and Eb from burdensome commitment. Barth may not defend male resentment, but the perception of woman as dead weight, dependent on man for definition, is central to his view. As symbol of undifferentiated reality, she echoes his inability to choose and yet forces him to do so. She becomes valueless in two senses: unpossessed, she is "empty," waiting for the chooser to confer value on her; once possessed, she loses her appeal and becomes a burden.

II

This use of woman as reality-symbol is of course not new in American fiction: think of Daisy Buchanan and Lolita, for example. And Barth's heroes face a problem similar to Gatsby's and Humbert's—the resistance of reality to purely subjective shaping. Refusal to choose is not finally a viable position for Barth; even Todd and Jake see that choices, no matter how arbitrary, are necessary for definition of world and self. So the hero must use what Jake learns to call "Mythotherapy" (ER 5): he must choose a point of view, create a self by choosing, and so define his relationship to the world. The "empty" woman, unshaped like external reality, invites this process. But once the hero has made the choice, the woman becomes a reminder of its arbitrariness. This is most often accomplished by pregnancy: Jane's, Rennie's, Joan's, and Anastasia's pregnancies all suggest the limiting consequence of choice, remind the hero that in selecting one path or one relationship over another he commits himself to unforeseeable and inescapable results. By acting on the woman, the hero takes on responsibility for what she becomes and bears. But, as the motif of pregnancy also suggests, all her existence is not the hero's creation. Rennie, for example, has no viewpoint outside Joe's or Jake's, and even physically cannot "handle her body in situations where there [are] no rules," but she does have her own "clumsy force" in both body and conversation (ER 54). Barth attributes no energetic will to woman, no identity that she can choose as a man does, no completed sense of self; but he gives her the power of inertia, of being preceding definition. She is the blank reality that must be given a human face—a man's. Thus Joan first resists Eb's attempt to idealize her because she accepts the identity—whore—conferred on her by McEvoy. But finally she represents to Eb a larger reality of failure and mortality that he must face and name without completely controlling. This depiction of female characters is progressively clarified by arth's development of an "Earth Mother" type. Giles must enter WESCAC's Belly with Anastasia in a mythical ceremony that combines (male) choosing self with (female) fleshly reality principle (GGB 672-3).[3] Eb must marry the pox-ridden, dying Joan before he can have his idealized relation with Anna; further, he must consummate the marriage (SWF 800-1). Anastasia and Joan—the Earth Mother and her negative version, the figure of disease and death—thus become more than reminders of the consequences of choice. They are physical reality, the aspect of life that underlies and balances human conceptualization.

Barth's female characters are threatened by the breakdown of their men's theories because they need the defining framework, but they are threatened also by the inadequacy of the male concepts. One example is Betty June Gunter, who tries to kill Todd for laughing at their copulation and later reminding her of it. It is not his power over her that she resents; indeed, at first the power seems to be hers, as she introduces him to sex. What she hates is his refusal to offer a definition of her and their relation that humanizes their roles. She is a reality-figure to Todd, the demonstration of human "animality" (FO 131); he can role-play with her (FO 129), but not offer her the dignity or romance she needs as part of the role. And she is unable to do the defining herself. Only as bodies do Barth's women defy male control: in sex, in pregnancy, in death. And even then they are not dynamic, for they represent and embody consequence without initiating it. They are not individuals, but forms of the non-individualized outer world. Barth's men, too, are types, but human types, choosers and definers; by separating women from men, he posits a self-Other distinction in which women are always Other. How deliberate the separation is may be seen in the short story "Night-Sea Journey," which uses the relation of sperm and ovum as the paradigm for male-female relations and offers the ultimate definition of the female principle: "*She*, which is to say, Other-than-a-he." As Simone de Beauvoir remarks in *The Second Sex*, the self-Other distinction—the schema that Barth accepts—places women outside the sphere of human choice and identity.

III

Chimera, however, seems to offer new possibilities. Here, Barth presents more varied women characters, many "feminists" in their resentment of male oppression, and heterosexual relations become a central concern. The language makes contemporary references to "raising consciousness" and "male sexist pigs," and all the couples persistently analyze their relations in terms of sex roles and sexual politics. Further, *Chimera*'s development through three novellas, each an elaborate extension of the preceding one,[4] is clearly linked to Barth's larger development by direct allusion to the earlier stories. For example, the description of Rennie Morgan "whipping her head from side to side" is transferred to several characters in *Chimera*, and Bellerophon's different versions of his sexual encounter with Anteia repeat language and situations from both the first two novels (C 201-2). Such connections encourage expectations that these stories will further explore some of the problems raised in previous works.

The foundation of *Chimera*'s sex-role patterning is described by the Genie in the "Dunyazadiad": "The teller's role, he felt, regardless of his actual gender, was essentially masculine, the listener's or reader's feminine, and the tale was the medium of their intercourse" (C 34). After admitting the possibility of (temporary) role-reversal, he adds that such "femininity" need not be "docile or inferior," that one could be a passive "sender" or an active "interpreter." There are two key concepts here: the idea that gender identity is defined by mode of being (receptive, communicative) rather than specific action or relative value, and a kind of Lawrentian idea of balance between equal but opposing polar principles. This view cannot be disposed of as "only" a metaphor, for it is repeatedly supported by situational patterns in these three novellas. The "Dunyazadiad" opens with a female narrator, but she describes a more "fitting" situation—Scheherazade receiving "her" tales from the Genie— and Dunyazade's narration is qualified by the two following sections of the novella, one dominated by Shah Zaman's story, and one in the voice of

Genie-Barth. In the following novellas, males (Perseus and Bellerophon) tell their life-stories to women. Both, through enfolded narratives, speak to two women at once; that is, Perseus repeats to Medusa almost exactly the tale he told earlier to Calyxa, and Bellerophon goes through the same process with Melanippe and Philonoe. Such double narration directs attention to the contrasts between the two types of women. Both types are still defined by reference to the central male, as his "listener" or "interpreter," and his choice between them reflects his choice of identity. The first type, seen in Perseus' nymph Calyxa and Bellerophon's wife Philonoe and many minor characters, is the devoted worshipper of the man, like Anastasia in *Giles Goat-Boy*. Such women find fulfillment in the man and accept him completely, knowing his weaknesses but needing a hero. They tend to take what Barth calls the "Tragic View of Sex and Temperament," believing that the dream of "perfect equality between men and women," while "the only defensible value in that line," is probably unattainable and even hinders the enjoyment of real, imperfect love. Seeing the gap between ideal and reality, and being "personally unsuited for independence," these women resign themselves to temporal mortal life; not expecting perfection, they accept simple "superiority" to themselves (C 53-54; see also 156). Despite their love, then, they are reminders of the fall from the ideal, so their admiration cannot sustain the hero. Perseus' friend Sibyl is another version of this form, restoring him to potency only by introducing him to sex, death and madness. His wife Andromeda is the worst extreme, devotion gone and only the ugly reminders of mortality left. This type is clearly an extension of Barth's early women, the symbols of external physical reality; once "both the cause of [the hero's] labor and its reward" (C 85), the demand for choice and consequence, they finally remind him of the arbitrariness and imperfection of the labor. So Jane, Rennie and Joan are the predecessors of Andromeda, Calyxa and Philonoe—all reminders of the consequence and death in temporal life.

But there is a second type of woman, heretofore incompletely developed in characters like Anna Cooke, but now very important, as the likeness of names suggests: Medusa, Melanippe, Melissa. This figure is ultimately the male's "true love" in *Chimera*, and she functions as a Muse rather than discouraging the heroic quest. Melissa, the Genie's absent mistress, is vaguely defined but partially identified with Scheherazade, his "inspiration." Medusa, in the "Perseid," is the purest form of the type; once the petrifying monster, now she can rejuvenate Perseus, though she risks becoming a monster again if he does not love her. In the novella's climax, she gives him the best of both worlds—immortal life as a constellation, mortal life as a man. The dual existence is the model for fulfillment in art and love, paralleling the Genie's dictum that nothing is ideal, nothing lasts forever, but "we must live as if it can and will" (C 35). That "as if" resonates throughout *Chimera*, offering its central paradox.

First, the ideal is seen as having its own reality; it is not life, but a distillation or shaping of it. Thus the co-existence of the two Perseuses, the danger that Medusa might petrify her hero, the consistent failure to make woman into the dream, the fiction's repeated separation of idea from reality. But the gap between the two worlds is not all: there is also a relation between them. "Some fictions," says the Genie, are "so much more valuable than fact" that they become "real" (C 25). The immortal form, in art or love, is not life itself, but is related to it, can affect it, sometimes even transform it. So one can choose to love "as if" the ideal were true, and the force of the attempt might even make it happen. Perseus and Medusa seem to succeed; their faith and love go beyond material fact, and the mortal woman, transformed by the "as if" into an ideal, in turn transforms the hero, and they exist on both the mortal and immortal planes. That possibility may explain the emphasis on commitment in the earlier works, despite the failures of the double view in Eb's relations with Anna and Joan—the untouchable sister and the all-too-real wife. Now the two are combined in one woman. But Melanippe is a less reassuring version of the Muse, and her story returns *Chimera* to the breakdown seen in the other fictions. Bellerophon sees her as ideal and immortal, but her vociferous denials and his pursuit of perfection lead to their separation and his failure.

The "as if," the delicate balance between reality and desire, fails, and Bellerophon admits that he has no talent for loving. By following the dualistic "Perseid" this ending seems to quash any hope for an integration of ideal and real, and casts an ironic light on the earlier story. Given Bellerophon's final failure to reach Olympus and the absolute disjunction between Perseus' two lives, the nature and power of the Muse become questionable. Her image contradicts the woman's existence in reality, and even her power seems derivative. Medusa's transformation of Perseus depends on his feeling for her; Bellerophon is inspired by an image of Melanippe that she rejects, and her quest is destroyed in his pursuit of his own. Any power the Muse has, then, is as catalyst or vehicle for the hero's imagination, not as independent element. Thus the early paradox of the shapeless and burdensome woman-as-reality is further exaggerated into open conflict by *Chimera*'s female types. The woman can drag a man down to physical mortal life, but cannot elevate him. Ultimately, she can only be a part of his transcendent vision by denying her own reality. Far from having an integrative effect, she becomes the symbol of dualism.

Chimera is not, of course, only "about" love, and it is certainly not intended to offer fully dimensional women characters, any more than its obsessed and flippant men are complex persons. But even allowing for the character typing of self-reflexive fiction, the kinds of limits the author places on his characters can reveal the problems of his position: the only successful relationship in *Chimera* (Perseus and Medusa) is clearly placed outside real life; the women are still extraordinarily passive, by choice or force subjected to male decisions, and they are truly functional only as symbols of the hero's choices. The male-female polarity makes conceptualization a male attribute, and so any sense of self a woman could have would be in imitation of a male model (like the Amazons) or in service of a male goal (as Muse). The only other alternative is to sink into the role of abiding flesh. Melanippe, for example, rejects Bellerophon's image of her to become wife and prolific mother. Over and over bright women, like Philonoe and Melanippe, give up thinking to have babies; magical women, like Medusa, derive identity and power from appearance and from male control; heroic women, like the Amazons, define themselves in imitation of and opposition to men. Outside male concepts, they have no identity but that of the unthinking physical realm. Nowhere do Barth's women have a role equal to men's; they neither determine their lives and define themselves as men do, nor exert, in their own distinct way, the irresistible influence on men that they themselves encounter. To call them "interpreters" of men's "stories" is no answer; their "interpretations" are rarely useful to anyone, including themselves. In fact, their "theories" are so often mere echoing of the man's views that they are more recorders than interpreters. (Barth's short story "Autobiography," whose "mother" is a dictaphone and "father" a human being, makes this pattern explicit.)

IV

This identification of woman with external physical world, however powerful, and man with conscious humanity is a dangerous dichotomy that becomes much more than a useful gimmick. Barth does sometimes try to make the division seem "merely" symbolic, by stressing the limits of his narrative; for example, Bellerophon's summary view of his women is modified by a reminder that it is "strictly from [his] viewpoint" (C 315), and the "impersonal" Melanippe who is "immortal" symbol is distinguished from her "private un-categorizable self" (C 247). Such elements suggest that the female-reality connection exists simply because these are male stories; thus the problem is the individual subject-object relationship, not gender identity. So woman is "reality" not as a role definition, but just from a man's point of view. But Barth's general approach belies that kind of justification. Even in Dunyazade's narration, men other than the narrator are not reduced to reality principles, but represent serious alternative views; even her own plan is finally made possible only by consent of her bridegroom. Only women are consistently reduced to vegetative life in Barth's fictions. Women who do long for more are punished; they end up bitter, like Anteia, or settle for non-heroic life after all, like Melanippe. Such is Barth's interweaving of myth and aesthetic that it is hard to tell whether he uses the pattern without clearly seeing its implications or actually attacks feminism by what he thinks are its spokeswomen. At any rate, the assumptions in the fiction are inconsistent, turning on the unnecessary and contradictory identification of individual woman with biological woman, of symbol with reality, of point of view with truth. In work so concerned with the relation of myth and reality, the confusion is especially striking. Barth's obsession with point of view holds the key; he accepts a male-oriented mythic structure, in which the male is human, the female everything else. He does not question those assumptions in the way that he questions others, but accepts a symbolic identification as literally true.

The emphasis on point of view and shaping perceiver, in fact, produces images that are even more reductive to women than the original myth. Having assigned man and woman to different poles with distinct philosophical and aesthetic meanings, Barth opts for only one side of the "balance." His protagonists, like himself, prefer myth and abstraction to reality, so they come alive as opposing characters do not. *Chimera* rationalizes the preference: "Since myths themselves are among other things poetic distillations of our ordinary psychic experience and therefore point always to daily reality, to write realistic fictions which point always to mythic archetypes is . . . to take the wrong end of the mythopoeic stick . . . . Better to address the archetypes directly" (C 207-8). Fiction is "truer" than particular reality, says Shah Zaman (C 61); but as both passages suggest, fictions and myths are so important because they "point to" reality, because the ideal shines through concrete circumstance. With Barth's heroes, however, the choice of the archetype does not lead back to daily reality, to combine idea and fact. His characters choose between the two, not acting "as if" the real were ideal, but surrendering one for the other. Even Perseus, who has both mortal and eternal life, finds no visible connection between the two levels, and Bellerophon leaves reality behind for his doomed flight to Olympus. They make a choice that Barth makes with his stylization and reworking of myth: to pursue the fiction and let the fact take care of itself. When such an approach is linked to the symbolic forms Barth uses, it is inevitable that women will be crushed or discarded by men.

In light of the emphasis on balance, such a result might seem a failure; but the real feeling of the novels does center on failure—in love and in other analogous situations. Barth wants to show the paradoxical nature of life, but keeps coming down on one side of the paradox, unable to resolve the polar tensions without surrender of one pole. A perspective so heavily weighted in favor of the "masculine," conceptual, creative pole can hardly celebrate "feminine" principles, particularly when the narrative itself displays the triumph of idea over fact, scheme over ambiguous life.[5] Barth's preference for the "male" side eliminates even the power suggested by the mythic dichotomy, reducing the potent innerness of the Earth Mother to the "vacuum" of the not-self, and reducing the energy of the Muse to the mimicry of the mirror-self. The result is female characters who are always seen from outside, who are reduced to symbols, symbols moreover of the non-human aspects of life, and who are denied power even in that area by narrative insistence on the creative male perceiver.

Notes

[1] Editions of Barth's works used are the 1956 Avon edition of *The Floating Opera* (cited as FO) and the 1972 Bantam edition of the same novel with "the original and correct ending"; Bantam editions of *The Sot-Weed Factor* (SWF), *The End of the Road* (ER), and *Lost in the Funhouse* (short stories identified by title), the Doubleday edition of *Giles Goat-Boy* (GGB), and the Fawcett-Crest edition of *Chimera* (C). Because Barth's work has been so much discussed, my citations from the earlier texts are exemplary rather than exhaustive. My notes indicate some of the work discussing the male-female pattern in single texts; I want to illuminate this area of the fiction as a whole. I have concentrated on the novels, and I have not made reference to the parts of *Letters* published to date because the pattern is not yet clear.

[2] Herbert F. Smith, "Barth's Endless Road," *Critique*, VI, 2 (Fall 1963), 72 and 75.

[3] For discussion of the Earth Mother in *Giles Goat-Boy* see Campbell Tatham, "The Gilesian Monomyth: Some Remarks on the Structure of *Giles Goat-Boy*," *Genre 3* (1970), 372; and John W. Tilton, "*Giles Goat-Boy*: An Interpretation," *Bucknell Review*, 1970, pp. 101-02.

[4] For structural connections in *Chimera*, see Cynthia Davis, " 'The Key to the Treasure': Narrative Movements and Effects in *Chimera*," *The Journal of Narrative Technique*, VI (1975), 105-115.

[5] In *To The Lighthouse*, a novel equally (though differently) stylized and equally concerned with mythic forms defined by relation to gender, Virginia Woolf manages to present a true sense of the power of the "feminine" qualities and also a clear balance of the two poles in the character of Lily Briscoe. It seems that it is not the myth itself that prevents resolution so much as a strong tendency toward exclusive choice of one pole and repression of another in Barth's work. One can work within the old patterns to offer new resolutions and to distinguish individual from symbol; Barth avoids such resolution.

Margaret Myers
The Lost Self:
Gender in *David Copperfield*

WHETHER *DAVID COPPERFIELD* is read as a *bildungsroman,* a novel of individual growth to artistic and moral maturity, or as an Oedipal drama in which David quests for an idealized version of the lost mother, it remains quintessentially a novel about the search for self.[1] Indeed both the Freudian interpretation of the novel and the more conventional literary exegesis share ground insofar as the autobiographical narrative voice articulates—and therefore imposes—a coherence upon his own experience. While criticism has amply expanded upon the moral, artistic and sexual content of David's narrative, it has at best only obliquely recognized the sequence of gender role-playing that vitally informs his journey to self-discovery. For the adult David Copperfield must re-discover and re-integrate into a coherent sense of self those aspects of his male selfhood culturally designated as feminine. It is a task finally too radical in its espousal of an achieved state of androgyny to be affirmed at novel's end, but until then *David Copperfield* clearly indicts the cultural extremes of masculinity and femininity. All that is best in David—his artistic and moral impulses—are identified as feminine, and these he loses in early adulthood when he adopts the culturally approved and strictly masculine persona. His rebirth in the Swiss Alps and his marriage to Agnes appear to reclaim the feminine aspects of that androgynous selfhood. Through David's development, his loss and recovery of selfhood, the key figures of Agnes Wickfield and Tommy Traddles act as harbingers of what should be and what may be. Moral barometers, both, they also offer the promise of reconciling the feminine with the masculine, the moral and the imaginative with the social, the private and the public.[2]

The novel itself, of course, structures the literal journey of self-discovery in David's symbolic rebirth during his Wordsworthian encounter with the grandeur of the Swiss Alps following Dora's death.[3] David's prolonged stay in Europe enables him to recover that which he had lost. The novel focuses that loss on Agnes as the appropriate wife for David, though many critics now argue that Agnes more significantly represents a selfhood which David also needs to discover and recover. J. Hillis Miller is one who sees Agnes as the creator of David's selfhood "without whom he would be nothing."[4] In the religious analogy which Miller uses, "David has that relationship to Agnes which a devout

Christian has to God." Alexander Welsh goes on to refine Miller's thesis by
noting that the definition of self "becomes crucial at death, after which he
[the hero] will be nothing unless the heroine can save him."[5] Finally,
Stanley Friedman in his subsequent discussion of the novel picks up
Welsh's delineation of Agnes as the familiar of death and argues that she
offers the necessary consolation to the older narrator as he confronts his
own death, and that in such consolation the narrator is able to reconcile
with a Providence over which he has no control.[6] All this criticism
correctly follows Dickens' lead in designating Agnes the "heroine" of the
novel.[7] She functions in the novel as the agent of male destiny rather than
as the creator of her own, although Friedman concludes his discussion by
quoting Milton, arguing that since, like Adam and Eve, "their state cannot
be sever'd," both David and Agnes "serve together as the hero of David's
life."[8]

This line of criticism invites further refinement. *David Copperfield* is
structured around the ironic juxtaposition of simultaneous loss and
achievement. At one crucial point in his life David acquires a
conventionally masculine demeanor, but he does so at the unrecognized
expense of a selfhood which at a later stage in his life is only recovered by
his wife's death. That lost selfhood is feminine-identified insofar as the
moral, the emotional and the artistic are culturally associated with the
feminine, an association which the novel itself confirms. Finally the novel
seeks to reconcile that feminine selfhood with a masculine identity, not
simply in individuals and their private relationships, but also by
implication in the larger social context. The last chapter overtly attempts
to expound a social optimism based on such a reconciliation. The attempt
proves futile. The story of conventional success, and even triumph, is
permeated with a sense of irrevocable loss so that even at its end the novel
holds true to the ironic pattern of its basic structure. While it attempts at a
covert narrative level to deny the pattern by which achievement is
inevitably alloyed with loss, a haunting sadness permeates the novel's end.
In part that sadness derives from the recognition in the final chapter of the
proximity and permanence of death, but death's closeness is a recognition
that has informed the novel from its beginning (and David's caul): in
David Copperfield birth always has death in attendance. There is, I think, a
further source for the subdued atmosphere of the final chapter, and that
can be found in the novel's inability to achieve an effective and convincing
optimism for life while it is lived. Whatever the promise of an androgynous
reconciliation, the masculine-identified world of *David Copperfield*
cannot finally admit the feminine-identified into the prevailing social and
economic structures. Psychological truth must give way finally to cultural
convention.

Modern criticism has marvelled at the psychological insight of the
novel, and there is no need here to recapitulate David's loss of Eden with

the intrusion of the sexually potent adult male, Murdstone. David's consequent expulsion to Salem House moves him into a "homosocial" world, an exclusively male company which in common with all such societies still divides experience into masculine and feminine domains. The emotional, the moral, and the artistic are all feminine-identified, and it is here as schoolboys that both Tommy Traddles and David Copperfield are most overtly identified with the feminine. In this enclosed environment, James Steerforth enacts the masculine role and here, as in later life and in the larger social world, he comes to represent the worst aspects of indulged cultural manhood. Socially successful, revered by his male peers, he is sensual, amoral, and self-absorbed. The moral and the emotional Tommy Traddles suffers much in this exclusively masculine community, and in Salem House his moral sensibility and his emotional sensitivity are contemptuously identified with the feminine. After Steerforth's public mistreatment of Mr. Mell, an incident in which Mell is not only humiliated but is also dismissed from his only means of livelihood, David feels "self-reproach" and "contrition," though he does not reveal his feeling for fear of Steerforth's contempt. Traddles, unlike David, is afraid neither to weep in sorrow for Mr. Mell nor to upbraid Steerforth for his cruel mistreatment of the impoverished teacher. Steerforth's response to Traddles is to call him "a girl," and "Miss Traddles," and all the other boys, on hearing that Steerforth plans to compensate Mr. Mell with money (the masculine substitute for feeling), are "extremely glad to see Traddles so put down" (Chapter VII).[9]

David's inability to act upon his best moral instincts, a weakness crucial to his subsequent life, does not deny that at Salem House, he too is feminine-identified. No sooner has he arrived at the school than the handsome Steerforth asks David if he has a sister:

> 'You haven't got a sister, have you?' said Steerforth, yawning.
> 'No,' I answered.
> 'That's a pity,' said Steerforth. 'If you had had one, I should imagine she would have been a pretty, timid, little, bright-eyed sort of a girl. I should have liked to know her. Good night, young Copperfield.'
>
> (Chapter VII)

Not for the only time in his life, David is identified with a mythic sister (although clearly Steerforth could just as well be describing David's surrogate sibling, Little Em'ly). Steerforth, from their first meeting, identifies a feminine in David which is central to the nature and development of their friendship. Moreover, this exchange takes place late at night in the bedroom David shares with several other boys, including Steerforth, and it follows the feast of cakes and wine which David's pocket-money has purchased under the magisterial supervision of Steerforth. The experience of secrecy and sensuality is very much in keeping with subsequent revelations of Steerforth's character, particularly in his treatment of Little Em'ly. Such secret sensuality is further associated with David's imagination and artistic abilities. While at Salem House, David is the "plaything" of his dormitory because of his night-time story-telling.

> Whatever I had within me that was romantic and dreamy, was encouraged by so much story-telling in the dark; and in that respect the pursuit may not have been very profitable to me.
>
> (Chapter VII)

The evaluative disassociation of the narrative voice from his "romantic and dreamy" youthful self seems curious given the nature of the adult's professional success as a writer—such earlier practice has indeed "proved profitable." It is a clue that the narrator is anxious about the feminine identification. Uncertain and ambivalent about both sensuality and artistic ability, the adult male artist distances himself from those "feminine" characteristics on which, ironically, his art and worldly success are founded. By the time David reaches cultural manhood, feminine art will have been transformed into masculine enterprise. The suspect will have been made culturally safe.

Meantime, David's boyhood continues to engage in gender role-playing. The enactment of male and female roles survives through the shared experience of Salem House to the renewal of David and Steerforth's friendship in London. The intervening years have been spent by David in a household where sexual role-playing does not conform to traditional precepts. Davey, the son of David and Dora, is transformed into Trotwood Copperfield, the adopted child of Mr. Dick and Betsey Trotwood. The emotional and artistic Mr. Dick, florid, full of childish delight, without a strong rational sensibility is in marked antithesis to the Victorian paterfamilias. Betsey Trotwood, on the other hand, is explicitly masculine-identified. When David first meets her in Dover, he describes her as "handsome," her dress is severe and neat with "linen at her throat not unlike a shirt-collar, and things at her wrists like little shirt-wristbands" (Chapter XIII). She wears a man's watch, with chain and seals, and when, much later, she visits Dora's aunts Lavinia and Clarissa, she is regarded as "an eccentric lady, and somewhat masculine with a strong understanding" (Chapter XL). In such an environment, David is not identified as exclusively masculine. Constantly encouraged to think and act as would his imaginary sister, Betsey Trotwood Copperfield, he is also confirmed in an identification with both natural parents, for he "would be as like his father as it's possible to be, if he was not like his mother, too" (Chapter XIII). Even his new name, Trotwood, defines gender identity.

Names play a telling role in David's life. Significantly it is not until they meet again as young men that Steerforth coins the nickname "Daisy"

for David Copperfield. In an act of sensitive generosity Betsey Trotwood
has given the eighteen-year-old David the freedom and the money to spend
a month as he wishes while travelling to visit Yarmouth. Stopping in
London for his first night, intimidated by waiters, abashed by the palpable
fact that he has no need of the hot shaving water the maid leaves outside his
door in the morning, David runs into Steerforth, now an Oxford
undergraduate. The dynamics of their boyhood friendship continue into
adulthood. Steerforth is masterful and knowledgeable while David is full
of romantic enthusiasm, "as fresh as a daisy at sunrise" (Chapter XIX),
ready to be tutored and eager to be liked by the older man. They visit
Steerforth's mother and spend a week "in a most delightful manner" with
Steerforth giving lessons in the manly arts of riding, boxing and fencing:

> The week passed rapidly, as may be supposed, to one entranced as I was; and yet it
> gave me so many occasions for knowing Steerforth better, and admiring him more
> in a thousand respects, that at its close I seemed to have been with him for a much
> longer time. A dashing way he had of treating me like a plaything, was more
> agreeable to me than any behavior he could have adopted.
>
> (Chapter XXI)

Steerforth, of course, then joins David in his visit to Yarmouth, thereby
initiating the sequence of events which leads to the seduction of Little
Em'ly, Steerforth's new "plaything," and all the betrayals of family and
friends attendant upon their elopement.

   Until that disillusionment, the friendship of David and Steerforth
continues in the pattern of their childhood. Steerforth is the dominant,
experienced, condescending superior in a relationship comfortable in its
operating assumption of inequality. Their relationship has only the
subtlest of moral content, and the nature of that content explicitly lies
within the power of the superior Steerforth. Though founded on genuine
love, the friendship of David and Steerforth hints at the corruption of
innocence in its best moral impulses. Thus David represses his sympathy
for Mr. Mell; thus Steerforth allows the inexperienced David to spend a
drunken night on the town. As Agnes warns David, Steerforth is his "bad
angel," a charge which at the time David vehemently denies. In so doing,
David is covertly defending that aspect of self which is most akin to
Steerforth: the social male self. Throughout their early relationship, David
is morally superior to Steerforth only in the innocence of his instinct, never
in an actual choice in terms of action or behavior.

   The loss of Steerforth marks David's movement from androgynous
boyhood to masculine adulthood. It is a loss which coincides with two
other markers in this rite of passage. The first is his love for Dora. The
second is David's initiation into cultural manhood when, with the news of

his aunt's financial ruin, he shoulders the traditional male burden of economic responsibility for his family. For David, social and cultural maturity means the adoption of a rigorously masculine role, a role which relies for its definition on the clear separation of the feminine from the masculine. David becomes earnest, rational and hardworking. He masculinizes his own selfhood. The art of writing is turned into the enterprise of Parliamentary reporting so that he can make a living. Simultaneously, David looks for his domestic and personal happiness to a woman who matches the extremity of his own cultural role-playing. Conforming to stereotype, their differences come to represent the separation of the instinctive from the rational; neither is able, however, to make moral or emotional coherence out of the polarity. As such their relationship develops into an indictment of extreme sexual roles, an indictment confirmed by the parallels which exist between their marriage and the friendship of David with Steerforth. While Doady is never Dora's "bad angel," their relationship, in its content, the dynamic of its development and even, in some measure, the nature of its eventual outcome, echoes the earlier and older friendship. In giving priority to a social male self, David diminishes his emotional sensitivity and blunts his moral sensibility. In so doing he hurts Dora, he betrays the child of nature, the "young innocence" whom experience cannot teach.

The audience of *David Copperfield* is warned from the outset of the inherent moral ambivalence of David's masculine role-playing. The famous incident of the beggar in the street calling "Blind! Blind! Blind" refers to the matrix of experience in which it occurs, not solely to David's choice of Dora over Agnes. Part of that matrix is his espousal of the work ethic, which happens simultaneously, and from which the narrator deliberately and ironically distances himself. Chapter XXXVI, "Enthusiasm," follows immediately upon the beggar's call of "Blind! Blind! Blind!" and opens:

What I had to do, was, to turn the painful discipline of my younger days to account, by going to work with a resolute and steady heart. What I had to do, was, to take my woodman's axe in my hand, and clear my own way through the forest of difficulty, by cutting down the trees until I came to Dora. And I went on at a mighty rate, as if it could be done by walking.

The single most important source of David's manifold "blindness" is his capacity for uncritical and exuberant enthusiasm. Agnes, who like the narrator is also a major source of moral comment in the novel, tempers David's youthfully passionate response to life, though she always does so with a gentle humor, as when, for example, she teases him by "threatening to keep a little register of [his] attachments with the dates, duration, and termination of each..." (Chapter XXV) when David confesses that he is half in love with Rosa Dartle. Unlike either his relationships with Agnes or Tommy Traddles, David's relationships with both Steerforth and Dora are characterized by an early passionate enthusiasm which blinds him to the moral implications of personality and behavior, both in himself and in those he loves. So it is with work.

Meanwhile, the loss of Steerforth intensifies David's passionate love for Dora, though, as with Walter Gay's devotion to Florence Dombey, his early love is centered on an ideal rather than an actuality:

All this time, I had gone on loving Dora, harder than ever. Her *idea* [italics mine] was my refuge in disappointment and distress, and made some amends to me, even for the loss of my friend. The more I pitied myself, or pitied others, the more I sought for consolation in the image of Dora. The greater the accumulation of deceit and trouble in the world, the brighter and purer shone the star of Dora high above the world. I don't think I had any definite idea where Dora came from, or in what degree she was related to a higher order of beings; but I am quite sure I would have scouted the notion of her being simply human, like any other young lady, with indignation and contempt.

(Chapter XXXIII)

It reads almost as purely as Ruskin and hence the parody. But the humor does not disguise the serious consequences of this culturally-condoned view of women. It is David's inability to comprehend the reality of Dora which causes his failure to mediate between her perceptions of life and his excessive enthusiasm, a failure compounded by his disastrous attempt at playing the teacher and mentor in Dora's life, which Steerforth has played in his.

David alone fails to understand Dora's essential nature, and, as becomes the pattern, their relationship is in fact mediated through other women: Julia Mills, Betsey Trotwood and Agnes Wickfield. David and Dora are thus trapped in the contradictions of their own culture. David has enthusiastically espoused the ideals of masculinity and femininity: he will work earnestly toward an inevitable worldly success while relying on a "Cottage of Content" for his domestic happiness. He has fallen in love with an ideal of decorative womanhood, a woman who is childish, without intellectual depth or strong understanding, but one who delights and pleases him, and who, by every implication, excites him physically. He is superior, she is inferior: he will teach her, she is his "plaything." It is one of the further ironies, of course, that David is attempting to amalgamate the divided maternal image of the two Claras. He wants Dora to acquire the domestic skills of Peggotty. The undoubted, if narratively unacknowledged, sensuality of David and Dora's relationship connects significantly with the secrecy of their engagement: it is a constellation of moral ambivalence which marks all the disastrous relationships in the novel, and one which is most clearly identified with Steerforth. In upbraiding David for this deceit towards Dora's aunts, Agnes serves to remind the audience of David's moral fallibility; it undercuts any claim David might make to moral superiority in his relationship with Dora.

The pleasures of courtship prove to be the dilemmas of marriage, and so David pursues the painful pedagogical course of attempting "to form Dora's mind." The profound unhappiness he causes her rests on David's conviction of the superiority of the rational, a conviction which operates in defiance of the "natural" realities of Dora's personality and capabilities. David, for all his sense of the superiority of the masculine-identified attribute, that of rationality, is the very last to comprehend the fixed nature of his marital relationship. Agnes, Betsey Trotwood, even Dora herself, all understand and warn David about the nature of his choice in marriage. The "instinctively" feminine has a moral sensitivity denied to the intellectually based. Thus Betsey Trotwood who, like David, regains a feminine selfhood which she had denied in the bitterness of experience, refuses to repeat the pattern of the past. She declines to interfere in the marriage by advising Dora on practical matters, as David had requested, and instead accepts "Little Blossom" as she is without criticism. It is Dora herself who asks to be called "child-wife"; she too comprehends that she can never be what David wants her to be. He, however, does not take the warning seriously, and so he sets about making Dora "reasonable," with the only palpable results being his own loneliness and her unhappiness. Finally deciding it had been a wrongheaded scheme, David brings home gifts and a good mood to reconcile himself to his wife. Their conversation works around the key polarities of the rational and the instinctive:

I sat down by my wife on the sofa, and put the ear-rings in her ears; and then I told her that I feared we had not been quite as good company lately, as we used to be, and that the fault was mine. Which I sincerely felt, and which indeed it was.

'The truth is, Dora, my life,' I said; 'I have been trying to be wise.'

'And to make me wise too,' said Dora, timidly. 'Haven't you, Doady?'

I nodded assent to the pretty inquiry of the raised eyebrows, and kissed the parted lips.

'It's not a bit of use,' said Dora, shaking her head, until the ear-rings rang again. 'You know what a little thing I am, and what I wanted you to call me from the first. If you can't do so, I am afraid you'll never like me. Are you sure you don't think, sometimes, it would have been better to have—'

'Done what, my dear?' For she made no effort to proceed.

'Nothing!' said Dora.

'Nothing?' I repeated.

She put her arms around my neck, and laughed, and called herself by her favorite name of a goose, and hid her face on my shoulder in such a profusion of curls that it was quite a task to clear them away and see it.

'Don't I think it would have been better to have done nothing than to have tried to form my little wife's mind?' said I, laughing at myself. 'Is that the question? Yes, indeed, I do.'

'Is that what you have been trying?' cried Dora. 'Oh what a shocking boy!'

'But I shall never try any more,' said I. 'For I love her dearly as she is.'

'Without a story—really?' inquired Dora, creeping closer to me.

'Why should I seek to change,' said I, 'what has been so precious to me for so long! You can never show better than as your own natural self, my sweet Dora; and we'll try no conceited experiments, but go back to our old way, and be happy.'

'And be happy!' returned Dora. 'Yes! All day! And you won't mind things going a tiny morsel wrong, sometimes?'

'No, no,' said I. 'We must do the best we can.'

'And you won't tell me, any more, that we make other people bad,' coaxed Dora; 'will you! Because you know it's so dreadfully cross!'

'No, no,' said I.

'It's better for me to be stupid than uncomfortable, isn't it?' said Dora.

'Better to be naturally Dora than anything else in the world.'

'In the world! Ah, Doady, it's a large place.'

She shook her head, turned her delighted bright eyes up to mine, kissed me, broke into a merry laugh and sprang away to put on Jip's new collar.

(Chapter LIII)

David, of course, is remarkably obtuse as to the hidden content of this conversation, which is founded on Dora's accurate perception that he regrets the marriage. The failure of David's "wisdom," of his male-identified rationality, to engage successfully with Dora's naturalness, represents the failure of the culturally-endorsed concepts of masculinity and femininity. There is appeasement, but there can be no reconciliation between such fixed extremes: David and Dora's marriage is a thorough-going indictment of the "Cottage of Content." It is only after the loss of such sexual extremes that a structure of possible reconciliation can be discovered when David regains those feminine aspects of selfhood which he has repressed or denied.

The deaths of Dora and Steerforth are narratively fortuitous. They relieve David of a life-long commitment to erroneous youthful choice, an instance of authorial generosity common in mid-Victorian novels. Their deaths, moreover, take on further significance if the characters do indeed represent the culturally-approved concepts of masculinity and femininity. Steerforth, readily admired, forever associated with money and easy social success, is without moral instinct, a lack he himself recognizes, and for which he blames his mother.[10] Dora, on the other hand, pretty and foolish, enjoys a moral innocence, a native inability for conscious malice, one which qualifies (if never actually compensates for) her complete lack of intellectual comprehension.[11] David, potentially androgynous, has loved them both and loses them both. Neither Daisy, the feminized male, nor Doady, the corrupted male, survives: it is Trotwood Copperfield who returns, renewed, from Europe. As Trotwood (the name which Agnes uses), David is able to make a living as an artist, he is able to weep openly (when he was married to Dora, David would weep only in secret), and perhaps most important of all, he is able to acknowledge his love for the "right" woman, Agnes. At the same time, David loses none of the quality of masculine enterprise; he retains his capacity for earnest hard work, an earnestness "thorough-going, ardent, and sincere" which David claims he owes all to Agnes (Chapter XLII).

Agnes is central to the significance of David's rediscovery of selfhood while in Switzerland, but the sequence by which David reaches Dover after his return to England is equally telling. Apart from Mr. Chillip, as much in attendance at this spiritual birth as he was at David's natural birth, the only people David visits in London en route to Agnes are Tommy Traddles and Sophy, "the dearest girl," whom Tommy has married. Tommy Traddles plays an extremely important role in *David Copperfield*, not least of which is his apparent representation of a social no less than personal reconciliation between the masculine and the feminine. In his selfhood, Tommy is posited as an ideal: emotional and intensely moral, Tommy is nonetheless capable of the hard work and intellectual endeavor necessary for eminence in the public domain. Thus he appears to reconcile internally the masculine with the feminine, the rational with the moral and the emotional, but even more significantly he appears to reconcile the private with the public. Married to the woman he loves, together they serve with maternal self-sacrifice the whole impoverished Crewler family. The image of Tommy Traddles in the dusty chambers of the Inns of Court surrounded by laughing women, all enjoying the best of communal and familial times, attempts a genuine optimism. Hidden away, at the very heart of the very driest male institution, an institution which deliberately excludes the emotional and the moral from the structure on which it rests, is a group of happy women chatting around a fire while a contented and busy man makes tea for everyone. The scene is as overtly optimistic as is Traddles' eventual success in law. The assumption, at novel's end, of his appointment to the Bench represents the most positive view of the law in Dickens' novels. With Traddles a judge, there would be an active moral agent at the highest levels of a major social institution. Moreover, that agent is identified as possessing the feminine qualities of sensibility and domesticity. The difficulty of the final chapter which embodies this social optimism, derives in part from its failure to make this optimism convincing. It is a failure which operates in conjunction with the portrayal of Agnes, a character who has always provoked critical unease.

It is a cliche of literary criticism that nothing is more difficult than to portray sympathetically and convincingly a positive idea of good. As with all cliches, it has a strong measure of truth to it. Certainly one of the difficulties surrounding Agnes Wickfield is that she is supposed to represent an ideal of womanhood, an ideal which has mercifully lost favor with the passing years. The ideal is of a woman who is domestically competent yet who has the "softened beauty of a stained-glass window"; a woman who embodies the best moral impulses, impulses which are instinctively structured on selflessness, yet one who simultaneously enjoys a calm and serious intelligence. Whatever the problems of this cultural ideal of womanhood, there are certain specific elements in the portrayal of Agnes which are essential to an understanding of the novel's final failure to carry through on its promise of espousing an unconventional sexual and social ideology.

Agnes Wickfield is the great lost character of *David Copperfield*. Although Dickens gives little real narrative substance to her extraordinary life, he was fascinated as an author with the nexus of family character and experience which constitute the main details of her biography. As with almost every other major Dickens character (and thus the exceptions become significant[12]), Agnes is motherless. Her mother, having married socially beneath her family and against its wishes, dies shortly after Agnes' birth. Throughout her childhood and early adulthood, Agnes has thereby provided the sole rationale for her alcoholic father's obsessive and criminally unethical behavior, much as Little Nell is her grandfather's own excuse for his compulsive gambling. The male burden of economically supporting women (and this seems especially so when the women are explicitly identified as "good angels") often takes a neurotic, and finally criminal cast in Dickens' novels. Simultaneously Agnes plays housekeeper to her widowed father, another key and recurrent relationship in Dickens' writings. Moreover, in love from childhood, Agnes must bear the additional burdens, not only of unrequited love, but of loving a man too blind to comprehend the nature of her feelings, and one who marries a woman thoroughly and entirely different from herself. In this sea of troubles other dangers lurk: she is desired by the morally odious and physically repulsive Uriah Heep, her father causes the bankruptcy of their dearest friends, and she must over a period of several years run a school to support herself and her father following the public revelation of his dubious work habits. Yet despite a life so ripe for artistic exploration and revelation, Agnes as an autonomous character remains hidden from the audience. We know nothing of her emotional or intellectual responses to these traumatic events; we never even discover what she feels about Uriah Heep and his courtship of her, or of her father's public disgrace. Agnes is presented entirely from David's point of view, a view which is always egocentric and often unperceptive.

In part the difficulty of revealing Agnes may derive from the nature of autobiographical technique. It is a technique which, as used by Dickens, inherently subordinates all other characters, limiting the audience's access to them to the agency of the first-person persona. David, unlike Nick Carroway, for example, is never off-stage: events and characters are all revealed through his presence, if not his consciousness. But the limitations of first-person narration cannot be blamed entirely for the unavailability of Agnes as an autonomous character. Dickens demonstrates, for example, an easy capability of using the possibilities of retrospective in the revelations of Steerforth: the superior knowledge of the narrator constantly qualifies the limited awareness and understanding of the character of David Copperfield at the various stages of the narrative. No such technique is ever used to generate a complexity of characterization for Agnes; not once does the narrator reflect or concede an enhanced understanding of Agnes as a character who has suffered great pain and humiliation: retrospective experience merely confirms the stereotype. Moreover, other characters are demonstrated to have experiences and feelings unknown to David Copperfield, and for the audience to be aware of the depth and significance of that unknown life, if ignorant of the details. Betsey Trotwood has enjoyed a complex and profound range of experience and emotions in her marriage to, separation from, and blackmail by a man she has loved passionately. It is as apparent to David as to the audience that her fear of fire is a symptom of this hidden life, that it reveals the presence, but not the nature, of deep feelings held under severe control. With the exception of her love for David, and then only at the very end when David himself is suffering the pangs of unrequited love, Agnes is never implicitly granted an autonomous moral or emotional life. Finally, it is a perverse comment on the significance which Agnes has in the novel that she must remain hidden from the audience, hidden, that is, except as David perceives her. If she were revealed as a character, Agnes Wickfield would threaten to displace David from the center of his own narrative, a displacement which would run counter to the egocentric nature of the novel's theme and structure.

Agnes, then, exists only as an idea in the mind of the narrator. What the idea of Dora is to the young David Copperfield, Agnes is to the older narrative persona: as the heroine of his life she exists only in relationship to him. Agnes, moreover, is not simply the heroine of the narrator's life; she is also, as Alexander Welsh has argued, the prefiguration of his death.[13] The last chapter of *David Copperfield* is haunted by a preoccupation with the inevitability of the narrator's own death, at whose dying and at whose wake Agnes will stand guard, harbinger and protector both. The fear of the feminine resides in part in the anxiety inspired by death and its human guardians. Even the feminine-identified Tommy Traddles doodles constantly the skeletal image of human morality. But the problem posed by the final chapter of *David Copperfield* resides not only (and perhaps not even primarily) in the fear of the feminine identification with death; that fear is significantly compounded by the male anxiety of feminization, an anxiety which helps create a conventionality at the novel's end which defies its own sexual radicalism. The portrayal of the Copperfield household in the last chapter is socially and sexually safe: he and Agnes (a soundly conventional couple) are blessed with healthy children, those they love are enjoying a golden old age, and David's writing, his "feminine" art, is acknowledged only in terms of successful worldly enterprise. The narrator has retreated from the true heroism of David Copperfield, the individual recognition of the complexity of sexual identity and the necessity of incorporating the feminine into that which is masculine identified. The intensity of Romantic experience, the self lost and found again in defiance of social convention and definition, is enbourgeoised: *David Copperfield* retreats from the radical into a safe domestic harbor, a Victorian middle-class home.

Notes

[1]For an excellent reconciliation of the "intentionalist" and psychoanalytic readings of the novel, see Gordon D. Hirsch, *Victorian Newsletter*, 58 (Fall 1980), pp. 1-5.

[2]Throughout this discussion of *David Copperfield*, I use the term "feminine" much as Marilyn French characterizes the "inlaw" (i.e. culturally approved) characteristics designated as feminine in "The Garden Principles," *Shakespeare's Division of Experience* (New York: Summit Books, 1980).

[3]*The Prelude* was of course published in the same year as *David Copperfield*. John Lucas argues that Dickens may well have read the poem (which appeared in July 1850) before beginning work on the number which includes Dora's death: *The Melancholy Man: A Study of Dickens' Novels* (London: Methuen and Company, 1970), pp. 169-70.

[4]J. Hillis Miller, *Charles Dickens: The World of His Novels* (Bloomington: Indiana University Press, 1969), p. 157.

[5]Alexander Welsh, *The City of Dickens* (Oxford: Clarendon Press, 1971), p. 181.

[6]Stanley Friedman, "Dickens' Mid-Victorian Theodicy," *Dickens Studies Annual*, 7 (1978), pp. 128-150.

[7]John Butt and Kathleen Tillotson, *Dickens At Work* (London: Methuen and Company, 1957), pp. 128-30.

[8]Friedman, p. 150.

[9]As Bert G. Hornback has noted, Dickens took some care over the choice of these epithets; Dickens changed the text in manuscript from "stupid" to "you girl," and the phrase "Miss Traddles" is an interlinear addition. *"The Hero of My Life": Essays on Dickens* (Athens: Ohio University Press, 1981), p. 82.

The text used is from *The Oxford Illustrated Dickens* (London: O.U.P., 1948). All subsequent references are by the chapter, and are included in parentheses in the text.

[10]Blaming the mother for a moral failure in self is not simply an abdication of individual reponsibility. It also represents an additional burden women bear in a culture which deems them the moral standard-bearers.

[11]The incident of the page finally transported after repeated revelations of theft from the Copperfield household is one small demonstration of the central differences between a rationally-based and an instinctively-held morality. David attempts to explain the moral "contagion" of their domestic incompetence (that it leads their servants into theft and other nefarious activities); Dora emotionally understands the accusation (that *she* is being blamed and compared to a transported page), but is incapable of understanding the intellectual concept of responsibility by default (Chapter XLVII).

[12]Arthur Clennam is the single most important exception to the general Dickens rule of motherless central characters.

[13]Welsh, pp. 180-183.

Patricia Merivale

The Search for the Other Woman:
Joan Didion and the Female Artist-Parable

JOAN DIDION'S FINEST NOVEL to date, *A Book of Common Prayer* (1977),[1] is by no means easy to understand or interpret, but two sets of analogies help to clarify the book's complex intentions. One is to the distinctively "feminine" variant of the contemporary identity quest as written, for instance, by Ruth Prawer Jhabvala, in *Heat and Dust*, Doris Lessing in *Memoirs of a Survivor* and especially Christa Wolf, in *The Quest for Christa T*. These women, and several others, write the sort of artist-parable which presupposes that the narrator can, and should at least attempt to, "find" herself through the act of writing a book, the overt subject of which is the search for the true biography of someone else—a feminine alter ego. The other analogy, which I shall discuss first, is to the almost exclusively "masculine" genre of the elegiac romance.[2]

I

An elegiac romance is, to abridge considerably, a fictional autobiography which must disguise itself as the biography of a person now dead. Books of this type have been written by Herman Melville, F. Scott Fitzgerald, Robert Penn Warren, Saul Bellow and Ken Kesey, among many others, but most notably by Joseph Conrad. Until now, the central relationship has almost always been a male bonding between narrator and subject; Didion seems to be the first (except for Christa Wolf) to make that central relationship a female bonding. All elegiac romances have "biographers" who disingenuously claim to be quite unimportant compared to their "heroes"; only in the end does the narrator emerge as the central character, assessing his *own* life in terms of his vicarious experience (at the time) and his fuller discovery (in retrospect) of the life of his subject.

I tell you these things about myself only to legitimize my voice. We are uneasy about a story until we know who is telling it. In no other sense does it matter who "I" am: "the narrator" plays no motive role in this narrative, nor would I want to .... I am interested in Charlotte Douglas only insofar as she passed through Boca Grande, only insofar as the meaning of that sojourn continues to elude me.

(*BCP*, 21)

133

Thus Didion's narrator, Grace Strasser-Mendana, temporizes at the beginning of the book; by the end she has realized at least this one thing: "I am more like Charlotte than I thought I was" (*BCP*, 268). Such a narrator is, as we shall see, ambivalently but obsessively devoted to his subject and liable to enlarge merits or defects past the point of realistic characterization. He is commonly (perhaps, as the above quotation suggests, "she" is too) a very "unreliable" narrator.

One elegiac romance in particular, Graham Greene's *The Quiet American* (1955),[3] is exemplary for our purposes. Similarities of theme, subject and narrative structure are so striking that I assume Didion chose it deliberately and explicitly as a model; if so, it should be of considerable help in extrapolating Grace's ironies into an understanding of Didion's.

Although Didion's mythical land of Boca Grande resembles Conrad's Costaguana (from *Nostromo*) and Garcia Marquez' Colombia, as revised in the light of her own Central American journey,[4] it chiefly appropriates the Greene-lands of Haiti, Paraguay and Viet Nam. The strange blend in Didion of shabby-exotic tropical setting, topical reference, political content and random explosions almost as inept as the inadvertent acts of heroism and the intense good deeds of the protagonists suggests an open willingness to seem indebted to Greene.

Greene-land, however, is a man's world. It is a tropical country where western white men are the outsider-exploiters and where the indigenous tyrants of banana republics are still subversively at the service of foreigners, even while they assert their nominal independence by overthrowing each other in yearly revolutions. Thus the basic political structure of Boca Grande is that of Conrad's Costaguana, updated and simplified almost to the point of caricature or abstraction. In these squalid tropics, the simpler moralities of "sojourners" like Alden Pyle (Greene's "quiet" and disastrously purposeful "American") or Charlotte Douglas (Didion's noisier and disastrously purposeless American) break or crumble under insidious moral pressures and oblique corruptions. Intermediary between Newcomer and Native in these books is the narrator, an outsider-who-really-knows-the-country ("the Far East, which he [Pyle] had known for as many months as I had years" *QA*, 12). Greene's Fowler is the reporter, who has no opinions and never takes sides; Didion's Grace Strasser-Mendana found anthropology not certain enough and turned to biochemistry in her search for measurable, objective truth to which she can bear witness. Both these narrators draw shrewd, cynical, detached conclusions from the fatal misadventures of the well-intentioned, but too naive and visible newcomers, caught in the cross-fire between revolutionary elements and unstable local tyrannies. Both narrators eventually realize that they are much more involved, both emotionally and causally, in the deaths of Pyle and Charlotte Douglas than they, or we, had supposed. As Fowler is eventually forced to acknowledge his emotional commitments, take decisive part in the action, and accept guilt for the consequences, so Grace allows us to infer that she is more concerned about and connected with Charlotte's unhappy destiny than she is willing to admit even to herself and, further, that the observer, by observing, alters what is to be observed. Pursuing the empirical evidence for biographical truth, Grace is forced to confess it inadequate to the mysteries, uncertainties and occasional magic power of human character and interrelationships.

As Didion says in a rather teasing interview (*New York Times Book Review*, April 3, 1977), the "narrator has got to be telling the story for a reason." Fowler's "reason" is quite evident: his complicity in Pyle's death, motivated by considerations ranging from jealousy to humanitarianism, has trapped him in a contrition that enforces confession upon him. The nature of Grace's concern with Charlotte can be sketched out in broad integrate terms, but is by no means so easy to integrate with the substance of the book's events.

For some reason (which I shall try to determine) Grace finds it not only worthwhile but essential to spend what she knows to be the last months of her life (she is sixty and dying of cancer) writing Charlotte's elegiac memorial, although she only knew Charlotte in her fortieth and last year and can by no means account for her deeds and nature. Her key question, which we too would like to have answered, is "Then why is it in my mind when nothing else is." (*BCP*, 214, Didion's punctuation). Why indeed? Can Grace account for herself by attempting to account for Charlotte, when she will not (or perhaps cannot) account for the relationship between them? "I will be her witness" opens the book; "I have not been the witness I wanted to be" closes it.[5]

Greene's bonding relationship is the usual one for elegiac romance: two men who are both friends and rivals are in competition for a woman who chiefly matters as the catalyst in the break-up of their bonding. The relationship between Charlotte and Grace seems not to follow that pattern, even though it is possible to see in the book a similar erotic triangle, with Grace's son, Gerardo, who is Charlotte's lover, as the unmoved catalyst. This possibility may be one of Didion's teases: both women feel explicitly "unconnected" to Gerardo; he does not matter to either of them emotionally as the beautiful Phuong matters to both Pyle and Fowler.

Their female bonding begins with Grace's quite unsympathetic mockery of Charlotte's aimlessness and naivete. She acknowledges contrary evidence, for which she cannot account; yet much of her description borders upon caricature, as to a lesser extent does Fowler's description of Pyle, another person who invites a national as well as a sexual stereotype. Nearer the end of the book, however, clues to a deep similarity between Grace and Charlotte begin to thicken, and Grace acknowledges resemblance and some grudging sympathy. Charlotte is conditioned from the beginning by the loss of two husbands, a fact which does not seem to matter very much, and of two daughters, a fact which matters a lot. Grace has also lost both husband and son (husband dead and son "unconnected"); these losses do not matter very much either, as far as she tells us. Her low capacity for emotional involvement seems to be, along with her intellectual defenses, the key respect in which she differs from Charlotte. In retrospect Grace comes very close, in the writing of this elegy, to acknowledging that she has now lost the daughter whom she barely found, never claimed, and could not save: Charlotte.

A "daughter" is perhaps that younger alter ego in whom the dying may fancy themselves reborn and in whom the living glimpse their immortality, as Charlotte glimpses it in her daughter Marin: "Charlotte ... believed that when she walked through the valley of the shadow she would be sustained by the taste of Marin's salt tears, her body and blood" (*BCP*, 69). The failure of the bonding between Grace and Charlotte is reduplicated in the next generation by Charlotte's loss of her daughter to "history"—North American terrorist activity in the manner of Patty Hearst. In both generations bonding is symbolically reasserted, first by Charlotte, as she seeks out the death that would justify her to her daughter, and then by Grace, as she writes the book of *Common Prayer* which at last admits the bond between them. Her book constitutes a prayer for both the dead and the dying, one based on the "truest" testimony the elegiast can gather.

These sweeping parallels in the generational pattern tend to oversweeten the story and must be counter-balanced by a consideration of ironic parallels of plot and situation. Both women are "Norteamericanas": Grace, long accustomed to living in Boca Grande, is more the Norteamericana than she realizes. They are both "sojourners" *de afuera*; both have some quality of taboo which has at times made the men of the country fascinated, or afraid, or both. They are subversive elements in the "man's world" of Boca Grande politics. Grace married into one of the country's "three or four solvent families" (*BCP*, 173) over thirty years ago; she now holds 59% of the land and the power—a fact which, in the absence of stated consequences, she does her best to allow us to forget. Evidently Edgar, her late husband, was fascinated; evidently her two brothers-in-law, whose shares of the family fortune she holds in trust, are a little afraid and very resentful: "Victor would have me arrested if he thought he could carry it off" (*BCP*, 211). She seems to have been, for thirty years, a more active and, from the men's point of view, maleficent "Mrs. Gould of Sulaco" (*Nostromo*), up to her eyebrows in the traditional changes and manipulations of power among the males of the ruling family. Antonio, the second brother-in-law, hates Charlotte for reminding him of that other "norteamericana cunt" (*BCP*, 204), his sister-in-law. Charlotte is "a version of me at whom he could vent his rage," says Grace (*BCP*, 216). Antonio can wait for Grace to die, but a healthy, barely middle-aged Charlotte, with excellent prospects of marrying Gerardo and recapitulating Grace's rule indefinitely, is a temptation to murder. In a manner of speaking, Charlotte dies as a surrogate for Grace; Antonio at least is in no doubt about the virtual identity between them.

The immediate cause of Charlotte's death, however, is that the revolutionary game is not going according to pattern. The guerillas usually give up on the fourth day, but this time they have "extra hardware" from somewhere, and on the ninth day (Grace has been safely in New Orleans since Day Minus One) Charlotte, who has refused to leave, is shot in the back while being interrogated in the stadium. That is what Gerardo tells his Mama, but who told Gerardo Grace "prefer[s] not to know" (*BCP*, 69).

Who is the "somebody" giving this extra twist to Boca Grande politics? Who is financing the "outside hardware" (*BCP*, 244) that has escalated the usual game? Grace dismisses several possibilities, including the (to us) obviously implicated Leonard, though not on "empirical" grounds (*BCP*, 264); some remain which she does not grapple with. Could it be Grace herself? Didion has warned us to beware of "deceptive surfaces" (*NYTBR* interview); Grace has often asserted that revolutions are made "entirely by people we know" (*BCP*, 29); Occam's razor, in the form of Didion's scrupulous economy of means, asks us to look within the story for the answer. Such sharply heightened complicity could well be among the several things of which Grace wishes us to be uncertain. She is already clearly complicit, though she never explicitly admits it, in the deadly corruptions of Boca Grande politics-as-usual. Had she promoted the extra hardware, she would still be guilty only of oblique complicity in Charlotte's death. Her role then would resemble that of Fowler, who directs Pyle to the place of his assassination, and her narrative obsession, which might be called contrition, would be amply accounted for.

A likelier alternative is that her "delusion" has consisted in not realizing that Boca Grande might well become part of the real political world, in which "outside forces" do operate, and that politics could no longer be confined to the "solvent families" of the murky Banana Republic, that mordant sub-Conradian operetta which molds Grace's assumptions about political life. Perhaps Didion's ironic turn against Grace, who was being ironic about Charlotte, is to give Charlotte the last word as early as page fifteen: "What I was overlooking entirely, Charlotte said, was what Boca Grande 'could become'."

The likeliest supposition, however, about the "hardware" is one in which Charlotte's view of herself as "passionate" comes to seem more valid than Grace's view of her as "deluded" (*BCP*, 11). "Unless the delusion was mine," Grace reflects at the end (*BCP*, 272). Perhaps her delusion took the form of not seeing that Charlotte really was rather like Greene's Quiet American, capable not only of a passionate idealistic commitment, but of turning that commitment into hardware, like Pyle's milky plastic. After Charlotte watches the shooting up of the cholera vaccine, a "steel" (*BCP*, 255) comes into her voice, which Grace does not hear at the time.

"Charlotte heard even more than I heard but Charlotte seemed not to listen. Charlotte seemed not to see" (*BCP*, 240). Grace's logic here, as elsewhere, is elliptical; she does not complete the syllogism—"Charlotte saw even more than I saw"—as we, at least upon re-reading the book, might wish her to do.[6] Nor does she follow out the implications of some of her other observations—for instance, on Charlotte at airports:

People who go to the airport first invent some business to conduct there . . . . Then one day they see a plane, "their" plane . . . . They buy the ticket . . . . Quite as if they were ordinary travelers. (*BCP*, 143)

Leonard, Charlotte's husband, "had just realized that she was walking not idly but towards a specific destination" (*BCP*, 246); Grace never realized as much, or at any rate never articulates it. Charlotte chooses to stay; she chooses to go to the stadium. She seems to expect to be killed (as if she knows that the government forces have good grounds to do so), for en route she sends Grace Marin's address, along with her emerald wedding ring. "The point was lost on [Grace]," we may assume (*BCP*, 268), for she "did not mention to Marin that the emerald was a memento from the man who financed the Tupamaros" (*BCP*, 271). That is to say, Grace did not realize that the purpose of the ring was to be deduced by analogy with its origins; it was to be recycled into buying extra hardware for Marin's terrorist group in the States. Charlotte had tried to make peace with her daughter by dying "on the [right] side of a 'people's revolution' " (*BCP*, 214) after all.

The "man who financed the Tupamaros" was Grace's late husband, Edgar, a fact she only finds out after Charlotte's death. Her destiny is thus more closely tied to Charlotte's than she knew, both through their marital ties to Leonard and Edgar, two traffickers in "extra hardware," and through the significant migrations of the emerald ring: from Edgar to Leonard to Charlotte to Grace, but *not* to Marin. If Grace's failure to deliver the message is inadvertent, she is what she most fears being, obtuse; if perhaps Grace did catch the point, and deliberately neglected to deliver the message that would reunite mother and daughter in joint commitment and sacrifice, then she has almost as much to be contrite about as Fowler has.

Marin has long felt betrayed by her mother; Charlotte, after many quasi-filial confidences to Grace (her largest single source of information about Charlotte's North American life), comes to see that, at the conspiratorial social tables of Boca Grande, manipulators were deciding how to deploy her, a latter-day Isabel Archer, an innocent fallen among mean sophisticates, *and that Grace was among them.* " 'You were there too,' she said finally" (*BCP*, 236). "Sometimes I forget that I was there too," Grace concedes (*BCP*, 228), but she says it to us, not to Charlotte.

"Mother" betrays "daughter" again; perhaps it is this betrayal that provokes Charlotte to her strange symbolic settlement with her own daughter. The only "settling" left for Grace to do is to write this book, in which ironically we are allowed (perhaps) to understand more than she herself can. Charlotte's other husband, Warren (also, like Grace, dying of cancer), is given another of the ambiguous wrap-up statements that punctuate the book: " 'You're in over your head,' he said [to Grace] finally, and that was all that he said" (*BCP*, 169).

There is considerable room for maneuver in the interpretation of Didion's sub-text,[7] even with the powerful assistance of analogies to *The Quiet American* in particular and the elegiac romance in general. In one important respect Didion goes beyond Greene, into the mode of the artist-parable. Fowler simply writes a book, which is, in itself, a quite unproblematic activity for him. His problem is his painful dialectic of detachment and complicity; the pain thereof can be partly exorcized by telling us, as he cannot tell his acquaintances, that he killed Pyle and is sorry for it. He grows into honesty with himself and is honest with us, in retrospect, throughout.

Didion's is not only a more ironic text than Greene's but also a more self-reflexive one. Fowler's book is true, as far as he knows the truth. Grace's is *about* what she cannot discover or make sense of; if there is one mystery even darker to her than Charlotte's nature, it is her own. Further, Grace does not intend to be even as candid with us as she could be; her effort, under these synergistically ironic handicaps, to sum up her own life through Charlotte's is thus an exemplary parable of the difficulty of writing a text with any useful correspondence to the "real world" at all. If we wish to use generic analogies to investigate Didion's intentions further, we should turn back to books like Wolf's, Jhabvala's and Lessing's. In *The Quest for Christa T., Heat and Dust* and *Memoirs of a Survivor*, books as excellent in their ways as Didion's, we find other accounts of how to seek a "mother" or a "daughter," or some other female image for oneself, and how to turn that search into a book which becomes one's own self as creating artist.[8]

II

Something curious happened to female artist-parables in the seventies, a decade which started, for my purposes, in 1968 and is not yet over. While many such fictions continue to be written, as always, as narratively linear searches for the self (Margaret Atwood's *Surfacing*, for instance), a number have turned up with binary narrative structures seemingly determined by the pressure of their chief plot element: female bonding, or the search for the Other Woman. The narrator, always first-person, always consciously writing down this story, can only find her "self" by first finding, rescuing, then re-creating in the fiction, her alter ego, a woman lost, dead, caught in the past, who must be sought "in another country," "druben," in a place which ironically counterpoints and satirizes the homeland from which the narrator follows the heroine into "foreignness." In each book two "Innocents Abroad," whether two Americans in Boca Grande (Didion) or in Nazi Germany and Austria (Hellman), two Canadians on St. Antoine (Atwood), two Englishwomen in India (Jhabvala), two Germans in a new Germany divided from itself by both geography and history (Wolf)—all follow a pattern of the doubling of self in a doubling of terrain, which seems, in turn, to encourage a doubling of structure: these stories are commonly either elegiac romances, in which, as we have seen, the autobiography of the narrator masquerades as the biography of the dead heroine, or antiphonal texts, in which two disjunct narratives repeatedly interrupt, yet seem to "answer" each other.[9] Such antiphonal narratives are not causally interconnected; they are on different levels of artifice (or of "reality"). An inner duplication, or erratic correspondence, between them echoes in its ambiguous tension the relationship of self and alter ego within the book as a whole. The final goal of the narrator's quest is to join self and alter ego; the final goal of the reader's quest is to persuade these two apparently unconnected narratives to yield up a single book.

Of the three female bonding stories which are elegiac romances (compared to well over seventy reasonably well-known "male" ones) two, those by Didion and Wolf, are also artist-parables. The third, Lillian Hellman's "Julia," is certainly an elegiac romance, though this was perhaps not as clear in the book (*Pentimento*, 1973) as it became in the film version, which foregrounded the autobiographical significance for Hellman of material which in the book was largely anecdotal in scope. In either form, the story is more like a section of a *Kunstlerroman*, Hellman's life-as-an-artist, than like an artist-parable, a genre which requires, rather, an obliquely expressed account of the quarrel between Art and Life, or (as in most of these stories) of the quest to turn Life into Text. Hellman's metaphor of "pentimento," a painterly way of "seeing and then seeing again,"[10] suggests more allegory than the tale supplies; "Julia" is merely, if I put it that way, "life."

Didion's book, on the other hand, is a masterpiece of artist-parable as well as of elegiac romance. Like *The Quiet American*, *A Book of Common Prayer* is a story of self-discovery through a gain in moral awareness, but it is also, like *The Quest for Christa T.*, an account of the problematic nature of any attempt to ascertain, let alone convey, the truth of Self or Other by way of a text: "I have not been the witness I wanted to be" (*BCP*, 272). Though theme and detail are much closer to Greene's, Didion might well have picked up some hints from Christa Wolf's book on how to persuade a genre to change gender.

The title of Christa Wolf's *Nachdenken uber Christa T* (1968) has in fact, like Proust's title, been mistranslated: "Nachdenken," meaning approximately "recollection" or "remembrance," is turned into "quest," very much as Proust's "recherche" (*A la recherche du temps perdu*) has become "remembrance" (*Remembrance of Things Past*). But both implications operate, in "elegiac" artist-parables, because "memory" (an arm of creative imagination) is what turns "recherche" into art or text. It is the narrator's "remembrance," working upon the heroine's own documents, letters, notes (as Grace interprets Charlotte's passport), which re-creates or brings Christa T. "back to life," thereby turning the Quest-which-is-recollection into the text we read; residual artifacts, via memory, become re-creative artifice; left-over documents strive to be turned into the "truest" story possible. The process of remembering her heroine, Christa T., both ratifies the identity of the narrator and gives it a new direction: "Tomorrow to fresh woods and pastures new," Wolf might have concluded, though her tone is in fact closer to that of Rilke's elegies than to that of Milton's. There are overtones of the poet-hero, Orpheus', descent into the Underworld to rescue his dead wife, Eurydice, in all these stories of a rescue from the dead, but perhaps Demeter's search for her lost daughter, Persephone, kidnapped by Pluto, god of the Underworld, would be a closer mythic paradigm for mother and daughter bonding stories like Didion's. Where the bonding is not "vertical," across generations, but "horizontal," i.e., between "sisters," as in Wolf's story, perhaps a still more appropriate paradigm is that of the sisters Procne and Philomela, in which the antiphonal or elegiac narrative from the past comes by way of an inner artifact made up, like Philomela's tapestry, of recollected pain and grieving. Another such story is found in Margaret Atwood's *Bodily Harm* (1981), which (although, unlike these other stories, it is told largely in the third person) is also both identity-quest and artist-parable. It seems to pick up not only its broad outline but also many details from *A Book of Common Prayer*, being set in a Caribbean Greene-land, very much like Didion's, which is ironically contrasted to Toronto and small-town Ontario much as Boca Grande is contrasted to Charlotte's San Francisco and Hollister. St. Antoine, like Boca Grande, is haunted by terrorism; the narrator, like Didion's, learns to "witness," in both senses, another woman's enacted pain and courage. " 'Tell someone what happened.' 'Who should I tell?' 'I don't know . . . . Someone'." Like Didion's narrator, Atwood's protagonist must make the moral decision to "be her witness," to be Procne to her Philomela.

Both Didion and Wolf ask *us* to sort out a narrator who is sorting out herself by sorting out a dead heroine who was sorting out herself in terms of her own relationships, whether aesthetic, political or personal. In Didion the pattern is Demeter and Persephone redoubled; the narrator, Grace, must come to terms with her surrogate daughter, the heroine, through aesthetic means, i.e., by writing down her story, while the heroine, Charlotte, has attempted to come to terms with her own daughter through political action. Didion, although a remarkably non-symbolic author, preferring to accrete symbolic import through a vocabulary of images private to the text, allows herself two allusive patterns, which correspond roughly to these two Ovidian myths. The significant migrations of Charlotte's square emerald (worn "in place of a wedding ring," *BCP*, 271) seem meant to lead to a reunion of mother and daughter: "By the end of the novel," says Didion, "the emerald is almost the narrative. I had a good time with that emerald."[11] It is all the more significant when linked to the *name* of the lost daughter, Marin, which is half a satirical topographical reference ("Marin County"), half an allusion to the story, in Shakespeare's *Pericles*, of the grief-filled search for Marina, daughter lost then found, and of her parents' joyful reconciliation, with the help of a token of recognition: "The King my father gave you such a ring" (V.iii.38). More Philomela-like is the image of "red shoes," which calls to mind Hans Christian Andersen's grim parable ("The Red Shoes") of the pain and punishment meted out to women who step across the line into self-indulgent creative self-expression, or into a Philomela-like protest against oppression.

Wolf's and Didion's heroines are oddly similar, both in character and in their effect on their respective narrators. Their often self-contradictory actions keep putting into question the narrators' preconceptions and judgments about their characters; both heroines are outsiders, who share a "deep vacuum of nervous exhaustion," who live "strenuously even when [they] seem lackadaisical," who are "never capable of keeping apart things that didn't belong together" (*QCT* 36, 55,64); both die "hopeful" (*BCP* 11). They share a curiously inadvertent charm and a deep inability to endure brutality to others; they have both held a small child, dead, in horribly empty places at night, one in a Mexican parking-lot (it is for her that the 'red shoes' are needed), one in an East German snow-field; both are in flight, perpetual refugees, always in motion, yet drifting and apparently purposeless; they blend self-doubt and spontaneity. Both have profound but largely concealed political commitments, brought about by their humanitarian sympathies.

It could be said of Didion's heroine, as it is of Wolf's, that "walking through other towns, with the same stride, the same amazed look in her eyes, [i]t always seemed that she'd taken it upon herself to be at home everywhere and a stranger everywhere . . . in the same instant; and as if from time to time it dawned on her what she was paying for and with" (*QCT* 13). The Germany of history is present by its very absence, as geographically divided off West Germany also is: "*druben*—over there. The trip there is unusual enough to make your heart beat faster: over there is where the opposite ideas for living are produced, where everything is the reverse— people, things, and thoughts...[Christa] spits on the memorial to the 'stolen territories in the East' " (*QCT* 125).

Similar though the heroines may be, the narrators could hardly be more different. Didion's is active in the plot, perhaps duplicitously so, and very fully characterized, despite her claims to be a mere witness. She stresses continually the unacceptable eccentricities of her heroine, as she has sardonically and cynically observed them; only towards the end does she grudgingly concede, "I am more like Charlotte than I thought I was." That strong ego to which such concessions come only with difficulty is paradoxically re-asserted in her final admission of her emotional and artistic insufficiency: "I have not been the witness I wanted to be." Wolf's narrator approaches her task with a self-effacing humility, for both her own validity as a witness—"So what testimony can I give?" and her own creative abilities: "Mightn't the net that has been woven ... for her ... be incapable of catching her?" (*QCT* 87, 117). Indeed so self-effacing is she that she is barely characterized at all; at times she almost blurs into the author; at times they both blur into Wolf's namesake, Christa T. To make a sharp distinction among the three—author, narrator, heroine—forcing ironic clashes among them, as Didion has done, is no part of Wolf's intention. Christa T., although a failed and fragmentary writer herself, is still engaged in the same sort of quest, an inner duplication of the narrator's and the author's and, by extension, the reader's: a search for self by way of a narrative made from the search for someone else.

Other female artist-parables, those which employ antiphonal texts to tell stories of female bonding, likewise account for the present in terms of the past. Ruth Prawer Jhabvala's *Heat and Dust* (1975) looks at first like a middle-brow realistic account of the imposing of two Englishwomen upon India, and their at times awkward assimilations into an environment which is both "home" and (emphatically, exotically) not-home. The book alternates sections from the narrator's first-person, present-tense account of her stay in contemporary India with her third-person account, re-created from diaries and letters, of the life of her step-grandmother, who lived and died in India fifty years earlier.[12] The analogies between relationships and events in Jhabvala's antiphonal narratives are too striking not to bulge the surface of her apparently seamless realism. They hint at allegory or fantasy (metempsychosis, perhaps, or a reincarnation of the older woman in the younger), so strong are the coincidences. The narrator learns what to do with her life by re-enacting, inadvertently at first, the main events of her step-grandmother's life, and then, like Didion's and Wolf's narrators, learns from recapitulating them in which direction she is to shape her own. The story is not elegiac romance; the life is discovered and duplicated, rather than shared and remembered, but, as in elegiac romance, it is the aesthetic action of re-telling the life of the Other Woman that makes *both* lives meaningful.

Doris Lessing and Margaret Atwood likewise write artist-parables antiphonally, forcing the reader into the writer's role of making the connections, of joining the texts into the book, as the self and the alter ego are joined like the new Self by the constructing of the book. Lessing, in *Memoirs of a Survivor* (1974), alternates her "present" world with a visionary or imagined world which supplies a past for her surrogate daughter, one clearly constructed from the memories of her own past, thus establishing a close identity between "mother" and "daughter" by the aid of the creative imagination, whose realm is the (temporal rather than spatial) "other" world "behind the wall." Atwood's *Lady Oracle* (1976), being a spoof of both artist-parable and identity quest, combines a "present" narrative with a narrative of pure artifice which is a comic-Gothic mirroring of it, giving us a Canada of which Italy itself (the Gothic land *par excellence*) is a comic-Gothic mirroring. Joan Foster speaks for all our narrator-heroines in their ironic relation to their doubled landscapes when she says,

Please rescue. I was here, in a beautiful southern landscape, with breezes and old-world charm, but all the time my own country was embedded in my brain, like a metal plate left over from an operation; or rather, like one of those pellets you drop into bowls of water, which expand and turn into garish mineral flowers .... There was no sense trying to get away, I'd brought them all with me.[12]

The relationship of self and alter ego is seemingly imaged in the relationship between the narrator and the heroine of the Gothic romance she is writing—but the fundamental relationship, again, is that of mother and daughter. The narrator's Gothic imagination had always provided an escape route from her mother's intolerable domination, but Art attacks Life when her dead mother's ghost returns to haunt her. The narrator has been an "escape artist" in both work and life; indeed her artifice, like many others in these books, refuses to stay where it "belongs"; her *life* turns into a potentially destructive Gothic romance. More explicitly than in Didion, the story of the Red Shoes (with a credit to the movie) is a key image in Atwood of the female artist's life:[13]

The real red shoes [are] the feet punished for dancing. You could dance, or you could have the love of a good man. But you were afraid to dance, because you had this unnatural fear that if you danced they'd cut your feet off so you wouldn't be able to dance. Finally you overcame your fear, and danced, and they cut your feet off.

Of course male authors also can write antiphonal stories of female bonding. The Quebec novelist Hubert Aquin, like Atwood, supplies an alter ego and a doubled topography for his female narrator within an invented text in her own story (*L'Antiphonaire*, 1969), but in a pessimistic proleptic intensification of Atwood's deliberately stereotyped comic-Gothic, Aquin fulfills the prophecy of the Red Shoes and makes sure that the story does destroy the story-teller; the Text does destroy the Life. Atwood trifles with self-reflexiveness; Aquin takes it to a desperate conclusion.

My conclusion is less desperate. William Gass, in *Willie Masters' Lonesome Wife* (1968), goes much further than Atwood or even Aquin in reifying the female alter ego into a text. His narrator, the Lonesome Wife, has another self who is *only* the text of the story she is telling, but the Wife makes the discovery that *she too* is only the text; it is the *text* that has been narrating, antiphonally at least, if not polyphonically. The "I . . . made so luckily of language"[14] sings a bawdy hymn of of praise to artifice, a hymn constructed from the metaphors that can describe, indifferently, both language and sexuality. As a Barthesian comic turn on some fairly contemporary critical theory embodying endless metaphoric interchanges between textuality and sexuality, this book is beyond our immediate scope, for it moves beyond the category of the artist-parable just as surely as Hellman's "Julia" does, but in the opposite direction. If Self finds its alter ego to be only text, and the Life has *become* the text, conflict, or even a search through symbolic geographies in the real world, let alone enough character to supply identity, are scarcely any longer relevant concepts. Perhaps it is significant that such "pure" identifications of artifice in terms of female sexuality as Gass's and Aquin's rendering of the female characters, in the end, as externalized objects—texts—are written by male authors; they are parables of the projection of the Self's imagination upon the outside world, like many other masculine artist-parables of the Discovered City, a very different sort of symbolic geography, but arguably as gender-determined a form as the parables of the search for the Other Woman seem to be. But that is another topic. Between "life," as in "Julia," and "art," as in Gass, lies the territory of the female artist-parable, the territory I have been exploring, where Didion and Wolf in one way and Lessing, Jhabvala and Atwood in another have told parables of the quest to renew Life by way of Text, in which Art and Life are reconciled as a woman may be reconciled with her alter ego, through the effort of search in strange lands, through the labor of memory, and through the creativity of an artistic re-telling.

Gass's concluding exhortation thus applies to our argument on several levels:

YOU HAVE
FALLEN
INTO ART
—RETURN TO
LIFE

We will doubtless find some more artist-parables—perhaps even androgynous ones—on the way back up.

Notes

[1]New York: Simon and Schuster. Page references will be given in the text, using the abbreviation *BCP*.

[2]This first section of the paper, on *BCP* as elegiac romance, has been adapted from an earlier version, "Through Greene-land in Drag: Joan Didion's *A Book of Common Prayer*," *Pacific Coast Philology* 15 (October, 1980), 45-52, which is reprinted here by kind permission of the editors.

Both the concept and the term "elegiac romance" are Kenneth Bruffee's. For a much fuller discussion, see his *Elegiac Romance: Cultural Change and Loss of the Hero in Modern Fiction* (Ithaca: Cornell Univ. Press, 1983), which gives readings of most of the major elegiac romances. See also my article, "The Biographical Compulsion: Elegiac Romances in Canadian Fiction," *Journal of Modern Literature* 8: 1 (Spring, 1980), 139-52.

[3]Harmondsworth: Penguin Books, 1975. Page references will be given in the text, using the abbreviation *QA*. Greene's entertainment, *The Third Man*, is also an elegiac romance.

The best critical article to date on *BCP*, Victor Strandberg, "Passion and Delusion in *A Book of Common Prayer*," *Modern Fiction Studies* 27 (Summer, 1981), 225-42, gives a full account of the book's relationship through *The Great Gatsby* and *A Portrait of a Lady* to the great tradition in American literature of redemptive sacrifice. He is not chiefly concerned with narrative structure, although *Gatsby*, of course, is another elegiac romance.

[4]Didion quotes, in her review article on another author of guerilla romances, V.S. Naipaul, lines from Conrad's "Karain" as quoted by Naipaul himself, lines which seem to apply to Boca Grande as well: "a land without memories ... where each sunrise, like a dazzling act of special creation, was disconnected from the eve and the morrow," *NYRB* (June 12, 1980), p. 21. Cf. "Every time the sun falls on a day in Boca Grande that day appears to vanish from local memory ... Boca Grande has no history" (*BCP*, 14).

[5]Cf. Margaret Atwood's *Bodily Harm* (1981) for a female identity quest (and probably an artist-parable) in the third person, which seems to pick up not only its broad outline but also many details from *BCP*. *Bodily Harm* is also set in a Caribbean Greene-land, haunted by terrorism, where the main character learns to "witness," in both senses, another woman's enacted pain and courage. " 'Tell someone what happened.' 'Who should I tell?' 'I don't know... Someone'." Cf. "I will be her witness" (*BCP*, 11).

[6]I owe this point to Katharine Odgers' "Why Grace Likes the Light in Boca Grande" (unpublished), which compares the "epistemologies" of *BCP* with those of the first great elegiac romance, Melville's "Bartleby the Scrivener."

[7]See Virginia Cox, "From Passivity to Passion: Woman as Revolutionary in Joan Didion's *A Book of Common Prayer*" (unpublished), for a cogent analysis of Leonard's central role in both the gun-running and the moral tangles of *BCP*.

[8]See Judith Kegan Gardiner, "The (US)es of (I)dentity: A Response to Abel on '(E)merging Identities," *Signs: Journal of Women in Culture and Society* (6:3, 1981, 436-442) for a valuable discussion of the "explicit historical and political aims" as well as the "fictional dimensions" of the female pairings in Jhabvala and Wolf. "This permeability between the author and her text," "the adult novel is brought up like a daughter," seem

particularly useful insights.

[9]I discuss the term "antiphonal text" in "Neo-Modernism in the Canadian Artist-Parable: Hubert Aquin and Brian Moore," *Canadian Review of Comparative Literature* (Spring, 1979), pp. 195-205.

[10]Wolf, tr. Christopher Middleton (1970) (New York: Dell, 1972). Hereafter abbreviated *QCT*. Hellman, *Pentimento: A Book of Portraits* (New York: Signet, 1974). See p. 1 for her explanation of the term "pentimento."

[11]"Joan Didion," *Writers at Work: Paris Review Interview*, 5th ser., ed. George Plimpton (New York: Viking Press, 1981), p. 354.

[12]If "step-grandmother" seems a bit far-fetched as a version of the Demeter and Persephone pattern (inverted, of course, into 'Persephone's' search for 'Demeter'), recollect that 1977 was a vintage year for *great*-grandmothers: identity is sought in female bonding across *three* generations in Caroline Blackwood's *Great Granny Webster* and Anita Desai's *Fire on the Mountain*. Another book which could well be analyzed in terms I have employed in this paper is Joy Kogawa's *Obasan* (Toronto: Lester & Orpen Dennys, 1981), in which the elegiac search for the narrator's mother takes the form of seeking the history of her surrogate mother, her aunt. The context is the doubled land of the Canadian Japanese, enemy aliens in their own country, Canada, during World War II.

[13]McClelland and Stewart (Seal, 1980), pp. 335-336.

[14](New York: Knopf, 1981), unpaginated.

George R. Bodmer

Sounding the Fourth Alarm:
Identity and The Masculine Tradition
in the Fiction of Cheever and Updike

I

IN JOHN CHEEVER'S STORY "The Fourth Alarm," the narrator is baffled by the strange actions of his rebelling wife. After becoming involved in amateur dramatics, she quits her job as a sixth grade social studies teacher, moves out of their house, and takes a part as a nude actor in an off-Broadway play. The husband realizes that a radical change is being made in his life but he is unwilling to understand what the transition is all about:

I sit in the sun drinking gin .... It is autumn. The leaves have turned. The morning is windless, but the leaves fall by the hundreds. In order to see anything—a leaf or a blade of grass—you have, I think, to know the keenness of love. Mrs. Uxbridge is sixty-three, my wife is away, and Mrs. Smithsonian (who lives on the other side of town) is seldom in the mood these days, so I seem to miss some part of the morning as if the hour had a threshold or a series of thresholds that I cannot cross. Passing a football might do it but Peter is too young and my only football-playing neighbor goes to church.

("The Fourth Alarm," p. 645)[1]

Such might be a good introduction to many of the "Cheever men." He is upper middle class American and lives in New England. He is quiet voiced, motivated by love or the sharp feeling of love and lust. He feels bewildered and irritated that his life would be nudged from its routine by the uncooperativeness of women to let things continue. Yet his approach is a cynical one; with his wife gone, he considers his housekeeper (too old) and his mistress (not in the mood). His response is to seek solace in the trappings of masculinity: drinking or throwing the football around. His feeling is one of loneliness and nostalgia; he casts his mood in an autumnal setting and he wishes things were not changing.

He talks to his wife, wonders vainly if he should hit her, and at last goes to a performance of her play *Ozamanides II*. There he sees her and the rest of the cast nude, performing simulated sex acts onstage. While watching, he thinks back to a movie which captivated him as a child. In this movie, *The Fourth Alarm*, a city is replacing its horse drawn fire engines with modern gasoline-powered trucks. When all the trucks prove inadequate in fighting a fire, the fourth alarm sounds and the few remaining horses save the day. Clearly the horses are out of date and doomed, but for one final moment the old order still operates. As the husband reminisces, his thoughts of the past and his childhood mingle with his desire that his wife not change his life.

At the end of the play the cast exhorts the audience to shed their clothes and join in onstage. The husband tries to do so but carries his wallet, keys, watch with him. He is further encouraged to shed everything, as actors and audience chant, "Put down your lendings, put down your lendings." Unable to, he redresses and slinks out of the theater. When he finds it snowing outside, he is consoled by the thought of his snow tires. It is significant that he has tried to join his wife. When she auditioned for the part she said,

> There I sat naked in front of these strangers and I felt for the first time in my life that I'd found myself in nakedness. I felt like a new woman, a better woman. To be naked and unashamed in front of strangers was one of the most exciting experiences I've ever had . . . .
>
> ("The Fourth Alarm," p. 646)

Conversely, his thought of snow tires "gave me a sense of security and accomplishment that would have disgusted Ozamanides and his naked court; but I seemed not to have exposed my inhibitions but to have hit on some marvelously practical and obdurate part of myself" ("The Fourth Alarm," p. 649).

The husband is aware of the irrelevance of his thought, yet it represents his stubborn clinging to an old order, one which like the horses, after all, is doomed. He tries the traditional approaches, but fails at trying to join in and fails at trying to leave her. "I asked for a divorce. She said she saw no reason for a divorce. Adultery and cruelty have well marked courses of action but what can a man do when his wife wants to appear naked on the stage?" ("The Fourth Alarm," p. 647). The world has changed for him, leaving him no recourse, no way to change, no way to cope.

II

In the fiction of Cheever and John Updike, the main characters, almost entirely males, confront a bewildering (for them) change in the social order. Their wives, their girlfriends, their female counterparts demand an equality of experience which the males seem unable to understand. Instead, these males retreat to an attitude of nostalgia for a time when, they think, life was simpler and more romantic. Nostalgia tinges the writing of both Cheever and Updike, but the heroes of each realize that they, like the fire department horses, are out of date and doomed.

Such heroes tend to see women as inspiration or even a romantic landscape on which their lives are played out. The main character of Updike's novel *Of the Farm* (1965) says, "My wife is wide, wide-hipped and long-waisted, and, surveyed from above, gives an impression of terrain, of a wealth whose ownership imposes upon my own body a sweet strain of extension; entered, she yields a variety of landscapes."[2] Likewise when Sarah Wapshot in Cheever's *The Wapshot Chronicle* sets up her own store, her husband Leander feels he is betraying his town and all its history which surrounds him. These men are inspired by "their" women, but they are paralyzed by their commitment to traditions which tie them into rigid and inoperable roles.

III

Cheever's fictive world concerns a modern New England, often beset by suburbia and its attendant tawdriness. Though he often writes about strong women, his viewpoint is clearly male, often focusing on men who are unaware their control has been usurped by a woman. These men are motivated by romance, by love and lust. Likewise they hold strong to a tradition of what they feel men should be like and, hence, what a woman should be like. All must support this system of the strong, dignified man, though in Cheever's fiction, it is usually most adamantly grasped by the man who is rapidly losing all dignity. Finally, all is suffused with a sense of nostalgia that the world of romance and dominant men no longer exists.

These concerns can be seen in Cheever's novels *The Wapshot Chronicle* (1957) and *The Wapshot Scandal* (1964) which deal with the Wapshot family of the New England seaport town of St. Botolphs. The rich old eccentric aunt is Honora Wapshot who stands for a traditional sense of right though she is brought down by the U.S. Government for paying no income taxes. Her nephew Leander runs a ferry for tourists until he is ruined when the ship runs aground and his wife Sarah takes up their support, with a gift shop. Their sons Moses and Coverly as much as possible try to break out of the St. Botolphs and heavy Wapshot traditions.

As romance is a yearning for a world in which the imperfection of human love is made perfect, so these characters who think themselves propelled by love find it is lust that moves them. It is rigidness that will not allow them to join the two. For instance,

... Coverly got vehemently to his knees but he was not halfway through his first prayer when the perfume of the woman in the pew ahead of him undid all his mortification and showed him that the literal body of Christ Church was no mighty fortress .... The devil ... urged him to peer down the front of Mrs. Harper's dress, to admire the ankles of the lady in front and to wonder if there was any truth in the rumors about the rector and the boy soprano.

(The Wapshot Chronicle, pp. 64-5.)[3]

A young girl, on the other hand, his counterpart, tries the sex without the love:

I mean it just seems that all I ever heard about was sex when I was growing up. I mean everyone told me it was just marvelous and the end of all my problems and loneliness and everything and so naturally I looked forward to it and then when I was at Allendale I went to this dance with this nice-looking boy and we did it and it didn't stop me from feeling lonely ....

(The Wapshot Chronicle, p. 49)

Dr. Cameron, the director of the missile base where Coverly works in *The Wapshot Scandal*, is one of those Cheever characters who uses sex as a hedge against aging and death:

He was one of those blameless old men who had found that lasciviousness was his best means of clinging to life. In the act of love his heart sent up a percussive beating like a gallows drum in the street, but lewdness was his best sense of forgetfulness, his best way of grappling with the unhappy facts of time. With age his desires had grown more irresistible as his fear of death and corruption mounted.

(The Wapshot Scandal), p. 130)[4]

In this dichotomy of love and lust, men who are attracted to women begin to suspect that they are the enemy, rather than men's counterparts. They love the pure, unphysical woman, but need the companionship of the physical. But to allow the physical woman equal status is to threaten the close fraternity of men that settled the country.

   This fraternity is marked by such defenses as throwing the football around. Leander fulfills his responsibility as a father by teaching his sons "to fell a tree, pluck and dress a chicken, sow, cultivate and harvest, catch a fish, save money, countersink a nail, make cider with a hand press, clean a gun, sail a boat, etc." *(The Wapshot Chronicle*, pp. 53-4). These are symbolic but in the tug of war between mother and father for possession of their children, Sarah gives her son a cookbook. "The sense was not only that he had failed himself and his father by bringing a cookbook to a fishing camp; he had profaned the mysterious rites of virility and had failed whole generations of future Wapshots as well ..." *(The Wapshot Chronicle*, p. 60). Coverly and Moses grow up in such a world and try to escape by moving away, living in the world of commerce, taking wives. They are the transition yet they carry St. Botolphs with them. Before telling a story of a man who urinates down his leg into a chamber pot to avoid bothering his wife with the noise, Coverley tells his New York City psychiatrist:

Well, sir, where I come from, I think it's hard to take much pride in being a man. I mean the women are very powerful. They are kind and they mean very well, but sometimes they get very oppressive. Sometimes you feel as if it wasn't right to be a man.

(The Wapshot Chronicle, p. 126)

   It is certainly difficult to be a man but not because the women are too strong. The women, subject to similar difficulties, seek love, find lust, attempt to help, and fail because they cannot be accepted in such a social order. For instance, Leander is the model of ruined upper class, incapable of earning a living or being practical, but he bases his self-concept on his roles as a *paterfamilias*. He is subsidized by Aunt Honora and allowed to think himself a ship's captain as he ferries tourists in the restored ship *Topaz*. When it runs aground, Honora refuses to fix it. The ship is a symbol of his masculinity as well as connecting him to the history of New England. To have Sarah support the family by turning the refloated ship into a gift shop makes him feel small in front of his town. By failing as a man, he is disappointing his history:

> To have his wife work at all raised for Leander the fine point of sexual prerogatives and having made one great mistake in going into debt to Honora he didn't want to make another .... The question went beyond sexual prerogatives into tradition, for much of what Sarah sold was ornamented with ships at sea and was meant to stir romantic memories of great days of St. Botolphs as a port.
>
> (*The Wapshot Chronicle*, p. 138)

Leander's plaintive cry—"I only want to be esteemed" (p. 204) is preparation for his drowning himself.

Connections between Cheever's life and his fiction have been drawn, especially in the family story of the Wapshot novels. Cheever's father's family was rooted in the New England sea commerce, and when his father's manufacturing business was destroyed in the Depression, his wife supported the family with a gift shop. Cheever has said, "I remained deeply disconcerted by the harm my mother's working did for my father's esteem."[5]

The theme these two novels pursue is one of nostalgia and new experience, characterized by the developing and changing of a family. In *The Wapshot Chronicle*, the remnants of the Wapshots are the spiritual Honora and the fleshly romantic Leander. His sons grow and are pushed out by Honora with the promise of her money if they marry and continue the name. Thus thrust out into the world they are robbed of support from the old order. By the end of *The Wapshot Chronicle*, each son has a wife, though Coverly's is subject to deep depression and often disappears, and Moses' is attracted to him only for sex. In *The Wapshot Scandal*, the story continues but the family is scattered. Leander has drowned himself. His wife Sarah, never a fully drawn character, has died and been dismissed from the narrative. Honora, facing a tax trial, flees to Italy and is brought back, where she starves herself to death.

The twentieth century has caught up with the family and shown them to be out of date and ineffectual. Their saga is a funny episodic one in these two novels, and the reader feels sympathy for characters who seek success and happiness through traditional though obsolete means. The Wapshot sons leave the family but are adrift without the sense of history and custom which alternately inspire and paralyze Leander. Each male character is drawn to a female but finds himself increasingly isolated. Attracted and frightened by the mystery of sex, attracted and frightened by the figure of the strong woman, inspired and paralyzed by the idea of what the woman could do if she had the power to be equal with men, these characters bob in a romantic pool. They wish for a return to a "he-man" existence where the unruly woman never raised her rebellious cry, never sought her own sexual fulfillment (that is, revealed it was lust, too, which motivated her), never grew powerful enough to leave the man alone and powerless. Cheever is not condemning strong women, nor the man who cannot accept them; he is only showing man, wavering between accepting, subduing or retreating. His male characters lost in their romantic ways, do in fact have to retreat, but they rage against their enemies, women, and strive to preserve their dignity.

Much is at stake here and the battle can be a violent, intense one. These men are in the prison of their male thought patterns and think to strike in any way possible. When a homosexual (and homosexuality is a recurring theme in Cheever's fiction) makes a pass at Coverly, he thinks "...it seemed that Pancras had offered him much more than friendship—that he had offered him the subtle means by which we deface and diminish the loveliness of a woman" (*The Wapshot Chronicle*, p. 257). The desperate nature of this struggle becomes apparent when the Cheever man is confined to an all-male society, in his prison novel *Falconer*.

IV

John Updike often covers the same ground as Cheever though he is a generation younger. His novels tend to take place in the locales Updike has lived in, from Pennsylvania to the Massachusetts of many of his later books, where he now lives. His novels all focus on a main male character, usually an adulterous man who is committed to an otherwise stable marriage. This theme of adultery—especially in the context of contemporary American society and contemporary Christianity—is common to most of the books, but is most elaborately described in the novel *Couples* (1968).

Perhaps analogous to Cheever's Wapshot novels are the three Rabbit novels in which Updike follows his hero Harry Angstrom over a twenty year period: *Rabbit, Run* (1960), *Rabbit Redux* (1971) and *Rabbit Is Rich* (1981).

In the first novel Harry Angstrom, known as "Rabbit," is established as a character. He is 26 years old, poorly settled with a pregnant wife and a son Nelson, and working in an uninteresting job as a supermarket demonstrator of the Magi-Peel Kitchen Peeler in Mt. Judge, Pennsylvania. He once enjoyed glory as a high school basketball star, but he feels trapped in his dull marriage to Janice. In this book his main approach to problems is to *run*, with the energy of the adolescent athlete. He runs away from his wife twice in the novel, once from his lover, and from most of his responsibility. The style of *Rabbit, Run* matches the energy of its main character; the story is told in present tense.

Thus Updike sets up the young man who once enjoyed fame and love as a boy and is now facing a problem of the transition to adulthood. As he grows less interested in his wife, sex is connected in his mind with that nostalgia for past glory. He remembers a high school girlfriend:

Mary Ann. Tired and stiff and lazily tough after a game he would find her hanging on the front steps under the school motto and they would walk across mulching wet leaves through white November fog to his father's car and drive to get the heater warmed and park. Her body a branched tree of warm nests yet always this touch of timidity. As if she wasn't sure but he was much bigger, a winner. He came to her as a winner and that's the feeling he's missed since.

(*Rabbit, Run*, p. 198)[6]

Rabbit uses this image to judge his home life and his wife, wishing she could be his girl again. By dint of his being a man, he feels he is free to run in search of what he feels he has lost. Though irresponsible, he brings great power to people, to renew their self-worth if not his. When he takes a part-time job to help a widow work her garden, she says,

You kept me alive, Harry; it's the truth; you did. All winter I was fighting the grave and then in April I looked out the window and here was this tall young man burning my old stalks and I knew life hadn't left me. That's what you have, Harry: life. It's a strange gift and I don't know how we're supposed to use it but it's the only gift we get and it's a good one.

(*Rabbit, Run*, p.224)

Likewise when he takes up with Ruth Leonard, a sometime prostitute, he is able to bring to her a sense of worthiness and grace in sex:

God she used to hate them with their wet mouths and little hands but when she had it with Harry she kind of forgave them all, it was only half their fault, they were a kind of wall she kept battering against because she knew there was something there and all of a sudden with Harry there it was and it made everything that had gone before seem pretty unreal.

(*Rabbit, Run*, p.146)

In some ways, Janice Angstrom his wife, on the other hand, is an extreme though less self-aware version of Rabbit; while he has the freedom to act and to escape, she as a mother can merely remain with her children. Her family, the Springers, run a successful car agency and she was a spoiled only child, while Harry's family is blue collar. She is unimaginative, a child Harry sees as needing protection, and she constantly watches television, often the Mickey Mouse Club. She was pregnant when they married and this contributes to Rabbit's sense of confinement. Abandoned by him, she drinks and in the novel's most powerful scene, she accidently drowns their newborn baby.

Rabbit in *Rabbit, Run* is a man who cannot deal with adulthood and so falls back on nostalgia for an earlier, simpler glory. This sense of loss he blames on the woman who he feels should make him feel the way Ruth does, "that she is so much his friend in this search" (p. 84). Since he also runs from the pregnant Ruth at the end, Rabbit is clearly no hero. But he does possess that unstoppable energy to act, as impulsively and instinctively as a rabbit.

Ten years later in *Rabbit Redux* Rabbit has lost much of his energy but is still fighting the same battles; this time, however, it is his wife who has the affair and moves out. Rabbit at 36 is "a pale tall man going fat" (*Rabbit Redux*, p. 57).[7] Moved to the suburbs and laid off from his job as a linotypist, he is here much touched by the events of the outside world in 1969. *Rabbit Redux* is Updike's most topical book, full of references to and evidence of the Vietnam war and its protest, space flights, race riots, drugs, and the younger generation's views on sex. In fact when Janice leaves, all these problems move into the house with Harry and his son Nelson. He takes in a Black revolutionary named Skeeter Farnsworth and an eighteen year old white girl, Jill, who becomes his mistress. These two indoctrinate him into the words and thoughts that he fears and that he hopes will help him to understand why the world is changing so radically.

Janice is a much stronger character in this book, if not so closely observed as Rabbit. Like the wife in Cheever's "The Fourth Alarm," she is motivated by her own sense of dissatisfaction. Partly because he is unsure where to place the blame for his daughter's drowning ten years before and partly because he fears his own death, Rabbit is uneasy in making love with his wife. He wonders, "Should he have let her have another to replace the one that died? Maybe that was the mistake. It had all seemed like a pit to him then, her womb and the grave, sex and death, he had fled her ... as a tiger's mouth" (*Rabbit Redux*, p. 27). In the old days Rabbit's method was not questing but merely running off; here his wife clearly possesses the sense of what she is running toward. She tells him, "I'm searching for a valid identity and I suggest you do the same" (p. 104). Perhaps he found his identity too soon and is locked into the adolescent ideal. Perhaps his desperation is caused by the feeling that he will always be behind, specifically in his dealings with love and sex and his family. In an earlier context, Janice says of her husband and the events between *Rabbit, Run* and *Rabbit Redux*, "Maybe he came back to me, to Nelson and me, for the old-fashioned reasons, and wants to live an old-fashioned life, but nobody does that any more, and he feels it. He put his life into rules he feels melting away now. I mean, I know he thinks he's missing something" (p. 53).

There is evidence in the novel to suggest that Updike sees the times as transitional for men. Josephine Hendin has written, "Updike is the first writer since D.H. Lawrence to define maleness as sexual and economic responsibility for women, and to connect the decline of society with the decline of masculinity."[8] When Harry watches a Black couple on a television show, he fantasizes about the stereotypic Black male sexual prowess: ". . . that's why white women need them, white men too quick about it. Have to get on with the job, making America great" (p. 18). Jill, the lover who is half his age and who accidentally calls him "Daddy," analyzes him in an evening discussion:

We all agree, I think, that your problem is that you've never been given a chance to formulate your views. Because of the competitive American context, you've had to convert everything into action too rapidly. Your life has no reflective content; it's all instinct, and when your instincts let you down, you have nothing to trust. That's what makes you cynical.

(*Rabbit Redux*, p. 228)

Rabbit himself is removed from this context when a reactionary neighbor, suspicious of his houseguests, burns down his house. Jill is killed, Skeeter flees, and Rabbit and Janice are rejoined.

The time is long past when in fact the American man had to use his energy settling the country and protecting his wife and family from attack by hostile natives and nature. Still with no arena for testing—as the basketball court provided—he has no way to prove his worth. The man is no longer the ruler of his family and Rabbit has lost faith in his ability to act and to move. Following "rules he feels melting away," Rabbit is paralyzed.

By becoming the manager of the Toyota dealership when Janice's father dies, Rabbit does succeed in the "competitive American context" in *Rabbit Is Rich*. He and Janice live in a world made hospitable by a country club, a son in college, a trip to the Caribbean. Both have settled down into a routine of success and drinking; any rebellious energy is channeled into an uncharacteristic episode of partner-swapping while on vacation at the end of the novel. The book communicates the sense that Rabbit has lived too long in a house of women, his mother-in-law's house, and it is still easy for him to blame his dissatisfaction on Janice. "It is her fault; at every turn she has been a wall to his freedom" (p. 42)[9] Settled into inaction, it is Rabbit's task to communicate to his son Nelson that he too once felt the rebelliousness and need to run that his son does.

Again the Updike man confronts woman as the friendly enemy, that person who ties you down with children and homes, who makes you work at boring jobs and do unsavory things to earn money. In all this, with little understanding, Rabbit still harbors the suspicion that he is being kept out, that women are less unhappy than he; he expresses it appropriately in a ball-game metaphor:

It is as when he was a boy in grade school, and there seemed to be a secret everywhere, flickering up and down the aisles, bouncing around like the playground ball at recess, and he could not get his hands on it, the girls were keeping it from him, they were too quick.

(*Rabbit Is Rich*, pp. 127-8)

This dream-like image intrudes on that basketball glory that once brought Rabbit his reinforcement; even that recedes in the distance of time, but it cannot be obliterated. It is Rabbit's equivalent to the American settling the country. And it is shown here to be a handicap. A girl Rabbit suspects is his long-separated child by Ruth Leonard tells Nelson at a party, "Some mothers ... think girls should be quiet and smart. Mine says women get more out of life. With men, it's if you don't win every time, you're nothing" (p. 328).

If this is a true pattern, it is one repeated in the next generation, for it is Nelson who has the energy to run in the third novel. He arrives from college at the Springer-Angstrom house and is soon joined by his pregnant fiancee. He marries, is pressured to return to college, tries to fit in with his father at the car lot. Finally, like the Rabbit of twenty years before, he bolts and runs. Before he goes, he argues with his father about returning to college. Rabbit is surprised he wants to stay in Mt. Judge:

"In my days kids *wanted* to get out in the world. We were scared but not so scared we kept running back to Mama. And Grandmama. What're you going to do when you run out of women to tell you what to do?"
"Same thing you'll do. Drop dead."

(*Rabbit Is Rich*, p. 208)

It is left for Nelson to rediscover the world he can't imagine his 46 year old father ever knew. He feels trapped by the circumstances of being a father and a husband and finds he's married to the enemy. He echoes Rabbit when he wonders, "Why can't a woman just be your friend, even with the sex? Why do you have to keep dealing with all this ego, giving back hurt just to defend yourself?" (p. 336). Like Rabbit, he disappears and the reader has every expectation he'll return and settle into that confused, uneasy truce that his father and mother share.

Updike describes the American man set securely in the context of marriage, a marriage that is rebelled against and is the focus of the husband's dissatisfaction. Since man has no longer to prove himself in hand-to-hand combat or against the elements, he adventures in adultery, in seeking love outside his marriage. It is even possible to institutionalize and sanction this, as the Angstroms have done with the spouse-swapping in *Rabbit Is Rich*. Because the author focuses so heavily on the male, his affairs seem silly, tawdry, routine—while his wife's usually take place out of the reader's view and therefore appear less silly and more sympathetic.

His drive to win, to score, makes man successful on the basketball court but makes him tragically unsuccessful in the relations between the sexes. He wishes to find a lover who will be the admiring friend he remembers from locker room days, but he puts his spouse in an adversary position and fights and fights. In Updike's fiction, the mechanism for rebelling, for continuing the battle and the testing is adultery. The man, lost and feeling useless without his daily proving of himself, is doomed to yearn with nostalgia for his youth, when such competition made him seem invincible and worthy.

V

Since the male characters in the books of these two writers live in such contention with their female counterparts it would seem natural to examine them in an environment free, or nearly free, of women, which is what Cheever does in *Falconer* (1977) and Updike in *A Month of Sundays* (1975). In the first the ex-professor Ezekiel Farragut is imprisoned in Falconer Correctional Facility for murdering his brother. In *A Month of Sundays*, the Rev. Thomas Marshfield, caught having affairs with several of his female parishioners, is sent to a desert retreat by his bishop. Each must deal with the imprisonment his character forces on him in the outside world.

Like the Wapshots, Farragut remembers a family with a rich father who had lost his money and had been supported by a mother who, among other things, pumped gasoline. "Farragut's father had taken him fishing in the wilderness and had taught him to climb high mountains, but when he had discharged these responsibilities he neglected his son and spent most of his time tacking around Travertine harbor in a little catboat" (*Falconer*, p. 58).[10] Farragut is married to a strong, unpleasant woman, Marcia, who taunts him on her visits to the prison. Like most of the marriages described, theirs is not happy: "It was partly because we stopped doing things together" (p. 24). As a defense mechanism, of course, separating himself emotionally from this wife is a natural consequence of incarceration. But with Farragut it is merely a continuation of the separation he naturally felt outside and blamed not on himself but on the changing of the times: "Marcia's thrust for independence was not, he knew, the burden of his company but the burden of history" (p. 27). Here he shifts the responsibility away from his own disinterest and neglect.

As in all of Cheever's books, the twin attractions of love and lust are a necessity to Farragut, and he with great fear and misgiving turns to homosexuality in the prison system. Desiring human contact, it is his only alternative. Such a move, however, threatens and causes him to question his masculine identity. Loving a man, he feels, robs him of his due:

But why did he long so for Jody when he had often thought that it was his role in life to possess the most beautiful women? Women possessed the greatest and the most rewarding mysteriousness. They were approached in darkness and sometimes, but not always, possessed in darkness. They were an essence, fortified and besieged, worth conquering and, once conquered, flowing with spoils.

(Falconer, p. 100)

He receives his comeuppance in loving the aggressive inmate Jody who uses him as he might use a woman on the outside. And, "... there was, since Jody was a man, the danger that Farragut might be in love with himself" (pp. 102-103). The key to his masculine identity is that Farragut is unable to see beyond himself and like other Cheever characters views women only as extensions of himself, that ideal to love and ignore, and that nether side to lust after and abandon. Marcia challenges him with his inability to deal with the actual woman:

Do you still dream about your blonde? You do, of course; that I can easily see. Don't you understand that she never existed, Zeke, and that she never will? Oh, I can see by the way you hold your head that you still dream about that blonde who never menstruated or shaved her legs or challenged anything you said or did.

(Falconer, p.121)

Farragut's problem is that while he will never meet that woman he can likewise not be satisfied with the woman who is real, who is capable of supporting him and being his equal.

Farragut escapes Falconer with the time-honored trick of substituting himself for the body of an inmate who has died. Once outside he rejoices at rising from the dead and walks, buoyed with the sense of love and friendship he has learned from the inmates inside. The novel ends positively but there is little to suggest he has escaped the prison of his thinking. His history is full of his father and his mother, his brother and his wife; it is harder to escape the tradition that tracks him.

VI

With a minister as a main character, it is natural that ethical and theological questions arise in Updike's *A Month of Sundays.* Thomas Marshfield, 41, leads a middle-class Protestant church in New England. As a child, he thought of God as being father-like and associated him with the joinery and carpentry of the church building. Likewise God also came to him in the singing and organ music of the church service. His mother and his first extramarital lover are church organists and he follows his father's vocation as minister. As a young seminarian, Marshfield seduces the daughter of his ethics professor, his wife-to-be Joan.

After almost twenty years of marriage, life slows to a natural routine. He complains, "under my good wife's administration sex had become a solemn, once-a-week business ritualized and worrisomely hushed" (*A*

Month of Sundays, p. 34).[11] He turns his attention outward, first having an affair with the organist Alicia Crick in an act of self-discovery. He finds "Alicia in bed was a revelation. At last I confronted as in an ecstatic mirror my own sexual demon" (p. 33). When he moves on she has an affair with the sexton Bork, and when this ends both men casually sack her. Glib, Marshfield is adept at justifying himself in clerical terms. He then turns to a deacon's wife and several other women of troubled marriages who come to him for counseling. When he is exposed, his bishop expels him to a retreat for errant churchmen for a month.

Here, in a womb-like complex of buildings in the desert he must follow a regimen which includes writing every morning until noon, at which time the bar opens and Marshfield plays golf and cards with the other internees: traditional masculine activities. The product of his writing every day for a month is the thirty-one chapters which comprise *A Month of Sundays*. These writings make a strange justification for adultery, which he calls "our inherent condition" (p. 44). This condition is a basis for life, as he sees it, and is even the basis for marriage: "Verily, the sacrament of marriage, as instituted in its adamant impossibility by our Saviour, exists but as a precondition for the sacrament of adultery" (p. 47). Marshfield reiterates the theme that here, in striving against the limits of marriage and infidelity, against the structures of society and God, is the last testing place for men:

Wherein does the modern American man recover his sense of worth, not as dogged breadwinner and economic integer, but as romantic minister and phallic knight, as personage, embodiment, and hero? In adultery.

(*A Month of Sundays*, p. 46)

Only one woman exists in this environment, and true to his nature he sets about seducing her, the stern proprietress of the retreat, Ms. Prynne. Suspecting she is reading his daily writing, he tries to win her through his words. His work is a confession and in addressing her as "Ideal Reader," he seeks her as he seeks God, someone to save him. In other words, he wants to meet a woman whom he can finally join as an angel or as a partner. When at last his term is up and he succeeds with Prynne (the ending is ambiguous), the experience is expressed in terms of prayer and revelation:

What is it, this human contact, this blank-browed thing we do for one another? There was a moment, when I entered you, and was big, and you were entirely wet, when you could not have seen yourself, when your eyes were all for another, looking up into mine, with an expression without a name, of entry and alarm, and of salutation. I pray my own face, a stranger to me, saluted you in turn.

(*A Month of Sundays*, p.228)

Like Farragut, Marshfield is at the point of returning to the world and he seems to have reached a breakthrough in which this woman has for the first time merged his ideas of the real and the ideal.

VII

Males in the fiction of Cheever and Updike often see their women as dependent. When they find themselves in need of protection and support they cling to the illusion of dominance all the harder. Such is Farragut's "burden of history" which, rightly or wrongly, projects the problem as the inheritance from the time when society and the environment required the strong impulsive man. The mechanism for passing the order is from father to son, through the Wapshots, from Rabbit to Nelson. Yet even when these characters see they are on the edge of a change, or on the edge of extinction, they cannot resist following their inner imperative, that "fourth alarm."

Notes

[1] John Cheever, "The Fourth Alarm," in *The Stories of John Cheever* (New York: Knopf, 1978), pp. 645-649. "The Fourth Alarm" first appeared in *Esquire*, April 1970.

[2] John Updike, *Of the Farm* (New York: Knopf, 1965), p. 46.

[3] John Cheever, *The Wapshot Chronicle* (New York: Harper & Brothers, 1957).

[4] John Cheever, *The Wapshot Scandal* (New York: Harper and Row, Perenniel Library Edition, 1964, 1973).

[5] Lynne Waldeland, *John Cheever* (Boston, Twayne, 1979), p. 17.

[6] John Updike, *Rabbit, Run* (New York: Knopf, 1960).

[7] John Updike, *Rabbit Redux* (New York: Knopf, 1971).

[8] Josephine Hendin, *Vulnerable People: A View of American Fiction Since 1945* (New York: Oxford, 1978), p. 89.

[9] John Updike, *Rabbit Is Rich* (New York: Knopf, 1981).

[10] John Cheever, *Falconer* (New York: Knopf, 1977).

[11] John Updike, *A Month of Sundays* (New York: Knopf, 1975).

Gender and Genre

Judith Spector

Science Fiction and the Sex War: A Womb of One's Own

MARY SHELLEY IS REGARDED by many science fiction aficianados[1] as the "mother" of the genre which, until the relatively recent feminist involvement,[2] was notably hostile toward women. Ambivalence toward one's mother, ambivalence marked by hatred, would not appear anomalous within any cultural context touched by the insights of Freud; yet in the case of Shelley and the subsequent traditions of science fiction, we may have discovered an Oedipal conflict more fundamental than a superficial inquiry might reveal.

Shelley's *Frankenstein*[3] explicitly concerns itself with the question of the creation of life through artificial means. Science fiction has subsequently concerned itself with related problems of an existential character ever since, in a way which suggests a reaction to its literary "mother." Deeply conservative, *Frankenstein* warns the reader that Victor Frankenstein's unnatural attempt to create life is an act of arrogance punishable by the deaths of Frankenstein's beloved family and friends, and by his own eternal guilt. There is some evidence that Shelley herself may have been employing the "creation of life" motif as a metaphor for man's—and her own disguised—involvement with work, with his frenzied and sublimated passion to create a cultural "baby." She has Victor Frankenstein warn his listener within the work, and his reader without, that an all-consuming pursuit of intellectual creativity is "Unlawful." He then goes on to describe his state of mind during his endeavors:

But my enthusiasm was checked by my anxiety, and I appeared rather like one doomed by slavery to toil in the mines, or any other unwholesome trade than an artist occupied by his favorite employment. Every night I was oppressed by a slow fever, and I became nervous to a most painful degree; the fall of a leaf startled me, and I shunned my fellow creatures as if I had been guilty of a crime.

(*Frankenstein*, p. 41)

Frankenstein is described not as a scientist, but as a guilty artist, and his crime is a social one. These facts have led more than one critic to

163

hypothesize that Shelley herself may have had a great deal of guilt over her own artistic pursuits, presumably unsuitable or "unnatural" for a woman,[4] and over the death of her actual babies before and during the period of time in which *Frankenstein* was written.[5] But the fact remains that she founded a genre which was to continue a preoccupation with the creation, continuation, variation and destruction of life through "unnatural"—scientific, technological and intellectual—means. She stated her own question about the suitability of artistic creation as an activity for women as a question about the suitability of a man's involvement in the creation of physical life through the intellect. Theoretically, it would be as unsuitable for a man to create a "baby," as it would be for a woman to create a work of art. Hence, Victor Frankenstein produces a "monster."

The male science fiction writers who followed Shelley, however, were to regard as monstrous only Shelley's attempt to delineate the male artist's proper endeavors. Many of these writers were quick to appropriate "mental motherhood" as their rightful and logical domain. They were to fight for the privilege of cultural sublimation, and to repudiate not just Mary Shelley as the "mother" of science fiction, but all mothers and women as well.

In the course of this claiming of science fiction as a genre by, for and about men of action, male authors have had some assistance from Freudian and Jungian psychology. Freud enables us to see the creation of culture and art as a masculine compensatory activity in lieu of woman's physical procreative function;[6] Jung declares that Logos or intellect is man's true function, and leaves Eros and its concomitant procreative activities to woman.[7] Understood prescriptively, both Freud and Jung send Mary Shelley and other women writers back to their nurseries to fulfill themselves through anatomy and Eros and to avoid the terrible guilt which might ensue should they pursue intellectual creativity to the exclusion of all else.

As soon as women are relegated to physical procreativity, men are free to claim intellectual creativity as their equal and opposite right. That claim is precisely what one male science fiction writer, Arthur C. Clarke, has contributed to the ongoing sex war in which he declares the male to be a superior creator and claims that "mental motherhood" must be a male preserve. Here again, we may draw upon psychology to identify the phenomenon. But this time we find that if Freud restricts the woman to her biological destiny, he also helps the feminist critic to understand the male science fiction writer's insecurities. Clarke's creation of "Star-Child," a fetus who rules outer space in *2001*,[8] may be symptomatic of Clarke's own womb envy.[9] If that theory does not seem suitable, we can assess Star-Child as part of a hero myth which Clarke has developed in response to anxieties related to birth trauma.[10] In either case, the hostility to the mother is evident in his suppression and/or elimination of women in the novel. The hostility, of course, also manifests itself in his choice of creation. He is not content to create culture or art within the novel, but insists upon bringing into being an actual child born of intellect, the supposedly "male" force. Victor Frankenstein's failure becomes for Clarke a function of Shelley's gender, and women as "mothers," as creators, are to be feared, punished or eliminated.

The first mother we encounter in *2001* is among the "man-apes," a pitiful and unenlightened species struggling with survival and led by Moon-Watcher, the prototypical hero who will save his tribe. The relationship between Moon-Watcher and the mother is clear:

> The two babies were already whimpering for food, but became silent when Moon-Watcher snarled at them. One of the mothers, defending the infant she could not properly feed, gave him an angry growl in return; he lacked the energy even to cuff her for her presumption.
>
> (*2001*, p.14)

The mother is inadequate as a source of nourishment for her infant, and her attitude toward the male in her implied criticism of his behavior to her infant is labelled "presumption." The novel (and film) go on to state that the salvation and nurture of the proto-human race will be through Moon-Watcher and will be explicitly phallic. Moon-Watcher himself contains the two elements necessary to human enlightenment—physical strength and intellect:

> Among his kind, Moon-Watcher was almost a giant. He was nearly five feet high, and though badly undernourished weighed over a hundred pounds. His hairy, muscular body was halfway between man and ape. The forehead was low, and there were ridges over the eye sockets, yet he unmistakably held in his genes the promise of humanity. As he looked out upon the hostile world of the Pleistocene, there was already something in his gaze beyond the capacity of any ape.
>
> (*2001*, p. 14)

A marvelous specimen of "macho" among the apes, Moon-Watcher only needs to be touched by the magic phallus, a crystalline monolith sent by intelligence beyond the Earth to teach proto-man:

> It was a rectangular slab, three times his height but narrow enough to span with his arms, and it was made of some completely transparent material; indeed, it was not easy to see except when the rising sun glinted on its edges.
>
> (*2001*, p. 19)

The monolith represents literal enlightenment; it teaches Moon-Watcher to visualize a better life, and to develop his phallic powers. These are first experienced by Moon-Watcher when he recognizes his first tool, which is, appropriately, "about six inches long":

> It was a heavy, pointed stone about six inches long, and though it did not fit his hand perfectly, it would do. As he swung his hand around, puzzed by its suddenly increased weight, he felt a pleasing sense of power and authority. He started to move toward the nearest pig.
>
> (*2001*, p. 26)

The use of tools, at least insofar as Clarke describes it, is primarily the development of weaponry in order to promote the killing of other carnivores and the employment of teeth upon meat. The phallic functions within this process of "enlightenment" and evolution are unmistakable. Clarke writes of man in the final phases of this evolutionary process:

> The spear, the bow, the gun, and finally the guided missile had given him weapons of infinite range and all but infinite power.
>
> Without those weapons, often though he had used them against himself, Man would never have conquered his world. Into them he had put his heart and soul, and for ages they had served him well.
>
> (*2001*, p. 37)

The weapons, however, become a danger to man's survival, and, at this point, Clarke must decide where to go beyond his intense phallic identification. The problem is that there isn't anywhere that is acceptable. Nor is a true regression to the primal state feasible, since mothers are still perceived with anger.

Clarke decides to eliminate the human mother, and to separate his hero, the descendant of Moon-Watcher, from "mother" Earth. In so doing, Clarke responds to the rivalry and hostility he feels relative to the primal state, by depicting the regression of his hero as a trip into the future rather than the past, and by depicting the phallus as a womb-like receptacle. These two features of dreams of rebirth are fairly common,[11] but the insistence upon the "mother" as a masculine force is an element which enhances the artist's concept of himself as the supreme creator and which allows Clarke to create, as well, a "masculine" rebirth. These concepts will become clearer in the course of our explication.

The first stage of Clarke's revision of biology involves the eradication of mothers. He shows us the male scientist, Heywood Floyd, on a trip to the moon. Floyd leaves "mother" Earth, receives a "baptism of space" (p. 42), and feels an elation which changes to depression:

> The mood passed swiftly, as he suddenly realized that he was leaving Earth, and everything he had ever loved. Down there were his three children, motherless since his wife had taken that fatal flight to Europe ten years ago. (p. 46)

The scientist's physical children are now "motherless," and we will see that the trip into extended "outer space" is undertaken not by Floyd but by his successor in the novel, the astronaut Dave Bowman, who will convert "outer space" to the space of the primal situation. Outer space will become the masculine equivalent of the inner space of the womb, and the source of life will be the intellect (masculine force) of the extraterrestrials.

Not only do we not require women as mothers for this regression-as-progress and subsequent rebirth fantasy; women are not tolerated as other than inferior creatures who exist for man's pleasure, but not for his procreation. Significantly, when the stewardess offers Dr. Floyd some coffee or tea on his space flight, he reacts:

> "No thank you," he smiled. He always felt like a baby when he had to suck at one of those plastic drinking tubes.
> The stewardess was still hovering anxiously around him as he popped open his briefcase and prepared to remove his papers. (p. 48)

Floyd refuses to acknowledge any of the maternal aspects of woman as necessary to him, and he separates out her functions which allow her to be sexually alluring. On his next flight he appreciates a "charming little stewardess":

> As Floyd quickly discovered, she came from Bali, and had carried beyond the atmosphere some of the grace and mystery of that still largely unspoiled island. One of his strangest, and most enchanting, memories of the entire trip was her zero-gravity demonstration of some classical Balinese dance movements, with the lovely, blue-green crescent of the waning Earth as a backdrop. (p. 58)

The character depreciates the value of women by perceiving them as inferiors. They are "little"; they are subservient; they are preferably from cultures "unspoiled" by modern civilization. The antagonism beneath the surface is not very well disguised, and it is a common observation that superficial contempt for women may reveal fear beneath the surface.[12] Even on the moon base where all personnel are trained and transported at a cost of $100,000 per person (p. 63), Floyd manages to find himself "back in the familiar environment of typewriters, office computers, girl assistants, wall charts, and ringing telephones" (p. 65). Floyd demonstrates that he doesn't need reassurance or assistance from girls when, on the space shuttle, amid strange surroundings and sensations, he manages to say "to himself, firmly and successfully; Go to sleep, boy. This is just an ordinary shuttle" (p. 59).

Though the incident is amusing, we must move away from Floyd's attempt to be his own mother if we are to encounter that phenomenon on a large scale. Once we move into the secret space flight to Jupiter, we are in the company of astronauts who have dispensed with females altogether and who are content to obtain "adequate, though hardly glamorous, substitutes" from "the ship's pharmacopoeia" (p. 104). Via the vision screen on the space ship, we see a tearful Mrs. Poole wishing her son a happy birthday, as the chapter entitled "Birthday Party" begins. What follows this separation through the good-byes on the screen is Frank Poole's permanent separation from Mrs. Poole and "mother" Earth as Poole is killed in space.

Clarke explains the episode with some introductory information about the space pods which will lead to Poole's unfortunate accident. We are told that these pods within the ship have been given female names, "perhaps in recognition of the fact that their personalities were sometimes slightly unpredictable" (p. 124). When Poole goes out into space to consider a minor repair to the ship, he is attached to "Betty" by an umbilical cord. "She" is not, however, under his sole control:

> There was one thing more to do before he left the pod. He switched over from manual to remote operation, putting Betty now under control of Hal. It was a standard safety precaution; though he was still secured to Betty by an immensely strong spring-loaded cord little thicker than cotton, even the best safety lines had been known to fail. He would look a fool if he needed his vehicle—and was unable to call it to his assistance by passing instructions to Hal. (p. 127)

Two things are very clear here: Betty is a mother figure who literally means life to Frank Poole; and Betty is not under Frank Poole's control. Clarke may well be warning his readers that a fellow just can't trust his mother. She's as unpredictable as any other vehicle, and as a human being her preference may be directed toward another man rather than oneself. In Poole's case, the results are tragic. On a subsequent trip with the pod, Betty runs him down:

> At the moment of impact, Betty was still moving quite slowly; she had not been built for high accelerations. But even at a mere ten miles an hour, half a ton of mass can be very lethal, on Earth or in space .... (p. 141)

Frank Poole, dead within his spacesuit and still attached to Betty, drifts off into space, accompanied by the description: "The pod and its satellite had vanished among the stars" (p. 142).

It is true that Betty was acting on Hal's orders rather than on Poole's. So much for the reliability of maternal preferences. However, Hal himself hearkens back to Victor Frankenstein's creations: Hal is a monster computer created by man. Clarke informs us of Hal's origins:

> Whatever way it worked, the final result was a machine intelligence that could produce—some philosophers still preferred to use the word "mimic"—most of the activities of the human brain, and with far greater speed and reliability. It was

extremely expensive, and only a few units of the HAL 9000 series had yet been built;
but the old jest that it would always be easier to make organic brains by unskilled
labor was beginning to sound a little hollow. (*2001, p. 96*)

Hal is a brain and his creation through "skilled" (intelligence) versus
"unskilled" (physical procreativity) labor is clearly documented. The
problem with Hal is that he is tainted by the duplicity of his creators who
ask him to conceal the purpose of the space flight from the astronauts.
Clarke describe's Hal's internal conflict:

Deliberate error was unthinkable. Even the concealment of truth filled him
with a sense of imperfection, of wrongness—of what, in a human being, would
have been called guilt. For like his makers, Hal had been created innocent; but, all
too soon, a snake had entered his electronic Eden. (*2001*, p. 148)

Hal is not free from Original Sin because he carries within him the
need for reinforcement through relationships with human beings. The
component of Eros, his need to save face with his colleagues, drives Hal to
madness and murder. He is the technological monster Clarke creates in
deference to Frankenstein's traditional failure; however, Clarke as author
will overcome his creative limitations when human Eros is eliminated and
pure Logos gains supremacy within Dave Bowman, the remaining
astronaut. Bowman, alone on the ship but for Hal, is in danger:

He was alone in an airless, partially disabled ship, all communication with
Earth cut off. There was not another human being within half a billion miles.
And yet, in one very real sense, he was *not* alone. Before he could be safe, he
must be lonelier still. (*2001*, p. 153)

Human relationships engender possibilities of treachery, rejection
and deceit. Bowman quickly pulls Hal's "ego-reinforcement" and "auto-
intellection" units, while he, Bowman, thinks to himself, "I am destroying
the only conscious creature in my universe. But it has to be done, if I am
ever to regain control of the ship" (p. 156).

David Bowman must make his trip into the vastness of space alone as
the hero who, according to Clarke's masculine version of the birth journey,
will be the son of pure intellect, free of mother, free of Earth, free of
relationship. Bowman must also free himself of matter, eventually, in
order to merge with the sort of God which Clarke envisions—pure
intellect, Logos, the male creator, and perhaps the male artist himself.

This rebirth, or ritual anti-birth, depending on one's perspective,
begins with Bowman's approach to Saturn and its moons and his sighting
of a gigantic phallic monolith on Japetus, a monolith "at least a mile
high" (p. 183). His journey has been engineered as long ago as Moon-
Watcher's time by the "lords of the galaxy," purely intellectual creatures

who have exceeded the limits of matter and are "beyond the reach of time" (p. 186). In order to become as they, he leaves his ship by means of a space pod and travels toward the monolith, which, he discovers, is a hollow shaft which can "turn inside out":

> That was happening to this huge, apparently solid structure. Impossibly, incredibly, it was no longer a monolith rearing high above a flat plain. What had seemed to be its roof had dropped away to infinite depths; for one dizzy moment, he seemed to be looking down into a vertical shaft—a rectangular duct which defied the laws of perspective, for its size did not decrease with distance . . . . (*2001*, p. 190)

Bowman exclaims, "The thing's hollow—it goes on forever—and oh my God—it's *full of stars!* (p. 191) and finds himself "dropping vertically down a huge rectangular shaft, several thousand feet deep" (p. 195).

Bruno Bettelheim and countless others have called attention to childish and sometimes willful misinterpretations of the penis as a vagina turned inside out, particularly in terms of masculine envy of the female organ.[13] More significantly, Bettelheim speaks of adolescent male puberty rites as ritual rebirths designed to free the emerging adult male from female domination:

Certain psychoanalytically oriented authors have gone further in stressing separation, claiming that the purpose of the ceremonies is to sever the Oedipal ties. Laubscher, for example, says that in order to pass from the childhood phase of female dominance into the second phase of male dominance and control the boy must experience a psychological rebirth into the world of men, severing all his attachments to the mother.

(*Symbolic Wounds*, p. 119)

In the context of the preceding statement, we may indeed see Bowman's transformational rebirth as an escape from Oedipal ties. He is now free of "mother" Earth, and of his human mother, and he is within the jurisdiction of the magical phallus of the monolith which will direct his further evolution into "outer" rather than "inner" space.

Even when Bowman emerges from the shaft of the monolith, he finds himself in space, and is briefly enclosed only by the walls of an illusion provided for his comfort as he makes the transition from man to superman. As Bowman drops toward a star, he finds himself enclosed first by "walls of some material like smoked glass" which suggest that the crystalline monolith has never left him, and then by—a hotel room! Clarke writes, "The space pod was resting on the polished floor of an elegant, anonymous hotel suite that might have been in any large city on Earth" (p. 208). Bowman emerges from the pod, to leave its protection forever, and goes into the room, where, after eating and showering, he climbs into bed to sleep "for the last time" (p. 215). This manufactured "womb" setting, complete with fear of sleep as death,[14] and provided by the courtesy of the logical forces, is apparently furnished in no-nonsense Howard Johnson style. At any rate, it allows Bowman to regress comfortably "down the corridors of time, being drained of knowledge and experience as he swept back toward his childhood" (p. 216):

> Now, at last the headlong regression was slackening; the wells of memory were nearly dry. Time flowed more and more sluggishly, approaching a moment of stasis—as a swinging pendulum, at the limit of its arc, seems frozen for one eternal instant, before the next cycle begins.
>
> The timeless instant passed; the machine reversed its swing. In an empty room, floating amid the fires of a double star twenty thousand light-years from Earth, a baby opened its eyes and began to cry. (*2001*, p. 217)

Bowman actually becomes a baby—a space fetus who represents the ultimate evolution of man away from female influence, away from the physical realm and physical modes of reproduction. If women possess an "inner space" and the power to procreate physically, Clarke appropriates intellectual procreativity and all of "outer space." His child is born of evolving Logos, a masculine being who has transcended the progressive forces of physical weaponry (as we shall see) and who is himself now a part of the purely phallic "monolithic" race of the extraterrestrials. Appropriately, the first entity which the space fetus perceives is the magic phallus: "A ghostly, glimmering rectangle had formed in the empty air" (p. 217). The object attracts the interest of the child which was once David Bowman:

> With eyes that already held more than human intentness, the baby stared into the depths of the crystal monolith, seeing—but not yet understanding—the mysteries that lay beyond. It knew that it had come home, that here was the origin of many races besides its own; but it knew also that it could not stay. Beyond this moment lay another birth, stranger than any in the past. (*2001*, p. 218)

The baby is "born" as "the protective walls [fade] back into the nonexistence from which they had briefly emerged" and

> the metal and plastic of the forgotten space pod, and the clothing once worn by an entity who had called himself David Bowman, flashed into flame. The last links with Earth were gone, resolved back into their component atoms. (*2001*, p. 218)

The destruction of any vestigial womb-like enclosures is passionately accomplished in a flash of flame. All that remains to the Star-Child is his newly acquired total domination of "mother" Earth.

Guided by the magic phallus, the crystal monolith representing the ultimate power of Logos, we are told that Star-Child:

put forth his will, and the circling megatons flowered in a silent detonation that brought a brief, false dawn to half the sleeping globe.

Then he waited, marshaling his thoughts and brooding over his still untested powers. For though he was master of the world, he was not quite sure what to do next. (*2001*, p. 221)

Whether his mastery of the world has involved the destruction of the human race or merely the destruction of its atomic weapons remains a matter of lively debate among Clarke's fans. We are only told for certain that Star-Child has detonated "the circling megatons" of the Earth. Although Clarke thus veils his conclusion in ambiguity, the clarity of Star-Child's destructive vengeance against all of Eros nevertheless shines through. Before Star-Child detonates the weapons, we are told that "history as men knew it would be drawing to a close" (p. 221). Furthermore, Star-Child's act parallels, word for word, Moon-Watcher's murder through weaponry of another ape-man. We are told of both Moon-Watcher and Star-Child: "Now he was master of the world, and he was not quite sure what to do next" (pp. 34 and 221). Both creatures, at that point, have vented their infantile rage against relationship, and against the primal mother.

However it is questionable whether such venting of hostilities is therapeutic at all, or whether it is even the point of the exercise. An earlier work by Clarke, *Childhood's End*,[15] has mentally advanced forces from space remove children from their parents. The children then coalesce into one entity, destroy the parents and all other Earthly life, and take off into the vastness of the galaxy. This development represents the end of childhood for the children, and for the entire human race which will be represented by the further evolution of the newly developed species. That novel, too, is marked by hostility toward women and toward mothers. A glimpse of "dialogue" between George and his wife is revealing:

> George looked down at her with sympathy, but nothing more. It was strange how much one could alter in so short a time. He was fond of her: she had borne his children and was part of his life. But of the love which a not clearly remembered person named George Greggson had once known towards a fading dream called Jean Morrel, how much remained?
>
> (*Childhood's End*, p. 165)

How much love, one might well ask, was there to begin with? George, the artist figure within the book looks upon Jean, the mother, with increasing hostility. If hostility toward the mother is never really overcome, in Clarke's case, his repetition of antagonism through art is either an ongoing attempt to work out his feelings, or something else entirely. That the contest is always between the artist and the mother ought to indicate that there is more to Clarke's method than an attempt to resolve the separation anxieties of a would-be space traveller. Clarke's repeated production of novels is, rather, a demonstration of the power of the "mental" masculine "womb."[16] The real Star-Child is the work of fiction as he defies "science"—the knowledge that only women can bear children.

The knowledge informs and enrages not only Clarke, who typifies Victor Frankenstein's male successors so well, but also many others. Science fiction asks us to consider where the human race is going, while it remembers where we have come from. Insofar as male authors feel that they have come from female "creators," resentments abound. The undisputed fact of mother's creativity in producing the author puts his own creativity to the test. He produces books, certainly, but also Star-Children and "babies" of other sorts.

Isaac Asimov, for example, in *I, Robot*,[17] brings forth a new race of beings made by man's intellect in the image of man. The robots, naturally, are referred to as "boys."[18] The "boys" have remarkable abilities, and the first robot we see—Robbie—far surpasses the one human mother in the book. Robbie is a nursemaid for little Gloria, the child of Mrs. Weston, a shrew who is more concerned about what the neighbors will think of Robbie than about her little girl's attachment to him. Mrs. Weston, we are told, "made full use of every device which a clumsier and more scrupulous sex has learned, with reason and futility, to fear" (*I, Robot*, p. 18).

The fear of the mother's capacity for "creating" life, the fear of castration, rejection and death are all here in the mental landscapes of male-oriented science fiction. And these fears produce resentment and anxiety. With regard to the latter, there is always the certain knowledge that mother preferred another man—presumably, the author's father. Identifying with that former rival, the author must now punish mother. Asimov undertakes this project in his treatment of the one female scientist in his book, Susan Calvin, robopsychologist and Ph. D. She is described in her younger days as "a frosty girl, plain and colorless, who protected herself against a world she disliked by a mask-like expression and a hypertrophy of intellect" (*I, Robot*, p. 7). Later, in a central episode of the book, thirty-eight year old Susan Calvin's last hopes of marrying are destroyed. The male scientist whom she adores tells her he is engaged to be married, while the reader is given a verbal picture of her humiliation as the blood drains from Calvin's countenance: "The inexpertly applied rouge made a pair of nasty red splotches upon her chalk-white face" (*I, Robot*, p. 95).

Similarly in Kurt Vonnegut, Jr.'s *The Sirens of Titan*,[19] the essential female character, Beatrice, is first described as a frigid, proud woman, immaculate and haughty. In the existential quest for the continuation of the race, and in Vonnegut's quest to punish mother for supplying him with life but not coming up with an explanation of what it all means, Beatrice is humbled and defeated. She is selected by chance, in spite of the fact that she is "plain-looking" (*Sirens*, p. 40), to be raped in outer space and to be "bred by the Martians—like farm animals [are]" (*Sirens*, p. 26). Vonnegut has Beatrice pronounce later on that it has all been worth it since the meaning of life—what little meaning there is—is "to be used" by others (*Sirens*, p. 310).

The hostility toward women in *Sirens* comes complete with a discussion by Malachi Constant, the earlier mentioned hero-rapist, of how his mother was a "whore," and of how all women are "whores" (*Sirens*, p. 61). The same character also has a womb-regression fantasy which, in his own mind, captures the spirit of his own perspective of sexuality:

Unk withdrew the rod and patch, slipped his thumb under the open breech, caught the sunlight on his oily thumbnail. The thumbnail sent the sunlight up the bore. Unk put his eye to the muzzle and was thrilled by perfect beauty. He could have stared happily at the immaculate spiral of the rifling for hours, dreaming of the happy land whose round gate he saw at the other end of the bore. The pink under his oily thumbnail at the far end of the barrel made that far end seem a rosy paradise indeed. Some day he was going to crawl down the barrel to that paradise. (*Sirens*, p. 109)

The three sirens, the triple goddess representing all of the aspects of woman,[20] reside within that paradise at the other end of the gun. It is an appropriate image with which to end our discussion of the science fiction sex war. It should seem remarkable to no one that feminist writers of science fiction have responded energetically to Vonnegut's, Clarke's and Asimov's attitudes and themes. Joanna Russ, in *The Female Man*[21] and *We Who Are About To....*[22] manages to create a female who is, socially at least, a man,[23] a robot in the form of a man who is employed solely for a woman's sexual pleasure,[24] and a woman who would rather kill the members of her landing party—and herself—than be a "walking womb[25] for the purpose of perpetuating a pointless group of human beings. As for the sex war itself, which is the offspring of Mary Shelley, Frankenstein, and his monster, perpetuation seems assured.

Notes

[1]See, for example, Robert Scholes and Eric S. Rabkin, eds., *Science Fiction: History—Science—Vision* (New York: Oxford, 1977), pp. 191-196 for a discussion of *Frankenstein*. Scholes and Rabkin also discuss the fact that "Until recently, most science fiction was written for men ...," p. 185.

[2]Authors such as Joanna Russ, Marge Piercy, Doris Lessing, Anne McCaffrey, and Kate Wilhelm are among the many current women science fiction writers.

[3]Mary Shelley, *Frankenstein: or the Modern Prometheus* (New York: Bantam, 1967). References to this text are by title and page number. *Frankenstein* was first published in 1818.

[4]See Mary Poovey, "My Hideous Progeny: Mary Shelley and the Feminization of Romanticism," *PMLA*, 95 (1980), pp. 332-347. Poovey argues that *Frankenstein* "expresses the tension [Shelley] feels between the self-denying offices of domestic activity and the self-

assertiveness essential to artistic creation," p. 343.

[5]Ellen Moers, *Literary Women* (New York: Doubleday, 1976), pp. 90-99. Moers explores the relationships between birth and death in *Frankenstein* in the context of Mary Shelley's elopement at sixteen with Shelley, and the subsequent deaths of her babies.

[6]Although the theory of male compensatory activity might be inferred from Freud's concept of sublimation alone, Bruno Bettelheim cites several individuals who have endorsed the theory of male envy of woman's procreative function: "Though male envy has not gone unrecognized, it has received relatively little notice in the psychoanalytic literature. To my knowledge, it was first discussed by Groddeck. Landauer referred to it in connection with his theory that it was men's disappointment at their inability to create human beings that led them to intellectual creation, a theory Chadwick had expressed earlier," Bruno Bettelheim, *Symbolic Wounds: Puberty Rites and the Envious Male* (New York: Collier, 1962), p. 56. Otto Rank, however. sees the creation of culture as an attempt to "deny the separation from the mother," Otto Rank, *The Trauma of Birth* (New York: Robert Brunner, 1952), p. 105.

[7]C.G. Jung, *AION: Researches into the Phenomenology of the Self*, Trans. R.F.C. Hull (New York: Pantheon, 1959). Also *Psyche and Symbol: A Selection from the Writings of C.G. Jung*, ed. Violet S. de Laszlo (New York: Anchor, 1958), p. 13:

I use Eros and Logos merely as conceptual aids to describe the fact that woman's consciousness is characterized more by the connective quality of Eros than by the discrimination and cognition of Logos. In men, Eros, the function of relationship, is usually less developed than Logos. In women, on the other hand, Eros is an expression of their true nature, while their Logos is often only a regrettable accident.

[8]Arthur C. Clarke, *2001: A Space Odyssey* (New York: Signet, 1968). All references by title and page number are to this text. The last chapter of the book is entitled "Star-Child." Those who have seen the film—and the text is based on the screenplay—will remember the visual depiction of "Star-Child" as a fetus in space.

[9]The concept of "womb envy" has had a good deal of psychoanalytic support. Most notably, Bruno Bettelheim sees womb envy as a legitimate neurotic problem in male children (see note 6). See also Daniel S. Jaffe, M.D., "The Masculine Envy of Woman's Procreative Function," in *Female Psychology: Contemporary Psychoanalytic Views*, Harold P. Blum, M.D., ed. (New York: International Universities Press, 1977), pp. 361-392, for a comprehensive list of source studies and an excellent technical discussion.

In literary terms, Kate Millet in *Sexual Politics* (New York: Avon, 1971), pp. 237-293, discusses the applicability of "womb envy" to some features of D.H. Lawrence's work.

[10]See Otto Rank, *The Trauma of Birth*, pp. 106-116 on "Heroic Compensation."

[11]Otto Rank, p. 79, discusses the interpretation of direction in birth dreams, as well as the apparent desire to go back into the father's body, a desire which he feels is a disguised womb phantasy.

Bettelheim, pp. 31-32, from a different perspective, explains the "penis as womb" idea in psychoanalytic studies.

[12]Otto Rank, p. 94, writes: "Woman has an antisocial influence, which gives psychological reasons for her exclusion from social as from political life in primitive (club houses) and in highly developed civilizations. Man depreciates her only consciously; in the Unconscious he fears her."

[13]See Bettelheim, note 11.

[14]Otto Rank, pp. 11-29, discusses "Infantile Anxiety" in terms of birth trauma.

[15]Arthur C. Clarke, *Childhood's End* (New York: Ballantine, 1953). References to this text are by title and page number.

[16]The masculine "mental womb" fantasy should be common knowledge by now; unfortunately, few have heard of it. Among mainstream modern writers, James Joyce creates the most explicit system. He has Stephen in *A Portrait of the Artist as a Young Man* (New York: Viking), p 217, declare: "O! In the virgin womb of the imagination the word was made flesh." An examination of Joyce's letters and the biography by Richard Ellmann will convince the staunchest skeptic that Joyce believed in mental wombs for men. The critic Mary Ellmann, in *Thinking About Women* (New York: Harcourt Brace, 1968), notes the mental womb phenomenon in Joyce and others. Her chapter on "Sexual Analogy" is especially enlightening (pp. 2-26).

---

[17]Isaac Asimov, *I, Robot* (Greenwich: Fawcett, 1950). References to this text are by title and page number.

[18]Asimov, p. 131, and elsewhere.

[19]Kurt Vonnegut, Jr., *The Sirens of Titan* (New York: Dell, 1959). References by title and page number are to this text.

[20]Wolfgang Lederer, M.D., in *The Fear of Women* (New York: Grune and Stratton, 1968), discusses the "Triple Goddess"—Aphrodite, Hera and Athena—pp. 28-29. The goddess represents the many aspects of woman as perceived by man.

[21]Joanna Russ, *The Female Man* (New York: Bantam, 1975).

[22]Joanna Russ, *We Who About To ...* (New York: Dell, 1975).

[23]Joanna Russ, *The Female Man.*

[24]See Russ, *The Female Man*, p. 185 and following, for descriptions of Davy, the "most beautiful man in the world."

[25]See Russ, *We Who Are About To ...*, p. 59.

Fritz H. Oehlschlaeger

Civilization as Emasculation:
The Threatening Role of Women in the Frontier Fiction
of Harold Bell Wright and Zane Grey

THE OPENING DECADE of the twentieth century brought the rise to popularity of a genre of American novels celebrating frontier life and the primitive virtues of strength, vigor and courage. Writers like Harold Bell Wright and Zane Grey enjoyed enormous success with a formula that combined the portrayal of a strong, silent hero with fast-paced plots, violence and romance. James D. Hart, historian of American popular fiction, suggests that the frontier novelist's audience consisted mostly of male readers who found a refreshing "escape from the complexities of modern life"[1] in the simple vision of clean air, picturesque mountains, and open plains. Hart argues further that the American esteem of Theodore Roosevelt also contributed to the popularity of frontier fiction. Male readers, "dreaming of rugged-individualistic successes that reality did not allow them," found the incarnation of Roosevelt's strenuous life in the heroic cowboys of Zane Grey or mountaineers of Harold Bell Wright.[2]

While the strenuous life primarily involved vigorous outdoor adventures, it usually included romance as well. A central focus of many frontier novels is on the primitive hero's relationships with women. What, then, did the predominantly male audience of the frontier novel want to be told about women?[3] The answer to that question can be found by looking at several of the highly popular novels of Wright and Grey.

Women in the frontier myth of Wright and Grey are nearly always associated with the forces of civilization that threaten the primitive world. This threat is often directly sexual: civilization threatens the primitive hero with emasculation. Never is the concern with emasculation more apparent, for instance, than in Grey's famous *Riders of the Purple Sage*, which dwells heavily on its heroine's attempt to civilize a notorious gunfighter by symbolically castrating him. A recurring pattern of the frontier novels involves the triumph of the primitive hero over the threatening, civilized woman. In novels like Wright's *When A Man's A Man* and *The Shepherd of the Hills*, the woman who yearns for civilization must learn to renounce her desires and embrace a primitive code demanding her complete subservience. The primitive woman receives two

177

compensations for her subservience: sexual gratification with her strong-man "mate" and his chivalric adoration. Such are the needs, the frontier novelist argues, of all "true" women. The frontier novelist's idea of women is perhaps nowhere better suggested than in Grey's consistent, though apparently unconscious, analogy between women and horses. Like a horse, the ideal woman should be fiery and spirited, but thoroughly responsive to her he-man's will. Excessive willfulness in women, as in horses, must be broken. All rebellious women in the frontier myth of Wright and Grey eventually learn their places and find satisfaction in their red-blooded mates.

One of Wright's celebrations of the primitive woman is *The Shepherd of the Hills*, an immensely popular tale of the Ozarks published in 1907. The major character of this novel is Daniel Howitt, an elderly Chicago minister who goes to the Ozarks to revitalize his Christian faith. As both James Hart and Frank Luther Mott have noted, Wright's religious message recalls Charles Sheldon's phenomenal bestseller *In His Steps*.[4] Like Sheldon, Wright criticizes the complacency and mercantile spirit of the urban churches. In the frontier Ozark setting, Reverend Howitt reestablishes close communion with God and finds simple virtue in the mountaineers. Although Wright strongly emphasizes his Christian theme, the novel's major masculine interest derives from a conflict between two primitive strong men of the mountains, Wash Gibbs and young "Matt" Matthews. In Wright's simple allegory, Wash Gibbs appears the incarnation of evil; he is a drunkard, thief and insane terrorist. Matt, on the other hand, is wholly virtuous—an innocent, upright child of the mountains. Matt prevails in this conflict of strong men by trouncing Wash Gibbs in a violent fist-fight. He then reigns supreme in the mountains, the dominant beast in the Darwinian jungle. Wash Gibbs is eventually killed while resisting a posse's attempts to arrest him.

The novel's heroine is Sammy Lane, a primitive mountain beauty. She is engaged to Ollie Stewart, a young weakling who leaves the mountains to acquire an education in the city. Through much of the novel, Sammy assumes she will marry Ollie and looks forward to moving with him to the city. But when Ollie returns to the mountains, Sammy is repulsed by his foppish effeminancy. She then refuses Ollie's offer of marriage, realizing that her "woman's heart" demands a virile mate. Eventually she marries the giant Matt Matthews, a natural superman engaged in a crudely Darwinian struggle for survival and dominance. Wright consistently describes Matthews in terms that suggest bestiality; of his hero's "splendid passion" for Sammy Lane, Wright comments, "it is the same instinct that prompts the panther to send his mating call ringing over the hills and through the forest, and leads the moose to issue his loud challenge."[5] Matt himself comments on his bestial nature: "I ain't no gentleman. I can't ever be one. I'm just a man. I'm a—a savage, a damned beast, and I'm glad of it" (171). Wright attempts to qualify his equation of manhood with brute strength through the Reverend Howitt, who counsels Matt, "your manhood depends on this, and upon nothing else, that you conquer and control the animal side of yourself" (172). Despite Howitt's insistence on the importance of Christian self-control, brute strength is the primary virtue Matt exhibits. In the primordial conflict with Wash Gibbs, Matt triumphs with his fists, not his Christian virtue.

Wright's conception of primitive womanhood is conveyed through Sammy Lane, who is the ideal "mate" for Matt Matthews. She also is portrayed as a vigorous, healthy animal, "strong as a young panther" (291). Wright's descriptions of her are always highly, if woodenly, sensual; she appears, for instance, "tall; beautifully tall, with the trimness of a young pine, deep bosomed, with limbs full-rounded, fairly tingling with the life and strength of perfect womanhood" (14). Sammy moves in a glow of erotic, fecund sexuality:

keenly alive to the life that throbbed and surged about her, her woman's heart and soul responded to the spirit of the season. The droning of the bees in the blossoms that grew in a cranny of the rock; the tinkle, tinkle of the sheep bells, as the flock moved slowly in their feeding; and the soft breathing of Mother Earth was in her ears; while the gentle breeze that stirred her hair came heavy with the smell of growing things (51.)

The language of the passages is without doubt stiff and conventional, but Wright's desire to evoke Sammy's vigorous sensuality is unmistakable.

Much of the novel focuses on Sammy's choice of a husband. Throughout the early sections of the novel, Sammy is engaged to Ollie Stewart and longs for the benefits of civilization that he represents. Sammy has no very clear idea about what city life means, but she does sense that being a "sure 'nough" lady will mean greater freedom and possibilities than she has in the Ozarks. She urges Matt Matthews, for instance, to leave the mountains for the city in order to avoid being "buried alive in these hills" (81). In her desire to learn the ways of a "sure 'nough" lady, Sammy begins regular visits with Daniel Howitt, who is experienced in the ways of city life. In his talks with the girl, Howitt presents the city as a realm of corruption, hypocrisy and superficiality. From her daily contact with this gentle teacher, Sammy learns the spiritual value of the simple mountain existence, the vanity of her desires for civilized life and the validity of the primitive code of womanhood.

Sammy Lane attempts to reconcile Howitt's spiritual teachings with her own instinctive sexuality. She rejects Ollie Stewart because "he is too little—body, soul, and spirit" (203). Sammy is attracted instead to Matt Matthews, in whom she sees sexual and spiritual virility. Sammy insists that Matt's manhood is not merely a matter of physical endowment, but of something "deeper...of which the brute strength was only an expression" (199). Yet when Sammy witnesses a furious fight between Matt and Wash Gibbs, her blood thrills at the feats of strength, and she sits "her beautiful figure tense, her lips parted, and her face flushed with excitement" (194). As Matt crushes the bones of the evil giant Wash Gibbs, Sammy emits a low orgastic groan, "Oh, *what a man!*" (195). Sammy's spiritual convictions appear feeble compared to this instinctive outburst. Despite Wright's interminable sermonizing about the value of spirituality, his characters remain basically animal types. Sammy refuses the civilized life Ollie Stewart represents because she realizes "that the only common ground whereon men and women may meet in safety is the ground of their manhood and womanhood" (290). Sex is enshrined, finally, as the only basis for a woman's relationship with a man.

Two interesting envoys from civilization in *The Shepherd of the Hills* are Ollie Stewart and Dr. Coughlan, a Chicago physician who goes to the Ozarks in search of Daniel Howitt. The prevailing note of Ollie Stewart's character is effeminacy. When he returns from the city, Ollie appears a "slender, pale-faced man, with faultless linen, well-gloved hands and shining patent leathers" (162). The dandified Ollie also speaks in a thin voice that contrasts sharply with the deep growls of the mountain he-men.

Throughout the novel, Ollie conforms to Wash Gibbs' estimate of him; he is a "dolly." Ollie's emasculation is responsible for his failure to win Sammy Lane. He is unable to play the man's role in defending her, as the chivalric code of the mountains requires. When Wash Gibbs threatens to attack Sammy, Ollie is impotent. In one scene Ollie threatens Gibbs with a tiny lady's pistol, only to have his nickel-plated phallus prove unserviceable as the evil giant knocks him to the ground.

Dr. Coughlan is another emasculated male from the cities. Whenever he considers an action, Coughlan wonders, "what would Sarah and the girls say?" (246). "Sarah and the girls" are a group of Coughlan's maiden aunts who ferociously regulate every aspect of his life in Chicago. Dr. Coughlan's presence in the novel clearly implies that city life is dominated by women who constrain a man's freedom and threaten his masculinity.

Another of Wright's novels that dwells on female sexuality and the emasculation of the civilized male is *When A Man's A Man*. This 1916 bestseller relates the adventures of Honourable Patches, a young Cleveland millionaire who travels to the Arizona desert to escape the effete life of the East. In Arizona, Patches becomes a bronc-busting, range-riding, rustler-hunting cowboy for the Cross Triangle Ranch. The novel's major romance involves Phil Acton, the Cross Triangle's foreman, and Kitty Reid, the daughter of a neighboring rancher. Kitty is this novel's version of the woman who yearns for civilized life. After three years of education in the East, Kitty returns to the West and finds its frontier strong men offensive. She repeatedly refuses Phil Acton's advances while becoming infatuated with an Eastern professor who is in Arizona to study primitive life. The professor is an emasculated Easterner—weak, feeble and sexually inadequate. When he proposes to Kitty, she realizes her need for sexual gratification with a virile strong man. Although she then agrees to marry Patches, she knows that Phil Acton is her perfect mate. In a final act of chivalry, Patches releases Kitty from the engagement, and she marries Acton.

When A Man's A Man insists on a chivalric code of behavior that establishes the strong man as protector of the helpless female. Patches violates this code when he asks Kitty Reid to marry him, for he takes advantage of her by appealing to her longing for education, culture and refinement. Although he knows Kitty does not love him, Patches promises her the life of civilized beauty and ease that she desires. Patches' realization of his sin against the code is presented as the novel's major climax; Helen Manning, a secondary character in the novel, tells him:

'When a man's a man there is one thing above all others that he cannot do. He cannot take advantage of a woman's weakness; he cannot tempt her beyond her strength; he must be strong both for himself and her; he must save her always from herself.'[6]

This statement makes the chivalric conception of women unpleasantly clear. Women are so weak and stupid that they cannot possibly know what they want; they must be protected against their own greatest enemies—their foolish, feminine desires.

As he does in The Shepherd of the Hills, Wright suggests that what every true woman wants is the love of a virile he-man. Kitty's desires for beauty and education are criticized for alienating her from the "simple, primitive, and enduring elements of life" (117). The values that she acquires from formal education are false standards that obscure her true womanly duties to home and family. Kitty's ultimate delusion lies in her affection for the effeminate professor of aesthetics, which is a perversion of her instinctive yearning for a virile mate. The professor's proposal of a marriage based on "the high, pure ground of a spiritual union" insults her "womanhood" (286). Kitty realizes finally that her "only lawful mate" (314) is the passionate primitive, Wild Horse Phil Acton, who says to her of his wooing: "I am going to win you—just as the wild things out there win their mates. You are going to come to me, girl, because you are mine—because you are my mate" (130). As he does in The Shepherd of the Hills, Wright contends that a true woman's happiness lies in sexual fulfillment with the primitive he-man.

When A Man's A Man also resembles The Shepherd of the Hills in its depiction of the civilized male. Like Ollie Stewart, Professor Parkhill is a weakling, a degenerate member of an "overcultured" race doomed to extinction. Wright strongly emphasizes the professor's sexual inadequacy;

his Eastern wife "ran away with a carpenter who had been at work on the house for some six weeks" (344). In the characterization of the professor, Wright again hints—as he does through Ollie Stewart and Dr. Coughlan—that the civilized world is dominated by women. Lacking primitive sexual vigor, the civilized male like Parkhill is unable to control either his wife or Kitty Reid.

A novel that clearly presents the civilized woman as a threat to male virility is Grey's *Riders of the Purple Sage*. In its attitudes toward women, *Riders of the Purple Sage* is perhaps the most revealing of all these frontier novels, for it focuses centrally on a woman of power and influence. The novel's heroine is Jane Withersteen, the Mormon owner of a large cattle ranch in Utah. The basic action of the novel involves Jane's attempts to defend her property against two groups—her Mormon brethren and a band of cattle rustlers. The chivalric code of manly behavior is again a crucial theme. Assisting Jane in her defense are two valorous knights of the sagebrush—Bern Venters, a range rider, and Lassiter, a gunfighter. Despite the noble efforts of these defenders, Jane ultimately loses her property. She receives compensation, however, for her loss of power and wealth. Through the course of her fight for the ranch, Jane becomes increasingly dependent on Lassiter and decides finally that happiness lies in submission to him.

There are two major romances in *Riders of the Purple Sage*. The more important of these brings together Jane Withersteen and the gunfighter Lassiter. When he arrives at Jane's ranch, Lassiter brings a reputation as a ruthless killer, a heartless murderer of Mormons. Jane, however, interprets his chivalric behavior toward her as evidence of a finer sensibility. She then determines to civilize him, to render him gentle and merciful. In order to tame Lassiter, Jane begins an elaborate program of coquetry. The symbolic objects of her assault are Lassiter's big black guns. In the climactic moment of their relationship, Jane threatens Lassiter with castration:

Jane slipped her hands down to the swinging gun-sheaths, and when she had locked her fingers around the huge, cold handles of the guns, she trembled as with a chilling ripple over all her body.

'May I take your guns?'

'Why?' he asked, and for the first time to her his voice carried a harsh note. Jane felt his hard, strong hands close round her wrists. It was not wholly with intent that she leaned against him, for the look of his eyes and the feel of his hands made her weak.

'It's no trifle—no woman's whim—it's deep—deep as my heart. Let me take them ....'

As if her hands had been those of a child, he unclasped their clinging grip from the handles of his guns, and, pushing her away, he turned his gray face to her in one look of terrible realization and then strode off into the shadows of the cottonwoods.[7]

After Jane's failure to emasculate Lassiter, the novel proceeds quite predictably. Jane begins to love the gunfighter and realizes that her desires for domination are "an infringement of her womanhood" (145). Still she manages to retain some independence by refusing to confess her love to Lassiter. In the novel's furious closing sequences, Jane and Lassiter flee from a band of Mormon vigilantes to the high ground of an isolated canyon. There, in the novel's final purple moment, Jane cries out, "*Lassiter, I love you*" (335), at which point he rolls a huge stone down upon the pursuing Mormons, closing the opening of the canyon forever. In the novel's final irony, Jane willingly accepts the subordinate role that the Mormons had consistently attempted to force upon her. The retreat to the canyon marks Jane's repudiation of civilization, and her cry of love for Lassiter indicates her submission to the strong man.

The novel's other important romance involves Bern Venters, a range rider and friend of Jane Withersteen. At the opening of the novel, Bern is an emasculated male who has willingly yielded his guns to Jane. The novel's opening scene clearly represents Bern's emasculation, as he grovels at the feet of a group of Mormons while they prepare to whip him. Significantly, Venters is saved from the Mormons by the intervention of Lassiter. Bern then begins a long process of regaining his primitive manhood.

Bern's love affair begins in curious fashion when he shoots the Masked Rider, a notorious rustler. Venters discovers the Masked Rider to be a woman, Bess, and carefully supervises her return to health in an isolated canyon. During her convalescence Bess is totally dependent on Venters for protection and security, a dependence that is instrumental in restoring Bern's lost masculinity. When Venters leaves the canyon to obtain supplies at the Withersteen ranch, Jane notes the change in her former employee:

she felt the difference she saw in him. Wild, rugged, unshorn—yet how splendid! He had gone away a boy—he had returned a man. He appeared taller, wider of shoulder, deeper-chested, more powerfully built (205).

Venters displays his new-found masculinity by freeing himself from Jane Withersteen and her foolish notions of kindness and non-violence. He becomes a terror to the Mormons and a fierce killer of rustlers. Venters even earns the recognition of Lassiter, who calls him "a good deal of a man" (228). Venters attributes his regained manhood directly to Bess. When he proposes marriage to her, Bern says, "I'm free! I'm a man—a man you've made—no more a beggar!" (233). Bess, then, contrasts directly with Jane Withersteen. Jane, the powerful civilized woman, threatens the virility of the primitive male, while Bess restores her mate's masculinity through submission to him.

Grey's *The Heritage of the Desert* also deals centrally with an effete male's return to primitive manhood. This novel's hero, John Hare, is a

New Yorker who moves to the Utah desert to seek relief from tuberculosis. In the desert, Hare is adopted by August Naab, the Mormon owner of a large cattle ranch. After regaining his health, Hare becomes one of Naab's trusted cowboys and distinguishes himself in a range war against rustlers. At the end of the novel, Hare marries Mescal, the adopted daughter of August Naab.

The major female figure in the novel, Mescal is clearly Grey's ideal primitive woman, a dark sensual beauty born to an Indian mother and a Spanish father. Fond of the "natural free life of the Indians, close to the earth,"[8] Mescal is sharply contrasted with Naab's white daughters, who "would rather have been in White Sage or Lund" (60). Yet despite her primitive passion, Mescal truly knows her place. Reared by the Naabs according to the strict Mormon code, Mescal fully accepts the subservience of women. This curious combination of native passion and feminine submissiveness makes of Mescal a "true woman," as she is called repeatedly throughout the novel.

Mescal's role in the novel is similar to Bess' in *Riders of the Purple Sage*. Along with the desert air and daily rations of deer meat, she is instrumental in restoring Jack Hare to vitality and manhood. In the first stage of his recuperation, Hare goes into the mountains with Mescal to tend a flock of Naab's sheep. During his months with Mescal in the mountains, Hare relinquishes his death wish and gains purpose from "what had come to him, of hope, of life, of Mescal's love, of things to be" (91). As his love for Mescal grows, Hare becomes her chivalric defender, protecting her repeatedly from the crude advances of August Naab's maverick son Snap, to whom Mescal is promised. After a long series of conflicts with Snap, Hare successfully proposes to Mescal; his proposal clearly suggests Grey's ideas about the function of women: "Mescal, I'm yours now. Your happiness—perhaps your life—depends on me. That makes a difference. Understand!" (221). In the western myth of Zane Grey, the woman's role is to somehow "make a difference" in the life of a man. She accomplishes this purpose through utter dependence, thereby giving her mate an object to defend and a reason to flex his primitive muscles.

Grey also conveys his ideas about women through a consistent analogy between the frontier woman and the cowboy's horse. Grey's he-men invariably respond to their horses in much the same way they respond to women. For Grey's cowboys, a hot, wild ride across the desert provides substitute sexual experience. The hard-riding cowboy generally experiences "savage delight"[9] or "the wild passions of wild men"[10] rising in his breast. In a riding sequence with distinctly sexual overtones, Grey describes Bern Venters:

cruelly he struck his spurs into Wrangle's flanks. A light touch of spur was sufficient to make Wrangle plunge. And now, with a ringing, wild snort, he seemed to double up in muscular convulsions and to shoot forward with an impetus that almost unseated Venters (246).

The he-man's response to Grey's hot-blooded beauties is similarly passionate. When a cowboy approaches a "true woman," he invariably feels "the mounting desire that thrill[s] all his blood."[11] Even Grey's figures of perverse passion burn equally for women and horses. The evil Mexican bandits of *Desert Gold* are characterized by two significant actions: they rape their abducted women and brutalize their stolen horses.

Grey's novels include additional suggestions of the similarity between women and horses. In *Desert Gold*, one of Grey's celibate cowboys transfers his passion for women onto horses, because, as he says, "I've had wimmen go back on me, but never no hoss!"[12] In *The Heritage of the Desert*, August Naab uses the same formula to break wild horses that he has used to tame the Indian girl Mescal. When Jack Hare attempts to break a wild stallion, Naab offers him advice that is meant to apply equally to women and horses: "you must make him love you, Jack. It can be done with any wild creature. Be gentle, but firm. Teach him to obey the slightest touch of rein, to stand when you throw your bridle on the ground, to come at your whistle."[13] The woman-as-horse motif operates in *Riders of the Purple Sage* as well. Jane Withersteen, the powerful castrater bitch, takes great pride in her horses, a pair of magnificent blacks that are reputedly the fastest in the territory. Throughout the novel, these horses symbolize Jane's power and independence. Like Jane, they must be broken and defeated by the primitive hero. An important event in Bern Venters' return to manhood is his triumph over Jane's favorite blacks in a furious race. Jane is allowed neither Lassiter's big, black guns nor her own strong, black horses.

Grey's consistent analogy between women and horses further clarifies his attitudes toward women and the ideal feminine type. Like a horse, Grey's ideal woman is an instinctive creature, passionate and spirited but ultimately submissive to the he-man's will. Grey's women also resemble horses in their tendency toward stupid willfulness. Like horses, Grey's women are often too stupid to know what is best for them; they often mistakenly yearn for power, freedom and the blessings of civilized existence. Such women, like Jane Withersteen, pose a powerful sexual threat to the primitive hero. Fortunately, as Grey's August Naab argues, both women and horses can be influenced by love. By flexing his primitive muscles, the strong man can arouse his mate's instinctive desires for dependence and sexual gratification. She will then realize the folly of her yearnings for freedom and civilization and never again attempt to throw him out of the saddle.

In their presentation of women, Grey's novels closely resemble Harold Bell Wright's. Both writers consistently associate women with the civilizing influences that threaten the primitive world. Wright and Grey argue that civilization emasculates the primitive hero and that contact with women is a fundamental part of that emasculation process. In the primitivist myth of Wright and Grey, the lesson for women—and for these novelists' primarily male audiences—is always the same. Women's desires for independence, power and civilized accomplishment are all delusions. The true woman's satisfaction lies in submission to her redblooded mate.

Notes

[1] James D. Hart, *The Popular Book* (Berkeley and Los Angeles: Univ. of California Press, 1963), p.214.

[2] Hart, p. 215.

[3] One should observe Hart's distinctions here between the audiences to which Wright and Grey addressed themselves. While grouping Wright with male novelists who wrote mainly for their own sex, Hart argues that Wright's immense popularity derived from his ability to combine "divergent appeals." Wright's specific contribution to the primitivist novel was "a simple muscular Christianity" that appealed to women readers as well as men. Grey, on the other hand, is classified by Hart simply as a writer of male escapist fiction. See *The Popular Book*, pp.214-216.

[4] Hart, p. 216. See also Frank Luther Mott, *Golden Multitudes* (New York: Macmillan, 1947), pp. 226-228.

[5] Harold Bell Wright, *The Shepherd of the Hills* (New York: Grosset & Dunlap, 1970), p. 169. Future page references will be included parenthetically.

[6] Harold Bell Wright, *When A Man's A Man* (Chicago: The Book Supply Company, 1916), p.327. Future page references will be included parenthetically.

[7] Zane Grey, *Riders of the Purple Sage* (New York: Grosset & Dunlap, 1912), pp. 146-47. Future page references will be included parenthetically.

[8] Zane Grey, *The Heritage of the Desert* (New York: Grosset & Dunlap, 1910), p. 89. Future page references will be included parenthetically.

[9] Grey, *The Heritage of the Desert*, p.238.

[10] Grey, *Riders of the Purple Sage*, p. 240.

[11] Grey, *The Heritage of the Desert*, p. 90.

[12] Zane Grey, *Desert Gold* (New York: Grosset & Dunlap, 1913), p. 90.

[13] Grey, *The Heritage of the Desert*, p. 115.

Joseph A. Boone

Male Independence and the American Quest Genre: Hidden Sexual Politics in the All-Male Worlds of Melville, Twain and London

THE ABSENCE OF WOMEN, courtship and marriage in classic American fiction—the absence, that is, of precisely those hallmarks of theme and form distinguishing the English tradition—has been a literary commonplace since the 1960 publication of Leslie Fiedler's *Love and Death in the American Novel*. It is, however, a commonplace in need of some rethinking. In the first place, as recent feminist critics have reminded us, those "classic" texts of men-without-women represent a minority deviating from a popular tradition in which women, courtship and marriage are very much in evidence.[1] And in the second place, as the hindsight of twenty-five years makes clear, Fiedler's argument is fueled by an unquestioning allegiance to certain Freudian assumptions about "normal" or "correct" male psychological development that predispose him, as a critic, to judge the quester's prototypical gesture of escape from society as a negative example of "arrested adolescence." I would propose a much more positive interpretation of the male quester's search for freedom of self than that offered by Fiedler, or, conversely, by those feminist critics who have assumed that the genre—as a literature written by men and about men—must inevitably valorize ideological concerns culturally designated as "masculine" or "patriarchal." Rather, concealed beneath the quest-romance's ostensibly rugged exterior there often exists a fascinating if sometimes ambivalent exploration of sexual politics, including a potentially radical critique of the patriarchal norms, restrictive roles, and sexual inequity characterizing nineteenth-century American familial and social life. What has been even less noted in studies of quest fiction—and which I will attempt to demonstrate in the cases of Melville, Twain and London—is the degree to which the experimental form of this "aberrant" fictional mode owes its existence to the presence of such a hidden sexual politics.

•The complex relation of gender to genre in the American quest is anticipated by Fiedler's study in two important ways which merit review at the onset of my own argument. First, Fiedler explains the rise of the American genre not merely as a reaction to the formal realism of everyday life espoused by the early English novel, but also as a rebellion against the ethos of sexual polarity pervading the countless tales of love and seduction that followed Richardson's achievement. The sentimental debasement of love ensuing shortly thereafter in early American fiction, Fiedler argues, sent the serious American writer scurrying in pursuit of alternate subject matters and modes—whence the accomplishments of authors ranging from Cooper and Hawthorne to Melville and Twain. Second, Fiedler forcefully argues that the mutual bonding of males repeated throughout the American canon came into being as an explicit alternative to the antagonistic heterosexual relationships emanating from the "sentimental love religion" dominating the conventional novel. However, in tracing the paradigmatic movement of the male quester away from societal structures—including marriage—Fiedler betrays the bias to which I have already referred: for, in his eyes, the freedom sought by the male protagonist "on the run" from society *necessarily* constitutes an adolescent avoidance of mature love, as epitomized in marital responsibility, and of adult identity.[2] Despite the partial truth of this assertion when applied, for instance, to figures such as Rip Van Winkle or Natty Bumppo, it does not follow that every unattached or independent quester lacks personal fulfillment simply because he avoids the constraints of patriarchically conceived marriage or traditionally defined manhood.

Indeed, several examples of the quest genre—*Moby-Dick* (1851), *The Adventures of Huckleberry Finn* (1884), *Billy Budd* (c. 1891), and *The Sea Wolf* (1904)—point in the opposite direction: the quester's linear projection outward from the closed circle of societal circumspection into undefined geographic and textual space "liberate[s] him," to paraphrase Henry James' definition of American romance, "from the conditions that we usually know to attach to [experience],"[3] and the consequence of that liberation, for a few of these unconventional protagonists, is the discovery of an affirming, multiform self that has broken through the strictures traditionally imposed on male social identity. Thus, the outwardbound voyage to confront the unknown that by definition comprises quest narrative simultaneously traces an inner journey toward a redefinition of self that defies social convention and sexual categorization. Lines from Melville's poem "After the Pleasure-Party" eloquently evoke the hidden or subconscious goal of many such quests:

> Could I remake me! or set free
> This sexless bound in sex, then plunge
> Deeper than Sappho, in a lunge
> Piercing Pan's paramount mystery!
> For, Nature, in no shallow surge
> Against thee either sex may urge,
> Why has thou made us but in halves—
> Co-relatives? This makes us slaves.
> If these co-relatives never meet
> Self-hood itself seems incomplete.[4]

Adapting Melville's terminology, we might say that the yearning to be "set free" from those inner and outer "bounds in sex" which threaten to stultify the self leads to a "plunge" into the "mystery" of sexual identity, the psychological terrain of Pan, that is analogous to the physical act of questing itself.

This goal, moreover, helps distinguish the American genre from archetypal patterns of quest-romance, such as those described by Northrop Frye. For in the traditional model the mythic wanderer most often returns from his perilous journeys to the world of the known as a culture-hero, his discovery of identity serving a *social* good that heals the wasted kingdom.[5] In spirit if not always in reality, the prototypical American quester remains a rebel-figure or social outcast whose true self can only exist *outside* the parameters of his culture; unlike the hero of the mythic pattern, he strives not so much for the reintegration into society as for the reintegration of his often fragmented identity, a bringing together of heart and mind as well as those severed "halves" of personality associated in "After the Pleasure Party" with the two sexes. The following pages will attempt to measure the radical implications—and psychic dangers—of the questing figure's departure from his prescribed sexual role by examining four fantasies of freedom and escape in which the provisional, "unfixed" quality of the structural organization of quest narrative facilitates the authorial exploration of non-traditional male identity. Instead of uncovering a univocal ideology of stereotypical manhood, we will find inscribed in the trajectories of these specific American quest narratives visions of individuality and mutual relationship that attempt to break down conventional sexual categorization by breaking through the limiting forms of culture and the conventions of love-literature at once. In a sense, the questing vision was ultimately limited by its chosen field of representation; for the decision to forego the world of male-female relations necessarily involved an absence of female reality that, as we shall see in adaptations of the genre in the twentieth century, could be used to support a misogynistic world-view. Nonetheless, the early *potential* of the mode was immense, for by presenting the figuratively all-male world as an *imaginative* alternative to existing social and literary constructs, the quest writer found himself empowered to express in "a bold and nervous lofty language," perhaps for the first time, a questioning of the dominant sexual order within which he too was trapped.

I

The male quest in American fiction represents only one branch, of course, of the larger fictional category self-consciously labeled the "Romance" by early promoters of the form. The quest formula shared with American romance the latter's repudiation of the strictly realistic methods associated with conventional English fiction;[6] but the quest variant went further in *also* repudiating the love emphases of traditional fiction—an inheritance from which few general American romancers were exempt. So the frequently stereotypical images of women, high degrees of etherealized eroticism, and reliance upon conventional love-plot mechanisms in writers as diverse as Cooper, Poe and Hawthorne indicate.[7]

The writer of quest-romance, in contrast to the general romancer, dealt by definition with a world largely void of women or normal social regulations, a world in which the male exploration of sea or desert provided a subject ideally suited for the novelist interested in working outside the thematic strictures of the literary marriage tradition. Historically, as Frye has demonstrated, the questing hero's physical movement away from civilized realms, often alone, makes the development of his independent, singular identity a paramount focus, and American adaptations continue this emphasis. What is different—and hence revealing—about American versions of the quest-romance formula is the extent to which the fair lady who typically figured as the medieval quester's goal or reward has been displaced by the more metaphysical objects of truth, absolute reality, the nature of authority, and similar lofty issues. Implicit in this shift, whether of conscious or unconscious design, are several very significant factors: first, having less reason to promulgate the objectification and idealization of woman inherent in most other literatures of the time, the quest skirts the historical perception of woman as man's opposite, leaving the universe instead to play the antagonistic role of "Other"; second, since the quester's virility is therefore less dependent on genital than heroic contact (as Fiedler puts it), his acquisition of adult male identity is freed from usual connotations of reproductive function and social good; and third, the "forward thrust of inquiry, the dynamic assertion of self in a progressive line of exploration" that John Seelye defines as the genre's underlying structural principle disassociates it from the closural constraints that the finality of return-and-marriage, even only as symbol, would impose.[8]

The quester's journey *into* the unknown simultaneously implies an escape *from* the known—that is, the context of nineteenth-century American culture. As we have seen, Fiedler argues that the quest writer's avoidance of themes of passion and marriage was a direct result of his society's extreme degree of sentimentalization and sexual bifurcation. This assumption is corroborated by Ann Douglas in *The Feminization of American Culture*, which analyzes the sentimental myth of absolute connubial love and of the wife's domestic role that took root in early nineteenth-century America and rapidly became *the* middle-class ideal.[9] The widely preached doctrine of the wife's sacred "influence" within the home arose as a response to the period's increasingly severe dichotomization of male and female spheres and roles: the more that the growth of capitalism encouraged "masculine" aggression and drive in its fledgling male entrepreneurs, the more society venerated traditional "feminine" values to compensate for the harsher realities. Given the importance of the marriage institution in maintaining these hierarchical roles, it is small wonder that the unmarried male, having freely chosen his independence from the blandishments of marriage and the "softer sex," came under attack by the moral guardians of society. "Does not your soul become chilled," the hero of the tract *Married or Single* warns a bachelor hero, "at the soul-revolting idea, that all the noble deeds ... of a Washington would have been lost ... to the world, if his father had acted the strange, unnatural, criminal part you propose to yourself?"[10]

If the quester sought to flee this marital ethos, the romance-quest writer also sought escape from the seeming banalities of much popular "women's fiction"—literature generally written by and for women that served as a tool for socialization into often unwittingly proper "feminine" roles.[11] The tendency of these sentimental writers to employ pat formulas to convey their messages of domestic and social order hinged on the shared belief that the marriage vow, as the novelist Mrs. E.D.E.N. Southworth put it, was "the most sacred tie on earth"; unravel that knot and not only "the peace of families, [but] the social welfare of the whole community" might fall apart.[12] Hence, as Herbert Ross Brown explains in the standard work on the sentimental tradition, these writers coerced the structural paradigms of courtship, seduction and marital trials inherited from English love fiction into serving their conservative aims with unabashed fervor:

The final solution was neatly reserved for the last chapter where the punishment was made to fit the crime, and the reward to equal the virtue. To achieve it, authors subjected the long aim of coincidence to the rack of expediency where it was stretched and fractured to suit every need of the plot.[13]

The domination of the American fictional market by these relatively uncrafted productions—inspiring Hawthorne's unkind reference to that "damned mob of scribbling women"[14]—intensified the sense of exclusion felt by those writers in search of unsentimental themes and uncontrived forms.

Instead of uncovering a univocal ideology of stereotypical manhood, we will find inscribed in the trajectories of these specific American quest narratives visions of individuality and mutual relationship that attempt to break down conventional sexual categorization by breaking through the limiting forms of culture and the conventions of love-literature at once. In a sense, the questing vision was ultimately limited by its chosen field of representation; for the decision to forego the world of male-female relations necessarily involved in absence of female reality that, as we shall see in adaptations of the genre in the twentieth century, could be used to support a misogynistic world-view. Nonetheless, the early *potential* of the mode was immense, for by presenting the figuratively all-male world as an *imaginative* alternative to existing social and literary constructs, the quest writer found himself empowered to express in "a bold and nervous lofty language," perhaps for the first time, a questioning of the dominant sexual order within which he too was trapped.

A later and contrasting literary context that sheds light on the exploration of masculine identity in the quest-romance is the male adventure story of the frontier or wild West, with its prototype in Cooper's wilderness tales. Only superficially resembling the romance-quests in which I am interested, this late-century development served the same ideological function for its male readers as the sentimental treatise did for the female audience: through its romanticized fantasies of supervirile heroism and strength, the western novel validated accepted notions of sexual hierarchy and male authority.[15] Telling in this regard—and radically at odds with the quest genre—is the fact that the frontier hero's rough-and-ready adventures are almost always governed by a crude manifestation of the courtship pattern. As one also finds in the Leatherstocking Tales, it is the inspiriting presence of women—as frail vessels to rescue and protect from the menacing wilderness environment, as signifiers of a civilization whose values can only be maintained by male prowess—that gives the frontier novel's hyper-masculine ethos its whole point.[16] From opposing vantage points, then, the western and sentimental genres—along with most "Romance" narrative in general—maintained an essentialist myth of sexual dichotomization from which the protagonists of Melville, Twain and London's quest novels attempt to escape.

Rather than directly challenge the falsifying stereotypes of the sexes promoted by this fictional system and its parent realist tradition, the prototypical romance writer simply abandoned the subject of "realistic" romantic involvement altogether; some romancers like Hawthorne and Poe turned to largely allegorical modes of narrative whose dichotomized images of light/dark heroines, in particular, were as "unreal" as those mythologized by sentimental fiction, while the quest writer sidestepped the social and literary problematic of the sexes by imagining world without women, hence ostensibly free of the gendered system creating a sexually bifurcated society. As we have noted, there may be at times a fine line separating innovative and conservative impulse in the writer's choice of the quest as narrative subject. By examining *how* the male world is used, however, whether it gives voice to dominant values, as in Cooper, or attempts through indirection to give voice to a hitherto silenced reality and alternative world, as in Melville, we can begin to filter the wishfully escapist from legitimately progressive variations within the genre. In the latter case, moreover, it is important to realize that the socially subversive content of the fiction is, as in much marginalized women's fiction, filtered first through the private realm of individual desire: rather than confronting the politics of sexuality head-on or in a public context, such texts often limit their explorations of the impingements of social and fictive structures of power to the personal level—a focus nonetheless opening up, for the quest writer, a hitherto unexplored geography of possibility underlying social myths of male identity and relationship.

II

While these various literary and social contexts help explain the genesis of the quest format, certain repeating thematic and formal tropes peculiar to the genre underline the uncommonness of its attempt to redefine masculine sexual identity. Paramount among three distinguishing characteristics is the ever-present male bond in the world of the quest. Fiedler first deduced that the genre's "manly friendships" represent "a kind of counter-matrimony"[17]: whence the relationships of Ishmael and Queequeg, Huck and Jim, Van Weyden and Wolf Larsen. As symbolic alternative to the conventions and constrictions associated with the social ideal of wedlock, the "pure marriage of males" facilitates bonds that are deeply committed yet—unlike hierarchically-ordered marriage—not detrimental to either partner's sense of personal freedom.[18] The mutuality of gender, it would appear, permits a level of equal interchange and individualism that the dualistic assumptions underlying conventional marital union negate. Unlike the male pairs represented in the British tradition of master and servant (one thinks of Crusoe and Friday, Pickwick and Sam Weller, Holmes and Watson, whose "unions" reflect the hierarchical order of society), the American comrades often present a more multifaceted model of loving relationship: their bonds simultaneously partake of brotherly, passionate, paternal, filial, even maternal qualities, without being restricted to one definition alone. Even when the paired questers comprise a racial duality—which Fiedler interprets as a symbolic union of the "primitive" or instinctual life and the questing ego[19]—the fact remains that the black-white opposition is only "skin-deep," as it were, since the true source maintaining the male bond is its mutuality—of spirit, of gender, of democratic fraternity.

The theoretical absence of women in the quest narrative provides a second indication of its untraditional status, but not in an expected fashion. For, although the male quest by definition excludes woman as major protagonist (the second half of London's *The Sea Wolf* will prove an instructive exception), her traces nonetheless resurface in the world of the quest to play a crucial role as symbol and image, as inner principle in the individual quester, and as external role imposed on weaker or androgynous men by repressive figures of authority.[20] As the lines cited from Melville's "After the Pleasure Party" indicate, the quest not only reaches "beyond" for a metaphysical explanation of existence, but may also reach "within for a psychogenic truth that reveals the falsity of the constructs of gender used to differentiate the sexes and distribute power unequally betwen them."[21] *Moby-Dick, Huckleberry Finn, Billy Budd* and *The Sea Wolf* all to some extent participate in a dialectic between those obsessed questers, filled with a will to power that blinds them to this truth, and those expansive selves—like Ishmael, Huck, Billy—whose inner equanimity rests upon their unselfconscious acceptance of the love and compassion traditionally associated with the female sphere and the heart. The dangers besetting such "openness" of personality are best illustrated in *Billy Budd,* where the eponymous hero's "androgynous" attributes become a "feminine" weakness to those authorities who fear loss of their male-identified powers and thus force the "handsome sailor" to assume a role analogous to that of woman's in society. The very existence of such "female-substitute" figures in the quest genre becomes a powerful textual signifier of the oppressiveness and potential destruction associated with an ethos equating power with masculinity.

A third distinguishing trait of the American male quest—noted by Chase, Brodhead, Seelye and others—is its unique narrative structure. What has gone unmentioned, however, is the degree to which the mode's textual organization, in replicating the quester's search for unboundaried self-definition, evolved as an important correlative of the radical thematic departures outlined above. In essence, the rejection of restrictive cultural formats that triggers the protagonist's desire to escape society simultaneously operates as a rejection of the concept of stable narrative centers: that is, the forward movement of the quest into unknown *geographic* space is so orchestrated as to create a linear projection into undefined *textual* space. Instead of a symmetrically unified pattern based on conflict, separation and resolution, the narrative organization of the quest novel is characterized by an open series of often jarring or startling narrative expansions and transformations. Related to Romantic theories of the organically proliferating text, the quest narrative thus has an effect of being always already in process, of forever reaching after new and unexpected plateaus of meaning. As Richard Brodhead has demonstrated, this effect is often achieved by the linking together of disparate representational modes (or sub-genres) of fiction, so that the reader gains the sense not merely of several types of narrative strung together, but of one mode after the other being left behind, traveled beyond, as the evolving quest carries both reader and protagonist into increasingly uncharted realms of discourse and plot. These transitions from one mode of narration to the next are often marked (1) by threshold moments that serve as springboard from which the narrative, like the quest itself, launches forward into the unknown, or (2) by symbolic moments of rebirth that propel the protagonist into new contexts and new identities.

Often accompanying these shifts in mode are abrupt refocusings of perspective, exemplified by the frequently discussed movement in *Moby-Dick* from Ishmael's narrating voice to omnisciently narrated scenes to which he has no access. This process of juxtaposing voices and viewpoints is not simply authorial idiosyncrasy or pyrotechnical display: more importantly, the technique reenacts a process happening on the psychological level as the hero's identity undergoes successive expansions towards an ideally inclusive openness. The representational and perspectival strategies structuring the quest thus function in concert with its thematic content; its innovative format embodies *both* the quester's escape from restrictive sexual convention and his subsequent expansion into a multiform sense of maleness. In the process, as the following examples of *Moby-Dick, Huckleberry Finn, Billy Budd* and *The Sea Wolf* will show, the movement of the quest forms an emphatic rejection of the narrative stability and fortuitously merging plot lines associated with nineteenth-century fiction in general and with the love-plot in particular.

III

A major secondary theme—and target of criticism—running throughout Melville's canon concerns the sexual polarity that can render wedlock a life-denying prison and selfhood a state of incompletion. At the same time, his novels and stories stage an unremitting attack on fictional conventions, particularly those formal constraints inherited from the literary marriage tradition.[23] Melville's evolution of the male quest narrative can be seen as a defiant response to these concerns: his strategic reformulation of the quest-romance genre, importantly, allowed his personal vision of *vital* male identity to emerge in healthy opposition to the sentimental literary ideology that countenanced an unbridgeable separation of male and female roles, powers and spheres.[24] In Melville's world of quest, in fact, individual authenticity depends on the effort to reconcile such antimonies, and this ideal of manhood is given concrete if brief representation in the avatars of the Handsome Sailor type recurring throughout the canon; these men (Marnoo of *Typee*, Jack Chase of *White-Jacket*, Billy) are most notable for their striking physical unions of masculine and feminine beauty.[25] But it is in *Moby-Dick*, the archetypal quest narrative, that Melville most allusively and deeply explores the psychological connection between self-sufficient male identity and an acknowledgement of the "feminine" within man; in the process the issue of sexual identity becomes an inseparable part of the text's subject-matter and narrative form. The result is a completely different mode of "love story," one in which unending quest (as pursued by Ishmael) rather than ultimate conquest (Ahab's goal) defines the independent self and its relationship to others.

Despite its lack of heterosexual romance, *Moby-Dick* exudes a powerful erotic energy that is manifested in a complex network of sexual innuendo, imagery and mythic allusion.[26] Ever since D.H. Lawrence's identification of the white whale as "the great American phallos," numerous psychoanalytic readings have focused on the battle of Moby-Dick and Ahab as an expression of the aggressive male libido. This emphasis, however, has tended to neglect the symbolic significance with which Melville imbues the feminine as well as the phallic.[27] Not only is the whale evoked in imagery suggesting a paradoxical union of masculine and feminine principles[28]; the encompassing universe of the novel—sea and sky—is figured in the suggestively titled chapter "The Symphony" as a primordial wedding of "hardly separable" elements iconographically represented as male and female. The polymorphous life-force at work in the natural world becomes an appropriate backdrop for Melville's depiction of a similar state existing in human nature and embodied in Ishmael, who progresses toward a psychic harmony and an elasticity of identity that is always in motion, never fixed by conventional rules of social roles. Significantly, Ishmael's bond with another man forms the text's opening paradigm of the means to inner unity. Beginning his narration in a state of self-division, Ishmael soon undergoes a "melting" that heals his "splintered heart" through the restorative influence of the self-possessed and loving Queequeg, his bed-companion in New Bedford.[29] The fact that Melville repeatedly identifies their sojourn as a kind of honeymoon (pp. 53, 54) points to the symbolic "marriage" taking place within Ishmael's psyche, as well as to the viability of the male bond in affirming the individual wholeness of the independent male quester.

Exactly *what* is being unified in Ishmael is given further symbolic representation in the "Grand Armada" chapter, which as many critics have noted presents a vision of internal union already prefigured in Ishmael's bonding with Queequeg.[30] For as his whaleboat inadvertently penetrates to the "innermost heart of [a] shoal" of gallied whales (p. 324), the young man has a revelation of the maternal love and feminine life-processes abiding at the secret heart of life. Within a circle of "enchanted calm" the boat is visited by sporting "cows and calves[,] the women and children of this routed host" (p. 324); in the translucent "watery vaults" below the craft there unfolds a "still stranger world" of "nursing mothers" (p. 325) and of "young Leviathan amours in the deep" (p. 326). What makes this glimpse of the sources of life so overpowering is Ishmael's immediate recognition of an analogous state existing within himself: "But even so, amid the tornadoed Atlantic of my being, do I myself still for ever centrally disport in mute calm ... deep down and deep inland there I still bathe me in eternal mildness of joy" (p. 326).

Although this actual moment passes as the herd of whales disperses, its interior vision of love echoes through the rest of the novel, perhaps most vividly dramatized as external possibility in the famous "A Squeeze of the Hand" chapter. In this simultaneously rhapsodic and comic scene, where the crew lovingly join hands while squeezing whale casing or sperm, the inner "mildness of joy" experienced in the Armada becomes a joyous embrace of all fellow-men. The male bond of two equivalent selves celebrated in the New Bedford chapters is thus transformed into a principle of fraternal democracy shared among several dozen men. Yet pointedly enough, as Chase and Shulman point out, this ideal of loving community exists *outside* the "settled social order" because its all-male constituency necessarily forms a "radically unorthodox alternative" to societal—and specifically marital—norms.[31]

The degree to which Ishmael's expanding identity depends upon his unquestioning acceptance of the "maternal" or "feminine" within himself is also central to the narrative's conclusion. It is the Rachel, after all, the loving mother "in her retracing search after her missing children" (p. 470), that reclaims Ishmael from the wreck of the Pequod. In a penultimate image of rebirth, Ishmael undergoes yet one more expansion of self as he survives to tell the tale. His salvation, however, is neither fixed nor permanently secured, like that of a traditional hero, at the novel's end. It will rather depend on a continuing series of "rebirths" into progressively new worlds: selfhood is realized, paradoxically, in the perpetual act of questing for it. Ishmael's expansive textual presence and narrating voice have reaffirmed this truth time and again, suggesting in the process his capacity for transcending socially-prescribed labels and for championing a revisionary definition of his independent subjectivity as a man.

The ideal wholeness toward which Ishmael moves contrasts vividly with Ahab's one-sided definition of his masculinity, as his tragically fixed purpose and fixated personality attest. Having concentrated all his energies, both emotional and libidinal, into one singularly aggressive goal, Ahab becomes the stereotype of the destructive "male" impulse, fueled by ultimately empty shows of vengeance, power and ego. In the process, the mad captain has replaced the potential for loving contact with his fellow beings with what Martin Pops has aptly termed "violent thrusts" against an imagined foe.[32] The aim of "quest," so perverted by Ahab's monomania, has become simply "conquest."

Ahab's defiant posturing specifically reveals the self-hatred that is unleashed when the softening influences of the heart, the soul, the identifies the soul's⸱ gender as female, Ahab's first mate mourns that "small touch of the human mother" and that "soft feeling of the that "small touch of the human mother" and that "soft feeling of the human" which he feels that Ahab, through his assumption of absolute mastery, has "overmanned" both in himself and in his crew (p. 148); a few chapters later the reader is made privy to Ahab's nightmare-ridden sleep when this very "soul" attempts to escape the "integral" of which it is part

(p. 175), an action metaphorically leaving Ahab a divided, incomplete man: in a pattern that will become increasingly familiar, will has triumphed over feeling. The degree to which patriarchal values of hatred and tumult finally supplant in Ahab the maternal ones of love and inner calm embraced by Ishmael becomes obvious when Ahab declares his satanic allegiance and "right worship" to "my fiery father" (pp. 416-17) during the terrifying storm-at-sea episode near the end of the novel. It comes as no surprise that in the shortly following "The Symphony" chapter Ahab once again rejects the momentarily softening emotions coaxed into life within him by the surrounding environment. By the time the climactic three-day chase begins, Ahab's identity has become more hardened than ever, impervious to change or emotion—the man has become a nightmarish embodiment of the erotic compulsion to subjugate lying behind the traditional male ethos that maintains its supremacy in a gender-divided world through power.

The contrast between Ishmael's acquisition of an open perspective that might be called androgynous and Ahab's imprisonment within a limited role forms a powerful critique of the male ethos ruling American society. The depth of this critique is extended, to a significant degree, by Melville's unconventional manipulation of narrative form in *Moby-Dick*. In defining the quester's pursuit of "open independence" as a rejection of the finality of port or harbor, the "safety" of home or hearthstone (p. 97), Melville suggests the manner in which the very trajectory of his text, a linear projection into the unknown, not only breaks from the closed world of shore values but also from the self-contained design and narrative ends of traditionally conceived fiction. But the structure of this narrative is not linear in a simply descriptive fashion. As Brodhead has perceived, the novel's sense of irrevocable forward motion results from the strategic arrangement of a series of continually transforming narrative modes and extending perspectival structures. As a result, the reader's sensation of traveling through and beyond a succession of texts and superimposed views of reality replicates that of the quester simultaneously plunging into the unknown in search of a new identity. Thus, the predominantly comedic mode of the initial shore chapters, ending with the "marriage" of Ishmael and Queequeg, gives way to a new form and new realm, that of supernatural romance, as the Pequod launches its mysterious quest into the "lone Atlantic" (p. 97); the world of romance is in turn interrupted and extended by a variety of representational modes—stage-drama, monologues, Montaigne-like essays, interpolated tales and more—whose shifts in format are accompanied by modulations in points of view. This organicism engenders an expansive textuality appropriate to the recording of Ishmael's growth toward inclusive, unlimited identity; for his chameleon shifts of tone, style and role—matching and accommodating the various structural modulations—attest to what Brodhead calls a "mazy dance of mind" capable of activating "a whole range of ... [hidden] potential within."[33] Structure, in effect, becomes as instrumental as characterization in conferring on Ishmael an identity that encompasses a radically untraditional conception of male selfhood.

The open pattern that Ishmael comes to view as more true to life and to the human personality ("There is no steady unretracting progress in this life; we do not advance through fixed gradations, and at the last one pause," he states in a famous passage [p. 406]) also becomes descriptive of Melville's textual enterprise: through Ishmael's narrating voice he constantly emphasizes the openness of a narrative technique which "promise[s] nothing complete" (p. 118). In juxtaposition to Ahab's enunciation of his madly fixed purpose in chapter 44, Ishmael declares at the beginning of chapter 45 that his own direction as narrator will be determined by impression and indirection rather than straightforward movement, and he thus voices an aesthetic credo that corresponds to the inconclusive openness of his own personality: "I care not to perform my task methodically" (p. 175). Nothing could be more removed from Ahab's desire for absolute finality—an "end" ironically attained in Ahab's final "reunion" in death with his antagonist, the White Whale. Although the literal action of the hunt reaches a close, the novel's meaning remains deliberately open. The mystery of the whale, which remains as inconclusive and enigmatic as ever, is matched by the opening affixed to Ishmael's story. His symbolic rebirth and rescue from the wreckage of the Pequod ("one did survive the wreck ... and I was he" [p. 470]), reactivating the continuing possibilities of self-discovery, moves Ishmael toward an open future and unknown point in the time from which he narrates the Epilogue. The "portrait" of Ishmael, therefore, eludes a final framing, just as his identity escapes restrictive definitions of masculine behavior. Melville's innovative break from fictional tradition in evolving the quest narrative, it becomes clear, has helped to give voice to an alternative vision of selfhood that similarly eludes social and sexual convention.

* * *

Themes of independent selfhood, non-restrictive sexual roles, and counter-traditional male bonds also figure prominently in the voyage of self-discovery charted in Twain's *The Adventures of Huckleberry Finn*. The degree to which this "innocent" novel of "boyhood" is actually a subversive document of social and political protest has often been pointed out; Huck's quest through the contrasting worlds of shore and river provides a devastating commentary on confrontation between enslavement and freedom in American life, race, and culture. Huck's quest, however, is also a response to a bifurcated sexual ethos that blocks individual wholeness or self-expression. In rejecting the shore world's negative models of masculine aggression and feminine piety alike, Huck embraces an independent truth of self, rooted in an ethos of compassionate love, that runs counter to all social hierarchies. For it is his loving relationship with the slave, Jim, above all else, that becomes the measure of Huck's status as a cultural misfit and of his unretraceable deviation from a traditional standard of manhood.

In contrast to a world enslaved in custom, Huck shares with Ishmael an innate flexibility and receptivity in face of the unknown. The multiple roles, identities, and fabricated biographies he invents during the course of his quest give him the figurative space within which to develop a more complete sense of self. Whereas the disguises donned by the charlatan Duke and Dauphin simply make clear their parasitic relationship to society, Huck's facile movement among multiple identities attests to his freedom from all fixed roles: he can cross boundaries of class, race and sex with startling ease.[34]

Like a younger Ishmael, Huck also undergoes a series of symbolic deaths and rebirths that, analogous to the various identities he assumes, illustrate his continually expanding personality. These rebirths, not coincidentally, mark progressive stages in the novel's structure, for its organization is predicated upon a series of modal and tonal shifts tracing Huck's geographic, then psychological, removal from societal structures that impede personal development. The first two stages of Huck's removal from the known define the twin sources of his oppression as sentimental and patriarchal in organization. First, Huck finds himself trapped in the "feminized" world of the Widow Douglas and Miss Watson who ply the tools of conventional morality and religious piety in an attempt to sanitize Huck's rebellious strain and thereby "fix" him within a norm of childhood predictability. With Pap's kidnapping and imprisoning of the boy in the woods at one remove from the decorous social order of St. Petersburg, Huck finds himself once again psychologically circumscribed—now by stupidly "masculine" force rather than "feminine" threats of conscience. Accordingly, the novel shifts from the genre of adolescent escape fiction to that of backwoods melodrama. But in both cases the power structure sanctioning Huck's oppression remains the same. For, anti-social as Pap may seem, he shares with the Widow Douglas a belief in familial and social hierarchy that justifies his parental brutality as well as his racial bigotry. In both cases the patriarchal power structure sanctioning Huck's oppression remains the same.

Staging his "death" to escape Pap's tyranny, Huck begins an odyssey—first to Jackson Island, then downriver with the runaway Jim—that inaugurates a third mode of narrative, the quest proper. The diametric opposition between Huck's values and the world he is attempting to elude becomes the text's basic structural principle from this point to the river-voyage's end in chapter 31. For the linear projection of the quest is periodically interrupted by digressive shore episodes and picaresque adventures that expose, time and again, the patriarchal and sentimental norms that have cooperated in corrupting American culture.[35] Juxtaposed with the power of oppression, however, is the potential power of love residing in the river idyll itself, an oasis of freedom to which Huck repeatedly returns after his disastrous adventures on shore.[36] As the one constant element in the fluid downriver movement, the raft comes to represent a more stable concept of "home" than its sentimentalized Victorian counterpart: "We said there warn't no home like a raft, after all," Huck comments upon escaping the gruesome aftermath of the Grangerford-Shepherdson feud, happy to feel "free and safe once more."[37]

And if this momentary paradise comprises an unconventional definition of home, its two members form an equally counter-traditional example of "family"—made as it is of two races and one sex. Similar to the bond shared by Ishmael and Queequeg, Huck and Jim's loving attachment is forged in a mutuality of spirit that, over time, becomes genuine, equitable and non-possessive: as such it transcends the structures defining the relation of man and wife, parent and child, white and black, in American society. If Huck's identity refuses to be fitted to one role, neither does this bond conform to a single need but rather embodies multiple dimensions. Fiedler rightly observes of this "counter-marriage of males" that

Jim is all things to [Huck]: father and mother and playmate and beloved, appearing naked and begowned and bewhiskered ... and calling Huck by names appropriate to their multiform relationship: 'Huck' or 'honey' or 'chile' or 'boss,' and just once 'white genleman.'[38]

Moreover, Jim also provides the boy with a positive model of male selfhood, the ideal goal of the quest; as he pronounces early in the text, "I owns myself" (p. 246), his words calling to mind the self-possession of Queequeg, "always equal to himself" (*MD,* p. 52). For Twain and for Melville the path to individual integrity lies through heartfelt compassion, and the stages by which Huck discovers the worth of his attachment to Jim simultaneously chart his progress toward a non-conforming identity that depends, ironically, on *not* being "man enough" (p 310) in the eyes of society to turn in Jim as an escaped slave.[39]

What, then, many critics have asked, happens to Huck's gains in self-knowledge in the final escapades at Phelps Farm? In stepping off the raft in chapter 31, Huck literally walks into another novel—one authored, in a figurative sense, by Tom Sawyer—and accordingly his character seems to transform dramatically as he becomes Tom's passive accomplice.

However, if we take into consideration the modal shifts typical of the quest genre in general, we can see that the episode at Phelps Farm, rather than marking a complete departure from the social criticism that has preceded, forms the final in a series of transforming modes of fictional representation: from its opening in a juvenile fantasy fiction that is presented as a spin-off of *Tom Sawyer*'s ending to quest idyll punctuated by the violent, the gothic, and the picaresque, the text now evolves into a scathing social satire that works to expose the "fictions" of authority by which a slave-owning society operates. For Master Tom's sadistic (and utterly ridiculous) scheme to rescue Jim from his new captivity at the Farm—worked out "regular" according to "what's in the books" (pp. 202, 203)—becomes Twain's satiric parody of the conventional plot formulas that Twain himself is violating in writing a romance-quest. The inadequacy of Tom's viewpoint is exposed when his regulated plot backfires—indeed, approaches tragedy—as Tom is shot and Jim recaptured to be hanged. Conventional novelistic form, Twain implies, may be the least effective way of "freeing" a subject—be that subject Jim or be it Twain's subversive themes.

Yet Tom's fantasies seem to carry the day, given the neatly contrived, happy ending and last-page revelation that Jim is a free man after all. But we simultaneously learn that Huck has also been "freed"—released by the death of Pap into sole possession of his named identity. Tom's earlier gripe that Huck "want[s] to be starting something fresh all the time" (p. 480), rather than going along with established conventions, becomes a prophecy of the text's final structural turn. For in the last lines Huck announces his intention of escaping the boundaries of conventional life and the closure of Tom's imposed fiction by lighting out for the Territory. With this penultimate gesture, Huck reaffirms both the forward-moving dynamic of the quest and his own counter-traditional opposition to growing up to fit a "sivilized" definition of manhood. One may question whether Huck will ever succeed in attaining true or total self-expression, however far West he moves, but this closing ambiguity only enhances the radical implications of Twain's social criticism and Huck's dream of unhampered freedom.[40]

*　　*　　*

As the nineteenth-century drew to a close, the sentimentalism that had long dominated American society began to give way to a more overtly masculinist ethos that venerated male power at the expense of the softer emotions of the heart celebrated by Ishmael and Huck. Melville's last and unfinished *Billy Budd, Sailor*, appraises the effects of this new set of values in an allegory of life and death aboard a man-of-war ship literally and figuratively adrift at sea. With damningly calm, clear simplicity, this text presents the death of Melville's personal ideal of independent manhood—

the Handsome Sailor prototype embodied in the androgynous Billy—at the hands of unfeeling justice and brute violence. In so doing, this interiorized version of the quest-romance unequivocally sets itself against a power-oriented culture whose univocal reading of "masculine" authority and "masculine" identity not only further disempowered women in general but also threatened to eclipse what Melville would identify in symbolic terms as the "feminine in man."[41]

The conjunction of masculine and feminine characteristics in Billy's appearance, coupled with his personality and its effect on others, indicates the extent to which a probing of sexual identity lies at the heart of the novella.[42] With a face "all but feminine in purity,"[43] Billy also boasts a "masculine beauty" (p. 53) and fine physical "mold" (p. 51) that "in the nude might have posed for a statue of young Adam before the Fall" (p. 94). For all the marks of the "heroic strong man, Hercules," in his physical bearing, Billy also calls to mind "something suggestive of a mother" favored by the goddess of Love, Venus (p. 51), and it is this latter characteristic, feminine-associated love, that Billy's personality most abundantly conveys, as his harmonizing role as "peacemaker" aboard the merchantship Rights-of-Man illustrates (p. 47).

The floating, idyllic and all-male comaraderie of the Rights-of-Man—evocative of the Edenic paradise temporarily established aboard Huck and Jim's raft—is only a memory, however, in *Billy Budd*, which opens after the foretopman's impressment into the King's service by the officers of the Bellipotent. Billy's transition from one ship to the other, as their names suggest, outlines a crucial rite of passage as he grows from a youthful state of freedom to an adult life in which martial power stands as the controlling metaphor for a state of male domination: the shipboard world of quest, hitherto an escape from social circumscription, has become a microcosm of the hierarchical world left behind.

The psychological action culminating in the eclipse of Melville's male ideal unfolds, appropriately, as a series of confrontations between the untraditional Billy and the Bellipotent's two representatives of entrenched power, the bullying "master-at-arms" Claggart and the authoritarian captain, Edward Fairfax Vere. Both men perceive Billy as a threat because his presence subconsciously reminds them of the emotive or loving faculty within themselves that has been suppressed to insure their superiority over and control of others.

Claggart's dual feelings of attraction for and subsequent hatred of Billy's physical beauty, for instance, amount to a profound "envy" (p. 78) of Billy's sensed difference. Thus, the master-at-arms' attraction becomes a smouldering "passion" of hatred (p. 77) that renders any mutual love on the order of that experienced by Huck and Jim, or Ishmael and Queequeg, impossible. As Georges Michel Sarotte and E. Grant Watson have realized, Claggart's ensuing attempt to dominate Billy through persecution—

precipitating Billy's tragedy—is a defensive mechanism to protect himself
against love, that very *non-aggressive* force embodied in Billy that
Claggart at once desires and fears.[44] In the sadomasochistic configuration
that Claggart and Billy form—a perverse parody of the romantic ideal of
complementary opposition—it is inevitable that words be replaced by
physical aggression as the only mode of communication possible between
the two men, for these are the terms that the "master" Claggart has
imposed on his victim. "I could only say it with a blow" (p. 106), Billy thus
testifies of his spontaneous rebellion against this tyranny, which results in
Claggart's death.

At this moment the narrative focus shifts to Vere, who embodies an
intellectualized version of the impulses underlying Claggart's brutality.
For Vere's is a "resolute nature" (p. 60) founded on self-control as
crippling as Claggart's repressed passions; his reasoned deliberations leave
him, "the most undemonstrative of men" (p. 60), an incomplete self
"lack[ing] in the companionable quality" (p. 63). Only in response to
Billy's crime does the extent of Vere's allegiance to authoritarian norms
surface, however, and then in a very telling substitution of terms: "The
father in him, manifested toward Billy thus far . . . was replaced by the
military disciplinarian" (p. 100). Although Vere may be justified in fearing
mutiny, given the politically unstable climate of the times, the extreme
"prudence and vigor" (p. 103) that he chooses to exercise in summoning
the drumhead court is extreme. For as his amazingly explicit summary
speech at Billy's trial indicates, his hardness and rejection of mercy are
directly linked to a fear of the "feminine in man," and all that term
connotes as dangerously subversive of masculine authority:

But let not warm hearts betray heads that should be cool . . . . Well, the heart here,
sometimes *the feminine in man* is as that piteous woman, and hard though it be,
she must here be ruled out. (p. 111; emphases added)

Not only is the jury being told to rule out "that piteous woman" in
themselves, but they are implicitly being directed to "rule out" Billy, who
has come to represent the "feminine in man," the signifier of difference
that must be expelled if the hierarchical supremacy of men is to be
maintained in the world of which the Bellipotent is a microcosm. For Vere
also stresses that Billy's crime has been to violate the whole concept of
traditional hierarchy by "strik[ing] his superior in grade" (p. 111). In a
man-of-war world, as well as in society, disciplinary action for this
infraction of order must "[take] after the father"—that is, the destructive
principle Vere identifies as "War" itself (p. 112). The purpose, then,
toward which Vere drives is nothing less than the erasure of the
"feminine," yet radically insubordinate, impulse embodied in Billy.

While patriarchal rule superficially triumphs in this confrontation—

for Billy is hanged—the male world without his harmonizing presence is left more incomplete than ever, a fact simultaneously registered in the novella's jagged narrative structure. Throughout the text Melville has made its formal attributes suggestive of an ever-deepening inquiry into the nature of male authority and identity. Hence the "voyage into the unknown" format presented here is depicted less as an external than psychological event, as the absence of all but minimal physical action suggests. Instead, the "movement" characteristic of the genre occurs as an intellectual or textual activity: one chapter will become an opening up, rather than linear extension, of the information conveyed in its predecessor; seeming digressions turn into the true trajectory of the narrative; the shifting of focus from Billy to Vere, then to Claggart and back to Vere, abets the disorienting sensation of an evolving movement whose destination is uncertain; Melville's use of a conjecture-filled narrative voice which can only hypothesize about but never penetrate the various characters' states of consciousness heightens the reader's experience of plunging blindly into a mystery—Billy's martyrdom—for which there is no final explanation.

The purposefully "ragged edges" (p. 128) of Melville's conclusion—a series of digressive "sequel[s]" (p. 128) that follow upon Billy's execution—therefore introduce several divergent impressions of Billy and his story in order to continue the questioning raised by the prior events; issues are refused the simplification inherent in a closed plot format.[45] As a result, the open-ended quest narrative utilized in *Billy Budd* unlocks a disturbing exploration into the far reaches of patriarchal power, revealing the all-male world to be an inferno of violence, domination and repression when traditional male authority is allowed to stamp out the "feminine in man." The tragic outcome of the confrontation between self-sufficiency and limited sexual roles, played out as psychodrama in this "inside narrative" (the novella's subtitle), foreshadows the advent of the male-oriented novel of the twentieth century, in which men bond together not to escape sexual dichomotization but to perpetuate its stranglehold on norms of identity.

*   *   *

The status of Jack London's *The Sea Wolf* as a quest novel falls somewhere between these extremes of male fiction. On one level London is as vitally concerned with issues of sexual identity as Melville; yet his attempt to chart a more positive ideal through male bonding is fraught with ambiguities that become not only thematically but textually problematic when, at the novel's end, the format of the quest dissolves into that of sentimental romance. The conflicting allegiances of *The Sea Wolf* offer an opportunity to assess, by way of summary, the potential and the liabilities of using the quest-romance mode as an expression of rebellion against literary and sexual norms.

London's novel shares with other male quest narratives a sea-journey into the literal and metaphysical reaches of the unknown, experienced by reader and protagonist alike as a process of defamiliarization. Opening with the shipwrecked Humphrey Van Weyden stranded "in the midst of a gray primordial vastness,"[46] the action shifts to Wolf Larsen's seal-hunter whose plunging movement "into the heart of the Pacific" seems to near the "bounds" of "the universe itself" (pp. 30, 166). Simultaneously, Humphrey is gradually divorced from the realm of the psychologically familiar as the nightmarish outbreaks of violence aboard the renegade ship increase in tempo. This process of removal is matched by another element common to quest narrative—Humphrey's immersion in an all-male environment that inspires a redefinition of his own manhood and realization of a supposedly more well-rounded identity. But here we can pinpoint an important difference between London's purpose and that of the preceding authors. Whereas Billy's identity has always been unselfconsciously androgynous and both Ishmael and Huck grow to accept the "feminine" as part of their integral selves, Humphrey's task is rather to incorporate the manly element lacking in his dilettantish, effeminate upbringing. "My muscles were small and soft, like a woman's" (p. 30), he confesses to the reader, explaining that "I had not been called 'Sissy' Van Weyden all my days without reason" (p. 64). Thus, while Melville and Twain reclaim the feminine from a stereotypical context in order to make it a symbol of a universal loving capacity that transcends gender, London continues to link femininity with weakness, passivity, inertia. The goal of Humphrey's quest for identity—theoretically at least—is a blending of his initial sensitivity with virile strength, but London's emphasis on the latter, as we shall see, ultimately circles back to a traditional view of the sexes.

Fished from the sea and rubbed back to life aboard Larsen's "brute-ship," Humphrey is reborn into a totally alien, all-male world where "Force, nothing but force obtained" (p. 32) and where all "Weakness is wrong" (p. 55). The hierarchy of domination that arises from this ethos of brute strength—an anarchic version of the iron-clad authoritarianism represented in *Billy Budd*—is embodied in Wolf Larsen, captain of the Ghost and Humphrey's immediate model for the elemental "potency" and "virility of spirit" (p. 16) characterizing the perfect "man-type" (p. 99). Despite Wolf's unfeeling cruelty, he is also a brooding thinker haunted by "that questing, that everlasting query...as to what it was all about" (p. 59). Hence he becomes Humphrey's emblem of the archetypal romantic quester as well as virile superman: "I could see him only as living always, and dominating always, fighting and destroying, himself surviving" (p. 120).

Although Humphrey's prognosis of Wolf's future turns out to be wrong, his relationship with Wolf provides the necessary spur to his own growth and survival. Metaphorically, Wolf becomes the very territory through which Humphrey's quest for manhood must lead: "I felt an elation of spirit," Humphrey says of the Captain's presence, "I was groping into his soul-stuff . . . I was exploring virgin territory. A strange, a terribly strange, region was unrolling itself before my eyes" (p. 56). So intimate a drawing together may seem to recall the affirming bonds of Ishmael and Queequeg, or Huck and Jim, but in fact Humphrey and Wolf's gravitation to each other is based on an antithetical norm of polarity and hierarchy. For Wolf is not only Humphrey's teacher but his total *master* in an arrangement closer to marital conventions than London realizes: "And thus it was that I passed into a state of involuntary servitude," Humphrey reports of the role he assumes in response to Wolf's domination. "He was stronger than I, that was all" (p. 23). The sexual undercurrents always present in Humphrey's physical attraction to Wolf also italicize the conventional dynamics implicit in their master-slave relationship. When Humphrey first sees Wolf in the nude, for instance, he is instantly mesmerized by his masculine beauty; and Wolf's "command" that the awed Humphrey feel "the great muscles [that] leapt and moved under [his] satiny skin" (p. 99) is an act of deliberate provocation, establishing Wolf's power at the same time it valorizes male virility above any other sexual expression. The homoeroticism that Melville makes a positive symbol of unconventionality in *Moby-Dick* here becomes, unconsciously for London, an extension of the destructive male-female dialectic from which Melville's questers flee.

The disquieting resonances of such a relationship inevitably mark Humphrey's development, calling into question the ideal of manhood that London has set up as the proper end of his protagonist's quest. As in most quest narrative, personal growth is measured in a succession of newly acquired identities and roles, a process initiated when the nearly drowned Humphrey is renamed "Hump" by Wolf and made to assume the role of cabin-boy with the promise that "It will be the making of you" (p. 18). Having plummeted from a privileged status in the outer world to lowest position in the shipboard hierarchy, Hump undergoes his first *rite de passage* when he beats up the bully Cooky, a man even more effeminate than—and hence hierarchically inferior to—himself.[47] Progressing to the coveted rank of "mate," Hump becomes "aware of a toughening or hardening I was undergoing" (p. 108). While he maintains enough of his former values to realize that brutality alone is wrong, he welcomes the fact that he can "never again be quite the same man" because he feels that in touching upon his masculinity he is encountering "the world of the real" for the first time (p. 108).

But simultaneous with this process is Hump's awareness of the inadequacies of Wolf's world and creed: namely, its "unnatural" exclusion of women and the crew's lack of any capacity for "softness, and tenderness, and sympathy" (p. 89). However, unlike the texts of Melville and Twain, which advocate a realization *within men themselves* of emotions and values traditionally associated with women, Hump means his solution literally: it is the *actual presence* of women as spiritual examplars that is needed, without which the inherent "brute" in man cannot be tamed nor a "balance to their lives" be added (p. 89). This essentially conservative estimate of male and female nature anticipates the next turn of the plot as the ship-wrecked Maud Brewster enters the hitherto all-male world of the Ghost and irrevocably upsets its psychological dynamics. The modal shift from quest format to erotic-seduction narrative accompanying Maud's arrival serves to underscore London's vision of "correct" male development for Hump. By becoming the "willing slave" (p. 133) of Maud rather than Wolf, Hump redirects his newly acquired "masculine" energy into the chivalric service of fragile womanhood—a sacred duty successfully carried out when he strikes a blow to Wolf, his former master, to keep him from ravishing Maud.[48]

Following this positive exertion of male strength, the narrative undergoes yet another modal shift as Hump engineers his and Maud's escape from Wolf's ship; a kind of New World narrative evolves as the two set up house on a deserted island, Maud playing Friday to Hump's increasingly resourceful Crusoe in a primitive version of the domestic plot. Hump's successes in sheltering and protecting the physically less competent Maud, confirming his new masculine identity, precipitates an inner recognition of his love for Maud and of his natural ascendance in the conventional sexual order: "instantly conscious I became of my manhood," Hump lyricizes upon embracing Maud for the first time, "I felt myself masculine, the protector of the weak, the fighting male. And, best of all, I felt myself the protector of my loved one" (p. 201). Hump's last rite of passage is accomplished when he defeats the now weakened Wolf—who has coincidentally drifted to the same island—and prepares to sail back to civilization with Maud. With this imminent return to social order, the rhetoric of the last pages of the novel, in which the lovers exchange declarations, becomes that of sentimental romance:

> 'My woman, my own small woman,' I said, my free hand petting her shoulder in the way all lovers know though never learn in school.
> 'My man,' she said, looking at me for an instant with tremulous lids which fluttered down and veiled her eyes as she snuggled her head against my breast with a happy little sigh. (p. 252)

It is telling that neither Hump's sense of himself as a "man" nor Maud's as a "woman" stands alone: the identity of each depends on a complementary other who is to be possessed rather than be appreciated for his or her individuality—"my" man, "my" woman. Unlike the self-possession characterizing the independent identities of Ishmael or Huck or Billy, the "new" definition of masculinity toward which London directs his quest becomes, in Hump's case, evidence supporting an already existing ethos. The "feminine" side of the male protagonist, represented by Hump's initial effeminacy and aesthetic capacities as a literary critic, is deflected to the female "half" of a literal conjunction of male and female—for Maud is no less than a female poet by profession. The union that takes place within Ishmael has once again become the union that takes place externally, and in being made simultaneous with the ending of the novel it brings to a halt the fictional movement and meaning synonymous with quest.

IV

The imminent return of Hump and Maud to civilization—transforming the text's originally infinity-bound quest into a circular voyage of return and a recuperation of the familiar—serves to remind us of the potential of earlier quest narrative to move in quite the *opposite* direction—into unknown spheres where a new ideal of manhood awaits discovery. For, at its most psychologically adventurous, the quest novel as conceived by Melville or Twain activates a vision of male autonomy and subjectivity that engages in a covertly revolutionary sexual politics of its time by departing from traditional sexual categories. From our vantage point, the positive attributes of the questing hero's escape into a world without women appear threefold. First, his removal from the social and sexual expectations of a marriage-oriented culture may set free an expansive sense of identity that, like Ishmael's or Huck's, is multiform, fluid and affirming in its integrity. Second, the elevation of mutuality—rather than polarity—in the male bond, rendering it a marriage of equals, presents an alternative to the inequality governing institutionalized heterosexual relationship. And, third, an understated but powerful critique of the sexual order left behind often lingers in image, symbol, and situation in the all-male world; thus, as in *Billy Budd*, the degree to which the world of quest replicates the negative aspects of the society from which the quester has flown can become the vehicle for acute social criticism of America's male-dominated structures of power. As all these analyses have indicated, furthermore, the genre's potential for exploring the various implications of male independence exists in proportion to the radically "unfixed," provisional status of its narrative form. Hence, *The Sea Wolf*'s lack of success in maintaining the open-ended imperatives of the mode—signalled in its return to the happy ending of conventional romance—also becomes a sign of its abandonment of the untraditional themes we have seen in other quest narratives.

London's rather confused alliances—holding to both a "progressive" sexual ethic and an overtly masculinist creed—help explain the failure, by and large, of modern quest fiction to explore the unorthodox potentialities unearthed by earlier Americanists. For twentieth-century versions of the male quest—and here I largely agree with Fiedler's analysis of modern American fiction—have become increasingly ambiguous and self-deceiving as the possibility of escaping into a womanless world has become only a symbolic reality. In turn, literary evocations of the male bond have ceased to function as positive expressions of alternative relationships; rather, the depiction of camaraderie among men often disguises a profoundly disturbing authorial desire to avoid female reality altogether, while the fantasy of escaping society with one's comrades becomes the protagonist's ultimate excuse for misogynist exclusivity. The underlying fear of losing power that motivates such attitudes—so well dramatized in the pathological cases of Ahab, Claggart and Wolf—has led not only to a new and destructive stereotype of femininity (the "castrating bitch" syndrome) but also to a new archetype of phallic manhood, epitomized in the supervirile and silent western hero impervious to overt displays of emotion but swift to take violent action.[49]

These negative manifestations of modern-day quest, emerging from what was initially a movement away from stereotypicality, have been complicated by another factor: the distrust, in a more self-conscious age, of the homosexual implications of relationships between men who flee women. The result has often been an increased representation of machismo in male relations, as if mere strength would allay such fears, and a shying away from the non-sexist ideal embodied in Billy, as if representing the "feminine in man" would constitute an admission of sexual "deviance." Ironically, the natural and unconscious celebration of homoeroticism in traditional quest narrative becomes the ultimate taboo in contemporary renderings of the form.[50]

It is illuminating to trace these various ambivalences at work in Hemingway's *The Sun Also Rises* (1926) and Mailer's *The Naked and the Dead* (1948), two modern adaptations of the genre preoccupied with issues of sexual identity and independence from women. The fragmented post-war world of *The Sun Also Rises* provides the setting in which Jake Barnes' aimless quest for self-renewal unfolds; his sexual war-wound, leaving him literally a man without women despite the hovering presence of Brett, becomes the symbol of a personal inner void as well as the sign of the impotence of the world at large. Counterposed with this despairing vision, however, is the center of values residing in the reduced, modern-day version of male quest—Jake's spiritually purifying fishing trip to Spain with Bill Gordon—that lies at the heart of the novel. Yet the negative effect of this necessarily momentary retreat is that it reinforces the men's tendency to see *all* the world as an exclusively male domain: Brett, indeed, can only participate in this world by playing (unsuccessfully) at being "one of the boys." The result is a misogynist universe in which any independently minded woman, because of the threat she poses to male superiority, is doomed to failure.

Mailer's novel, on the other hand, exposes a hellish underside of Hemingway's nostalgic dream of an untroubled male Eden. Set in the all-male environment of a Pacific war zone, its central action a monomaniacal quest through the defamiliarizing reaches of the island Anopopei's jungles and mountains, *The Naked and the Dead* uses conventions of the quest format to show that there is *no escape*, however far one journeys, from the power-structures that rule society and dictate human behavior. All of Mailer's characters, in attempting to leave behind their disastrous personal relationships with women at home, have only found in war another battlefield, where they can continue to vent their frustrations in acts of meaningless aggression; even their own in-group relationships are simply power plays, demonstrating a "universal" compulsion to dominate and control others.

Thus, Mailer makes the quest into war—and his inquiry into the psychology of power—a scorching indictment of a destructive ethos associated with masculine aggression. But at the same time he seems to view the urge to fight and conquer as an inescapable aspect of maleness, and in the process he denigrates the alternative value of what we have been calling the "feminine" as saving inner principle or outer reality.[51] The novel's strongest point is at once its true weakness: for the oppressive vision of aggressive force that Mailer discloses simultaneously eclipses his perception of other possibilities.

These modern versions of the quest would seem to confirm Eve Kosofsky Sedgwick's thesis in *Between Men: English Literature and Male Homosocial Desire* that men form socially permissible bonds in order to perpetuate patriarchy.[52] The patriarchal order, that is, carries on its functions as if it were a "world without women," whether or not women are actually present to participate in its transactive desires. In a sense, then, even the earliest imaginings of the world of male quest are not without a certain potential ambiguity. But this is where it becomes crucial for us to distinguish between, say, the pairing of Natty-Chingachgook, who recuperate the wilderness for the white man and that of Ishmael-Queequeg, who plunge into its mystery in search of their own untapped potential. For as long as the possibility of breaking completely with the world of the known could be imagined *as actuality* by the nineteenth century quest writer, the symbolic value of venturing into the unknown with other men held the power of meaning *differently*, other than the pattern that Sedgwick sees as pervasive. Indeed, the unlikely heroes that we find in Ishmael, Billy and Huckleberry attest to the fact that outside the boundaries of social constriction exists the possibility of re-imagining male identity; outside the boundaries of social discourse, an innovative language of the self; outside the boundaries of conventional literary texts, the forward momentum of an ever-unfolding narrative form that we now call the "quest."

By way of conclusion, I would like to turn to a fictional model that we might not suspect of drawing on the American male quest: Charlotte Perkins Gilman's utopian-feminist *Herland*, written in 1915. For in the parodic narrative action framing this fantasy of an all-*female* world, three male explorers inadvertently dash headlong into the circumference of a hidden Amazonian kingdom; this act of discovery simultaneously triggers an opposing form of narration which absorbs all forward motion and reformulates it in the non-linear patterns that comprise the Herlanders' non-patriarchal way of life. This brilliantly arranged opening sequence, of course, deliberately appropriates the movement associated with quest in order to debunk the aggressive ethos that Gilman categorically equates with it. But the trajectory that her own opening chapters inscribe, fascinatingly enough, reproduces on a slightly larger scale that of the psychological progress that Ishmael, the archetypal American quester, undergoes in the Grand Armada chapters of *Moby-Dick*—a linear entrance into an "enchanted circle" within which the feminine secrets of life and ongoing creation unfold. It is this prospect of interior recovery, this wedding-within of those unequal "co-relatives" without which "Self-hood itself seems incomplete," then, that forms the true goal and unorthodox "love story" of Melville and Twain's versions of the male quest. Gilman's feminist message turns out to be not so far removed, indeed, from that of quest-romancers who made of the symbolic act of questing a *modus vivendi* and of its literary method a counter-traditional genre.

Notes

[1]See, for example, Nina Baym's *Woman's Fiction: A Guide to Novels by and about Women in America, 1820-1970* (Ithaca: Cornell Univ. Press, 1978), p. 11ff.

[2]For Fiedler's description of the sexual combat or polarity inherent in sentimental ideology, see *Love and Death in the American Novel* (New York: Stein and Day, 1966), pp. 62-71; for his summary of the effect of its "debasement" on the anti-bourgeois American novelist, see pp. 74-93. Fiedler's assumptions about the immaturity of the American writer/quester's attitude toward women and sex echo throughout his analysis, reflected in generalizations such as "It is maturity above all things that the American writer fears, and marriage seems to him its essential sign" (p. 388); the theme of arrested adolescence is implicit in his diagnosis as well of the "Good Bad Boy" syndrome in much American fiction (pp. 270-290). The "anti-bourgeois" genre that Fiedler sees rising in America consists not only of quest elements, but also of a heavily gothic strain (one thinks of C.B. Brown, Poe, certain Hawthorne and Faulkner works); in regard to such "fictions of terror," Fiedler's analysis of the guilt over and evasion of sexuality as a psychologically regressive tendency seems more apt.

[3]Preface to *The Americans*, quoted from *The Art of the Novel* in Michael David Bell, *The Development of American Romance: The Sacrifice of Relation* (Chicago: Univ. Press, 1980), p. 8.

[4]*Selected Poems of Herman Melville*, ed. Henig Cohen (Carbondale, Ill.: Southern Ill. Univ. Press, 1964), p. 134.

[5]*Anatomy of Criticism: Four Essays* (Princeton: Princeton Univ. Press, 1957), see "The Mythos of Summer: Romance," pp. 186-205.

[6]The anti-realist aspects of American "Romance" are presented by Richard Chase in *The American Novel and its Tradition* (Garden City: Doubleday, 1957), pp. 12-13; Lionel Trilling in "Manners, Morals, and the Novel," in *The Liberal Imagination: Essays on Literature and Society* (New York: Scribners, 1976), p. 212; and Richard Brodhead in *Hawthorne, Melville, and the Novel* (Chicago: Univ. of Chicago Press, 1973), pp. 18-24. Brodhead argues that Chase's complete separation of (English) novel and (American) romance is too extreme, since one of the strategic disunities characterizing American romance is its *inclusion* of "realism," but as only one mode and angle of vision among many.

[7]My reasons for excluding Cooper's works, in particular, from the following discussion of male "quest" novels deserve a word of explanation. Despite the "masculine" adventures seeming to dominate his romances of the American wilderness, Cooper's sagas of male bonding are shot through with courtship subplots in which the protection of frail maidenhood provides the underlying structure—and proves a clue to Cooper's true ideological allegiances. For, as Nina Baym has incisively demonstrated in "The Women of Cooper's *Leatherstocking Tales*," in *Images of Women in Fiction: Feminine Perspectives*, ed. Susan Koppelman Cornillon (Bowling Green, Ohio: Popular Press, 1972), pp. 135-154, marriage is central to each of the tales, its function that of validating Cooper's conservative social message by imprinting the codes of civilization onto the "virgin" face of the wilderness. If *The Last of the Mohicans* is the most obvious example of the importance of women and marriage to Cooper's romances, *The Pathfinder* is the most telling. For even as Natty Bumppo forfeits his chance to marry Mabel Dunham in order to remain a bachelor in a world of men, he acts in the greater service of the patriarchal order; since Mabel's father has been suddenly killed, Natty as his loyal friend must step in as her paternal guardian, and it is in this fatherly role that Bumppo hands Mabel over to a younger suitor, who has been fretting impatiently in the wings since the story opened and now steps forward to frame the courtship action.

Poe's view of the sexes, akin to that of the English Romantic poets, was particularly stereotypical in its view of women as spiritual beings or destroyers of men; his stories reveal an obsession with sex as a means of possession and self-destruction. Hawthorne, as America's literary heir to the Puritan and Miltonic vision of holy marriage as a positive good, promotes in countless "Romances" marriage as the means by which "man and woman together can momentarily restore Paradise on earth" (Fiedler, p. 223). Thus, the allegorical trajectories of romantic involvement in *The Blithedale Romance, The House of the Seven Gables* and *The Marble Faun* achieve equilibrium in "mitigated happy endings" that echo the last lines of *Paradise Lost*: innocence is a sad but fortunate fall as long as it culminates in the salvation of bourgeois marriage.

[8]Seelye, *Melville: The Ironic Diagram* (Evanston, Ill; Northwestern Univ. Press, 1970), p. 5.

[9]*The Feminization of American Culture* (New York: Knopf, 1977),. pp. 10-13, and 45-46. Nancy F. Cott in *The Bonds of Womanhood: "Women's Sphere" in New England 1780-1835* (New Haven: Yale Univ. Press, 1977) documents a similar process occurring in the earliest years of the century.

[10]T.S. Arthur, *Married or Single* (1843), quoted in Herbert Ross Brown, *The Sentimental Novel in America, 1789-1860* (Durham: Duke Univ. Press, 1940), p. 282.

[11]Some critics of the sentimental genre include Brown; Henri Petter, *The Early American Novel* (Columbus: Ohio State Univ. Press, 1971); Henry Nash Smith, "The Scribbling Women and the Cosmic Success Story," *Critical Inquiry*, 1 (1974), 47-70; and Baym, *Woman's Fiction*, which argues for a less pernicious influence of the genre upon its readers: in Baym's view, the heroine achieves a relative degree of self-autonomy, signified by the successful accomplishment of marriage, that presented its female audience with a positive model of individual development. I would, however, counter that the admitted "formulaic constraints" (p. 12) structuring the genre similarly limited the "feminine" roles its heroines were allowed to represent or experience.

[12]*The Minister's Wooing*, quoted in Brown, p. 285.

[13]Brown, p. 176.

[14]Letter, dated Jan. 19, 1855, Liverpool, in *Letters of Hawthorne to William D. Ticknor*, 2 vols. (Newark, N.J., 1910), 1:75.

[15]For descriptions of the frontier or western genre, see Ann-Janine Morey-Gaines, "Of Menace and Men: The Sexual Tensions of the American Frontier Metaphor," *Soundings*, 4 (1981), 133-47, and Fritz H. Oehlschlaeger, "Civilization as Emasculation: The Threatening Role of Women in the Frontier Fiction of Harold Bell Wright and Zane Grey," *The Midwest Quarterly*, 20 (1981), 346-59.

[16]On the proximity of the frontier ethos to Cooper, see Baym, "The Women of Cooper's *Leatherstocking Tales*," previously cited, p. 146.

[17]Fiedler, p. 211.

[18]Fiedler, pp. 211, 367-8.

[19]Fiedler, pp. 365-6.

[20]I owe the concept of the role played by the "missing woman" in the all-male world to the suggestive study of all-male casts in drama written by Robert H. Vorlicky, "America's Power Plays: The Traditional Hero in Male Cast Drama," Diss. Univ. of Wisconsin, 1981; see especially chapter 2, "The Power of the Invisible Woman."

[21]Martin L. Pops applies such a Jungian method to Melville's canon in *The Melville Archetype* (Kent, OH: Kent State Univ. Press, 1970), pp. 7-9, 17.

[22]Brodhead, pp. 18-22.

[23]Pierre the would-be writer acknowledges precisely these formal constraints when faced with the "unravelled plot" of Isabel's past: "By infallible presentiment he saw ... that not always doth life's beginning gloom conclude in gladness; that wedding-bells peal not ever in the last scene of life's fifth act ... [but] have no proper endings." See *Pierre, or The Ambiguities*, ed. Harrison Hayford, et al. (Evanston: Northwestern Univ. Press and the Newberry Library, 1971), p. 141. Examples of Melville's critique of wedlock roles include the satiric portrayal of the native couple, Samoa and Anatoo, in *Mardi*, and the truly disturbing marital warfare in the story, "I and My Chimney."

[23]Douglas, in comparing Melville's achievement with that of Margaret Fuller, notes that because "genuine sexual identity becomes ... illicit" in any society prone to sexual stereotyping, "Melville conceived masculinity, as Fuller understood feminism, essential as resistance to sentimentalism, as an effort at a genuinely political and philosophical life" (p. 284).

[25]Richard Chase elaborates on this point in *Herman Melville: A Critical Study* (1949; rpt. New York: Hafner, 1971), p. 17.

[26]The pioneering study of sexual reference in the novel is that of Robert Shulman, "The Serious Functions of Melville's Phallic Jokes," *American Literature*, 33 (1966), 179-94.

[27]For such Freudian readings, see Lawrence, *Studies in Classic American Literature* (1923; rpt. New York: Anchor, 1951), pp. 156-74; Harry Slochower, "Freudian Motifs in *Moby-Dick*," *Complex*, 3 (1950), 20; Newton Arwin, *Herman Melville* (n.p.: William Sloane, 1950), 128; and Henry A. Murray, "In Nomine Diaboli," *Moby Dick Centennial Essays*, (ed. Tyrus Hillway and Luther S. Mansfield (Dallas: Southern Methodist Univ. Press, 1953), pp. 3-21. Two critics employing a Freudian method yet focusing on the "feminine" are Fiedler and Mark Hennelly, "Ishmael's Nightmare and the American Eve," *American Imago*, 30 (1973), 274-93. Noting that although it is true that "on the surface the novel seems almost totally lacking in reference to things feminine," Hennelly correctly directs the reader to trace the "various mutations [of feminine reference] through the novel's structure, imagery and characters" (p. 278).

[28]In "The Battering Ram," the whale's impervious forehead, destroying all enemies, first seems a personification of masculine aggressive force; yet this surface member actually protects an inner sanctum filled with the "effeminacy" of a "most delicate oil." If the whale's head is described in rather startlingly bisexual imagery, so too is its opposite anatomical member, the tail, which combines Titanic strength and delicate grace in one consistent movement.

[29]*Moby-Dick*, ed. Harrison Hayford and Hershel Parker (New York: Norton, 1967), p. 53. All further references to this edition will appear in parenthesis in my text.

[30]For instance, see Fiedler, p. 382, and Julian Rice, "Male Sexuality in *Moby-Dick*," *American Transcendental Quarterly*, 39 (1978), p. 241.

[31]These quotations are from Chase, *Herman Melville*, p. 106, and Shulman, p. 184, respectively.

[32]Pops, p. 73.

[33]Brodhead, pp. 154, 156.

[34]When Mrs. Loftis discovers he isn't "Sarah Williams," Huck becomes "George Peters" and when that fails, "Sarah Mary Williams George Alexander Peters" (p. 263); to the raftsmen in chapter 16 he proclaims himself the "Charles William Allbright" of Ed's ghost-tale, then admits he is "really" only "Alex James Hopkins" (p. 306). The Grangerfords know him as "George Jackson," he parades as the English valet "Adolphus" in the Wilks home, and Tom's rescue-scheme calls for him again to impersonate a woman as the "yaller servant-girl" (p. 511). Kenneth Lynn equates Huck's spontaneous fictional biographies with his search for identity in "Huck and Jim," *The Yale Review*, 47 (1958), 427.

[35]The feud waged by the Grangerford-Shepherdson men, for example, exposes meaningless aggression as a component of Southern-style patriarchy, while their women-folk illustrate lives of domestic triviality; the Duke and Dauphin provide an example of absolutely corrupt power; the Pokeville revival scheme, like Peter Wilks' funeral scene, ridicules the sentimental piety of the indiscriminately sobbing crowd that can just as easily turn into a senseless mob howling blindly for blood and vengeance, as in the Colonel Sherburne incident.

[36]Tom Towers in "Love and Power in *Huck Finn*," *Tulane Studies in English*, 23 (1978), 17-37, makes the dialectical alternation between these two forces the subject of his study, citing Huck's exchanges with Pap, the Grangerfords, and the Duke and Dauphin as significant markers of this rhythmical pattern.

[37]*The Adventures of Huckleberry Finn*, in *The Portable Mark Twain*, ed. Bernard DeVoto (1946; rpt. New York: Viking, 1972), p. 340. All further references to this edition will appear in parentheses in my text.

[38]The lines I have quoted from Fiedler's excellent analysis of the Huck-Finn bond are preceded by these equally illuminating observations:

... In Jim, Huck finds the pure affection offered by Mary Jane without the threat of marriage; the escape from social obligations offered by Pap without the threat of beatings; the protection and pettings offered by his volunteer foster-mothers without the threat of pious conformity; the male companionship offered by the Grangerfords without the threat of combat of honor; the friendship offered by Tom without the everlasting rhetoric and make-believe. (pp. 352-353)

[39]Here I refer to the episode in chapter 16 in which Huck has a chance to prove his loyalty to Jim's love—and thus his nonconforming individuality—when he lies to a group of slave-hunters about the race of his raft-companion. The terminology used to express this snap decision suggests the extent to which Huck's nonconformity is a disavowal of traditional norms of masculinity: "*I warn't man enough*, hadn't the spunk of a rabbit. I see *I was weakening*; so I just give up trying, and up and says 'He's white' " (p. 310; emphasis added). Likewise, Huck's famous decision in chapter 31 to "go to hell" rather than "pray a lie" comes as the result of being overwhelmed by a series of memories of his and Jim's idyllic life together that figuratively "unman" the boy: "somehow I couldn't seem to strike no places *to harden me* against [Jim]" (p. 450; emphasis added). Again, Huck's growth toward nonconforming identity expresses a rejection of traditional masculine associations (strength, hardness) and a simultaneous awareness of the depth of his love for Jim.

[40]An excellent article regarding the "future" growth of Huck is Paul Delaney's "You Can't Go Back to the Raft Ag'in, Huck Honey! Mark Twain's Western Sequel to *Huckleberry Finn*," *Western American Literature*, 11 (1976), 215-229, which evaluates the failure of Twain to finish the "Huck Finn and Tom Sawyer Among the Indians" manuscript (begun 1884) because of the particularly brutal sexual realities, along with a growingly bleak existential dilemma, that must face Huck as a maturing young adult in a vicious world.

[41]On this subject, see the Epilogue to Douglas' previously cited *The Feminization of American Culture*, pp. 327-329.

[42]Mary E.B. Fussell's research into the novella's composition in "*Billy Budd:* Melville's

Happy Ending," *Studies in Romanticism*, 15 (1976), 43-47, undercovers several reasons for assuming that Melville's earlier investigations into sexual identity were on his mind during its conception. For one, the early manuscript leaf upon which Melville plotted his essential creative "breakthrough" by inventing the mediating figure of Vere ("Look at it. Look at it," Melville exclaimed in the margin) is inscribed on its reverse with the dedication to that "great heart," Jack Chase, an avatar of the Handsome Sailor apotheosized in *White Jacket* as "the man who, in a predominantly masculine world, has successfully integrated the 'female' side of his nature with his more overtly 'male' side, losing by neither, gaining by both" (Fussell, p. 47). In addition, Melville composed three of the most provocative later leaves on the backs of the holograph copy pages of the poem, "After the Pleasure Party," which as we have seen contains a crucial articulation of Melville's belief in the need to break through restrictive sexual roles in order to achieve individual harmony (pp. 45-46). Hence, it is not unreasonable to assume, along with Fussell, that the associations roused by this poem and the memory of Chase may have helped spark Melville's creation of *Billy Budd* as an investigation into the nature of masculine identity and authority.

[43]*Billy Budd, Sailor (An Inside Narrative)*, ed. Harrison Hayford and Merton M. Sealts, Jr. (Chicago: Univ. of Chicago Press, 1962), p. 50. All further references to this edition will appear in parentheses in my text.

[44]Sarotte, *Like a Brother, Like a Lover: Male Homosexuality in the American Novel and Theatre from Herman Melville to James Baldwin*, trans. Richard Miller (New York: Anchor-Doubleday, 1978), and Watson, "Melville's Testament of Acceptance," *New England Quarterly*, 6 (1933), 324-325.

[45]These "sequels" not only precipitate a series of modal transformations (from quasi-scientific explication to newspaper account to verse ballad) typical of quest-structure, but also underscore the issues of sexual identity and authoritarian power raised throughout the text. This series of five "endings" has been analyzed well by Mary Foley in "The Digressions in *Billy Budd*," in *Melville's Billy Budd and the Critics*, ed. William T. Stafford (San Francisco: Wadsworth, 1961), pp. 220-222.

[46]*The Sea Wolf* (New York: Bantam, 1963), p. 7. All further references to this edition will appear in parentheses in my text.

[47]For this exercise of physical force, Humphrey earns Wolf's words of approbation, "You've got *spunk*" (p. 65; emphasis added)—which, ironically, is that very quality that Huck feels guilty for lacking in not betraying Jim to the slave-hunters (*HF*, p. 310).

[48]Also telling is the fact that Hump's *chivalrous* love comes into being the instant he realizes Wolf's *sexual* desire for Maude; that is, Wolf's sexual desire awakens Hump's "purer" love, in a paradigmatic situation of mediated or triangular desire with the woman as mediator between men. See pp. 147-8.

[49]Morey-Gaines provides a telling example of the equation of virility, violence and selfhood in the western genre by citing the moment in *Shane* when the hero, who has been in disguise, puts his "guns" back on. Simultaneously his identity as a "real" man resurfaces: "They were part of him, part of the man ... for the first time this man was complete, was himself, in the final effect of his being" (p. 140).

[50]Another product of the modern quest writer's homophobia is the tendency to make the "villain" in the all-male world a homosexual: hence General Cummings' repressed homosexual yearnings in *The Naked and the Dead*. Melville, of course, also exploited this stereotype in his depiction of Claggart in *Billy Budd*, but with a qualitative difference since the psychological motivations underlying Claggart's repressed desires are regretted rather than condemned.

The writer's fear of the homosexual implications of the male bond is tied to a larger narrative problem, namely, the limited fictional possibilities of representing men together in interpersonal situations other than those traditionally "male" ones of exploration, sports or war. As Robert Kiely insightfully notes of *Women in Love* in *Beyond Egotism: Fiction of James Joyce, Virginia Woolf, and D.H. Lawrence* (Cambridge: Harvard Univ. Press, 1980), pp. 156-168, the narrative simply stops, has no place to go, when Gerald and Rupert find themselves alone together. The generic implications of this spatial issue are fascinating when we note that the two fictional sub-genres overwhelmingly concerned with relationships between men—the American quest-romance and twentieth century gay fiction—inscribe between men—the American quest-romance and twentieth century gay fiction—inscribe totally opposite trajectories; for the soaring movement of quest narrative contrasts vividly to the symbolic center of much gay fiction—the room or circumscribed space where all important action takes place (see, for example, Baldwin's *Giovanni's Room*, the prison cell of Puig's *The Kiss of the Spiderwoman*, the largely interior scenes of Mary Renault's "war" novel, *The Charioteer*, from which the battlefields are never glimpsed).

[51] The women of the novel, only "present" in the "Time Machine" flashbacks, are almost always seen as antagonistic "Others" who are either stereotypically naive, frigid, lascivious or conniving and whom Mailer seems to hold equally responsible for the inherent sexual warfare that drives men to violent extremes. And the one male character explicitly linked with "feminine" feelings, General Cummings (whose father used to beat him for acting "like a goddam woman") is depicted as a homosexual fascist whose repressed desires are directly responsible for the doomed mission on which he sends the recon team. The "villain" wrecking the quest, that is, is the "feminine" in man, personified by Mailer as homosexual and antithetical to his conception of masculinity.

[52]*Between Men* (New York: Columbia University Press, 1985), pp. 21-27.

Norine Voss

"Saying the Unsayable": An Introduction to Women's Autobiography

IN NO OTHER LITERARY GENRE as in autobiography have women produced such a varied and rich canon, yet received so little recognition for their achievements. Since 1436, when the controversial religious mystic Margery Kempe told her life story, women have written countless volumes of autobiography. Despite the extraordinary interest and high merit of many of these works, critics have ignored female autobiographers far more than they have disregarded women novelists and poets. Surveying books about American autobiography might lead one to conclude that Gertrude Stein was the only American woman to write an autobiography, nor would reading English criticism yield a more balanced picture. Starting with an understandable interest in the better-known, men's autobiographies, critics have focused attention on these works. As a result, however, definitions of the genre, ideas about the nature of the self, and aesthetic standards have been based on a handful of examples exclusively white and male, among them Augustine, Rousseau, Franklin, Goethe, Mill, and Adams. Not surprisingly, critics have then found women's autobiographies to deviate from the masculine norm, and have further excluded them from the accepted canon.

As readers and students of women's autobiography, we cannot understand the female tradition by adopting without question a critical theory and methodology that grew out of a reading of men's autobiographies. We must first understand the limitations, as well as the strengths of existing criticism before we can comprehend how women have struggled with and reshaped a recalcitrant genre, faced the problem of autobiographical truth and developed new forms. Once women's works are appreciated on their own terms, we can better understand women's autobiography.

Sustained interest in autobiography as a genre dates from the 1950s. The critics who have been the most influential on autobiographical theory, as well as the most elitist and implicitly sexist, are those whom Francis Hart terms the "traditionalists": Wayne Shumaker, Roy Pascal, Georges Gusdorf and Barrett John Mandel. Even though recent critics have begun to disagree with them, the ideas of the traditionalists still remain the starting point for younger critics. As Mandel defines it,

"Autobiography is a retrospective account of a man's whole life (or a significant part of a life) written as avowed truth and for a specific purpose by the man who lived the life."[1] The crucial terms here are "restrospective account" and "specific purpose," for these create the form and the shape of what the traditionalists term "true autobiography."

The act of retrospection creates a superimposition of two temporal planes, a universal feature which, Shumaker believes, "makes autobiographical form possible" and distinguishes it from forms such as the diary.[2] According to the traditionalists, to achieve artistic form, the autobiographer determines his identity, often selecting one facet of himself to stand for the whole person, the artist or the seeker of education, for example. He then decides on his purpose, the informing principle that will give a shape to his life story and govern the selection of material. A writer who defines himself as the artist, for example, should then select only those memories revealing his artistic development. The kind of autobiography preferred by the traditionalists results in what Shumaker calls "a literary simplification of an extremely complex reality" (p. 40), and leads to a critical obsession with orderliness. In Pascal's words, autobiography "imposes a pattern on a life, constructs out of it a coherent story."[3]

Nowhere has the androcentric bias of traditional criticism so severely affected the evaluation of women's autobiography as in the matter of form, since it is by standards of form that autobiographies are usually judged superior or inferior. The traditionalists place enormous importance on the retrospective stance and the resulting temporal duality as the touchstone of a superior work. Wayne Shumaker imagines this act of retrospection as a "moment of apparently permanent elevation above passion and ambition." He continues, "Life has been lived, and is now to be recorded in tranquility, with a serenity and honesty that would have been impossible in the thick of the struggle" (p. 128). This picture of the autobiographer— cool, serene, standing somehow apart from the life—does not adequately describe many women's autobiographies; in fact, it may be an artificial construct not representative of all men's lives either.

Shumaker assumes here a state of full self-knowledge free from conflict, a condition that women's status in a patriarchal culture often prevents them from attaining (or that, if attained, their vulnerability to attack makes them hesitant to reveal). *The Life of Margery Kempe* (1432, 1436) reveals simultaneously a life dedicated to religion and the rebellion of a woman whose religious vocation allowed her a freedom of speech and action the oppression of the fifteenth century would never have otherwise permitted. The work threatens to fly apart under the pressure of two such antithetical impulses, earning critical condemnation. Yet no other alternative was possible. If Kempe had clearly seen and defined herself as a rebel against the confines of woman's place, she might have produced a more coherent work and earned a larger place in literary history. She would certainly have earned a place at the stake.

Even now, when writers feel freer to analyze themselves and to risk more than Kempe, female autobiographers often choose "disorderly" forms and reject the traditionalists' demand for a retrospective stance aloof from the life. Kate Millett refuses to emulate Shumaker's picture of autobiography as "the stepping back of a painter to have a look at the finished canvas" (p. 103), by making the act of recording her life an integral part of her autobiography. Midway through *Flying* (1974), Millett informs her audience that she has begun to write *Flying*, and periodically reminds us of the writing process by describing the increasing bulk of the manuscript, the time she nearly lost it in London, and her difficulties in writing some sections. By suggesting that her writing and our reading of the autobiography are occurring, as it seems, simultaneously, Millett refuses to create an autobiographical self static and aloof, knowing both the beginning and the end. Unlike Shumaker's metaphor of the painter and the canvas, life is not tidy and artistically simplified, nor can one distance oneself, even momentarily.[4] *Flying* thus affirms the validity of an art that embodies the complexity, multiplicity and continuum of life.

The selective persona and distanced stance of the male autobiographers, features most critics prefer, usually result in a linear form as the autobiographer selectively traces his development as an artist, a politician, or some other self-definition. Yet a linear view of life is more apt to characterize those men whose socialization has been toward a career or toward pursuing a specific goal. Most women, on the other hand, have been taught that their lives revolve around the needs of others; they are not taught the single-minded pursuit of long-term goals. Compared to the lives of famous male autobiographers, women's lives seem disjointed, non-linear.

Roy Pascal plays amateur sociologist in a passage which unintentionally reveals the androcentric bias behind a preference for linear form: "Great autobiographies are all by men of acknowledged achievement and distinction; they have already asserted their personalities and can fairly securely see their lives as the reaching of the present defined personality, a personality which is socially established—as scientist, philosopher, businessman, statesman, poet—as well as psychologically established. (Should one believe that here lies the reason why scarcely any great autobiographies have been written by women?)."[5] Pascal does not realize that the aesthetic standards distinguishing a great autobiography are strongly reinforced, if not totally created, by the social standards marking a great life. If we were to imagine a society that valued personal relationships much more highly than money, fame or distinction, then we would find aesthetic standards radically different, corresponding to the changed social standards. In this imagined society critics would judge Lillian Hellman's *Pentimento*, structured around personal relationships, as far superior to *The Education of Henry Adams*, which omits the twenty-year period that included his marriage. No criticism of Adams himself is implied here; an autobiographer may exclude what he or she wills, and Adams may well have found memories of his wife's suicide too painful to reawaken. However, in this hypothetical, gynocentric society, Adams' failure to emphasize personal relationships would be considered a major *artistic* flaw because aesthetic values are not absolutes, but translations of social values.

By androcentric standards female autobiography seems disorderly. Estelle Jelinek prefers the term "discontinuous," and she and Suzanne Juhasz have pointed out that women's lives are not usually linear, but rather, cyclical, repetitive, disjointed and other-directed. Progress toward a goal often proceeds erratically, usually because of exigencies beyond the individual's control, such as a family crisis. As Jelinek argues, women's autobiographies reflect this discontinuity: "The narratives of their lives are usually not chronological and progressive [like men's] but disconnected or organized into self-sustained units rather than connecting chapters."[6]

For some writers discontinuous form is unintentional, forced by their cultural position. The narrative of Margery Kempe is torn by her repressed rebellion against oppressive confines. Even Edith Wharton, a vastly more polished writer, cannot unify her experiences. After presenting the author's childhood, *A Backward Glance* (1934) splits into material relating to Wharton's writing career (largely contained in a chapter called "The Secret Garden") and anecdotes expected from a lady in high society. Her disjointed narrative reflects the cultural truism that woman and artist are mutually exclusive categories. In the autobiography, as well as in her life, her writing career and the social roles appropriate to a lady with a pedigree remained in different compartments.

The discontinuity unintended in some earlier writers has become a conscious artistic choice for such recent autobiographers as Kate Millett, Nikki Giovanni and Alta. Alta's discontinuous form represents her effort to embody the texture of female lives. In *Momma* (1974), which chronicles her years as a housewife and mother, Alta suggests the rhythm of her daily existence; often she informs us that between the paragraph we are reading and the one preceding, she has stopped writing in order to wash dishes or to deal with a bloody nose. Since her life is cyclical and prone to interruption, her segmented, disorderly form perfectly embodies the reality of her life: "retyping this, i stopped to read the rest of this section & forgot to put the pages in order. so they are no longer in the same order i wrote them. in order, as if my life were in order. who am i kidding."[7] Even her style, a kind of shorthand, reflects a woman who must snatch spare moments for writing.

Alta's radical literary form asserts the validity of hitherto hidden female lives and experiences, indifferent to the fact that neither they nor the form that expresses them are appreciated by the dominant culture. Rejecting an autobiographical form that demands unity and what Shumaker has called an "artistic simplification of an extremely complex reality," Alta presents her life in all its variety and frequent chaos. But those accustomed to more conventional forms should not mistake her method for an inartistic, literal copy of her life. Using for comparison Shumaker's metaphor for the autobiographer and the work as a painter and a finished canvas, one could picture Alta's book as a photograph. Good photographers do not simply point their cameras and shoot; they compose their shots and later carefully develop and crop them. The result, though more realistic than a painting, remains art. Like any artist Alta has shaped her material, but still retains the immediacy and vitality of her life. As in the works of her sister autobiographers, Mary McCarthy, Lillian Hellman and Maya Angelou, who present their lives in vividly realized segments, Alta's discontinuous form implies that meaning inheres, especially for women, in the individual events and diurnal details of a life.

Wayne Shumaker, Roy Pascal and Barrett John Mandel focus largely on British or other European autobiographies. No one has yet attempted a history of American autobiography with the scope of Shumaker's history of European autobiography, but several book-length studies of selected American autobiographies and a few articles which attempt an overview have been written. An examination of these works reveals a canon of exemplary American autobiographies forming a tradition of white, male works. According to these studies, the most important autobiographers before 1900 are Jonathan Edwards, Benjamin Franklin, Henry David Thoreau, Henry Adams, Henry James and by some standards Walt Whitman. In dealing with the twentieth century, these scholars display a little more variety in their selection. In a few of these studies Gertrude Stein appears, the only woman to be accepted into the pantheon of important American autobiographers. Even though these works do not claim to be definitive studies of American autobiography as a whole, the authors' virtual exclusion of women and black male autobiographers creates implicit assumptions about what constitutes great American autobiography. Theories formulated after a study of autobiographies by men in turn tend to further exclude women.

Nina Baym argues a similar point in a detailed and convincing article on the ways critics of the American novel have developed theories that exclude American women novelists. One tendency that Baym notes in novel criticism can be a pitfall for scholars of American autobiography as well—evaluating works according to their "Americanness," searching for works that embody a distinctively American theme or myth. Such themes and myths are usually masculine, as Baym argues. Although America has always been a diverse and pluralistic society, "the matter of American experience," according to Baym's study of the critics, "is inherently male."[8] For example, James M. Cox, like many seeing Franklin as the father of American autobiography, believes that he created "the form which would realize the revolution and thus stand for it. That form was the autobiography—the life of a self-made, self-governing man."[9] Though Cox does include Gertrude Stein (everyone's favorite token) in his article, his image of the exemplary American character is more masculine than feminine. In a recent article on American autobiography, Robert Sayre argues that the great autobiographies are those which have pondered the idea of America and contributed to the national character.[10] The question remains: whose idea of America and which American character should be espoused?

Afro-American autobiography is usually treated as a tradition separate from white autobiography. Two books on black autobiography each include a chapter on women and provide an example of the results that occur when theories developed from men's autobiographies are applied to women's. Stephen Butterfield sees the early slave narratives defining a tradition of struggle and rebellion in black autobiography. In his chapter on Ida B. Wells, Anne Moody and Maya Angelou, Butterfield praises the autobiographies of Wells, who crusaded against lynching and Jim Crow laws, and of Moody, who fought many of the civil rights struggles in Mississippi in the 1960s. He finds Angelou's work disapponting by comparison, a judgment based not on the merit of Angelou's book, but on the militant, aggressive, politically active model he has come to expect from reading black men's autobiographies.[11] Sidonie Smith, on the other hand, considers a less masculine theme in black autobiography. She explores patterns of escape toward freedom, or in the case of Richard Wright, exhaustion of "the possibility of flight to geographical freedom." She evaluates Angelou more highly than Butterfield does, as one who "dramatize[s] the possibility of . . . liberation through the creative act of writing autobiography itself."[12] By selecting a theme in black American experience that is not predominantly masculine, Smith's study can fully appreciate Angelou's work. Because much criticism of American literature has been based on tracing predominantly masculine themes, myths and experience, this approach does not prove useful for studying American women's autobiography.

A group of recent critics has begun to express reservations about tranditionalist theories. Although they seem little more aware of women's autobiography than Shumaker and his colleagues, their writings sometimes point out general lines of thought useful when considering women's autobiography. Francis Hart argues that the traditional categories of apology, confession, and memoir are too rigid, and that the critic must be sensitive to the writer's often multiple and shifting intentions and allow the work to define its own form.[13] Hart's caution against coming to a work with preconceived expectations and trying to impose concepts of form on it offers useful advice when studying a genre as protean as autobiography. Like Hart, Elizabeth W. Bruss finds narrow, prescriptive definitions of limited usefulness. Autobiography, she argues, is an "act," not a form. By this she means that the meaning of the concept of autobiography is an understanding shared by the author and the contemporary readers, an understanding determined by their shared cultural context.[14] Understanding what contemporary readers expected autobiography to be aids in studying autobiography from earlier periods. Bruss' insight also proves useful in considering works such as the experimental autobiographies by Kate Millett, Nikki Giovanni, and Alta, who carry on a dialogue with their readers, anticipating the audience's expectations and trying to reshape its response.

Reacting against those who treat autobiography from different centuries and cultures as essentially similar, Karl Weintraub stresses the importance of historical context in shaping autobiography. He considers selected texts from St. Augustine to twentieth-century works, studying the ways autobiography has changed, and arguing that the modern concept of autobiography was itself the product of historical factors that created "the recognition of a strong historical dimension of all human reality and a modern mode of self-conception as an individuality."[15] John M. Morris understands that the nineteenth-century milieu of Wordsworth and John Stuart Mills fostered, if not created, the "unity of self" found in their autobiographies.[16] He thus indirectly supports the assertion that the unity admired in some of the great men's autobiographies is not an aesthetic universal but a feature of a particular historical period.

Although Weintraub and Morris do not deal with women's autobiography, their emphasis on the formative influence of the historical context remains an important point. Women's autobiographies cannot be fully understood in isolation from women's status and experiences within particular cultures and historical periods. One must remember, however, that women's history does not always follow the same contours, the same hills and valleys, as men's. For example, the late nineteenth-century must have seemed for many American men an era of increasing constriction with the closing of the frontier and the change from self-employed farmer to urban wage laborer. For many women the same period meant greater access to education, more variety in employment, and increased social activity. For these women, the decades surrounding the turn of the century proved a period of freedom, not constriction, and many autobiographies by women who lived through this era reveal patterns of escape toward freedom.

Although the revisionist criticism can sometimes prove generally useful, its focus on male autobiography means that it has little direct application to women's autobiography. Interest in autobiographies by women began in the mid 1970s, and published criticism remains sparse. Almost half of the published criticism can be found collected in one anthology, *Women's Autobiography: Essays in Criticism,* published by Indiana University Press in 1980 and edited by Estelle C. Jelinek. Aside from occasional studies of one autobiography, scholars have taken three main approaches. Some undertake archeological studies, essential to the early stages of any literary field of study; much effort must be expended to search out autobiographies, many of them long out of print and forgotten, in order to describe what is there. Some essays focus on a few autobiographers who share a feature, such as race or historical period, or trace a theme such as matrilinealism through selected autobiographies. Other essays raise such questions as whether differences exist between men's and women's autobiographies or what distinctive features women autobiographers share.

The question of whether women's autobiography differs substantially from men's may finally prove impossible to answer for practical reasons, and may not be a useful question to ask on theoretical grounds. In her paper "Discontinuity and Order," presented at the 1976 Modern Language Association's convention, Jelinek notes some general differences. Her study included only thirty-five autobiographies, however, and any conclusions based on such a limited sample must be regarded with caution, as Jelinek realizes. Practical considerations make sex-related differences difficult to prove. Even if one limited the study to men's and women's autobiographies in a particular historical period, one would have to read at least a few hundred autobiographies to provide an adequate sample, locate the differences, quantify the results, and then attempt to determine which differences resulted from the author's sex and not from race, religion, class, or period of time in which the author lived. Even if such a task could be completed, the results could legitimately be applied only to the men and women studied. More importantly, a comparative study might unintentionally give support to theories of biological determinism. And since literary criticism has traditionally seen male literature as the norm, including many men's autobiographies might tempt the readers or the writer to fall unconsciously into the trap of seeing the works by women as different, deviations from the norm. Autobiographers remain an individualistic group despite features they share. Even though many have noticed the frequency of discontinuous form in women's autobiographies, some women have written orderly autobiographies that would fit the traditionalist model, while some men have experimented with an apparently disorderly form.

Studying women's autobiographies in relation to one another can reveal insights unavailable when an autobiography is treated in isolation or read in the context of men's autobiography. Without arguing that features common to several women's autobiographies stem solely from the authors' sex, one can still watch patterns and themes emerging, note how they responded to the changing position and status of women, or see how women in different decades grappled with problems common to all autobiography. When writing autobiography, both men and women must confront problems that seem inherent in the nature of the genre: combining the revelation of the inner with an account of the outer person, feeling uncomfortable with the possibility of seeming conceited, and overcoming the obstacles standing in the way of telling the truth about the self. Although both sexes face these problems, womens' socialization has made their experience with these autobiographical problems somewhat different from men's. It is, however, a difference in degree rather than in kind.

As traditionally defined and practiced, autobiography has not been a congenial form for women. A public act of personal recollection, it poses the problem of welding both private and public experience. But unlike men, who are allowed to move in both spheres, women historically have been relegated to the private realm of home, personal relationships and emotion, a sphere they leave at their peril. Not surprisingly, many have chosen the diary form, which both Mary Jane Moffat and Suzanne Juhasz see as an analogue to women's lives within a patriarchal society: private, amateur, cyclical and concerned with daily experience.[17]

For those women who have chosen the more public mode of autobiography, the gap between the outside world of career, activity and ideas, and the private world of home, family and emotions (as the dichotomy is usually stated) often proves difficult to bridge. In her comparative study of thirty-five women's and men's autobiographies, Estelle C. Jelinek finds that most of the women write very little about the careers that made them famous.[18] An autobiography such as Elizabeth Gurley Flynn's *Rebel Girl* (1955) complements Jelinek's findings by virtually omitting private experience, concentrating instead on the "more important" outside world: after recounting her childhood, Flynn devotes approximately ten pages to her personal life out of the 282 remaining pages. Some autobiographers include both public and private experience but find connections difficult. In *Blackberry Winter* (1972), Margaret Mead seems unable to apply her anthropological work on sex roles to the sexual politics disastrously at work in her second marriage. The insightful, sometimes controversial anthropologist seems a different person from the woman proud of her ability to do the onerous housework under her husband's nose without his noticing it.

Autobiography is not only a public but also an egoistical genre, implying both a strong interest in oneself and a life which seems important enough to record. For both men and women in our culture, excessive concern with one's own self-importance remains an object for censure; the appearance of modesty must be maintained. This social prohibition falls more heavily on women than on men, however. For women, autobiography is not just egoistical, but *egotistical,* utterly incompatible with the conventional definition of femininity. The qualities of the ideal feminine woman should be passivity, humility, unselfishness bordering on self-annihilation, and self-display only to please a husband or a lover. The act of writing autobiography reawakens and exacerbates the autobiographer's life-long conflict between rigid definitions of femininity and her need for self-esteem and a vocation. The conflicts between egoism and unselfishness, self-love and self-effacement can affect the narrative mode and the form of the autobiography.

In the works of Margaret Cavendish and Arvazine Angeline Cooper, the authors' ambivalence toward the autobiographical act is reflected in formal confusion. Cavendish's 1656 autobiography (modestly appended to a biography of her husband) reveals her desire to be remembered as an individual rather than merely another Duchess of Newcastle. But this need for selfhood wars with her fear that the audience will find her autobiographical intrusion presumptuous and unfeminine. The resulting work is formally self-deprecating, amorphous, and other-directed. In an excellent discussion of Cavendish's autobiography, Patricia Meyer Spacks describes the effect of the writer's self-depreciation on its form: "Its form is formlessness: another disclaimer of self-assertion. The sequence of self-description demonstrates little coherent order. Successive paragraphs begin, 'As for my breeding,' 'As for our garments,' 'As for tutors,' 'As for my brothers.' The apparently random sequence, mingling the trivial with the important, does not issue from any genuine stream of consciousness; the Duchess, wondering what someone might conceivably want to know about her, answers always that her circumstances matter, not herself."[19] Several social strata lower than the Duchess, and centuries and an ocean away, another autobiographer also found that her fears of displaying self-esteem overpowered narrative coherence. Telling in old age of crossing the plains in a covered wagon, Arvazine Cooper shifts abruptly from the first- to the third-person narrative voice when her second child (but first son) is born. She fears she will otherwise appear "so personal as to seem egotistical."[20]

The self-love Cavendish and Cooper feared to express invites attack because it threatens to undercut the ideals of feminine unselfishness and devotion to others. Unselfishness, for some, seems the cement holding a patriarchal, capitalistic society together. In an acquisitive, individualistic culture dedicated to success, women's unselfishness has come to be seen as an ameliorating force. Women are thus taught to define themselves in relation to others rather than as autonomous selves. Any evidence of female "unselfishness," pursuit of one's own priorities, is severely censured.

Faced with a common condition, autobiographers have responded with structural techniques and narrative methods that sometimes assert the ego, but often conceal, diffuse or displace it. Jade Snow Wong not only disarms possible criticism with an apologetic preface but also narrates in the third person. This "submergence of the individual" stems partly from her Chinese heritage but more importantly protects this recent college graduate from what she calls her own "audacity."[21] At the opposite extreme, Emma Goldman, a rebel in autobiography as in life, asserts her autonomy by beginning *Living My Life* (1931) at the age of twenty, her past "cast off like a worn-out garment."[22] In a series of flashbacks to her unhappy childhood and youth Goldman soon suggests the reason for her literary choice. Before the autobiography opens, she had been defined in terms of others—as daughter, sister, wife, victim. Only at twenty did she truly begin living *her* life. The beginning of her autobiography represents both a personal and social manifesto: Goldman claims for women the right to live as autonomous beings.

Without falling into the trap of self-annihilation that Goldman sees clearly, other writers have explored the idea of the female self at the center of a web of relations by using this sense of self as a structuring principle. Catherine Drinker Bowen writes an autobiography-family biography, appropriately named *Family Portrait,* (1970), in which she presents her self within the context of a web of familial relationships.[23] Margaret Mead defines a "human unit of time" as the scope of her autobiography: her grandparents' memories and her granddaughter's childhood become the organic beginning and end of *Blackberry Winter.*[24] Using familial and other personal relationships, Lillian Hellman diffuses her autobiographical self by structuring *Pentimento* around family members and friends. Her group of character studies both affirms the principle of human connection and paradoxically allows Hellman to assert her ego.

This veiled self-assertion can be seen more clearly in Gertrude Stein's displacement of her autobiographical voice into the persona of Alice B. Toklas, thus enabling "Alice" to make her famous statement about having met only three geniuses in her life, one of them, of course, being Gertrude Stein. From Cavendish's sense of becoming lost in her relationship with her husband, to Goldman's radical assertion of autonomy, to Stein's and Hellman's ironic assertion of self within a form that emphasizes personal connectedness, women have responded in diverse ways to the tension between assertion of the ego and the definition of women through relationships with others.

Stein's duplicitous appropriation of Alice's voice or the veil of fiction Agnes Smedley, Sylvia Plath and Zelda Fitzgerald draw over their lives indicates the tension between truth and fiction in autobiography, a genre that is a somewhat uneasy wedding of history and subjective interpretation. Francis Hart perceptively discusses the meaning of autobiographical truth. Noting that readers expect an autobiography to give a truthful account of a person's life, he continues, "Truth is a definitive but elusive autobiographical intention.... Seeking to be history, autobiography must be fictive."[25] Because autobiography is a creative act that goes far beyond recording the past, truth proves a difficult problem that Hart and the autobiograhers he discusses must grapple with. Andre Maurois lists more practical reasons why truth in autobiography becomes a difficult goal, reasons ranging from a faulty memory to a desire to protect others.[26]

Male autobiographers find complete truthfulness a difficult task, but because of women's vulnerable position in patriarchal society, female autobiographers add an additional dimension to the question of autobiographical truth. Deception means survival for the powerless: to be successfully feminine means to learn concealment, deceit, the graceful falsehood. Hiding the signs of aging, flattering a boss, suppressing unfeminine emotions of anger or rebellion, depreciating or concealing intellectual and athletic ability, playing roles that have little connection with the real person—all these are part of almost any woman's repertoire.

Isadora Duncan, her feminine socialization augmented by her career as a performer, provides a striking illustration of feminine posing. Whether she is conning desk clerks to win her family beds for the night, dressing in tunics and attempting to build a temple in the ancient Greek fashion, or reclining in her "veritable domain of Circe," a chamber done in black velvet, Duncan never leaves the stage.[27] Theatricality as a pervasive theme, reinforced by her exclamatory, somewhat flowery style, provides a fitting medium for a life she describes as "more interesting than any novel and more adventurous than any cinema" (p. 1). Watching her perform, on and off the stage, the reader begins to question the literal truth of her narrative, to wonder if "Isadora Duncan" is not, in fact, a fictional projection—or projections. Duncan herself understands the autobiographical impulse toward fiction, specifically in terms of women's life-stories, and rejects the selective, tidy self favored by the traditionalist critics: "Is it [her persona] to be the Chaste Madonna, or the Messalina, or the Magdalen, or the Blue Stocking? Where can I find the woman of all these adventures? It seems to me there was not one, but hundreds—and my soul soaring aloft, not really affected by any of them" (p. 2). Her autobiography embodies the role-playing central to feminine experience.

"No woman has ever told the whole truth of her life," Isadora Duncan maintains (p. 3). The reasons lie even deeper than the role-playing women's survival demands, originating in the vulnerability of their powerless position. As Patricia Spacks suggests, "self-exposure is dangerous."[28] Emotions such as anger and rebellion and certain areas of female experience remain virtually taboo, even in this supposedly liberated age. In *The Book of Margery Kempe*, the narrative of this religious mystic seethes with a suppressed rebellion she could not admit even to herself. More than five centuries later, artist Judy Chicago remembers her initial terror at revealing her own anger. Prompted by the beginnings of the women's movement, she began relating in public lectures her experiences as a woman artist: the isolation, the experience of being used and abused sexually, and the denigration of her sometimes explicitly female imagery. After the lectures, she recalls, "I drove home and trembled in terror at the fantasies that told me that something terrible was going to happen because I was saying the unsayable. I was telling the truth about my experiences as a woman, and I felt sure that I would be punished for it, that someone would break into my studio and destroy all my paintings or would shoot me or beat me up." Even at the time of writing her autobiography, she continues, "the fears" of revealing her emotions can still "engulf" her.[29]

Some subjects as well as emotions are only now becoming autobiographical material, particularly female sexuality. Of course, isolated, earlier examples of frankness exist, notably Agnes Smedley's *Daughter of Earth* (1929). Assuring her audience that she has not evaded the truth, Smedley offers as evidence her openness in dealing with rape, illicit relationships, and the messy break-up of her second marriage. Yet her very honesty depends on the novelistic element in the work. Without the protective fiction, the supposition that this is the life of a "Marie Rogers," Smedley could never have told the truth about herself. As in her childhood, when she learned to lie in order to avoid punishment, Smedley would instead have told her audience what she thought it wanted to hear.[30]

To further illustrate the difficulty in speaking truth about female experiences, one could trace the portrayal of lesbianism (or its absence)—from earlier writers' complete omission, to Stein's safe, aesthetic incorporation of her relationship into her unusual narrative method, to Kate Millett's frank exploration of female relationships in *Flying* (1974) and *Sita* (1976). The recent tendency toward greater honesty in female self-expression could not exist without the supportive climate the feminist movement has fostered as an alternative to patriarchal repression. More and more frequently women have been saying the unsayable, thinking unthinkable thoughts, exploring taboo subjects.

Several concerns and themes preoccupy many women autobiographers, themes which might all be summed up by Judy Chicago's assertion that the autobiographical process involves saying the unsayable. Any woman who publishes an autobiography, no matter how modest and self-deprecating, implicitly contradicts traditional definitions of womanhood: women who define themselves exclusively as wives and mothers within the home tend not to publish autobiographies. How to express their non-traditional lives in the form of autobiography proves a question that interests many autobiographers. The autobiographers often deal with taboo emotions and subjects. One of the most important of these is anger, an emotion women have been taught to repress or to redirect against themselves or other women. Frequently, anger becomes a destructive force in a woman's life, and its expression in a literary work is usually seen as an artistic flaw. But many writers have discovered the creative potential of anger, in life and in art.

One target of anger has often been the mother. One would expect scenes between the autobiographers and a stern, patriarchal father, and such struggles do exist. But many autobiographers also reveal a less explored subject, the often troubled and ambivalent relationship between mothers and daughters in our culture. The act of re-examining their own lives, frequently at the same age as their mothers were when the autobiographers were young girls, may be what impels many autobiographers to reconsider their relationship with their mothers. Sometimes the mother metaphorically chokes and restricts the daughter's development, a situation acted out literally in naturalist Sally Carrighar's *Home to the Wilderness* (1973) when her mother attempts to strangle her. The mother can become a kind of anti-Muse, as in Kate Millett's work, representing the chastising voice of society that the adult writer has internalized, a force hindering her from writing. Reconciliation with the mother proves a difficult task, but one necessary before the writer can discover her full strength. Thus, much of Maxine Hong Kingston's *The Woman Warrior* (1976) concerns her discovery of a whole mother line, a source of power, strength, and creativity.

Repression of anger and the fears of which Judy Chicago speaks result in voicelessness. Over and over, autobiographers recount literal and metaphorical instances of being silenced, unable to speak, invisible. After being raped by her step-father, Maya Angelou does not speak for almost a year. Maxine Hong Kingston weaves many variations on the themes of voicelessness and invisibility, and she too remains virtually speechless and immobilized after she engages in a nightmarish torment of another dumb, passive, Chinese girl, a kind of mirror image of herself. Even as an adult, Kingston distrusts her speaking voice. Breaking through the silence becomes imperative for women autobiographers, who recount, often publicly for the first time, memories long buried: Charlotte Perkins Gilman, her descent into the near madness of mental breakdown; Katherine Dunham, the disturbing memory of her encounter with an exhibitionistic tramp; Sally Carrighar, her destructive and nearly fatal relationship with her mother. For many women, autobiography becomes a way of emerging from silence, a way of saying the unsayable.

Notes

[1]"The Autobiographer's Art," *Journal of Aesthetics and Art Criticism,*" 27 (Winter 1968), 217.

[2]*English Autobiography: Its Emergence, Materials, and Form* (Berkeley: Univ. of California Press, 1954), p.115. Subsequent references to Shumaker will be cited parenthetically within the text.

[3]*Design and Truth in Autobiography* (London: Routledge & Kegan Paul, 1960), p. 9.

[4]Charlotte Perkins Gilman provides one of the few exceptions to the obvious fact that one cannot know and thus write about the end of one's life. Suffering from cancer, she incorporated her planned suicide into the last chapter of *The Living of Charlotte Perkins Gilman*(1935; rpt. New York: Colophon-Harper, 1975).

[5]"Autobiography as an Art Form" *Stil- und Formprobleme in der Literature*, ed. Paul Bockmann Vortrage des VII Kongresses der Internationalen Vereinigung fur Moderne Sprachen un Literaturen in Heidelberg (Heidelberg: Carl Winter, 1959), p. 115.

[6]"Discontinuity and Order: A Comparison of Women's and Men's Autobiographies," paper presented at MLA convention, Dec.1976, pp. 10-11.

[7]*Momma: A Start on All the Untold Stories* (New York: Times Change Press, 1974), p. 37.

[8]"Melodramas of Beset Manhood: How Theories of American Fiction Exclude Women Authors," *American Quarterly*, 33 (Summer 1981), 130.

[9]"Autobiography and America," *Virginia Quarterly Review*, 47 (Spring 1971), 259.

[10]"Autobiography and the Making of America," in *Autobiography: Essays Theoretical and Critical*, ed. James Olney (Princeton: Princeton Univ. Press, 1980), p. 168.

[11]*Black Autobiography in America* (Amherst: Univ. of Mass. Press, 1974), pp. 201-17.

[12]*Where I'm Bound: Patterns of Slavery and Freedom in Black American Autobiography*, Contributions in American Studies, No. 16 (Westport, CT: Greenwood Press, 1974), p. ix and x.

[13]"Notes for an Anatomy of Modern Autobiography," *New Literary History*, 1 (Spring 1970), 490-91.

[14]*Autobiographical Acts: The Changing Situation of a Literary Genre* (Baltimore: Johns Hopkins Press, 1976), pp. 4-19.

[15]"Autobiography and the Historical Consciousness," *Critical Inquiry*, 1 (June 1975), 847.

[16]*Versions of the Self Studies in English Autobiography From John Bunyan to John Stuart Mill* (New York: Basic Books, 1966), p. 11.

[17]Moffat, Foreword, *Revelations: Diaries of Women*, ed. Moffat and Charlotte Painter (New York: Random House, 1974), p. 5; and Juhasz, " 'Some Deep Old Desk or Capacious Hold-All': Form and Women's Autobiography," paper presented at MLA convention, Dec. 1976, p. 3. Despite the quality of many published diaries, Shumaker judges the form inferior and implicitly feminine; the diary, he says, exemplifies "a wish to preserve experience, as a married woman may preserve the letters of her rejected suitors" (p. 103).

[18]Jelinek, "Discontinuity," pp. 8-9.

[19]*The Female Imagination* (New York: Knopf, 1975), p. 193.

[20]"From Her Unpublished Manuscript, *Journey Across the Plains*," in *Growing Up Female in America: Ten Lives*, ed. Eve Merriam (1971; rpt. New York: Dell-Laurel, 1973), p. 149.

[21]*Fifth Chinese Daughter* (New York: Harper & Row, 1950), p. vii.

[22]*Living My Life*, rev. ed. Richard and Anna Maria Drinnon (New York: Meridian-New American Library, 1977), p. 3. *Living My Life* was first published in 1931 in 2 vols.; by omitting material Goldman's publisher insisted she add, the Drinnons have attempted to restore the autobiography to what Goldman originally intended.

[23]Delores Gros-Louis sees a nineteenth-century analogy to Bowen's autobiography cast as family biography. While compiling a bibiography of American women's autobiographies, she discovered several masked as the story of the author's town or region, perhaps because these writers felt that their lives alone did not merit an entire book or because they feared that terming their books "autobiographies" seemed too presumptuous. Personal communication April 1978.

[24]*Blackberry Winter*, (1972; rpt. New York: Kangaroo-Pocket Books, 1975), p. 311.

[25]Hart, p. 486.

[26]*Aspects of biography*, trans. S.C. Roberts (London: Cambridge Univ. Press, 1929), pp. 132-45.

[27]*My Life* (New York: Boni & Liveright, 1927), p. 52 (episode at the hotel); pp. 123-28 (Greek temple episode); p. 261 (the black velvet room). Subsequent references to Duncan will be cited parenthetically within the text.

[28]"A Chronicle of Women," *Hudson Review*, 25 (Spring 1972), 157. Spacks makes this comment in the context of reviewing autobiographies by actresses.

[29]*Through the Flower: My Struggle as a Woman Artist* (1975; rpt. Garden City, NY: Anchor-Doubleday, 1977), p. 60.

[30]*Daughter of Earth* (1929; rpt. Old Westbury, NY: The Feminist Press, 1976), p. 350 (Smedley's avowal of the truth of her narrative); pp. 7-8 (the childhood episode about lying).

Joanna Russ

Amor Vincit Foeminam:
The Battle of the Sexes in Science Fiction

THAT THE SAME POST SHOULD BRING Parley J. Cooper's SF
novel, *The Feminists,* and Joan Bamberger's "The Myth of Matriarchy" is
not surprising[1]: modern feminist or anti-feminist concerns both turn
predictably to role-reversals in the group relations between the sexes; and
literal sex war, from civil war to secret cabal to street riots, does indeed
appear in modern SF. What is surprising is that the myth of the matriarchy
Bamberger describes as current among aboriginal South American tribal
societies is the same myth given flesh by Pinnacle Books in 1971. Since it is
highly unlikely that Cooper has been reading Bamberger (or vice versa)
one must conclude that similarly sexist societies produce similar fantasies.
As Bamberger puts it:

> ... the secret objects belonging to men (masks, trumpets, ritual lodge songs, and the like) ...
> are badges of authority, permitting one sex to dominate the other. However begun, the myths
> invariably end with the men in power. Either the men have taken from the women the
> symbols of authority or have installed themselves as the rightful owners of the ceremony ....
> In no versions do women win. (p. 274)

Surprisingly, however, "concerns with female reproductive
distinctions are nowhere in evidence .... The mythical message ...
stresses moral laxity and an abuse of power rather than any physical
weakness or disability" (p. 279). According to Bamberger, the "ideological
thrust" of the South American myths is "the justification ... for male
dominance through the evocation of a vision of a catastrophic alternative"
(p. 279).

To summarize: the men's Sacred Objects—the badge of authority and
means of domination over others—are stolen or contaminated by women,
who then become dominant over men. (Or the story begins with the
women dominant.) Women lose because they abuse this power or are
immoral (in various ways, e.g. incest), whereupon the men seize or reclaim
the Sacred Objects, sometimes with supernatural aid. The purpose of the
story is to show that women cannot handle power, ought not to have it, and
cannot keep it. This is the natural order of things. It is also extremely
precarious. According to Bamberger, throughout the Amazon area women
are punished by gang rape and sometimes by death for such misdemeanors
as viewing the sacred male paraphernalia (p. 275).

In my subsequent remarks, I will be discussing the following ten tales from 1926 to 1973, all by male writers, as well as one tale by "Tiptree":

Thomas Berger, *Regiment of Women*. NY: Simon & Schuster, 1973.

Nelson S. Bond, "The Priestsss Who Rebelled," in *When Women Rule*, ed. Sam Moscowitz. New York: Walker, 1972. (Originally in *Amazing Stories*, October 1939.)

Edmund Cooper, *Gender Genocide*. NY: Ace Books, 1972. (Originally published in the UK as *Who Needs Men?*; Hodder & Stoughton, n.d.)

Parley J. Cooper, *The Feminists*. NY: Pinnacle, 1971.

Thomas S. Gardner, "The Last Woman," in *When Women Rule* (see no. 2). (Originally in *Wonder Stories*, April 1932.)

David H. Keller, M.D., "The Feminine Metamorphosis," in *When Women Rule* (see no. 2). (Originally in *Science Wonder Stories*, August 1929.)

Keith Laumer, "War Against the Yukks," *Galaxy*, April 1965.

Bruce McAllister, "Ecce Femina!," *Fantasy and Science Fiction*, February 1972.

Booth Tarkington, "The Veiled Feminists of Atlantis," in *When Women Rule* (see no. 2). (Originally in *The Forum*, March 1926.)

James Tiptree, Jr., "Mama Come Home," *Ten Thousand Light Years from Home*. New York: Ace, 1973. (Originally in *If* in 1968 under the title "The Mother Ship.")

Wallace G. West, "The Last Man," in *When Women Rule* (see no. 2). (Originally in *Amazing Stories*, February 1929.)

The modern SF writers, disregarding their South American brothers' indifference to biological distinctions, make biology itself the guardian of the Sacred Object: they install the Sacred Object on their own persons. All the stories to be discussed (with the possible exception of James Tiptree's "Mama Come Home") use as their Sacred Objects the male genitalia; possession thereof guarantees victory in the battle of the sexes. This victory is therefore a victory of nature, and so the battle may be won without intelligence, character, humanity, humility, foresight, courage, planning, sense, technology or even responsibility. So "natural" is male victory that most of the stories cannot offer a plausible explanation of how the women could have rebelled in the first place. In three of the ten stories women are not actively engaged in fighting men; they have merely withdrawn from men's company—but the challenge to male domination is seen as identical. The confict is resolved—either for all women or for an exemplary woman—by some form of phallic display, and the men's victory (which is identical with the women's defeat) is not a military or political event but a quasi-religious conversion of the women. Although women in these stories constantly plan to do away with men, men (it seems) are not willing to do away with women—that is, do without women. But they certainly do not want angry, defeated women who might secretly plan how to start the conflict all over again. Unfortunately the illogicality of the solution requires reliance on mystified biology, which makes hay of real biology. Every human motive becomes a sexual motive, and the authors are forced to falsify their characters, especially the men. Since a likeable man might be liked (by a woman) for his likeableness and not for his Sacred Object, the men in these stories (with perhaps one exception) are either sadistic supermen, who incarnate the power of the penis, or lackwits who have nothing but their penises to offer. A human reacting to a human would ruin the whole business; the only pure test case is vagina acknowledging a godlike phallus, which is attached to nobody. In the overdetermined world of the Sex War economics do not exist, everything everybody does is sexually motivated, promiscuity is frigidity and vice versa, and the cure for rape is rape. As we move from the 1920s and '30s to the modern versions (*The Feminists, Gender Genocide* and "Ecce Femina!" overt violence increases and coherence decreases, the men are more and more on the defensive, and in two ("Ecce Femina!" and *Gender Genocide*), the men win individual victories but are doomed as a group. But the story remains the same story.

1. The first question one might ask about The Rule of Women, as Bamberger puts it, is how it began. The stories' answers are uniformly meager. For example, the only explanation offered by *The Feminists* (it is the longest of any) is:

> It was a quirk of fate .... Women did not intend to take total control. Their takeover is the fault of the passive male. He allowed himself to be controlled for the price of sex and then emasculated .... Women ... originally wanted only equality, but when they realized the ease with which they achieved it, they broadened their goals. (pp. 20-21)

The Feminists is a very badly-written book, and for that reason the baldest example of the myth in the whole collection. In the world of 1992, which has no futuristic details whatever, "the poison of the atmosphere had completely destroyed the vegetation" (p. 8), the subways have collapsed in New York City, the buses run infrequently, there is no snow-clearing equipment, and the US has become a police state with military rule and curfews. All women (including army soldiers) wear skirts; sex without permission of "The Committee" is punishable by death; and the gynocracy is pure high-society matriarchy. The hero, a member of the masculinist underground, is wounded in the *thigh* and feels great pain "shoot up ... *into his groin*" (p 118; italics added). He is captured by a tall soldier with "a masculine swagger to her walk" and "bushy eyebrows" (p. 129) who is witness to the first explicitly phallic display in the novel:

Instinctively he had covered his naked loins with his hands but now, realizing that she was laughing at his modesty, he removed his hands and boldly thrust his loins forward.

She continued to smile, but he knew the gesture annoyed her. (p. 129)

Bushy-browed Captain Luttrell ("I want to see if you disprove my theory of the male's inferiority .... The foundation [of it] may already have begun to crack"—p. 154) sends him back to New York City where the Mayor wants to use him as a scapegoat. So threatening (but fascinating) is his mere photograph that she has dreamed up a special execution for him; he finds himself facing "the gigantic blade of a guillotine" (p. 179). This symbolic castration is averted by the Mayor's discovery that he is in reality her long-lost son. She faces the mob herself. The Mayor's loyal aide explains: "The mayor discovered that she possessed *the major feminine weakness* she despised in others. *Before she was a Feminist, she was a Mother!*" (p. 187). Italics spent, the book goes on to tell us that the regime is crumbling and that the men will win.

The incoherence of *The Feminists* is right on the surface. Yet the Sex War myth produces some degree of nonsense in all the stories; centrally, the collapse of a gynocracy that is both impressively powerful and totally incompetent, before what might most politely be called the Sacred Object. (*The Feminists* is the only story in which the hero converts to normality not a potential sweetheart but his own mother.)

2. Keith Laumer's picture of the Rule of Women, "War Against the Yukks," is intentional comedy. The two heroes are a scatterbrained professor called Elton and a British game warden called Boyd. The two stumble upon, and are kidnapped by, an 8000-year-old space module directed by a Lunar Battle Computer buried under the Moon's Mount Tycho, which adapts itself to their language within seconds and takes them to an automatically-run dome on Callisto populated solely by women. Those are the remnants of an ancient sex war, started (as Elton says) by "some idiotic feminist movement somewhere" (p. 185), presumably the same idiots who built the Lunar Battle Computer. However, memory of the ancient war has degenerated into religion, as one Girl explains:

The terrible power they [the men, i.e., the Yukks] had was that they made perfectly nice Girls want them to do ... Strange Things. Even now, there's always the danger that a Girl will fall into Strange Ways—like dreaming about a Yukk chasing her, with all six hands reaching for her .... That's what makes the Yukks so terrible. (p. 183)

As in *The Feminists*, there is no masturbation or lesbianism among the Girls; instead there is perpetual blushing at the idea of Strange Thoughts and comic, innocent suggestions to sleep, bathe, or wrestle with the new "girls." But despite the Girls' naivete, nature wins again; the two Girls' Strange Thoughts become uncontrollable, and all four try unsuccessfully to escape in a spaceship. Just as Mother is about to despatch them, we learn that the installation's frozen sperm providentially ran out 20 years before and our heroes subside into a harem fantasy. "It should take us a year or so to work our way through, and then start over" (p. 194).

The oddest thing about "Yukks" is that atmosphere of super-heated sexuality among the Girls, with (simultaneously) total passivity. Whatever Strange Thoughts women may have, they can only wait (blushing and taking cold baths for 8200 years) for the bearers of the Sacred Object to come along and start something.

3. Nelson Bond's "The Priestess Who Rebelled" is tragic in tone, and the heroine lives in a primitive matriarchy (in the year 3482 A.D., after WW III). The biology is badly mystified—e.g., in this society modeled on bees and termites (a common pattern for matriarchies in SF) not only have the Men gone hairless, high-voiced and soft (moulting, perhaps) but the Warrior-class women have "tiny thwarted breasts, flat and hard" and the Mother-women are "full-lipped" with soft, white skins and humid eyes "washed barren of all expression by desires too oft aroused, too often sated" (pp. 108-9). Since all women choose which caste to enter after puberty it is hard to understand why the warriors' breasts have become thwarted—or why often-pregnant women develop full lips or why they spend a lot of time in sexual intercourse or why a lot of sexual intercourse makes your eyes blank.

The story begins when Meg, who has become a priestess and is therefore vowed to virginity, undertakes a pilgrimage to what the reader soon recognizes as Mount Rushmore (the tribes' gods are Jarg, Ibrim, Taamuz and Tedhi). Matriarchal woman meets patriarchal man when Meg is rescued from a "Wild One" (a homeless male) by Daiv, whose first words are : " 'You,' said the man-thing ... 'talk too much'." His next words: " 'You women!' he spat. 'Bah! You do not know how to train a horse ....' " And his next: " 'You talk too much!' repeated the man-thing wearily" (pp. 208-9).

He propositions her casually; she refuses but is forced to his campfire to get food. "Priestess" has the most coherent (and morally respectable) account of the rise of the matriarchy of any of these tales; it was, we are told, a women's revolt against men's endless war-making. Finally the women become settled citydwellers and the men homeless Wild Ones. How the Wild Ones generate more Wild Ones all by themselves is never explained. There is considerable quarreling over whether the Gods are male or female, which ends in "a mating custom which you do not know" (says Daiv) and the obligatory phallic display, here a kiss:

She struggled and tried to cry out, but his mouth bruised hers .... Suddenly her veins were running with liquid fire. Her heart beat upon rising, panting breasts like something captive that would be free .... A vast and terrible weakness trembled through Meg. She knew, fearfully, that if Daiv sought to mate with her, not all the priestessdom of the gods could save her. There was a body-hungry throbbing within her that hated his Manness ... but cried for it!. (p. 216)

Meg proceeds to Mt. Rushmore and receives the final blow:

The gods—were men!
    ...Even the curls could not conceal the inherent masculinity of Jarg and Taamuz. And Tedhi's lip was covered with Man-hair .... (p. 219)

Against the psychedelic kiss, the discovery that God is male, and the attraction of a life which consists mainly of being told she talks too much, Meg's friends, family, her lifelong loyalties, her own traditions and her religion, count as nothing. The Sacred Object triumphs—with a little help from the gods.
4. The defeat of the rebellious women in "The Feminine Metamorphosis" is due entirely to God, who invents for the purpose a special strain of syphilis which afflicts only Chinese, does not show up on Wasserman tests, and ends up driving into terminal paresis 5000 American businesswomen who have masculinized themselves with Chinese androgens in an attempt to take over the world. At first the women's complaints look sensible:

'I cannot understand why I was not promoted! ... I am more competent than the man you appointed to that position, and ... I have been in full charge of the department during the illness of the late occupant.'
'You were not promoted because you were a woman ....' (p. 149)

This explanation of female rebellion quickly segues into the plot described above, with the Sacred Object taking on an erratic, wandering life of its own, and smiting down the female thieves who have attempted to approximate it. With fewer and fewer boy babies born (due to the machinations of the women) and parthenogenesis in the offing ("the Government laboratories and nurseries," p. 187), it is time to bring out the heavy artillery. As the detective hero says: "... you forgot God. He had certain plans for the human race .... You took five thousand of our best women, girls who would have made loving wives and wonderful mothers ... and ... you have changed them into five thousand insane women" (pp. 195-96).
    Although the five thousand were dedicated businesswomen when the story began (many with "bachelor apartments," p. 152), the moral is clear: women who remain unsubjugated *in vivo* ("loving wives and wonderful mothers") will be raped *in vitro* and will die of venereal disease. And nobody human is responsible.

5. Bruce McAllister's "Ecce Femina!" is a story of women in motorcycle gangs; they shoot up "Vitamin E9—the 'ultravitamin that isn't really a vitamin'" (p. 119) thus endowing themselves with superhuman strength and sadism. Their favorite pastime is castrating and killing men, episodes commemorated by jacket patches of the female symbol with a skull placed inside the circle (p. 121). There are "hundreds of chapters" of "The Women's League" in California (p.119); and although Vitamin E9 may explain how the Rule of Women began (is the echo of "estrogen" intentional?) why it persists is a mystery:

> Soon I had him telling me about his wife, about how he had gotten sick and tired of supporting her—her bike, her E9, her arrogance, her appetite, her perversions [unnamed] .... He, like thousands of husbands each day, had found himself a weapon and gone nomad, traveling solo from tract to tract .... *The police never did anything. The courts never did anything. No one ever foreclosed.* (p. 133; italics added).

The biggest, toughest woman of all, known as "Ripper Jack" (sic) because she has killed 200 men (p. 142), nurses a wounded man back to health, defends him against the gang, and finally flees with him. Here is Jack before her conversion, as the narrator, who has been *wounded in the leg* in Cambodia, sees her.

> She was a tower of strength .... Her boots were like hooves. Her levis ... were like the tough, weathered hide. Her legs were like those of a buffalo. Her chest bulged like a truck's cab. Her arms were like swollen pistons and her long-sleeve Pendelton was like steel wool .... She was a god. From the waist down she was a bull; from the waist up, a man. (p. 132)

After the flight with the man she has come to love (because he is the only man she tries to fight who will not fight back—love is more effective in taking the zing out of Amazons than any number of battles) the narrator receives a snapshot of Jack with her man and her baby. Jack now looks like this:

> ...a heavyset woman, her muscle gone to fat, her breasts flabby under her flowerprint blouse. In her lap her big hands are cradling a baby, which is so young it's still pink.
> ... And you can't tell whether she's smiling or not.
> But then you never could. (p. 144)

In short, A Hell's Angel turns into Mona Lisa in only one year and the reason is biology; not only is Jack a mother, but, of all the women, only she never shot up Big E. Again we have the degradation of men, the lack of an explanation for the women's dominance (the explanation given is magic, considering the absolute lack of resistance to what are, after all, only

motorcycle gangs), the view of the narrator as "emasculated" because
he is terrified by a group of superhumanly strong, sadistic persons
who are determined to torment him, the insistence that women's
domination of men is unnatural (though presumably the pre-Big E
situation was not), and the final redemption by heterosexual love. There is
also, as in all these stories, the lack of any other kind of love or sex.
6. If the author of "Ecce Femina!" merely stumbled on the myth, Edmund
Cooper, in *Gender Genocide*, is doggedly insistent about it. In this world
set 250 years in the future, an all-female, technologically advanced society
occupies Southern England and periodically sends exterminators North to
kill the primitive survivals of patriarchy in Northern Scotland. Cooper
knows what started the Rule of Women: present-day feminists, who are
trying to build a world in which women kill men to enter adulthood and, if
they are especially brave, are awarded the Silver Nipple. (Cooper's London
contains a monument called "Germaine's Needle.") Cooper allows female
homosexuality into his future world only to spend 195 pages denying that
it's any fun; the story suffers even more than most from the usual
contradiction: if love conquers women so automatically and dependably,
how did the Amazon state ever come into existence? Indeed, Rura (the
heroine) is a traitor to her nation, her upbringing, and her comrades by
page 20; on her first expedition to kill "pigs" (and their "sows" and
"piglets") she finds she cannot do it, and even bandages the wounds of the
man whose first wife and child were killed by her now-dead comrades:

> Why was she doing this for a pig whose sow had just killed Moryn? She did not
> know. Perhaps it was because sunlight and death were incongruous .... She did
> not know.
> 'You were trained to kill, yet you do not. Why is this?'
> 'I don't know.' (p. 21)

The man (not some knock-kneed little crofter, mind you, but
MacDiarmid, the leader of the entire rebellion) then knocks her down,
spares her life, and announcing his determination to make a traitor of her,
kisses her: "It was like no other kiss she had ever known. It was
humiliating, it was degrading, it was disturbing. It drained strength from
her limbs, filled her head with nightmares" (p. 25).

The kiss is followed by a meeting back in the South with an old
woman whose story unsettles Rura completely. As usual, the reliance on
mystical biology includes the most extraordinary nonsense: that rape is
impossible, that first intercourse in the missionary position (after having
been bruised and beaten) invariably produces ecstasy, that a woman can
feel a man's semen enter her, that a vagina is a womb, and that clitorises are
inferior in sensitivity to cervixes:

> No woman—particularly an exterminator—who is conscious and uninjured

can be raped .... The revulsion and feeling of sickness just sort of died. And the weight on top of me seemed to be—well, interesting. And when he pinioned my arms and bit my throat and dug his fingers into my breast, it all hurt like hell but it aroused me .... So I let him enter .... I tell you, I never knew what a climax was until that red-haired animal squirted his semen into my womb. (p. 49)

A long period of inner conflict follows. Even the re-writing of history does not avail against nature, and when Rura goes out on another mission, and again can't fire her gun, she is gang-raped, called "hellbitch" and "screwmeat" (p. 77), taken to MacDiarmid, claimed by him to replace his dead wife, ordered to be quiet (some authors seem to think this is standard wooing procedure), slapped, and told: "You have entered a man's world. You have much to learn" (p. 84).

After a feeble attempt to kill him she collapses into his arms with the words: "I love you" (p. 92). The next day, with his original wound still unhealed, suffering from stab wounds he got in a fight with a follower the day before, and with Rura only 24 hours away from having been gang-raped into insensibility, he teaches her "what it is like to be a woman" (p. 91).

It was not like the rape of the previous day. It was not like lying with women. It was not like anything she had ever known.

It was warm, it was disturbing, it was exciting, it was humiliating, it was proud .... A man—this man by her side—had washed away twenty years of conditioning. He had loved her; and ... semen had pulsed excruciatingly, wonderfully, through her vagina. (pp. 114-16)

Rura's conversion occupies the first half of the book; the second half is an idyllic honeymoon, threatened constantly by "hellbitches." One of the most instructive omissions in the novel is the absence of social relations between the primitive Highlanders; men are rivals or subordinates in the feudal hierarchy (the way in which the men vie for power by dueling to the death with one another is hardly efficient for a community threatened by extinction), and social relations between women don't exist. In fact, there are no women except Rura.

What remains is to confirm Rura's conversion before the lovers die in a final *liebestod*, thus avoiding the question of what will happen to their idyll after Rura has had her baby and must, perforce, pay less attention to the Laird than to his son (both characters discuss the coming baby on the absolute presumption that it will be a boy)—or God forbid, when she meets other Highlanders and finds out that heterosexuality does not necessarily mean monogamy. Cooper's novel is one long proof that, for women, heterosexuality is so much physically pleasanter than lesbianism that it binds a woman not only to sexual pleasure but to one man in particular and to a whole ideology of male dominance. Other possible alternatives— promiscuity for one—are simply unthinkable.

7. I think it is clear by now that these stories are not only not written for women; they are not written about women. To quote Michael Korda, in *Male Chauvinism*: "[Men] don't as a rule hate [women] .... They just don't want to know anything about them."[2]

Elsewhere Korda says that men make women play roles "in a psychodrama that isn't even theirs" (p. 225). Perhaps the psychodrama of the Sacred Object is intended less to keep women down than to keep men up. (Sorry!) Penis worship *solus* is a lonely business and unconvincing. In this secular religion one cannot find another man to worship one's penis— he, after all, has got one of his own and is looking for a worshipper himself. (About the relation of homosexual men to the myth I do not know and therefore cannot speak.) So women are drafted as a permanent class of worshippers. Under the hatred and fear of women evident in the myth there is, I believe, a desperate appeal for *collusion*—the male victory, in every one of these fictions, is abjectly dependent on the female reaction. Without the women's adoration, the men's genitals are not sacred or impressive but only a means to male sensual enjoyment, a self-indulgence strikingly absent in these tales. *Gender Genocide* describes Rura's passion at length but not the Laird's; "Priestess" (at the moment of conversion) describes Meg's arousal, which is taken as defeat. (For Daiv to be similarly disturbed would be a defeat and so cannot happen—he might then be converted to matriarchy.) Only in the comic stories can men be sexually aroused, but there it is the women who become overwhelmed and lose their heads, while the men (as in "Yukks") coolly exploit the women's excitement.

You'd think these authors had been reading Ti-Grace Atkinson. They certainly agree with her that heterosexual love is an institution designed by men to subjugate women. What they add is that it anesthetizes men.[3] And inculcates in them an immense fear of expendability—perhaps the reason why these stories simply and flatly equate an all-female world with female domination of men. The remedy in both cases is to link heterosexual pleasure inextricably to female subjugation.

8. In the fictional worlds in which the women have refused this equation there is no sexual pleasure at all and the world is in decay, as in West's "The Last Man," one of the stories in Sam Moscowitz's *When Women Rule*. "The Last Man," published in 1929, portrays a world of decaying technology and devolving intellect; the atavistic couple in the story flee into the wilderness and survive, the woman tempting the man with fruit (her name is Eve). Although there is no present-day Sex War in "The Last Man," there was one in the past, the woman's world is tyrannical and sexless, and the real woman—a throwback—initiates natural love and the couple's subsequent flight because she can't stand the all-female society's lack of liveliness and love. An interesting answer to the story, written in 1932, is "The Last Woman" by Thomas S. Gardner, in which the atavistic couple (led by the man; the woman is passive and beautiful) is recaptured

and executed. The all-female world is carefully presented as the creation of one abnormal man. The all-female world is decaying, inept and had to be produced by radical biological changes which are irreversible; the all-male world is scientifically brilliant, powerful, productive and has been produced by the action of a drug whose results are temporary and reversible. The asymmetry of the stories is striking. It is hard to escape the conclusion that these "worlds" are really portraits of the two sexes as seen by the two authors.

9. In "The Veiled Feminists of Atlantis" Booth Tarkington presses the familiar charge that women will not be content with equality but will desire superiority. After wheedling the secrets of magic out of one of their benevolent men, the ruling-class women of Atlantis become the men's superiors. The women's unjust insistence on retaining the veil (symbol of mysterious sexual power) produces a battle of magic which sinks the island. Only the "uninitiated populace" (p. 103) survives. The great question, says the story, is who won, but considering that the Atlanteans' descendants are patriarchal (that the women go unveiled among neighboring tribes is a red herring), the "great question" seems deliberately mystificatory, especially in view of an earlier, very striking image: "One might say that a Kabyle woman's eyes are the eyes of a woman who has seen her grandmother beaten to death, but has not been tamed by the spectacle" (p. 100).

Under the occult details and exotic atmosphere, one discerns the familiar charges: that the rule of women over men is unjust (but the rule of men over women was benevolent), and that women's use of power will be immoral and destructive. Tarkington does not defeat his women with the Sacred Object; rather he assumes it by predicting that feminists cannot have sexual power. He takes from his women what he sees as their Sacred Object—the veil—thus implicitly rendering them unattractive. The condescending mystification of "Who won?" is the comment of a gentleman (one European gentleman tells the story to another *about* a primitive tribe) fairly sure of his privileges. He does not, it seems, need the reassurance of a Sacred Object, except implicitly.

10. Thomas Berger's *Regiment of Women*, a role-reversal world in which women bind their breasts and rape men anally with dildoes, is cheery and inane, a world of diesel dykes and screaming faggots (all imagined by a very naive writer). It has hardly more overall coherence than *The Feminists*, although it is infinitely better written in its single scenes.

The book betrays the conviction that a woman cannot dominate a man unless she has a penis somewhere about her (even if she keeps it in her bureau drawer) and that a man cannot be subjugated unless he acquires breasts, for which purpose silicone implants will do perfectly well. The year is 2047 but the clothes and props are late 1960s. The transvestism and artificial breasts seem to be in the service of rewritten history, although when the hero has his breasts removed late in the book, an army sergeant (female) only comments, "You boys! . . . cosmetic surgery has a tough time keeping up to date" (p. 146). Embryos are brought to term in artificial wombs, although the book doesn't say who raises the children, a very betraying omission. The biology and sociology are zany: men who are totally anorgasmic and have never masturbated can be forced to ejaculate by machines, women rape men artificially, and the gynocracy, as usual, is totally in control and extremely incompetent, kneeing men in the groin or castrating them at adulthood, which ruins their minds and makes them fat and willess. Men's Liberation is a single underground organization which cannot attract young men but only old ones, and the gynocracy triumphed because "men once had power but lost it through pity for women" (the only explanation ever given, p. 175). In short, we are back in the usual world in which the rule of women is sexless and tyrannical, and all this with a literalness that destroys the role-reversal intention. The story ends with a misfit couple fleeing to the wilderness, where the heroine makes the hero into a man by teaching him to drive, running down her own accomplishments, insisting he hold up a gas station, and telling him nature meant him to dominate because his penis is shaped like a weapon. Their final love-making is engineered by little Harriet (who seems to shrink constantly during the last few chapters as George realizes more and more how tiny she is) but the author, who has the sophistication to see that George needs collusion, cannot imagine that Harriet might actively make love to George. She can only taunt him into making love to her, an act he experiences as both rape and murder.

Berger calls the relation they eventually settle into "a reciprocal arrangement" (p. 345), but here is the end of the book:

> She tried to stay on top. 'You're too damned heavy!'
> But he easily rolled her over.
> 'It's time I caught the rain,' he said. And he inserted himself this time. If he was going to be a builder and a killer, he could be boss once in a while.
> Also, he was the one with the protuberant organ. (p. 349)

11. One of the few attempts to write thoughtfully about the Sex War that I can find is "Mama Come Home" by James Tiptree, Jr. Although the story contains eight-foot-tall women, they are part of a race from Capella of which we are a neotenic mutation; in its "mature" (i.e., Capellan) form, the women of the human race are two feet taller than men and dominate them, partly because they have the ability to rape men, which they do on Earth in parks and other deserted places, also murdering their victims afterwards. When we learn that with their super-technology the Capellans "plan to turn off the sun a little, as they leave" (p. 68) in order to "kick us back to the ice age" (p. 69), it becomes clear that these ladies are very bad indeed; "The men of Capella were slaves .... A cargo of exotic human

males was worth a good deal more than ore" (p. 68).

So far we are strictly in Sex-War Land. But the author (unlike others treated in this paper) explicitly observes: "The Capellans overturned our psychic scenery, our view of ourselves .... Look at their threat to our male-dominant structure" (p. 71). Then, pushing the myth rather far, the hero himself is raped.

> The navigator leaned down and said something in a velvety contralto. I didn't need a translator—I'd seen enough old flicks .... She casually twisted my arm until things broke .... The ensuing minutes I made a point of not remembering except when I forget not to wake up screaming .... I was discovering some nasty facts about Capellan physiology through a blaze of pain. (Ever think about being attacked by a *musth* vacuum cleaner?) .... Presently there was, blessedly, nothing. (p. 65)

Still, in "Mama Come Home" the real struggle is not between Earth men and Capellan giantesses. One of the hero's C.I.A. colleagues is Tillie, a woman under five feet in height who happens to look exactly like a Capellan, and whose impersonation of one is what saves Earth.

The real struggle is for Tillie's loyalty, and it is her conversion to loving the hero that is the center of the story. Gang-raped, knifed and left for dead as a teenager, she becomes the Capellans' translator and mascot:

> She was different these days—her eyes shone and she had a kind of tense, exalted smile....
> 'Tillie, it's dangerous. You don't know them.'
> ... She gave me the bare-faced stare.
> '*They're* dangerous?' (p. 59)

As the hero remarks, it was "permanent guerilla war inside" with "a six-inch layer of ice between her and everybody who shaved" (p. 59). The story sees this both as an "irrational sex phobia" (p. 72) and as something else; at one point the hero says:

> 'You think your big playmates are just like yourself, only gloriously immune from rape. I wouldn't be surprised if you were thinking of going home with them. But you don't know them .... *Did you ever meet any American blacks who moved to Kenya?* (p. 63; italics added)

Elsewhere his reasoning is explicitly political: "The American black who goes to Kenya often discovers he is an American first and an African second, no matter what they did to him in Newark" (p. 70).

Only after the news about the new ice age does the hero see "mad dreams dying in her [Tillie's] eyes" (p. 70). He concludes, with immense relief, "we had Tillie" (p. 71). The heroine's decision to throw in her lot with the male-dominant society which has raped her—a decision partly dependent on the hero's having also been raped—results in a symbolic re-living of her own rape (she pretends to be a raped Capellan in the faked film, which scares away the Capellans). She is then able to touch the hero and comment, "It's all relative, isn't it?"; and finally, "My mama came home with me" (p. 78).

If the story treats the Sex War scenario oddly, both inverting some of its elements and commenting critically on others, the reason is not far to seek. As the SF community now knows, "James Tiptree, Jr." is the pseudonym of Alice Sheldon. A woman does not, obviously, have the same stake in the myth as male authors may have. Eight years after this story, Tiptree published another story, "Houston, Houston, Do You Read?" in which present-day men who expect to take over a future, all-female world (a utopia, in fact) are competently and dispassionately killed. As one character says, "We simply have no facilities for people with your emotional problems."[4]

12. When women fight men, the battle is won by men because women are loyal to men. This piece of doublethink is made possible by splitting the female enemy into two: thus there are Capellan women and Earth women, as in "Yukks" there are sexy young women who are sympathetic, and unsexy old ones; as in *Gender Genocide* there are man-hating Lesbians and real women; as in "The Feminine Metamorphosis" there are good wives and mothers and unnatural businesswomen; as in "Ecce Femina!" there are women who shoot up Big E and women who don't. The real conflict is evaded. Moreover, solidarity among women either does not exist or is ruled out from the beginning; for example, Tillie is presented as without family, without friends, indeed without a social context of any kind. Thus her choice is—as it is in all these stories, for all the heroines—between evil (or in some cases decaying and sterile) female tyranny and some version of the hero, i.e., men. As Michael Korda says: "We need women . . . and hope that we can somehow ensnare, entrap, charm, hold one of them, as if by making our peace (on our terms) with one woman we can hold her captive in our camp, a prisoner of our side."[5] However neither in marriage nor in the myths of the Rule of Women will this strategy work. Transferring the Sacred Object to one's own person and calling upon biology (or nature) to guard it only shifts the area of precariousness and consequent terror from the realm of artifacts to that of fantasy. Without such a shift (a very old ploy in Western history) phrases like "penis envy," "castrating bitch," and "emasculated male" would be meaningless as metaphors; "screw you" would not be an insult; and medieval "witches" could not have caused their "victims'" genitals to disappear. The centuries of coercion that lie behind the stories described here are not funny—heteroinstitutionality (as against freely-chosen heterosensuality, which does not appear in these stories) is quite as dreadful as Ti-Grace Atkinson says it is.

Yet how unintentionally funny these stores are! Bruce McAllister's motorcylcle gang member, "Queen Elizabeth," using "soda pop for strange purposes" (never specified, p. 127); Edmund Cooper's determinedly charging into his favorite formula ("It was X. It was Y. It was Z. It was Q"); or Nelson Bond's teenage heroine who sobs, sticks out her chin, recognizes George Washington's essential maleness, and flings herself at the hero. The male ignorance betrayed by such fictions is appalling; the male wishes embodied in them are little short of soul-killing. But consider the title I almost used for this paper (and a very good one it is, too): *The Triumph of the Flasher.*

13. Not all SF concerned with role-reversals, all-female worlds, or male domination, is, of course, of the Flasher variety. Some of the material mentioned in Moskowitz's introduction to the book cited appears to be pro-feminist in intention, as is Frederik Pohl's *Search in the Sky* (which contains a brief satiric sketch of a role-reversal society), Theodore Sturgeon's *Venus Plus X* (a human, hermaphroditic society) and Mack Reynolds' *Amazon Planet,* in which the author sets up a role-reversal facade very like Berger's—armed female warriors and simpering men— only to reveal beneath it a peaceful and substantially egalitarian world. And the all-female world of John Wyndham's "Consider Her Ways" is a pro-feminist discussion of romantic love and the feminine mystique (although Wyndham creates another of those beehive-like societies structured by biological engineering). More doubtful is Poul Anderson's *Virgin Planet,* an all-female world in which the women span the whole range of human temperaments and activities. However, what will happen when men return to the planet (the women wished to be worthy of their vanished men, who died of a plague, and so became warriors, ship captains, etc.) is unclear. John Boyd's *Sex and the High Command* is a Sex War story of the cheerful-inane school in which the women win, having found a drug which produces both orgasm and pregnancy, i.e., a substitute for the Sacred Object.[6]

However, the above stories pale before an extraordinary phenomenon of the last few years—a number of feminist utopias, all but one written by women and all in every way the opposite of the Flasher books.[7] The feminist utopias, to the degree that they are concerned with the "battle of the sexes" (and most are) see it as a long, one-sided massacre whose cause (not cure) is male supremacy. They are explicit about economics and politics, sexually permissive, demystifying about biology, emphatic about the necessity for female bonding, concerned with children (who hardly exist in the Flasher books), non-urban, classless, communal, relatively peaceful while allowing room for female rage and female self-defense, and serious about the emotional and physical consequence of violence. The Flasher books perceive conflict between the sexes as private and opt for a magical solution *via* a mystified biology. The feminist utopias see such conflict as a public, class conflict, so the solutions advocated are economic, social and political. Strikingly, no Flasher book I was able to find envisioned a womanless world (or dared to say so); about half the feminist Utopias matter-of-factly excluded men.

Notes

[1]Parley J. Cooper, *The Feminists* (NY: Pinacle Books, 1971); Joan Bamberger, "The Myth of Matriarchy: Why Men Rule in Primitive Society," in Michell Zimbalist Rosaldo and Louise Lamphere, eds. *Woman, Culture, and Society* (Stanford, 1974).

[2]Michael Korda, *Male Chauvinism! How It Works* (NY, 1973), p. 232.

[3]Ti-Grace Atkinson, *Amazon Odyssey* (NY, 1974), pp. 13-24; Philip E. Slater, "Sexual Adequacy in America", *Intellectual Digest* (Nov. 1973): 17-20.

[4]James Tiptree, Jr. (pseud. of Alice Sheldon), "Houston, Houston, Do You Read?" in *Star Songs of an Old Primate* (NY: Ballantine, 1978).

[5]Korda, p. 222.

[6]Frederik Pohl and C.M. Kornbluth, *Search the Sky* (NY: Ballantine, 1954); Theodore Sturgeon, *Venus Plus X* (London: Gollancz, 1969); Mack Reynolds, *Amazon Planet* (NY: Ace, 1975); John Whyndham, "Consider Her Ways," in *Sometimes, Never* (NY: Ballantine, 1956); John Boyd, *Sex and the High Command* (NY: Weybright & Talley, 1971); Poul Anderson, *Virgin Planet* (NY: Avalon Books, 1959).

[7]I have treated a group of these works in a paper entitled "Recent Feminist Utopias," presented at the MLA panel on women and SF in Chicago, 1977. The paper has been accepted for publication in an anthology edited by Marleen Barr of the State University of New York at Buffalo, to be published by the Popular Press, Bowling Green, OH. The works are: Monique Wittig, *Les Guerillieres* (NY: Viking Press, 1971); Ursula Le Guin, *The Dispossessed* (NY: Harper & Row, 1974); Joanna Russ, *The Female Man* (NY: Bantam Books, 1975); Suzy McKee Charnas, *Motherlines* (NY: Putnam & Berkley, 1978); Samuel Delany, *Triton* (NY: Bantam, 1975); Marge Piercy, *Woman on the Edge of Time* (NY: Knopf, 1976); Marion Zimmer Bradley, *The Shattered Chain* (NY: Daw Books, 1976); Catherine Madsden, "Commodore Bork and the Compost," *The Witch and the Chameleon*, No. 5-6 (1976); James Tiptree, Jr. (pseudo. of Alice Sheldon), "Houston, Houston, Do You Read?" and Racoona Sheldon (also a pseud. of Alice Sheldon), "Your Faces, O My Sisters," both in *Aurora: Beyond Equality*, ed. Susan Janice Anderson and Vonda McIntyre (NY: Fawcett World Library, 1976); and Sally Gearhart, *The Wanderground* (Watertown, MA: Persephone Press, 1978).

[8]This paper is much indebted to Sam Moscowitz's collection, *When Women Rule*, which does a considerable service to SF not only by the stories he reprints but also by those discussed and listed in the Introduction. The author is personally indebted to David Hartwell for calling her attention to and making available a copy of *When Women Rule*.

About the Authors

Jane E. Archer is Assistant Professor of English at Birmingham-Southern College where she teaches courses in twentieth century British and American literature, comparative literature, critical theory, women authors and feminist critical theory. She has written extensively on Virginia Woolf and on feminist pedagogy.

George R. Bodmer teaches professional writing and American literature at Indiana University Northwest. He has written on Updike, Hawkes, Robert Penn Warren, Maurice Sendak, and technical writing.

Joseph A. Boone, a 1982 Ph.D. recipient from the University of Wisconsin-Madison, is an assistant professor in the English and American Literature Department at Harvard University, where he specializes in the novel as genre. A book on the relationship between marital ideology and narrative structure in nineteenth and early twentieth century fiction titled *Tradition Counter Tradition: Love and the Form of Fiction* is forthcoming from the University of Chicago Press as part of its women and culture series.

Cynthia Davis received the 1981 Florence Howe Award in Feminist Criticism for her essay, "Archetype and Structure: On Feminist Myth Criticism." She has published articles on John Barth, Margaret Drabble, Stanley Kunitz, Robin Morgan, and Toni Morrison. She is currently a writer and editor specializing in women's issues.

Janice L. Doane and **Devon Leigh Hodges.** Janice L. Doane was a 1983-84 doctoral fellow at the Pembroke Center for Teaching and Research on Women, Brown University and is currently on the faculty of St. Mary's College of California. Her book on Gertrude Stein entitled *Silence and Narrative* has just been published by Greenwood Press; her other co-authored articles with Devon Hodges are on Christopher Lasch and D. W. Winnicott.

Devon Leigh Hodges is Assistant Professor of English at George Mason University where she has taught courses on feminist criticism and theory. Her articles have appeared in journals such as *ELR* and *Enclitic*. She is the author of *Renaissance Fictions of Anatomy* (University of Massachusetts Press, 1985).

Judith Fetterley is Associate Professor of English at SUNY, Albany and author of *The Resisting Reader: A Feminist Approach to American Fiction* (Indiana University Press, 1978). She has also edited a book entitled *Provisions: A Reader from Nineteenth Century American Women* (Indiana Univ. Press, 1985).

Sandra M. Gilbert and **Susan Gubar.** Sandra M. Gilbert is on the faculty of Princeton University. She has completed a book of poems, *Emily's Bread,* (April, 1984) from Norton Press and is co-editor with Susan Gubar of the *Norton Anthology of Literature by Women.*

Susan Gubar is Professor of English at Indiana University. She and Sandra Gilbert have co-authored *The Madwoman in the Attic* (Yale Univ. Press, 1979), and are working on a sequel, *No Man's Land: The Place of the Woman Writer in the Twentieth Century.*

Patricia Merivale, Professor of English and Comparative Literature at the University of British Columbia, is interested in a wide variety of narrative structures with thematic implications, particularly those (like elegiac romance) relevant to artist parables in modern fiction. She is the author of *Pan the Goat-God: His Myth in Modern Times* (Harvard Comparative Literature Series) and of articles on comparative topics in *PMLA Comparative Literature, Journal of Modern Literature* and many others.

Margaret Myers is an Assistant Professor in the College of Business at Northern Kentucky. She continues to pursue her interests in the Victorian novel and feminist criticism while teaching marketing courses.

Fritz H. Oehlschlaeger is Associate Professor of English at Virginia Polytechnic Institute and State University. He has co-edited *Toward the Making of Thoreau's Modern Reputation* and published widely on various subjects in American literature. At present he is writing about Willa Cather.

Ann Parsons is an Assistant Professor of English at the University of Utah. She teaches courses mainly in American literature, fiction, and literature by and about women; writes mostly about women writers; and has worked with the Utah Women's Studies Program since its inception.

Joanna Russ has had eight novels published, as well as many reviews and essays. Her most recent novel is *Extra (Ordinary) People,* from St. Martin's Press.

Judith Spector is Associate Professor of English at the Columbus extension of Indiana University where she has taught courses on sex and science fiction, marriage as a problem in the contemporary novel, and sexual aesthetics. Her articles have appeared in *The Midwest Quarterly, Literature and Psychology* and *College English.*

Norine Voss has taught at the Indiana Women's Prison, the University of

Wisconsin-River Falls, and Stephens College. She has recently completed a book-length study of twentieth century American women's autobiography.